McGRAW-HILL's

CONQUERING GMAT MATH

McGRAW-HILL's
CONQUERING GMAT MATH

Robert E. Moyer, Ph.D.

New York   Chicago   San Francisco   Lisbon   London
Madrid   Mexico City   Milan   New Delhi   San Juan
Seoul   Singapore   Sydney   Toronto

The McGraw·Hill Companies

Library of Congress Cataloging-in-Publication Data

Moyer, Robert E.
    McGraw-Hill's conquering GMAT math / Robert E. Moyer. — 2nd ed.
        p.   cm.
    Originally published: McGraw-Hill's conquering GRE/GMAT math, c2007.
    ISBN-13: 978-0-07-148503-6
    ISBN-10: 0-07-148503-1
    1. Mathematics—Examinations, questions, etc.   2. Graduate Record
Examination—Study guides.   3. Graduate Management Admission Test—
Study guides.   4. Universities and colleges—Graduate work—
Examinations—Study guides.   I. Moyer, Robert E. McGraw-Hill's
conquering GRE/GMAT math.   II. Title.
QA43.M868   2008
510'.76—dc22   2008042530

1 2 3 4 5 6 7 8 9   QPD/QPD   0 1 4 3 2 1 0 9 8

ISBN-13 978-0-07-148503-6
MHID-10 0-07-148503-1

Printed and bound by Quebecor/Dubuque

McGraw-Hill books are available at special quantity discounts to use as
premiums and sales promotions, or for use in corporate training programs. For more information, please write to the Director of Special
Sales, McGraw-Hill Professional, Two Penn Plaza, New York, NY 10121-2298.
Or contact your local bookstore.

PREFACE

In recognition of the fact that the people preparing to take the GMAT have widely varying backgrounds and experiences in mathematics, this book provides an orientation to the mathematics content of the test, an introduction to the formats used for the mathematics test questions, and practice with multiple-choice mathematics questions. There is an explanation of the data sufficiency questions that are on the GMAT. Many of the questions on the test are general problem-solving questions in a multiple-choice format with five answer choices.

The mathematics review is quite comprehensive with explanations, example problems, and practice problems over arithmetic, algebra, and geometry. The mathematics on the GMAT is no more advanced than the mathematics taught in high school. The topics are explained in detail, and several examples of each concept are provided. After a few concepts have been explained, there is a set of practice problems with solutions. At the end of each of the four mathematics review units, there is a 50-question multiple-choice test covering the concepts of the unit. The answers and solutions to the questions on each unit test are provided in a separate section following the test. The review materials are structured so that you may select which topics you want to review. The unit tests may also be used to determine what topics you need to review.

After the unit tests there are two new features: GMAT Solved Problems and GMAT Practice Problems. These are sets of 10 items using the GMAT item formats and the content of the math review chapter. Thus, you become familiar with the format of the GMAT mathematics questions as you check your understanding of the mathematics content of the review chapter. These can be viewed as miniature GMAT practice tests.

There are two tests modeled after the GMAT mathematics section. Each test is followed by the answers and solutions for the questions on the test. The recommended time limit for each test is the same as that for the GMAT, 75 minutes. Each GMAT practice test has 37 questions as does the actual GMAT. The concepts on the practice tests are similar to those of the actual test, and the proportion of questions on each area is also similar to that of the actual test. Information on the most recent changes to the GMAT can be found on the www.mba.com website.

Using this book to review your mathematics knowledge, check your understanding of mathematics concepts, and practice demonstrating your math skills in a limited time frame will help you become prepared for the GMAT.

Robert E. Moyer, Ph.D.
Associate Professor of Mathematics
Southwest Minnesota State University

ABOUT THE AUTHOR

Dr. Robert E. Moyer has been teaching mathematics and mathematics education at Southwest Minnesota State University in Marshall, Minnesota, since 2002. Before coming to SMSU, he taught at Fort Valley State University in Fort Valley, Georgia, from 1985 to 2000, serving as head of the Department of Mathematics and Physics from 1992 to 1994.

Prior to teaching at the university level, Dr. Moyer spent 7 years as the mathematics consultant for a five-county Regional Educational Service Agency in central Georgia and 12 years as a high school mathematics teacher in Illinois. He has developed and taught numerous in-service courses for mathematics teachers.

He received his Doctor of Philosophy in Mathematics Education from the University of Illinois (Urbana-Champaign) in 1974. He received his Master of Science in 1967 and his Bachelor of Science in 1964, both in Mathematics Education from Southern Illinois University (Carbondale).

ACKNOWLEDGMENT

The writing of this book has been greatly aided and assisted by my daughter, Michelle Moyer. She did research on the tests and the mathematics content on them, created the graphics used in the manuscript, and edited the manuscript. Her work also aided in the consistency of style, chapter format, and overall structure. I owe her a great deal of thanks and appreciation for all the support she lent to the completion of the manuscript.

CONTENTS

SECTION I
INTRODUCTION

Graduate business schools consider a variety of factors when making decisions about which applicants to admit to their programs. These factors include educational background, work experience, recommendations, personal essays, and interviews. One factor often considered in admissions decisions is the applicant's performance on a standardized examination. The most common graduate business school admissions test is the Graduate Management Admission Test, generally called the GMAT®.

The Graduate Management Admission Council oversees the GMAT. The GMAT is developed by ACT, Inc., and delivered by Pearson VUE. The GMAT is designed to help graduate schools assess the qualifications of applicants for advanced study in business and management. The test is intended to be only one predictor of academic performance in the core curriculum of a graduate management program. The GMAT does not assume that test takers have specific knowledge of business or any other content areas.

The GMAT consists of three sections: Analytical Writing Assessment, Quantitative, and Verbal; this book focuses on the Quantitative section. The Quantitative section of the GMAT measures your ability to solve problems, to reason mathematically, and to interpret data. The two general types of item format on the Quantitative section of the GMAT are problem-solving and data sufficiency.

The GMAT uses a computer-adaptive format to deliver the questions. The computer selects a question based on whether the previous question was answered correctly. If the previous question was answered correctly, the difficulty level of the new question will be greater than that of the previous question; if the previous question was answered incorrectly, the next question will be easier. The content area of the question is the same whether a more difficult or an easier question was selected. Your score on the test is based on both the number of questions answered correctly and the level of difficulty of those questions.

The computer-adaptive format imposes some very important conditions on the testing situation. First, you may not go back to a question, so you must answer each question as you get to it. If you are not sure of the answer, eliminate as many answer choices as you can and then select the best choice from the smaller list. Second, you need to answer all questions, or there will be a penalty for not completing the section. In the Quantitative (mathematics) section, you are given 75 minutes to answer 37 questions, or about 2 minutes per question. You need to keep your eye on the time left and the number of questions remaining. You will do much better if you pace yourself rather than rush through the last few items. Missing several questions in a row, as you may if you rush, will hurt your score in two ways: your number of correct answers will be lower, of course, but also the questions you answer correctly after that point will affect your score less because the difficulty level will be lower.

When you prepare for the test, try to do three things: make sure you know the mathematics content of the test, familiarize yourself with the format of the test and questions, and practice the procedures so that you are able to complete the test in the allotted time. This book is designed to help you meet these three goals as you prepare for the Quantitative section of the GMAT; the practice tests will let you know if you have accomplished these goals.

For general information about registering for and taking the GMAT, visit the GMAT website at www.mba.com.

CHAPTER 1

THE GMAT MATHEMATICS SECTION

The GMAT is given as a computer-adaptive test. The Quantitative (mathematics) section of the test is presented as a set of multiple-choice questions with five answer choices each.

The computer presents you with one question at a time. The computer then scores the current question and uses that information to select the next question. If the question is answered correctly, the next question selected from the list of questions for the content area is slightly more difficult than the question answered correctly. If the previous question was answered incorrectly, the question selected is less difficult than the one just missed. Because the computer scores each question before presenting the next one, you must complete one question before you can go on to the next. Since you must answer a question before proceeding to the next question in a computer-adaptive test, you are asked to confirm your answer before going on to the next question.

Time management is important. The computer will show an on-screen clock that counts down the time remaining on the section. The clock can be hidden, but unless the clock is a distraction, leaving it visible is generally helpful in managing your time. Whether or not you hide the clock, it will alert you when there are 5 minutes left to work on the current section.

The GMAT Quantitative section contains 37 questions with a 75-minute time limit. To complete the section in the time allotted, you need to answer each question in an average time of about 2 minutes. Not completing the section will result in a penalty and could significantly lower your Quantitative score. **Failing to answer a question has a greater negative impact on your score than answering the question incorrectly.** A steady pace is the best way to achieve your highest possible score because rushing at the end means you may miss questions covering content that you know very well.

The GMAT measures mathematics skills that are acquired over a period of many years. Many of the skills are developed through the curriculum of the average high school. The purpose of the Quantitative section is to determine whether you have the knowledge and skills needed in a graduate business program. You have previously learned the mathematics needed for the test, and you only need to review it to be prepared for the Quantitative section.

The questions come in two basic formats: problem solving and data sufficiency. Problem-solving questions should be familiar to you; a question with five answer choices is presented, and you choose the correct answer. This format is used on most standardized tests. The data-sufficiency format is unique to the GMAT. In this format, you are given two statements and a question. You must decide if each of the statements is sufficient to answer the question alone, if the two statements taken together are sufficient to answer the question, or if the statements, even taken together, are not sufficient to answer the question.

CHAPTER 2

THE MATHEMATICS YOU NEED TO REVIEW

Since the GMAT is taken by people with a wide variety of educational backgrounds, the test uses mathematical skills and concepts that are assumed to be common for all test takers. The test questions use arithmetic, algebra, geometry, and basic statistics. You will be expected to apply basic mathematical skills, understand elementary mathematical concepts, reason quantitatively, recognize information relevant to the problem, and determine if there is sufficient information to solve a problem.

You will **not** be expected to know advanced statistics, trigonometry, or calculus, or to write a proof. The GMAT does not test specialized or advanced knowledge of mathematics. In general, the mathematical knowledge and skills needed do not extend beyond what is usually covered in the curriculum of the average high school.

You will be expected to recognize standard symbols such as = (equal to), ≠ (not equal to), < (less than), > (greater than), || (parallel to), and ⊥ (perpendicular to). All numbers used will be real numbers. Fractions, decimals, and percentages may be used. The broad areas of mathematical knowledge needed for success on the GMAT are number properties, arithmetic computation, algebra, geometry, and some basic statistics.

Number properties include such concepts as even and odd numbers, prime numbers, divisibility, rounding, and signed (positive and negative) numbers.

Arithmetic computation includes the order of operations, fractions (including computation with fractions), decimals, and averages. You may also be asked to solve word problems using arithmetic concepts.

The **algebra** needed on the GMAT includes linear equations, operations with algebraic expressions, powers and roots, standard deviation, inequalities, quadratic equations, systems of equations, and radicals. Again, algebra concepts may be part of a word problem you are asked to solve.

Geometry topics include the properties of points, lines, planes, and polygons; you may be asked to calculate area, perimeter, and volume, or to explore coordinate geometry.

When units of measure are used, they may be in English (U.S. Customary System) or metric units. If you need to convert between units of measure, the conversion relationship will be given, except for common ones such as converting minutes to hours, inches to feet, or centimeters to meters.

Although simple graphs or tables may be used in a question, you will not be asked to construct the graph or table; you will only need to interpret the data in a given graph or table. Since constructing graphs is not part of the GMAT, those procedures are not included in the mathematics review.

When answering any question on the GMAT, you first need to read the question carefully to see what is being asked. Then recall the mathematical concepts needed to relate the information you are given in a way that will enable you to solve the problem.

If you have completed an average high school mathematics program, you have previously been taught the mathematics you need for the GMAT. The review of arithmetic, algebra, and geometry provided in this book will help you to refresh your memory of the mathematical skills and knowledge you previously learned.

If you were not satisfied with your previous level of mathematical knowledge in a given area, then review the material provided on that topic in greater detail, making sure you fully understand each section before going on to the next one.

SECTION II

ITEM FORMATS

The GMAT mathematics section has only multiple-choice questions. There are 37 questions on the mathematics section. The questions fall into two major categories: problem solving, with approximately 22 questions, and data sufficiency, with approximately 15 questions.

Since the time limit for the mathematics section is 75 minutes, you need to complete each item in 2 minutes or less. Because of the computer-adaptive format, you need to start each question knowing that you need to answer it before going on. There is no chance to go back, so it is your only opportunity to answer the question. Read the question, consider the relevant mathematics you know, and apply logical reasoning to the situation. This should either allow you to answer the question or eliminate some of the answer choices so you can pick one of the remaining choices. Answer one question, then go on to the next. You need to do this rather quickly since you only have an average of about 2 minutes per question.

The GMAT has approximately 60% problem-solving questions and 40% data-sufficiency questions. Each problem-solving question has five answer choices. Below is an example of a problem-solving question.

1. **Isabella has a total of 534 points on her tests in music class and her test average is an 89. How many tests are included in her average?**

   - 5
   - 6
   - 7
   - 8
   - 9

The data-sufficiency questions measure your ability to determine how much information is needed to solve a problem. Below is an example of a data-sufficiency question.

2. **Noah has a can of 100 mixed nuts. The mixture contains only peanuts, almonds, and cashews. How many almonds are in the can?**
   (1) The ratio of peanuts to almonds to cashews is 6:1:3.
   (2) There are 60 peanuts in the can.

   - Statement (1) ALONE is sufficient, but statement (2) is not sufficient.
   - Statement (2) ALONE is sufficient, but statement (1) is not sufficient.
   - BOTH statements TOGETHER are sufficient, but NEITHER statement ALONE is sufficient.
   - EACH statement ALONE is sufficient.
   - Statements (1) and (2) TOGETHER are not sufficient.

The key to data-sufficiency questions is to determine if the data allows you to answer the question, not to actually find the answer. You just need to work far enough to determine that you have enough information to yield an answer.

CHAPTER 3
GMAT PROBLEM-SOLVING QUESTIONS

ITEM FORMATS

About two-thirds of the 37 questions on the Quantitative section of the GMAT are of the general problem-solving type. Each question has five answer choices. The questions focus on the given information and reasoning that you supply to select the best answer. A good strategy is to eliminate at least two answers and, if you cannot eliminate any more, to select the best answer from the remaining choices.

Any number in the problems will be a real number unless there is a further restriction on the variables. Operations among real numbers are assumed.

Figures show general relationships such as straight lines, collinear points, and adjacent angles. In general, you cannot determine measures of angles or line segments based on a figure alone. In a few cases, you will be told that a figure has been drawn to scale. When a figure has been drawn to scale, you may use the lengths in the drawing to help you solve the problem. Similarly, angle measures can be estimated from figures drawn to scale.

Example 1

If $\dfrac{b}{a+b} = \dfrac{7}{12}$, then what does $\dfrac{a}{b}$ equal?

A. $\dfrac{5}{12}$

B. $\dfrac{5}{7}$

C. $\dfrac{7}{5}$

D. $\dfrac{7}{19}$

E. $\dfrac{19}{12}$

Solution

Because $\dfrac{b}{a+b} = \dfrac{7}{12}$ is a proportion, you can use two properties to transform it. First, use the reciprocal property to get $\dfrac{a+b}{b} = \dfrac{12}{7}$; then use the subtraction property to get $\dfrac{a+b-b}{b} = \dfrac{12-7}{7}$. So $\dfrac{a}{b} = \dfrac{5}{7}$, and answer **B** is correct.

Example 2

In circle P, the two chords intersect at point X, with the lengths as indicated in the figure. Which could **not** be the sum of lengths a and b, if a and b are integers?

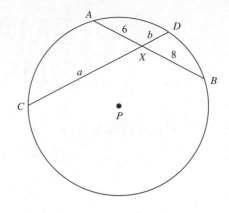

A. 49
B. 30
C. 26
D. 16
E. 14

Solution

When two chords intersect within a circle, the product of the segments on one chord is equal to the product of the segments on the other chord. Since the segments of the first chord are 6 and 8, the product of the lengths is 48. Thus, the product of the lengths a and b must be 48, and possible lengths are 48 and 1, 24 and 2, 12 and 4, and 8 and 6. So 49, 26, 16, and 14 are possible values for $a + b$. The correct answer is B, since 30 is not the sum of two integer factors of 48.

Example 3

In one can of mixed nuts, 30% is peanuts. In another can of mixed nuts that is one-half the size of the first one, 40% is peanuts. If both cans are emptied into the same bowl, what percentage of the mixed nuts in the bowl is peanuts?

A. $16\frac{2}{3}\%$

B. 20%
C. 25%

D. $33\frac{1}{3}\%$

E. 35%

Solution

Let the first can contain 16 ounces of nuts, so the second can contains 8 ounces of nuts. Thirty percent of 16 ounces is 4.8 ounces of peanuts, and 40% of 8 ounces is 4.2 ounces of peanuts. In the bowl there is $(4.8 + 3.2)$ ounces of the $(16 + 8)$ ounces in the bowl, and $\frac{8}{24} = \frac{1}{3} = 33\frac{1}{3}\%$. So $33\frac{1}{3}\%$ of the nuts are peanuts, and D is the correct answer.

Example 4

What is the sum of the prime numbers between $\frac{1}{2}$ and $9\frac{1}{5}$?

A. 15
B. 16
C. 17
D. 18
E. 25

Solution

The prime numbers between $\frac{1}{2}$ and $9\frac{1}{5}$ are 2, 3, 5, and 7. The sum of these prime numbers is 17, so the answer is C.

Example 5

A paint store mixes $\frac{3}{4}$ pint of red paint and $\frac{2}{3}$ pint of white paint to make a new paint color called Perfect Pink. How many pints of red paint would be needed to make 34 pints of Perfect Pink paint?

A. 9
B. 16
C. 18

D. $25\frac{1}{3}$

E. $28\frac{1}{2}$

Solution

First, determine how much paint the recipe for Perfect Pink will make. $\frac{3}{4}$ pint $+$ $\frac{2}{3}$ pint $=$ $\frac{9}{12}$ pint $+$ $\frac{8}{12}$ pint $=$ $\frac{17}{12}$ pints, or $1\frac{5}{12}$ pints. The ratio of red paint in the recipe is the same as it will be in the 34 pints of paint. Let N be the number of pints of red paint needed.

$$\frac{3/4}{1(5/12)} = \frac{N}{34}$$

$$\frac{3}{4}(34) = 1\frac{5}{12}(N)$$

$$\frac{102}{4} = \frac{17}{12}N$$

$$\frac{102}{4} \div \frac{17}{12} = N$$

$$18 = N$$

Thus, 18 pints of red paint are needed, and the answer is C.

SOLUTION STRATEGIES

1. **Apply a general rule or formula to answer the question.**
    In Example 2, you can apply a property from geometry that says that when two chords intersect inside a circle, the segments formed have lengths such that the product of the segment lengths is the same for each chord.

2. **Apply basic properties of numbers.**

   In Example 4, you can use the definition of a prime number so that you do not include 1, but do include 2.

3. **Eliminate as many answers as possible so that you can select from a smaller set of answer choices.**

   In Example 3, you can eliminate some of the answers by noting that since each can of mixed nuts is at least 30% peanuts, the mixture of the two cans will be least 30% peanuts. Thus, before doing any computation, you could eliminate answers A, B, and C. Therefore, if you need to guess, you only have two answer choices left and have increased your odds of guessing correctly.

4. **Substitute answers into the given question to see which one produces the correct result.**

   In Example 1, you are given $\dfrac{b}{a+b} = \dfrac{7}{12}$, and you want the value of $\dfrac{a}{b}$. You can divide the numerator and denominator of $\dfrac{b}{a+b}$ by b to get $\dfrac{1}{\dfrac{a}{b}+1}$.

   Now you can substitute the answer choices into the expression to see which answer produces a value of $\dfrac{7}{12}$. Answer A produces $\dfrac{12}{17}$, so it is wrong. Answer B produces $\dfrac{7}{12}$, so it is correct. Since this type of question has only one correct answer, you know the correct answer is B. You do not have to test the rest of the answer choices.

   This strategy cannot be employed on the majority of questions, but you can use it when you can see a way to quickly test the answer choices.

5. **Break down the situation into individual steps.**

   In Example 5, you have an everyday situation of mixing paint. Break the problem down into steps. First, find the total amount of paint the formula makes. Then set up a proportion to find the increased amount of red paint. Taking word problems one step at a time makes them more manageable.

EXERCISES

1. If a jewelry store wants to sell a necklace for $179.95 next week at a 60% off sale, how much is the price of the necklace this week?
   A. $71.98
   B. $251.93
   C. $287.92
   D. $399.92
   E. $449.88

2. Find the median for this set of data: 9, 2, 5, 7, 10, 9, 2, 8, 11, 10.
   A. 8
   B. 8.5
   C. 9
   D. 9.5
   E. 10

3. Which number is divisible by 3, 4, 5, and 6?
   A. 30
   B. 48
   C. 75
   D. 120
   E. 160

4. The length of a rectangle is 4 centimeters longer than the width, and the perimeter is 96 centimeters. How many square centimeters are there in the area of the rectangle?
   A. 48
   B. 396
   C. 572
   D. 1,760
   E. 2,288

5. Which quadratic equation has roots of 4 and $\frac{1}{2}$?

   A. $4x^2 - 9x + 2 = 0$
   B. $2x^2 - 9x + 4 = 0$
   C. $2x^3 - 9x^2 + 4x = 0$
   D. $2x^2 + 9x + 4 = 0$

   E. $x^2 - 2x + \frac{1}{2} = 0$

SOLUTIONS

1. **E** First, eliminate as many answers as possible so that you can select from a smaller set of numbers. If 60% off the original price leaves $179.95, then the original price is more than twice the sale price—greater than $360. Eliminate choices A, B, and C. Then substitute answers into the question to see which one produces the correct result. Try choice E. Now 60% of $449.88 is $269.93, and $449.88 − $269.93 = $179.95, so choice E is correct.

2. **B** Apply basic properties of numbers. In this case, apply the definition of the median as the middle value in the ordered sequence of values. To find the median, you need to arrange the data in order from lowest to highest: 2, 2, 5, 7, 8, 9, 9, 10, 10, 11. Since there is an even number of values, you average the two middle values to get the median Md.

   Md = (8 + 9) ÷ 2

   Md = 8.5

3. **D** Apply basic properties of numbers. In this case, apply the divisibility rules for 3, 4, and 5. Since any number divisible by 3 and 4 is divisible by 6, there is no need to check separately for divisibility by 6. When a number is divisible by 5, its units digit must be either 0 or 5. If a number is divisible by 3, then the sum of the digits must be divisible by 3. To be divisible by 4, the last two digits must form a number divisible by 4. Since you want an answer that ends in 0 or 5, answer B can be eliminated. The sum of the digits must be divisible by 3, so answer E can be eliminated. Finally, the last two digits of the number must be divisible by 4, so answers A and C can be eliminated. The correct answer is D.

4. **C** Break the situation down into individual steps. Apply the formulas for perimeter and area of a rectangle. The perimeter of a rectangle is given by the formula $P = 2l + 2w$, and the area is given by the formula $A = lw$. First, find the length and width. Let w equal the width of the given rectangle. The length can then be represented as $w + 4$.

   $$2w + 2(w + 4) = 96$$
   $$2w + 2w + 8 = 96$$
   $$4w + 8 = 96$$
   $$4w = 88$$
   $$w = 22$$

   Now find the length by adding 4.

   $$l = 26$$

   Now apply the formula for area.

   $$A = lw = 26(22) = 572$$

5. **B** Apply a general rule or formula to answer the question. In this case, apply the factoring procedure, and then find the solution for each factor. Note that answer C is not a quadratic equation and can be eliminated immediately. If the roots of a quadratic equation are 4 and $\frac{1}{2}$, then $x = 4$ and $x = \frac{1}{2}$ will yield $x - 4 = 0$ and $2x - 1 = 0$. The quadratic equation is therefore $(x - 4)(2x - 1) = 0$, which is $2x^2 - 9x + 4 = 0$. The correct answer is B.

CHAPTER 4

GMAT DATA-SUFFICIENCY QUESTIONS

ITEM FORMATS

GMAT data-sufficiency questions have as their focus not finding the solution to the problem, but determining whether or not there is enough information to solve it. In each item, you are given a situation and then two statements, and you are asked to determine whether one of the statements, both of the statements, or neither of the statements provides enough information to solve the problem.

Data-sufficiency questions occur only on the GMAT. About one-third of the 37 mathematics questions are of this type.

Once you practice a few of this type of question, you will see that they often take much less time than do the problem-solving questions. You do not have to solve the problem, just decide whether it can be solved.

The answer choices are the same for each question of this type:

A Statement (1) ALONE is sufficient, but statement (2) is not sufficient.
B Statement (2) ALONE is sufficient, but statement (1) is not sufficient.
C BOTH statements TOGETHER are sufficient, but NEITHER statement ALONE is sufficient.
D EACH statement ALONE is sufficient.
E Statements (1) and (2) TOGETHER are NOT sufficient.

Important points to remember when answering this type of question are that all numbers in the problem are real numbers; figures are always consistent with the given information but may conflict with either or both statements; all lines in the figures are straight lines; the position of points, line segments, and angles in a figure exist in the order shown; and angle measures are all greater than zero.

In a data-sufficiency question that asks for a numerical answer, it must be possible to determine that quantity's value exactly for a statement to be sufficient. You do not have to find the value, just know that with the given information and one or both statements, the value can be determined.

Study the following examples to see how the directions below apply to each item.

Directions: The following questions are data-sufficiency problems consisting of a question and two statements, labeled 1 and 2, in which certain data is given. You have to decide whether the data given in the statements is sufficient for answering the question. Using the data given in the statements plus your knowledge of mathematics and everyday facts (such as the number of days in July or the meaning of counterclockwise), you must indicate whether

A Statement 1 ALONE is sufficient, but statement 2 alone is not sufficient.
B Statement 2 ALONE is sufficient, but statement 1 alone is not sufficient.

C BOTH statements TOGETHER are sufficient, but NEITHER statement ALONE is sufficient.
D EACH statement ALONE is sufficient.
E Statements 1 and 2 TOGETHER are NOT sufficient.

Example 1

A rectangle has a perimeter of 96 centimeters. What are the dimensions of the rectangle?

1. The area is 572 square centimeters (cm^2).
2. The width is 4 centimeters shorter than the length.

☐ A. ☐ B. ☐ C. ☐ D. ☐ E.

Solution

For statement 1, if the area is 572 cm^2, then you have $lw = 572$ and $2l + 2w = 96$. If you have two equations with the same two variables, you can solve. For example, solving the system, you get $l = 26$ cm and $w = 22$ cm or $l = 22$ cm and $w = 26$ cm. The dimensions are 22 and 26 cm; thus, statement 1 is sufficient. Note that you do not need to actually solve it, just know that you can solve it.

For statement 2, if the width is 4 less than the length, you have $w = l - 4$ and $2l + 2w = 96$. Again, you can solve. For example, solving the system, you get $l = 26$ cm and $w = 22$ cm. The dimensions of the rectangle are 22 and 26 cm; thus, statement 2 is sufficient.

Since each statement is sufficient alone, the answer is D.

Example 2

Here G, H, I, J, and K are consecutive whole numbers. When is $G \times H \times I > 12$?

1. $G \geq 2$
2. G is odd.

☐ A. ☐ B. ☐ C. ☐ D. ☐ E.

Solution

Using statement 1, if $G \geq 2$, then $G \times H \times I = 2 \times 3 \times 4 = 24$, at least, and $24 > 12$. Statement 1 is sufficient.

Using statement 2, if G is odd, then G can be 1. If $G = 1$, then $G \times H \times I = 1 \times 2 \times 3 = 6$, and $6 < 12$. Also G could be 3, and then $G \times H \times I = 3 \times 4 \times 5 = 60$, and $60 > 12$. Statement 2 is not sufficient.

Thus, the correct answer is A.

Example 3

Lisa bought $50 worth of gas for her truck. How far can Lisa travel in her truck using this amount of gas?

1. The gas Lisa bought cost $2.75 a gallon.
2. Lisa's truck gets 24 miles per gallon of gas.

☐ A. ☐ B. ☐ C. ☐ D. ☐ E.

Solution

To determine how far Lisa can travel on $50 worth of gas, you need to know the number of gallons of gas that she purchased and the number of miles per gallon (mpg) Lisa's truck gets. (miles per gallon) × (number of gallons of gas) = distance traveled.

Using statement 1, knowing that gas cost $2.75 a gallon, you can determine the number of gallons of gas purchased: $50 ÷ $2.75, which is about 18.18 gallons. This is not sufficient to determine how far Lisa can travel.

Using statement 2, knowing that her truck gets 24 miles per gallon is not sufficient to determine how far Lisa can travel.

However, knowing the cost per gallon of gas yields the number of gallons of gas Lisa purchased (about 18.18), and knowing the mpg for her truck is 24, you can determine the distance that Lisa can travel: $24 \times 18.18 = 436.32$ miles.

Since it takes both statements together to be able to determine the distance, the answer is C.

Example 4

If $x^3 + y^3$, what is the value of x?

1. $y = 3$
2. $x < 0$

□ A. □ B. □ C. □ D. □ E.

Solution

For statement 1, knowing $y = 3$ just yields $x^3 + 27$, which is not an equation; you cannot determine x. Thus, statement 1 is not sufficient.

For statement 2, knowing $x < 0$ does not yield a value for x. Thus, statement 2 is not sufficient.

Combining $y = 3$ and $x < 0$ still does not let you determine the value of x, so together, statements 1 and 2 are not sufficient. Thus, the answer must be E.

Example 5

David has 26 coins in a jar, and all the coins are dimes and nickels. How many nickels are in the jar?

1. David spent part of the money on a soft drink.
2. The value of the coins is $1.85.

□ A. □ B. □ C. □ D. □ E.

Solution

For statement 1, the fact that David spent some of the money does not allow you to determine the number of nickels he has, so statement 1 is not sufficient.

For statement 2, if the value of the coins is $1.85, then if you let n be the number of nickels and d be the number of dimes, $0.05n + 0.10d = 1.85$, and $n + d = 26$. Solving the system of equations tells you that there are 15 nickels and 11 dimes, so statement 2 is sufficient to solve the problem.

Since statement 2 is sufficient and statement 1 is not, the answer is B.

SOLUTION STRATEGIES

1. **Work only as far as you must to be sure the question has an answer.**
   In Example 3, once you are sure you can determine the number of gallons of gas purchased and the number of miles per gallon, you know the answer is C because it takes both statements to get an answer.

2. **Be sure to try each statement *separately* to get an answer to the question.**
   In Example 1, after statement 1 yields an answer, there is a tendency to stop and say the answer is A. However, the answer could also be D, if statement 2 also yields an answer. To be sure whether the answer is A or D, you must try each statement separately.

3. **If statement 1 does not yield an answer to the question, check statement 2 to see if it will yield an answer to the question.**
   The tendency is to mark answer B, but when statement 1 does not yield a solution, the answer could be B, C, or E. When you try statement 2 and it yields an answer to the question, the correct answer is B as in Example 5. If it does not yield an answer, then the answer choice could be C or E as in Example 3 and Example 4, respectively.

4. **If neither statement alone yields an answer to the question, be sure to consider them together.**
   In Example 3, it takes both statements together to get an answer to the question.

5. **Remember that when both statements fail to yield an answer individually, they can still fail to yield an answer when taken together.**
   In Example 4, the statements individually do not yield an answer to the question, and when taken together, they still don't yield an answer to the question. Often people assume that when both statements fail individually to produce an answer, the answer is always C or is always E. Neither assumption is valid. You must check the two statements taken together to determine which is actually the correct answer. If, when taken together, they produce an answer to the question, the correct answer is C. If, when taken together, they fail to produce an answer to the question, the correct answer is E.

EXERCISES

Directions: The following questions are data-sufficiency problems consisting of a question and two statements, labeled 1 and 2, in which certain data is given. You have to decide whether the data given in the statements is sufficient for answering the question. Using the data given in the statements plus your knowledge of mathematics and everyday facts (such as the number of days in July or the meaning of counterclockwise), you must indicate whether

A Statement 1 ALONE is sufficient, but statement 2 alone is not sufficient.
B Statement 2 ALONE is sufficient, but statement 1 alone is not sufficient.
C BOTH statements TOGETHER are sufficient, but NEITHER statement ALONE is sufficient.
D EACH statement ALONE is sufficient.
E Statements 1 and 2 TOGETHER are NOT sufficient.

1. What is the value of $x^3 + y^3$?

    1. $x + y = 12$
    2. $x - y = 8$

    ☐ A. ☐ B. ☐ C. ☐ D. ☐ E.

2. What is the area of triangle *ABC*?

    1. $\angle ABC$ and $\angle CAB$ have the same measure.
    2. $AB = 9$, $BC = 12$, and $CA = 15$.

    ☐ A. ☐ B. ☐ C. ☐ D. ☐ E.

3. The mean (average) of w, x, and y is z. Is $z = w$?

    1. $\frac{1}{2}(x + y) = w$
    2. $w = x = y$

    ☐ A. ☐ B. ☐ C. ☐ D. ☐ E.

4. What is the area of square *PQRS*?

    1. The perimeter of *PQRS* is 28.
    2. The diagonal *SQ* is $7\sqrt{2}$.

    ☐ A. ☐ B. ☐ C. ☐ D. ☐ E.

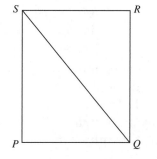

5. A piece of wood is cut into three pieces that have lengths in the ratio $x : y : z = 1 : 2 : 3$. What is the length $x + y + z$?

    1. $x + z = 16$
    2. $x < y < z$

    ☐ A. ☐ B. ☐ C. ☐ D. ☐ E.

SOLUTIONS

1. **C** Knowing that statement 1, $x + y = 12$, is true is not enough to determine the value of $x^3 + y^3$. Also statement 2, $x - y = 8$, is not enough to determine the values of $x^3 + y^3$. Strategy 5 tells you to consider statements 1 and 2 together. When you know both $x + y = 12$ and $x - y = 8$, you can determine that $x = 10$ and $y = 2$. Thus, the value of $x^3 + y^3$ is 1,008. The answer to the problem is C.

2. **B** Simply knowing that two angles of the triangle have the same measure does not allow you to find the area of the triangle, so statement 1 is not

sufficient. Using statement 2, knowing that $AB = 9$, $BC = 12$, and $CA = 15$ allows you to determine that triangle ABC is a right triangle. Since $AB^2 + BC^2 = 9^2 + 12^2 = 15^2 = CA^2$, triangle ABC is a right triangle. The legs of the right triangle, AB and BC, can be the base and altitude of the triangle, so the area of triangle ABC is $\frac{1}{2}bh = \frac{1}{2} \cdot 9 \cdot 12 = 54$. Thus, statement 2 is sufficient alone. As indicated by strategy 3, you must check statement 2 alone. Since it is sufficient, the answer is B.

3. **D** For statement 1, if $\frac{1}{2}(x + y) = w$, then $x + y = 2w$ and $w + x + y = 3w$, so the average of w, x, and y is $3w \div 3 = w$ and $z = w$. Thus, statement 1 is sufficient. Using strategy 2, you need to check statement 2 alone to determine if the answer is A or D. For statement 2, if $w = x = y$, then $w + x + y = 3w$ and $(w + x + y) \div 3 = 3w \div 3 = w$. Thus, w is the average and $w = z$, so statement 2 is sufficient. Since each statement is sufficient alone, the answer is D.

4. **D** For statement 1, if the perimeter of the square is 28, then $4s = 28$ and $s = 7$. The area of a square is s^2, so $s^2 = 7^2 = 49$. Thus, statement 1 is sufficient. Using strategy 2, you need to see if statement 2 alone is sufficient. The diagonal forms an isosceles right triangle with two of the sides of the square. If the diagonal is $7\sqrt{2}$, then $s^2 + s^2 = (7\sqrt{2})^2$ and $2s^2 = 98$. So $s^2 = 49$. Thus, statement 2 is sufficient. Since each statement alone is sufficient, the answer is D.

5. **A** As stated in the problem, if the ratio of $x : y : z = 1 : 2 : 3$, then $y = 2x$ and $z = 3x$. Thus, $x + y + z = 6x$. For statement 1, if $x + z = 16$, then $x + 3x = 16$, and $x = 4$. So $x + y + z = 6x = 6(4) = 24$. Thus, statement 1 is sufficient. From strategy 2, you know to check each statement. Statement 2 does not provide any additional information. Since the ratio is $1 : 2 : 3$, you can already conclude that $x < y < z$. Thus, statement 2 is not sufficient alone. Since only statement 1 yielded a result for the question, A is the correct answer for this question.

Note: The exercises in this chapter were worked out to the point where a solution to the problem was found (if possible), which is not needed to answer a data-sufficiency question on the GMAT. It was done here to make sure the justification for the answer was clear.

In general, you only have to work a data-sufficiency problem to the point at which you know there will be (or definitely will not be) a meaningful answer. When an answer is found that is not acceptable for the problem, you do not have sufficient data to solve the problem.

SECTION III

BASIC MATHEMATICS REVIEW

The mathematics section on the GMAT requires a knowledge of mathematics that is acquired over a period of years. This section will review topics in arithmetic, algebra, and geometry that could form the content of the mathematics questions on the GMAT.

Each chapter includes definitions of key concepts, worked-out examples, and practice exercises with explanations. Chapters conclude with a chapter test in multiple-choice format. The examples let you review the concepts and recall information you had learned previously. The practice exercises enable you to demonstrate your understanding of the concepts. Finally, you apply your knowledge to questions in a format similar to test questions.

Chapter 5, Number Properties, reviews the number line, the types of real numbers, rounding numbers, computing with signed numbers, and the properties of numbers. The properties of the special numbers 0, 1, and -1 are reviewed, as well as those of even and odd numbers. Number theory properties such as prime and composite numbers, multiples, factors, and divisors are covered as well as least common multiple, greatest common divisor, and prime factorization.

In Chapter 6, Arithmetic Computation, the order of operations, properties of operations, fractions, decimals, ratios, proportions, percents, averaging, powers, and roots are discussed. The associative, commutative, and distributive properties are reviewed and applied. Converting among fractions, decimals, and percents shows the relationships among the various forms of rational numbers. Word problems will allow you to apply information you know about numbers.

In Chapter 7, Algebra, you can review the basic concepts of algebra. You will evaluate expressions, solve equations, and solve inequalities. Computation with algebraic expressions will include monomials, binomials, and polynomials. Graphs of points and linear equations will be discussed. The solution of quadratic equations by factoring and by using the quadratic formula will be demonstrated. Algebraic word problems will include consecutive integer problems, age problems, mixture problems, and motion problems.

Chapter 8, Geometry, will review the fundamental concepts of geometry. Proofs will not be part of the GMAT, so they will not be considered. Angles, angle relationships, the relationship between lines, and types of polygons will be reviewed. Properties of triangles, parallelograms, rectangles, squares, and circles will be discussed. Formulas for area, perimeter, and volume of common geometric figures will be used in problems.

CHAPTER 5

NUMBER PROPERTIES

THE NUMBER LINE

A number line is a line with a scale for locating numbers indicated. The scale is determined when two numbers have their location indicated on the line. Usually, 0 and 1 are located first, but that is not a requirement.

The **origin** of a number line is the location of zero on that number line.

The **coordinate** of a point on a number line is the number associated with that point.

Figure 5.1 is an example of a number line. The space between two consecutive numbers is equal everywhere on the number line. On this number line, the integers from negative 5 to positive 5 are shown, but all integers can be located by using the scale shown.

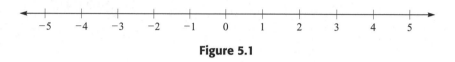

Figure 5.1

Numbers not shown on the number line can be represented by estimating their location between two consecutive numbers.

Example 1

Locate $A = \dfrac{1}{2}$, $B = \sqrt{2}$, and $C = 3.1$ on a number line, shown in Figure 5.2.

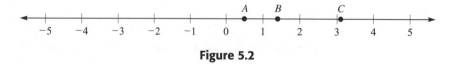

Figure 5.2

Solution

Since $A = 1/2$, it is located midway between 0 and 1. Since $B = \sqrt{2}$, you have to approximate $\sqrt{2}$ to get $\sqrt{2} \approx 1.414$. You locate B at about 1.4, which is a little less than halfway between 1 and 2. For $C = 3.1$, you locate C just to the right of 3 on the number line.

In working out the above example, you used a common practice of having the numbers increase as you go from left to right. Unless you are told otherwise, you may assume this is true for all number lines you encounter in this book and on the GMAT. Also, there are an infinite number of points between any two of the indicated coordinates. In general, you attempt to locate the number by thinking of the interval between two numbers as divided into halves. Then in each half, you locate the number by deciding if it is closer to the left end of the space, in the middle of the space, or closer to the right end of the space.

If greater accuracy is needed on the number line, the space between two numbers can be enlarged and subdivided into tenths of a unit. See Figure 5.3.

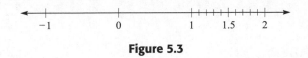

Figure 5.3

For even greater accuracy in locating points, the space between 1.2 and 1.3 could be enlarged and subdivided into 10 parts, or hundredths of a unit.

Number Line Exercises

A. Graph the numbers $3, \frac{1}{2}, -5, 8, 1\frac{1}{4}$, and $-\frac{2}{3}$ on a number line.

B. What are the coordinates of the points A, B, C, D, and E on the number line in Figure 5.4?

Figure 5.4

Solutions

A.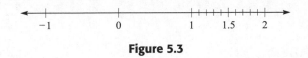

B. $A = 3, B = -1\frac{1}{2}, C = 7, D = 4\frac{1}{2}, E = 1$

THE REAL NUMBERS

A **real number** is any number that can be the coordinates of a point on a number line. The numbers $3, -4, 2.3, 5\frac{1}{3}, -7.21, -\frac{2}{3}, \sqrt{2}, 5$, and $\frac{5}{7}$ are all examples of real numbers.

The set of **counting numbers** is the set of numbers 1, 2, 3, 4, ... Counting numbers are evenly spaced on the number line. Each number is 1 more than the previous number, except for 1, which is the smallest counting number. The counting numbers are also known as the **natural numbers**.

The **whole numbers** are the counting numbers plus zero.

The **integers** are made up of the counting numbers, zero, and the negatives of the counting numbers. The integers are $\{\dots, -4, -3, -2, -1, 0, 1, 2, 3, 4, \dots\}$.

The **rational numbers** are all the numbers that can be written as the ratio of two integers a and b, when b is not zero. The rational numbers include all the integers, since you can let a be any integer and b be 1. You also get fractions such as $\frac{2}{3}, -\frac{1}{4}, \frac{6}{5}$, and $-\frac{11}{7}$. These fractions can also be written as decimals through division: $\frac{1}{4} = 1 \div 4 = 0.25$; $\frac{1}{3} = 1 \div 3 = 0.333\dots$.

Thus, you have rational numbers that yield finite or terminating decimals and rational numbers that yield infinite repeating decimals. Every rational number can be written in decimal form.

The **irrational numbers** are the real numbers that are not rational. The irrational numbers you are most familiar with include $\sqrt{2}$, $\sqrt{3}$, π, and e. Irrational numbers can be written as infinite, nonrepeating decimals. There are decimal approximations for $\sqrt{2} \approx 1.41421\cdots$, $\sqrt{3} \approx 1.73205\cdots$, $\pi \approx 3.14159\cdots$, and $e \approx 2.71828\cdots$. However, these approximations do not clearly show that the decimals are nonrepeating. To show a decimal that is both infinite and nonrepeating, you need a pattern that is not based on repetition. One such pattern is to start with 1, then 01, then 001, then 0001, with each step in the pattern adding another zero. You get $0.101001000100001\cdots$. Another pattern yields $0.1121231234\cdots$.

The real numbers are made up of the combination of all rational numbers and all irrational numbers. Thus, the set of real numbers is the set of all decimals, finite and infinite.

Number-Type Exercises

1. Change each number to its decimal form.

    A. $\dfrac{4}{5}$ B. $\dfrac{3}{4}$ C. $\dfrac{5}{6}$ D. $\dfrac{17}{10}$ E. $\dfrac{11}{20}$

2. Classify each of these numbers. Include **all** number types the number belongs to.

    A. $\sqrt{5}$ B. -3 C. 0 D. $\dfrac{2}{3}$ E. 8

Solutions

1. A. $\dfrac{4}{5} = 4 \div 5 = 0.8$

    B. $\dfrac{3}{4} = 3 \div 4 = 0.75$

    C. $\dfrac{5}{6} = 5 \div 6 = 0.8333\cdots$

    D. $\dfrac{17}{10} = 17 \div 10 = 1.7$

    E. $\dfrac{11}{20} = 11 \div 20 = 0.55$

2. A. $\sqrt{5}$ is irrational, real
    B. -3 is integer, rational, real
    C. 0 is whole number, integer, rational, real
    D. $\dfrac{2}{3}$ is rational, real
    E. 8 is counting number, whole number, integer, rational, real

■ ROUNDING NUMBERS

When numbers are approximated, the results need to be **rounded** to maintain the accuracy of the data. For example, frequently, when you work on problems with money, you get results that contain a fractional part of a cent. In these cases, you round the result to the nearest cent. In general, the accuracy is specified in the problem.

To round a number, first locate the digit that has the accuracy wanted; then examine the digit to the right. If the digit to the right is 5 or more, round up by increasing the accuracy digit by 1 and dropping all digits to the right of it. If the digit to the right of the accuracy digit is 4 or less, round down by leaving the accuracy digit the same and dropping all digits to the right of it.

If the digits dropped are to the left of the decimal point, they are replaced with zeros.

Example 2

Consider the number 2,643.718.

A. Round the number to the nearest tenth.
B. Round the number to the nearest hundredth.
C. Round the number to the nearest thousand.
D. Round the number to the nearest unit.
E. Round the number to the nearest hundred.

Solution

A. There is a 7 in the tenths digit, and the digit to the right of the tenths digit is a 1. Thus the tenth digit stays the same, and the digits to the right of it are dropped. When 2,643.718 is rounded to the nearest tenth, you get 2,643.7.
B. There is a 1 in the hundredths digit and an 8 in the next place to the right. Thus, you increase the 1 by 1 and drop all digits to the right. When rounded to the nearest hundredth, 2,643.718 becomes 2,643.72.
C. There is a 2 in the thousands place, and the digit to the right is a 6, so you add 1 to the 2 and drop all digits to the right. Since the thousands place is to the left of the decimal point, you have to fill in zeros for the dropped digits between the thousands digit and the decimal point. Thus, when you round 2,643.718 to the nearest thousand, you get 3,000.
D. When rounding 2,643.718 to the nearest unit, you have a 3 in the units place and a 7 in the place to the right. The result of the rounding is 2,644.
E. When rounding to the nearest hundred, you note that there is a 6 in the hundreds place and a 4 in the place to the right. Thus, you leave the 6 unchanged, and you drop the digits to the right of the hundreds place. Since the hundreds place is to the left of the decimal point, you must fill in zeros for the dropped digits between the hundreds place and the decimal point. The answer after rounding to hundreds is 2,600.

Rounding Exercises

A. Round 4.536 to the nearest tenth.
B. Round 5.8165 to the nearest thousandth.
C. Round 76,472 to the nearest hundred.
D. Round 268.463 to the nearest ten.
E. Round $486.238 to the nearest cent.
F. Round 4,563.75 to the nearest unit.
G. Round 1,436.3 to the nearest whole number.

Solutions

A. 4.5
B. 5.817
C. 76,500
D. 270
E. $486.24
F. 4,564
G. 1,436

EXPANDED NOTATION

Place value is used to write numbers in expanded notation. Each digit in the number is multiplied by the place value of that digit.

$300 = 3 \times 100$ or $300 = 3 \times 10^2$ since $10^2 = 100$

$50 = 5 \times 10$ or $50 = 5 \times 10^1$ since $10^1 = 10$

$7 = 7 \times 1$ or $7 = 7 \times 10^0$ since $10^0 = 1$

$357 = 300 + 50 + 7 = 3 \times 100 + 5 \times 10 + 7 \times 1$ or

$357 = 300 + 50 + 7 = 3 \times 10^2 + 5 \times 10^1 + 7 \times 10^0$

Example 3

Write 568 in expanded notation.

$568 = 500 + 60 + 8 = 5 \times 100 + 6 \times 10 + 8 \times 1$ or

$568 = 500 + 60 + 8 = 5 \times 10^2 + 6 \times 10^1 + 8 \times 10^0$

Example 4

Write 25,653 in expanded notation.

$25{,}653 = 20{,}000 + 5{,}000 + 600 + 50 + 3$
$= 2 \times 10{,}000 + 5 \times 1{,}000 + 6 \times 100 + 5 \times 10 + 3 \times 1$ or

$25{,}653 = 20{,}000 + 5{,}000 + 600 + 50 + 3$
$= 2 \times 10^4 + 5 \times 10^3 + 6 \times 10^2 + 5 \times 10^1 + 3 \times 10^0$

Example 5

Write 2,019 in expanded notation.

$2{,}019 = 2{,}000 + 10 + 9 = 2 \times 1{,}000 + 1 \times 10 + 9 \times 1$ or

$2{,}019 = 2{,}000 + 10 + 9 = 2 \times 10^3 + 1 \times 10^1 + 9 \times 10^0$

Note: Since there was a zero in the hundreds place, you can also include it in the expanded notation.

$2{,}019 = 2{,}000 + 0 + 10 + 9 = 2 \times 1{,}000 + 0 \times 100 + 1 \times 10 + 9 \times 1$ or

$2{,}019 = 2{,}000 + 0 + 10 + 9 = 2 \times 10^3 + 0 \times 10^2 + 1 \times 10^1 + 9 \times 10^0$

Example 6

Write 21,000 in expanded notation.

$$21{,}000 = 20{,}000 + 1{,}000 = 2 \times 10{,}000 + 1 \times 1{,}000 \quad \text{or}$$

$$21{,}000 = 20{,}000 + 1{,}000 = 2 \times 10^4 + 1 \times 10^3$$

    Expanded notation also applies to decimals. Fractions or 10 with a negative exponent is used to indicate the place value to the right of the decimal point.

$$0.1 = \frac{1}{10} = 10^{-1}$$

$$0.01 = \frac{1}{100} = 10^{-2}$$

$$0.001 = \frac{1}{1{,}000} = 10^{-3}$$

$$0.352 = 0.3 + 0.05 + 0.002 = 3 \times 0.1 + 5 \times 0.01 + 2 \times 0.001$$

$$= 3 \times \frac{1}{10} + 5 \times \frac{1}{100} + 2 \times \frac{1}{1{,}000} \quad \text{or}$$

$$0.352 = 0.3 + 0.05 + 0.002 = 3 \times 0.1 + 5 \times 0.01 + 2 \times 0.001$$

$$= 3 \times 10^{-1} + 5 \times 10^{-2} + 2 \times 10^{-3}$$

Example 7

Write 0.582 in expanded notation.

$$0.582 = 0.5 + 0.08 + 0.002 = 5 \times \frac{1}{10} + 8 \times \frac{1}{100} + 2 \times \frac{1}{1{,}000} \quad \text{or}$$

$$0.582 = 0.5 + 0.08 + 0.002 = 5 \times 10^{-1} + 8 \times 10^{-2} + 2 \times 10^{-3}$$

Example 8

Write 0.804 in expanded notation.

$$0.804 = 0.8 + 0.004 = 8 \times \frac{1}{10} + 4 \times \frac{1}{1{,}000} \quad \text{or}$$

$$0.804 = 0.8 + 0.004 = 8 \times 10^{-1} + 4 \times 10^{-3}$$

Example 9

Write 0.007 in expanded notation.

$$0.007 = 7 \times \frac{1}{1{,}000} \quad \text{or}$$

$$0.007 = 7 \times 10^{-3}$$

    A number that has both a whole number and a decimal point can also be written in expanded notation.

Example 10

Write 147.23 in expanded notation.

$$147.23 = 100 + 40 + 7 + 0.2 + 0.03$$

$$= 1 \times 100 + 4 \times 10 + 7 \times 1 + 2 \times \frac{1}{10} + 3 \times \frac{1}{100} \quad \text{or}$$

$$147.23 = 100 + 40 + 7 + 0.2 + 0.03$$

$$= 1 \times 10^2 + 4 \times 10^1 + 7 \times 10^0 + 2 \times 10^{-1} + 3 \times 10^{-2}$$

Example 11

Write 230.08 in expanded notation.

$$230.08 = 200 + 30 + 0.08 = 2 \times 100 + 3 \times 10 + 8 \times \frac{1}{100} \quad \text{or}$$

$$230.08 = 200 + 30 + 0.08 = 2 \times 10^2 + 3 \times 10^1 + 8 \times 10^{-2}$$

Expanded Notation Exercises

A. Write 2.364 in expanded notation.
B. Write 2,871 in expanded notation.
C. Write 0.349 in expanded notation.
D. Write 42.34 in expanded notation.
E. Write 728,000 in expanded notation.
F. Write 80.0005 in expanded notation.

Solutions

A. $2.364 = 2 + 0.3 + 0.06 + 0.004 = 2 \times 1 + 3 \times \frac{1}{10} + 6 \times \frac{1}{100} + 4 \times \frac{1}{1,000}$

or

$2.364 = 2 + 0.3 + 0.06 + 0.004 = 2 \times 10^0 + 3 \times 10^{-1} + 5 \times 10^{-2} + 4 \times 10^{-3}$

B. $2,871 = 2,000 + 800 + 70 + 1 = 2 \times 1,000 + 8 \times 100 + 7 \times 10 + 1 \times 1 \quad$ or

$2,871 = 2,000 + 800 + 70 + 1 = 2 \times 10^3 + 8 \times 10^2 + 7 \times 10^1 + 1 \times 10^0$

C. $0.349 = 0.3 + 0.04 + 0.009 = 3 \times \frac{1}{10} + 4 \times \frac{1}{100} + 9 \times \frac{1}{1,000} \quad$ or

$0.349 = 0.3 + 0.04 + 0.009 = 3 \times 10^{-1} + 4 \times 10^{-2} + 9 \times 10^{-3}$

D. $42.34 = 40 + 2 + 0.3 + 0.04 = 4 \times 10 + 2 \times 1 + 3 \times \frac{1}{10} + 4 \times \frac{1}{100} \quad$ or

$42.34 = 40 + 2 + 0.3 + 0.04 = 4 \times 10^1 + 2 \times 10^0 + 3 \times 10^{-1} + 4 \times 10^{-2}$

E. $728,000 = 700,000 + 20,000 + 8,000$
$= 7 \times 100,000 + 2 \times 10,000 + 8 \times 1,000 \quad$ or

$728,000 = 700,000 + 20,000 + 8,000 = 7 \times 10^5 + 2 \times 10^4 + 8 \times 10^3$

F. $80.0005 = 80 + 0.0005 = 8 \times 10 + 5 \times \frac{1}{10,000} \quad$ or

$80.0005 = 80 + 0.0005 = 8 \times 10^1 + 5 \times 10^{-4}$

PRACTICE PROBLEMS

1. Graph the points $A = 2\frac{1}{2}$, $B = -4$, $C = 0$, $D = \frac{3}{4}$, $E = 5$ on a number line.

2. What are the coordinates of points F, G, H, I, and J in Figure 5.5?

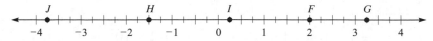

Figure 5.5

3. Which of these numbers are counting numbers?

    $3,\ 0,\ -5,\ \frac{2}{3},\ 0.4,\ 1\frac{1}{2},\ 8,\ -\frac{1}{2},\ \sqrt{2}$

4. Which of these numbers are whole numbers?

    $-2,\ 4,\ \frac{3}{4},\ 1\frac{1}{2},\ 6,\ \sqrt{5},\ -\frac{1}{3},\ 0,\ 0.8$

5. Which of these numbers are integers?

    $-4,\ 3,\ \frac{1}{4},\ \sqrt{8},\ 0,\ -\frac{1}{3},\ 2,\ 1\frac{3}{5},\ \frac{5}{4}$

6. Which of these numbers are rational?

    $2,\ 1\frac{1}{3},\ \sqrt{6},\ -5,\ 0.333\cdots,\ 0.51,$

    $0.5152253335\cdots$

7. Which of these numbers are irrational?

    $0,\ 2\frac{1}{5},\ \sqrt{15},\ -2,\ 0.525252\cdots,$

    $0.010010001\cdots,\ 0.86,\ 9$

8. Which types of numbers contain 18?

9. Which types of numbers contain -15?

10. Which types of numbers contain $\frac{7}{3}$?

11. Which types of numbers contain 0?

12. Which types of numbers contain 0.64?

13. Which types of numbers contain $0.672672672\cdots$?

14. Round 26,854 to the nearest thousand.

15. Round 0.6384 to the nearest tenth.

16. Round \$112.465 to the nearest cent.

17. Round 435.982 to the nearest unit.

18. Round 264.382 to the nearest hundredth.

19. Round 468,451 to the nearest ten.

20. Round 751.364 to the nearest hundred.

21. Write 3,471 in expanded notation.

22. Write 258,000,000 in expanded notation.

23. Write 37.42 in expanded notation.

24. Write 516.4 in expanded notation.

25. Write 0.8724 in expanded notation.

SOLUTIONS

1. See Figure 5.6.

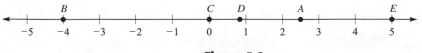

Figure 5.6

2. $F = 2, G = 3\frac{1}{4}, H = -1\frac{1}{2}, I = \frac{1}{4}, J = -3\frac{3}{4}$

3. 3 and 8 are counting numbers.

4. 0, 4, and 6 are whole numbers.

5. −4, 0, 2, and 3 are integers.

6. $-5, 0.333\cdots, 0.51, 1\frac{1}{3},$ and 2 are rational numbers.

7. $0.010010001\cdots$ and $\sqrt{15}$ are irrational numbers.

8. 18 is a whole number, a counting number, an integer, a rational number, and a real number.

9. −15 is an integer, a rational number, and a real number.

10. $\frac{7}{3}$ is a rational number and a real number.

11. 0 is a whole number, an integer, a rational number, and a real number.

12. 0.64 is a rational number and a real number.

13. $0.672672672\cdots$ is a rational number and a real number.

14. To the nearest thousand, 26,854 is 27,000.

15. To the nearest tenth, 0.6384 is 0.6.

16. To the nearest cent, $112.465 is $112.47.

17. To the nearest unit, 435.982 is 436.

18. To the nearest hundredth, 264.382 is 264.38.

19. To the nearest ten, 468,451 is 468,450.

20. To the nearest hundred, 751.364 is 800.

21. $3{,}471 = 3{,}000 + 400 + 70 + 1 = 3 \times 1{,}000 + 4 \times 100 + 7 \times 10 + 1 \times 1$ or

    $3{,}471 = 3{,}000 + 400 + 70 + 1 = 3 \times 10^3 + 4 \times 10^2 + 7 \times 10^1 + 1 \times 10^0$

22. $258{,}000{,}000 = 200{,}000{,}000 + 50{,}000{,}000 + 8{,}000{,}000 = 2 \times 100{,}000{,}000 + 5 \times 10{,}000{,}000 + 8 \times 1{,}000{,}000$ or

    $258{,}000{,}000 = 200{,}000{,}000 + 50{,}000{,}000 + 8{,}000{,}000 = 2 \times 10^8 + 5 \times 10^7 + 8 \times 10^6$

23. $37.42 = 30 + 7 + 0.4 + 0.02 = 3 \times 10 + 7 \times 1 + 4 \times \frac{1}{10} + 2 \times \frac{1}{100}$ or

    $37.42 = 30 + 7 + 0.4 + 0.02 = 3 \times 10^1 + 7 \times 10^0 + 4 \times 10^{-1} + 2 \times 10^{-2}$

24. $516.4 = 500 + 10 + 6 + 0.4 = 5 \times 100 + 1 \times 10 + 6 \times 1 + 4 \times \frac{1}{10}$ or

    $516.4 = 500 + 10 + 6 + 0.4 = 5 \times 10^2 + 1 \times 10^1 + 6 \times 10^1 + 4 \times 10^{-1}$

25. $0.8724 = 0.8 + 0.07 + 0.002 + 0.0004 = 8 \times \frac{1}{10} + 7 \times \frac{1}{100} + 2 \times \frac{1}{1{,}000} + 4 \times \frac{1}{10{,}000}$ or

    $0.8724 = 0.8 + 0.07 + 0.002 + 0.0004 = 8 \times 10^{-1} + 7 \times 10^{-2} + 2 \times 10^{-3} + 4 \times 10^{-4}$

◼ SIGNED NUMBERS

A **signed number** is a numeral preceded by a plus or minus sign. A numeral preceded by a "+" sign is a positive number, such as $+4, +\sqrt{10}$, or $+\frac{3}{4}$. A numeral preceded by a "−" sign is a negative number, such as $-4, -\sqrt{10}$, or $-\frac{3}{4}$.

On a number line (see Figure 5.7) the positive numbers are to the right of zero, and the negative numbers are to the left of zero.

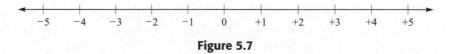

Figure 5.7

Zero is the only number that is neither positive nor negative. Preceding zero with a "+" sign or a "−" sign does not make it positive or negative.

The **absolute value** of a number is the distance a number is from zero on a number line.

The absolute value of a is denoted by $|a|$.

Example 12

Find the absolute value of each number.

A. $|+5|$ B. $|-3|$ C. $|0|$ D. $\left|-\dfrac{2}{3}\right|$ E. $\left|+\dfrac{1}{2}\right|$

Solution

A. When you look at the number line in Figure 5.7 and locate +5, you find that the distance from +5 to 0 on the number line is 5. Thus $|+5| = 5$.
B. When you look at Figure 5.7 and locate −3, you see that the distance from −3 to 0 is 3 units. Thus $|-3| = 3$.
C. When you look at Figure 5.7 and locate 0, you see that the distance from 0 is 0 units. Thus, $|0| = 0$.
D. $\left|-\dfrac{2}{3}\right| = \dfrac{2}{3}$
E. $\left|\dfrac{1}{2}\right| = \dfrac{1}{2}$

Adding Signed Numbers

To add two numbers with like signs, you add the absolute value of the numbers and precede the value with the common sign.

Example 13

Add these numbers.

A. $\begin{array}{r} +5 \\ +2 \\ \hline \end{array}$ B. $\begin{array}{r} +7 \\ +6 \\ \hline \end{array}$ C. $\begin{array}{r} -3 \\ -2 \\ \hline \end{array}$ D. $\begin{array}{r} -5 \\ -4 \\ \hline \end{array}$ E. $\begin{array}{r} -8 \\ -3 \\ \hline \end{array}$

Solution

A. $|+5| = 5$, $|+2| = 2$, and $5 + 2 = 7$. The answer is positive.
   $(+5) + (+2) = +7$
B. $|+7| = 7$, $|+6| = 6$, and $7 + 6 = 13$. The answer is positive.
   $(+7) + (+6) = +13$
C. $|-3| = 3$, $|-2| = 2$, and $3 + 2 = 5$. The answer is negative.
   $(-3) + (-2) = -5$
D. $|-5| = 5$, $|-4| = 4$, and $5 + 4 = 9$. The answer is negative.
   $(-5) + (-4) = -9$
E. $|-8| = 8$, $|-3| = 3$, and $8 + 3 = 11$. The answer is negative.
   $(-8) + (-3) = -11$

To add two numbers with unlike signs, you find the absolute value of the two numbers and subtract the smaller absolute value from the greater absolute value. The sign of the answer is the sign of the number with the greater absolute value.

Example 14

Add these signed numbers.

A. +3   B. −4   C. +4   D. −6   E. −3
   −2   +1   −7   +2   +6

Solution

A. $|+3| = 3$, $|−2| = 2$, and $3 − 2 = 1$. The sign is positive, since $3 > 2$.

   $(+3) + (−2) = +1$

B. $|−4| = 4$, $|+1| = 1$, and $4 − 1 = 3$. The sign is negative, since $4 > 1$.

   $(−4) + (+1) = −3$

C. $|+4| = 4$, $|−7| = 7$, and $7 − 4 = 3$. The sign is negative, since $7 > 4$.

   $(+4) + (−7) = −3$

D. $|−6| = 6$, $|+2| = 2$, and $6 − 2 = 4$. The sign is negative, since $6 > 2$.

   $(−6) + (+2) = −4$

E. $|−3| = 3$, $|+6| = 6$, and $6 − 3 = 3$. The sign is positive, since $6 > 3$.

   $(−3) + (+6) = +3$

Two numbers are **opposites** if they have unlike signs but the same absolute value. The unique property of opposites is that their sum is zero. $+4 + (−4) = 0; −5 + (+5) = 0$.

When adding more than two signed numbers, you consider whether the numbers all have the same sign. If they all have the same sign, then add the absolute values of the numbers and the sign of the result is the common sign. If the numbers have different signs, add all the positive numbers and add all the negative numbers. Then the two sums are added by using the procedure for adding two numbers with unlike signs.

Example 15

Add these signed numbers as indicated.

A. $(+5) + (+3) + (+7) + (+4) + (+2)$
B. $(−3) + (−7) + (−8) + (−2)$
C. $(+5) + (−3) + (+4) + (+3) + (−7) + (−8)$

Solution

A. $(+5) + (+3) + (+7) + (+4) + (+2) = +(5 + 3 + 7 + 4 + 2) = +21$
B. $(−3) + (−7) + (−8) + (−2) = −(3 + 7 + 8 + 2) = −20$
C. $(+5) + (−3) + (+4) + (+3) + (−7) + (−8) = +(5 + 4 + 3) + [−(3 + 7 + 8)]$
   $= (+12) + (−18) = −(18 − 12) = −6$

Subtracting Signed Numbers

To subtract the signed number a from the signed number b, you add the opposite of a to b.

Example 16

Subtract these signed numbers.

A. $+5$	B. -6	C. $+4$	D. -6	E. -4
$-\underline{-4}$	$-\underline{+2}$	$-\underline{+3}$	$-\underline{-5}$	$-\underline{-4}$

Solution

A. You change from subtraction of -4 to addition of the opposite of -4, which is $+4$. Your new problem is $(+5) + (+4)$. $|+5| = 5$ and $|+4| = 4$. So $5 + 4 = 9$, and the sign is positive.

   $(+5) - (-4) = +9$

B. You change from subtracting $+2$ to adding the opposite of $+2$, which is -2. Your new problem is $(-6) + (-2)$. $|-6| = 6$ and $|-2| = 2$. So $6 + 2 = 8$, and the sign is negative.

   $(-6) - (+2) = -8$

C. You change from subtracting $+3$ to adding the opposite of $+3$, which is -3. Your new problem is $(+4) + (-3)$. $|+4| = 4$ and $|-3| = 3$. So $4 - 3 = 1$, and the sign is positive, since $4 > 3$.

   $(+4) - (+3) = +1$

D. You change from subtracting -5 to adding the opposite of -5, which is $+5$. Your new problem is $(-6) + (+5)$. $|-6| = 6$ and $|+5| = 5$, so $6 - 5 = 1$. The sign is negative, since $6 > 5$.

   $(-6) - (-5) = -1$

E. You change from subtracting -4 to adding the opposite of -4, which is $+4$. Your new problem is $(-4) + (+4)$. $|-4| = 4$, $|+4| = 4$, and $4 - 4 = 0$. Since $4 = 4$, the answer is 0.

   $(-4) - (-4) = 0$

Multiplying Signed Numbers

To multiply two signed numbers with like signs, multiply the absolute values of the numbers. The sign of the answer is positive.

Example 17

Multiply these signed numbers.

A. $+4$	B. -6	C. -8	D. $+9$
$\times \underline{+2}$	$\times \underline{-5}$	$\times \underline{-3}$	$\times \underline{+4}$

Solution

A. $|+4| = 4$, $|+2| = 2$, and $4 \times 2 = 8$. The sign is positive.

   $(+4) \times (+2) = +8$

B. $|-6| = 6$, $|-5| = 5$, and $6 \times 5 = 30$. The sign is positive.

   $(-6) \times (-5) = +30$

C. $|-8| = 8$, $|-3| = 3$, and $8 \times 3 = 24$. The sign is positive.

   $(-8) \times (-3) = +24$

D. $|+9| = 9$, $|+4| = 4$, and $9 \times 4 = 36$. The sign is positive.

   $(+9) \times (+4) = +36$

To multiply two signed numbers with unlike signs, multiply the absolute value of the numbers. The sign of the answer is negative.

Example 18

Multiply these signed numbers.

A. $\begin{array}{r} -4 \\ \times\ +5 \end{array}$ B. $\begin{array}{r} +6 \\ \times\ -3 \end{array}$ C. $\begin{array}{r} -8 \\ \times\ +4 \end{array}$ D. $\begin{array}{r} +7 \\ \times\ -9 \end{array}$

Solution

A. $|-4| = 4$, $|+5| = 5$, and $4 \times 5 = 20$. The sign is negative.
   $(-4) \times (+5) = -20$
B. $|+6| = 6$, $|-3| = 3$, and $6 \times 3 = 18$. The sign is negative.
   $(+6) \times (-3) = -18$
C. $|-8| = 8$, $|+4| = 4$, and $8 \times 4 = 32$. The sign is negative.
   $(-8) \times (+4) = -32$
D. $|+7| = 7$, $|-9| = 9$, and $7 \times 9 = 63$. The sign is negative.
   $(+7) \times (-9) = -63$

When either number or both numbers in the product are zero, the product itself is zero.

When a product of signed numbers has an odd number of negative factors, the sign of the product is negative. When a product of signed numbers has an even number of negative factors, the sign of the product is positive.

Example 19

Find the indicated product of signed numbers.

A. $(+5) \times (-3) \times (-2) \times (+7) \times (-4)$
B. $(-3) \times (-5) \times (+2) \times (+6)$
C. $(-2) \times (-6) \times (-2) \times (-3)$
D. $(-3) \times (-2) \times (-1) \times (+2) \times (-3) \times (-5)$
E. $(-3) \times (-6) \times (0) \times (+4) \times (-7)$

Solution

A. There are three negative factors, so the answer is negative.
   $-(5 \times 3 \times 2 \times 7 \times 4) = -(840) = -840$
B. There are two negative factors, so the answer is positive.
   $+(3 \times 5 \times 2 \times 6) = +(180) = +180$
C. There are four negative factors, so the answer is positive.
   $+(2 \times 6 \times 2 \times 3) = +(72) = +72$
D. There are five negative factors, so the answer is negative.
   $-(3 \times 2 \times 1 \times 2 \times 3 \times 5) = -(180) = -180$
E. Since one of the factors is zero, the product is zero.

Dividing Signed Numbers

When you divide two signed numbers with like signs, the sign of the answer is positive, and the answer is the quotient of the absolute values of the numbers.

The division problem "a divided by b" can be written as $\dfrac{a}{b}$, $a \div b$, a/b, or $b\overline{)a}$.

Example 20

Do the indicated division of signed numbers.

A. $\dfrac{+3}{+1}$ B. $(+8) \div (+2)$ C. $\dfrac{-6}{-3}$ D. $(-18) \div (-2)$

Solution

A. The answer is positive. $\dfrac{+3}{+1} = +3$

B. The answer is positive. $(+8) \div (+2) = +4$

C. The answer is positive. $\dfrac{-6}{-3} = +2$

D. The answer is positive. $(-18) \div (-2) = +9$

To divide two numbers with unlike signs, the sign of the answer is negative, and the answer is the quotient of the absolute values of the numbers.

Example 21

A. $\dfrac{-16}{+8}$ B. $(-14) \div (+7)$ C. $(+15) \div (-3)$ D. $\dfrac{+56}{-8}$

Solution

A. The quotient is negative. $\dfrac{-16}{+8} = -2$

B. The quotient is negative. $(-14) \div (+7) = -2$

C. The quotient is negative. $(+15) \div (-3) = -5$

D. The quotient is negative. $\dfrac{+56}{-8} = -7$

When zero is divided by any nonzero number, the quotient is always zero. $\dfrac{0}{+6} = 0$; $0 \div (-13) = 0$.

Division by zero is not defined. Thus $\dfrac{5}{0}$ is not defined, and $(-3) \div 0$ is not defined.

Properties of Zero

- For any real number a, $a \times 0 = 0$.
- For any real number a, $a + 0 = a$.
- For any real number a, $a - 0 = a$ and $0 - a = -a$.
- For any nonzero real number a, $0 \div a = 0$.
- For real numbers a and b, if $a \times b = 0$, then $a = 0$ or $b = 0$.

Properties of 1 and −1

- $1 \times 1 = 1$
- $(-1) \times (-1) = 1$
- $(-1) \times (1) = -1$
- For all real numbers a, $a \times 1 = a$.
- For all real numbers a, $a \times (-1) = -a$.
- For all real numbers a and b, $-1(a \times b) = (-a) \times b = a \times (-b)$
- For all real numbers a, $-1 \times (-a) = a$.
- For all real numbers a, $a \div 1 = a$.
- For all real numbers a, $a \div (-1) = -a$.
- For any integer n, $n + 1$ is the next larger integer.
- For any integer n, $n + (-1)$ is the next smaller integer.
- The smallest counting number is 1.
- $1 + (-1) = 0$
- For any real number a, $(1 \times a) + (-1 \times a) = a + (-a) = 0$.

Example 22

Perform the indicated operations.

A. $3 + 0$	B. $5 + (-1)$	C. $3 \div (-1)$	D. $-3 \div 1$
E. $0 \div (-1)$	F. 7×0	G. -1×-1	H. $7 + (-7)$

Solution

A. $3 + 0 = 3$
B. $5 + (-1) = 4$
C. $3 \div (-1) = -3$
D. $-3 \div 1 = -3$
E. $0 \div (-1) = 0$
F. $7 \times 0 = 0$
G. $-1 \times -1 = 1$
H. $7 + (-7) = 0$

   To simplify problems, $+1$ is often written as just 1, and $+(-1)$ as -1. Thus, $+1 + (-3)$ can be written more simply as $1 - 3$. Also $(-2) \times (+3)$ is frequently written as $(-2)(3)$. A positive 3, $+3$, can be written as 3. You write $(-7) + (+5)$ as $-7 + 5$.

PRACTICE PROBLEMS

1. Find the absolute value of each number.

   A. $|-3|$ B. $|+7|$ C. $|2|$

   D. $\left|-\dfrac{1}{2}\right|$ E. $\left|1\dfrac{1}{3}\right|$

2. Add these signed numbers.

   A. $4 + (-2)$ B. $-3 + (-8)$ C. $-5 + 3$
   D. $4 + 8$ E. $-9 + (-8)$

3. Subtract these signed numbers.

   A. $3 - (-4)$ B. $-7 - 5$ C. $-8 - (-3)$
   D. $6 - (-9)$ E. $7 - 15$

4. Multiply these signed numbers.

   A. -5×3 B. 8×4 C. -4×-3
   D. 10×-8 E. -11×7

5. Divide these signed numbers.

   A. $-4 \div 2$ B. $8 \div (-4)$ C. $15 \div (-3)$
   D. $-14 \div (-7)$ E. $20 \div 4$

6. Compute as indicated.

   A. $4 + (-4)$ B. $16 \div (-2)$ C. $3 - 4$
   D. $13 - (-6)$ E. $5 - 0$ F. $0 \div (-8)$
   G. $(-5)(-6)$ H. $(3)(-11)$ I. $(-8)(5)$
   J. $(-4) \div (-4)$ K. $-7 - (-4)$ L. $3 \div (-1)$

7. Compute these sums.

   A. $3 + (-5) + (-2) + 4 + 7 + (-3)$
   B. $5 + 2 + (-5) + (-4) + 3 + (-7) + 4 + (-9)$
   C. $(-2) + (-3) + (-5) + (-7) + (-9)$
   D. $(-2) + 0 + (-2) + 8 + (-4) + (-11)$
   E. $(-10) + 6 + (-4) + 10 + 4$

8. Compute these products.

   A. $(-2)3(-4)(-3)(-5)$

   B. $2(3)(5)(9)(-11)$

   C. $3(0)(-8)6(-4)(-13)7$

   D. $(-4)(-3)(-5)(-6)(-2)(-1)$

   E. $(-7)1(-10)(-3)3$

9. Compute as indicated.

   A. $8 + (-8)$ B. $(-3)0$ C. $0 + (-4)$
   D. $0 \div (-14)$ E. $(-1)6$ F. $(-2)(+2)$
   G. $(-1)(-8)$ H. $4 \div 0$ I. $(-3) \div (-1)$
   J. $(-17)(+1)$ K. $(-13) + (+13)$ L. $16 \div (-16)$
   M. $(-7) \div (+1)$ N. $8 \div (-1)$ O. $5 \div (5)$
   P. $0 + (-8)$

■ SOLUTIONS

1. A. $|-3| = 3$
    B. $|+7| = 7$
    C. $|2| = 2$
    D. $\left|-\dfrac{1}{2}\right| = \dfrac{1}{2}$
    E. $\left|1\dfrac{1}{3}\right| = 1\dfrac{1}{3}$

2. A. $|4| = 4$, $|-2| = 2$, $4 - 2 = 2$. The signs are unlike, with $4 > 2$, so the sign is positive. $4 + (-2) = 2$
    B. $|-3| = 3$, $|-8| = 8$, $3 + 8 = 11$. The signs are both negative, so the answer is negative. $(-3) + (-8) = -11$
    C. $|-5| = 5$, $|3| = 3$, $5 - 3 = 2$. The signs are unlike, with $5 > 3$, so the answer is negative. $(-5) + 3 = -2$
    D. $|4| = 4$, $|8| = 8$, $4 + 8 = 12$. The signs are both positive, so the answer is positive. $4 + 8 = 12$
    E. $|-9| = 9$, $|-8| = 8$, $9 + 8 = 17$. The signs are both negative, so the answer is negative. $(-9) + (-8) = -17$

3. A. Change to adding $+4$. The new problem is $3 + 4$. $|3| = 3$, $|4| = 4$, $3 + 4 = 7$. The signs are both positive, so the answer is positive. $3 - (-4) = 7$
    B. Change to adding -5. The new problem is $-7 + (-5)$. $|-7| = 7$, $|-5| = 5$, $7 + 5 = 12$. The signs are both negative, so the answer is negative. $(-7) - 5 = -12$
    C. Change to adding $+3$. The new problem is $-8 + 3$. $|-8| = 8$, $|3| = 3$, $8 - 3 = 5$. The signs are unlike, with $8 > 3$, so the answer is negative. $(-8) - (-3) = -5$

D. Change to adding $+9$. The new problem is $6 + 9$. $|6| = 6$, $|9| = 9$, $6 + 9 = 15$. The signs are both positive, so the answer is positive. $6 - (-9) = 15$

E. Change to adding -15. The new problem is $7 + (-15)$. $|7| = 7$, $|-15| = 15$, $15 - 7 = 8$. The signs are unlike, with $15 > 7$, so the answer is negative. $7 - 15 = -8$

4. A. $|-5| = 5$, $|3| = 3$, $5 \times 3 = 15$. The signs are unlike, so the answer is negative. $(-5) \times 3 = -15$
    B. $|8| = 8$, $|4| = 4$, $8 \times 4 = 32$. The signs are like, so the answer is positive. $8 \times 4 = 32$
    C. $|-4| = 4$, $|-3| = 3$, $4 \times 3 = 12$. The signs are like, so the answer is positive. $(-4) \times (-3) = 12$
    D. $|10| = 10$, $|-8| = 8$, $10 \times 8 = 80$. The signs are unlike, so the answer is negative. $10 \times (-8) = (-80)$
    E. $|-11| = 11$, $|7| = 7$, $11 \times 7 = 77$. The signs are unlike, so the answer is negative. $(-11) \times 7 = -77$

5. A. $|-4| = 4$, $|2| = 2$, $4 \div 2 = 2$. The signs are unlike, so the answer is negative. $(-4) \div 2 = -2$
    B. $|8| = 8$, $|-4| = 4$, $8 \div 4 = 2$. The signs are unlike, so the answer is negative. $8 \div (-4) = -2$
    C. $|15| = 15$, $|-3| = 3$, $15 \div 3 = 5$. The signs are unlike, so the answer is negative. $15 \div (-3) = -5$
    D. $|-14| = 14$, $|-7| = 7$, $14 \div 7 = 2$. The signs are like, so the answer is positive. $(-14) \div (-7) = 2$
    E. $|20| = 20$, $|4| = 4$, $20 \div 4 = 5$. The signs are like, so the answer is positive. $20 \div 4 = 5$

6. A. The numbers are opposites, so the sum is 0. $4 + (-4) = 0$
   B. $|16| = 16, |-2| = 2, 16 \div 2 = 8$. You are dividing unlike signs, so the answer is negative. $16 \div (-2) = -8$
   C. Change to adding -4. The new problem is $3 + (-4)$. $|3| = 3, |-4| = 4, 4 - 3 = 1$. You are adding unlike signs, with $4 > 3$, so the answer is negative. $3 - 4 = (-1)$
   D. Change to adding $+6$. The new problem is $13 + 6$. $|13| = 13, |6| = 6, 13 + 6 = 19$. You are adding like signs, both positive, so the answer is positive. $13 - (-6) = 19$
   E. You are subtracting 0, so the number is unchanged. $5 - 0 = 5$
   F. You are dividing zero by a nonzero number, so the answer is zero. $0 \div (-8) = 0$
   G. $|-5| = 5, |-6| = 6, 5 \times 6 = 30$. You are multiplying like signs, so the answer is positive. $(-5) \times (-6) = 30$
   H. $|3| = 3, |-11| = 11, 3 \times 11 = 33$. You are multiplying unlike signs, so the answer is negative. $3 \times (-11) = -33$
   I. $|-8| = 8, |5| = 5, 8 \times 5 = 40$. You are multiplying unlike signs, so the answer is negative. $(-8) \times 5 = -40$
   J. $|-4| = 4, |-4| = 4, 4 \div 4 = 1$. You are dividing like signs, so the answer is positive. $(-4) \div (-4) = 1$
   K. You change to adding $+4$. Your new problem is $-7 + 4$. $|-7| = 7, |+4| = 4, 7 - 4 = 3$. You are adding unlike signs, with $7 > 4$, so the answer is negative. $(-7) - (-4) = -3$
   L. You are dividing by -1, so the answer is the opposite of 3, which is -3. $3 \div (-1) = -3$

7. A. Add the positive numbers: $3 + 4 + 7 = +14$
      Add the negative numbers: $(-5) + (-2) + (-3) = -10$
      Now add $+14$ and -10: $(+14) + (-10) = +(14 - 10) = +4$
      $3 + (-5) + (-2) + 4 + 7 + (-3) = +4$
   B. Add the positive numbers: $5 + 2 + 3 + 4 = +14$
      Add the negative numbers: $(-5) + (-4) + (-7) + (-9) = -25$
      Now add $+14$ and -25: $(+14) + (-25) = -(25 - 14) = -11$
      $5 + 2 + (-5) + (-4) + 3 + (-7) + 4 + (-9) = -11$
   C. All the numbers are negative, so the answer is negative.
      $(-2) + (-3) + (-5) + (-7) + (-9) = -26$

   D. Add the negative numbers: $(-2) + (-2) + (-4) + (-11) = -19$
      Now add 8 and -19: $(+8) + (-19) = -(19 - 8) = -11$
      Now add -11 and 0: $-11 + 0 = -11$
      $(-2) + 0 + (-2) + 8 + (-4) + (-11) = -11$
   E. Add the positive numbers: $6 + 10 + 4 = +20$
      Add the negative numbers: $(-10) + (-4) = -14$
      Add $+20$ and -14:
      $20 + (-14) = +(20 - 14) = +6$
      $(-10) + 6 + (-4) + 10 + 4 = +6$

8. A. There is an even number of negative factors, so the answer is positive. Find the product of the absolute values of the factors. $2 \times 3 \times 4 \times 3 \times 5 = 360$, so $(-2)3(-4)(-3)(-5) = +360$.
   B. There is an odd number of negative factors, so the answer is negative. Find the product of the absolute values of the factors. $2 \times 3 \times 5 \times 9 \times 11 = 2,970$, so $2(3)(5)(9)(-11) = -2,970$.
   C. There is a factor of zero in the product, so the answer is 0. $3(0)(-8)6(-4)(-13)7 = 0$.
   D. There is an even number of negative factors, so the answer is positive. Find the product of the absolute values of the factors. $4 \times 3 \times 5 \times 6 \times 2 \times 1 = 720$, so $(-4)(-3)(-5)(-6)(-2)(-1) = +720$.
   E. There is an odd number of negative factors, so the answer is negative. Find the product of the absolute values of the factors. $7 \times 1 \times 10 \times 3 \times 3 = 630$, so $(-7)1(-10)(-3)3 = -630$.

9. A. This is the sum of opposites, so it is 0. $(8) + (-8) = 0$
   B. One factor is zero, so the product is 0. $(-3)0 = 0$
   C. You are adding zero, so the number is unchanged. $0 + (-4) = -4$
   D. Dividing zero by a nonzero number has an answer of zero. $0 \div (-14) = 0$
   E. Multiplying a number by -1 gives its opposite. $-1(6) = -6$
   F. You are multiplying two numbers with unlike signs. The answer is negative. $(-2)(+2) = -4$
   G. Multiplying a number by -1 gives its opposite. $(-1)(-8) = 8$

H. Dividing by zero is undefined. $4 \div 0 =$ undefined

I. Dividing a number by -1 gives its opposite. $(-3) \div (-1) = +3$

J. Multiplying by $+1$ leaves the number unchanged. $(-17)(+1) = -17$

K. This is the sum of opposites, so the result is 0. $(-13) + (+13) = 0$

L. A number is divided by its opposite, so the answer is -1. $16 \div (-16) = -1$

M. Dividing by $+1$ leaves the number unchanged. $(-7) \div (+1) = -7$

N. Dividing a number by -1 gives its opposite. $8 \div (-1) = -8$

O. Dividing a nonzero number by itself gives 1 as the answer. $5 \div 5 = 1$

P. Adding 0 to a number leaves the number unchanged. $0 + (-8) = -8$

ODD AND EVEN NUMBERS

An **even number** is an integer that is divisible by 2.

An **odd number** is an integer that has a remainder of 1 when divided by 2.

An even number can be written in the form $2n$, where n is an integer. The even numbers are $\ldots, -6, -4, -2, 0, 2, 4, 6, \ldots$. To get the positive even numbers, restrict n to the counting numbers.

An odd number can be written in the form $2k + 1$, where k is an integer. The odd numbers are $\ldots, -5, -3, -1, 1, 3, 5, \ldots$.

Every integer is either even or odd. No integer can be both even and odd. Zero is an even number. The smallest positive odd number is 1. The smallest positive even number is 2.

An even number added to another even number always yields a third even number. $2 + 6 = 8$, $0 + (-4) = -4$, $16 + (-4) = 12$.

An even number subtracted from another even number always yields a third even number. $4 - 12 = -8$, $16 - 2 = 14$, $0 - 8 = -8$, $10 - (-8) = 18$.

When an even number is multiplied by an even number, the result is an even number. $4 \times 6 = 24$, $8 \times 0 = 0$, $-4 \times 2 = -8$, $-6 \times -10 = 60$.

However, when you divide an even number by another even number, you do not always get an even number, and you may not get an integer at all. $18 \div (-2) = -9$, $24 \div 6 = 4$, $6 \div 2 = 3$, $4 \div 8 = \dfrac{1}{2}$, $6 \div 0 =$ undefined.

Summary:
  even + even = even
  even − even = even
  even × even = even

An odd number added to an odd number is an even number. $3 + 7 = 10$, $-5 + 11 = 6$, $-3 + 3 = 0$, $1 + 1 = 2$.

When an odd number is subtracted from an odd number, the answer is an even number. $7 - 13 = -6$, $5 - 3 = 2$, $7 - 7 = 0$, $11 - 3 = 8$.

When two odd numbers are multiplied, the product will be an odd number. $3 \times 5 = 15$, $7 \times -5 = -35$, $7 \times (-9) = -63$.

When two odd numbers are divided, the result is always defined, but may not be an integer. It may be odd or not an integer at all. $21 \div 3 = 7$, $15 \div (-5) = -3$, $11 \div 5 = \dfrac{11}{5}$, $5 \div 7 = \dfrac{5}{7}$.

Summary:
  odd + odd = even
  odd − odd = even
  odd × odd = odd

Adding an even number and an odd number always gives an odd number for the answer. $3 + 4 = 7$, $8 + (-5) = 3$, $11 + 12 = 23$, $15 + 0 = 15$, $8 + 5 = 13$.

When you subtract an even number and an odd number, the result is an odd number. $5 - 2 = 3$, $6 - 1 = 5$, $-2 - (-3) = 1$, $8 + (-3) = 5$, $-7 + 6 = -1$.

If an even number and an odd number are multiplied, the answer is an even number. $3 \times 6 = 18$, $-7 \times 2 = -14$, $0 \times 3 = 0$, $5 \times 8 = 40$, $6 \times 11 = 66$.

When you divide an even number and an odd number, the answer **will not** be an integer when the divisor is an even number, and the answer **may not** be an integer when the divisor is an odd number. $7 \div 0 =$ undefined, $5 \div 2 = \dfrac{5}{2}$, $11 \div 14 = \dfrac{11}{14}$, $18 \div 3 = 6$, $10 \div 7 = \dfrac{10}{7}$.

Summary: odd + even = odd
even + odd = odd
odd − even = odd
even − odd = odd
odd × even = even
even × odd = even

Odd and Even Exercises

1. Which of these are even?

A. $3 + 3$	B. $5 + 6$	C. $8 - 2$	D. $7 - 3$
E. $4 + 6$	F. $7 + (-3)$	G. $5 + (-6)$	H. $4 + 5$
I. 3×5	J. 4×3	K. 5×6	L. -2×4
M. 5×1	N. $8 + 2$	O. $18 \quad 14$	P. $3 - 10$

2. Which of these are odd?

A. $3 + 7$	B. $5 - 2$	C. $2 + 7$	D. 5×6
E. 7×3	F. $9 + 4$	G. $8 + 3$	H. $-8 + 3$
I. 2×0	J. $5 - 3$	K. $7 + 5$	L. $4 - 5$
M. $5 + 7$	N. $9 + 0$	O. $3 + 5$	P. 8×7

Solutions

1. A. odd + odd = even $3 + 3$ is even
   B. odd + even = odd $5 + 6$ is NOT even
   C. even − even = even $8 - 2$ is even
   D. odd − odd = even $7 - 3$ is even
   E. even + even = even $4 + 6$ is even
   F. odd + odd = even $7 + (-3)$ is even
   G. odd + even = odd $5 + (-6)$ is NOT even
   H. even + odd = odd $4 + 5$ is NOT even
   I. odd × odd = odd 3×5 is NOT even
   J. even × odd = even 4×3 is even
   K. odd × even = even 5×6 is even
   L. even × even = even -2×4 is even
   M. odd × odd = odd 5×1 is NOT even
   N. even + even = even $8 + 2$ is even
   O. even − even = even $18 - 14$ is even
   P. odd − even = odd $3 - 10$ is NOT even

2. A. odd + odd = even $3 + 7$ is NOT odd
   B. odd − even = odd $5 - 2$ is odd
   C. even + odd = odd $2 + 7$ is odd
   D. odd × even = even 5×6 is NOT odd

E. odd × odd = odd	7×3 is odd
F. odd + even = odd	$9 + 4$ is odd
G. even + odd = odd	$8 + 3$ is odd
H. even + odd = odd	$-8 + 3$ is odd
I. even × even = even	2×0 is NOT odd
J. odd − odd = even	$5 - 3$ is NOT odd
K. odd + odd = even	$7 + 5$ is NOT odd
L. even − odd = odd	$4 - 5$ is odd
M. odd + odd = even	$5 + 7$ is NOT odd
N. odd + even = odd	$9 + 0$ is odd
O. odd + odd = even	$3 + 5$ is NOT odd
P. even × odd = even	8×7 is NOT odd

PRIMES, MULTIPLES, AND DIVISORS

A counting number a is a **multiple** of a counting number b if there is a counting number c such that $b \times c = a$.

To find the multiples of 3, multiply 3 by each counting number in turn. $3 \times 1 = 3$, $3 \times 2 = 6$, $3 \times 3 = 9$, $3 \times 4 = 12 \ldots$. Therefore, the multiples of 3 are $3, 6, 9, 12, 15 \ldots$.

The **least common multiple** of two or more counting numbers is the smallest positive number that is a multiple of each of the numbers.

The least common multiple of 6 and 10 is found by listing the multiples of each number and finding the smallest number that is in each list. The multiples of 6 are $6, 12, 18, 24, 30, 36, 42, 48, \ldots$ and the multiples of 10 are $10, 20, 30, 40, 50, 60, \ldots$. Since 30 is the smallest number that is in both lists, the least common multiple (LCM) of 6 and 10 is 30. You can write this as LCM $(6, 10) = 30$.

Example 23

Find the first five multiples of each number.

A. 7   B. 8   C. 9   D. 10   E. 15

Solution

A. $7 \times 1 = 7$, $7 \times 2 = 14$, $7 \times 3 = 21$, $7 \times 4 = 28$, $7 \times 5 = 35$ 7, 14, 21, 28, 35
B. $8 \times 1 = 8$, $8 \times 2 = 16$, $8 \times 3 = 24$, $8 \times 4 = 32$, $8 \times 5 = 40$ 8, 16, 24, 32, 40
C. $9 \times 1 = 9$, $9 \times 2 = 18$, $9 \times 3 = 27$, $9 \times 4 = 36$, $9 \times 5 = 45$ 9, 18, 27, 36, 45
D. $10 \times 1 = 10$, $10 \times 2 = 20$, $10 \times 3 = 30$, $10 \times 4 = 40$,
   $10 \times 5 = 50$ 10, 20, 30, 40, 50
E. $15 \times 1 = 15$, $15 \times 2 = 30$, $15 \times 3 = 45$, $15 \times 4 = 60$,
   $15 \times 5 = 75$ 15, 30, 45, 60, 75

Example 24

Find the least common multiple of each pair of numbers.

A. 4 and 6   B. 30 and 24   C. 8 and 15

Solution

A. The multiples of 4 are $4, 8, 12, 16, 20, 24, 30, 32, 36, \ldots$.
   The multiples of 6 are $6, 12, 18, 24, 30, 36, 42, \ldots$.
   12, 24, and 36 are three common multiples of 4 and 6. So 12 is the smallest number common to both lists, and LCM $(4, 6) = 12$.

B. The multiples of 30 are 30, 60, 90, 120, 150, 180, 210, ...
The multiples of 24 are 24, 48, 72, 96, 120, 144, 168, 192, ...
120 is the only number common to both lists. LCM (30, 24) = 120.
C. The multiples of 8 are 8, 16, 24, 32, 40, 48, 56, 64, 72, 80, 88, 96, 104, 112, 120, 128, ...
The multiples of 15 are 15, 30, 45, 60, 75, 90, 105, 120, 135, 150, ...
The only number in both lists is 120. LCM (8, 15) = 120.

Notes:

- If you do not have a multiple in common in your lists, extend your list of multiples until one is reached.
- For counting numbers a and b, LCM $(a, b) \leq a \times b$. This means that the least common multiple of two numbers is less than or equal to the product of the two numbers.

Example 25

Find the least common multiple for these sets of three numbers.
A. 5, 12, 8   B. 10, 25, 15

Solution

A. The multiples of 5 are 5, 10, 15, 20, 25, 30, 35, 40, 45, 50, 55, 60, 65, 70, 75, 80, 85, 90, 95, 100, 105, 110, 115, 120, 125, ...
The multiples of 12 are 12, 24, 36, 48, 60, 72, 84, 96, 108, 120, 132, 144, ...
The multiples of 8 are 8, 16, 24, 32, 40, 48, 56, 64, 72, 80, 88, 96, 104, 112, 120, 128, 136, ...
The number common to all three lists is 120. LCM (5, 12, 8) = 120.
B. The multiples of 10 are 10, 20, 30, 40, 50, 60, 70, 80, 90, 100, 110, 120, 130, 140, 150, 160, 170, 180, ...
The multiples of 25 are 25, 50, 75, 100, 125, 150, 175, 200, ...
The multiples of 15 are 15, 30, 45, 60, 75, 90, 105, 120, 135, 150, 165, 180, ...
The number common to all three lists is 150. LCM (10, 25, 15) = 150.

Factors and Greatest Common Divisors

A counting number a is a divisor of a counting number b if there is a counting number c such that $a \times c = b$.

Since $a \times c = b$, we also say that a is a **factor** of b.

In most cases the terms *factor* and *divisor* are used interchangeably; however, there are times when they have a slight difference. Since you are using counting numbers, this difference is not relevant on the GMAT.

The **greatest common divisor (GCD)** for two or more counting numbers is the largest counting number that is a divisor of each of the counting numbers.

To find the divisors of a counting number such as 12, write down the factors, which come in pairs. However, when both factors are the same, you list it just once. The divisors of 12 are 1 and 12, 2 and 6, and 3 and 4. You usually list the divisors in numerical order. Thus, you say that the divisors of 12 are 1, 2, 3, 4, 6, and 12. Since 12 is equal to the number itself, you say that 12 is an **improper divisor** of 12, and 1, 2, 3, 4, and 6 are the **proper divisors** of 12.

Example 26

List all the divisors of the given numbers.
A. 16   B. 20   C. 21   D. 23   E. 36

Solution

A. $1 \times 16 = 16$, $2 \times 8 = 16$, $4 \times 4 = 16$
   The divisors of 16 are 1, 2, 4, 8, 16.
B. $1 \times 20 = 20$, $2 \times 10 = 20$, $4 \times 5 = 20$
   The divisors of 20 are 1, 2, 4, 5, 10, 20.
C. $1 \times 21 = 21$, $3 \times 7 = 21$
   The divisors of 21 are 1, 3, 7, 21.
D. $1 \times 23 = 23$
   The divisors of 23 are 1, 23.
E. $1 \times 36 = 36$, $2 \times 18 = 36$, $3 \times 12 = 36$, $4 \times 9 = 36$, $6 \times 6 = 36$
   The divisors of 36 are 1, 2, 3, 4, 6, 9, 12, 18, 36.

Example 27

Find the greatest common divisor of each pair of numbers.
A. 8 and 12   B. 15 and 40   C. 30 and 24   D. 8 and 15   E. 7 and 14

Solution

A. $1 \times 8 = 8$, $2 \times 4 = 8$ The divisors of 8 are 1, 2, 4, 8.
   $1 \times 12 = 12$, $2 \times 6 = 12$, $3 \times 4 = 12$ The divisors of 12 are 1, 2, 3, 4, 6, and 12.
   1, 2, and 4 are the common divisors of 8 and 12. The greatest common divisor of 8 and 12 is 4. You can also write this as GCD (8, 12) = 4.
B. $1 \times 15 = 15$, $3 \times 5 = 15$ The divisors of 15 are 1, 3, 5, 15.
   $1 \times 40 = 40$, $2 \times 20 = 40$, $4 \times 10 = 40$, $5 \times 8 = 40$ The divisors of 40 are 1, 2, 4, 5, 8, 10, 20, 40. The common divisors of 15 and 40 are 1 and 5. GCD (15, 40) = 5.
C. $1 \times 30 = 30$, $2 \times 15 = 30$, $3 \times 10 = 30$, $5 \times 6 = 30$ The divisors of 30 are 1, 2, 3, 5, 6, 10, 15, 30.
   $1 \times 24 = 24$, $2 \times 12 = 24$, $3 \times 8 = 24$, $4 \times 6 = 24$ The divisors of 24 are 1, 2, 3, 4, 6, 8, 12, 24.
   The common divisors of 30 and 24 are 1, 2, 3, and 6. GCD (30, 24) = 6.
D. $1 \times 8 = 8$, $2 \times 4 = 8$ The divisors of 8 are 1, 2, 4, 8.
   $1 \times 15 = 15$, $3 \times 5 = 15$ The divisors of 15 are 1, 3, 5, 15.
   The only common divisor of 8 and 15 is 1. GCD (8, 15) = 1.
E. $1 \times 7 = 7$ The divisors of 7 are 1, 7.
   $1 \times 14 = 14$, $2 \times 7 = 14$ The divisors of 14 are 1, 2, 7, 14.
   The common divisors of 7 and 14 are 1 and 7. GCD (7, 14) = 7.
   The greatest common divisor of two counting numbers is at least 1 and never larger than the smaller of the two numbers.

Example 28

Find the greatest common divisor for each set of three numbers.
A. 8, 10, and 12   B. 39, 65, and 91   C. 250, 375, and 625

Solution

A. $1 \times 8 = 8$, $2 \times 4 = 8$ The divisors of 8 are 1, 2, 4, 8.
   $1 \times 10 = 10$, $2 \times 5 = 10$ The divisors of 10 are 1, 2, 5, 10.
   $1 \times 12 = 12$, $2 \times 6 = 12$, $3 \times 4 = 12$ The divisors of 12 are 1, 2, 3, 4, 6, and 12.
   The common divisors of 8, 10, and 12 are 1 and 2. GCD (8, 10, 12) = 2.

B.　$1 \times 39 = 39,\ 3 \times 13 = 39$　　　The divisors of 39 are 1, 3, 13, 39.
　　$1 \times 65 = 65,\ 5 \times 13 = 65$　　　The divisors of 65 are 1, 5, 13, 65.
　　$1 \times 91 = 91,\ 7 \times 13 = 91$　　　The divisors of 91 are 1, 7, 13, 91.
　　The common divisors of 39, 65, and 91 are 1 and 13. GCD (39, 65, 91) = 13.
C.　$1 \times 250 = 250,\ 2 \times 125 = 250,\ 5 \times 50 = 250,\ 10 \times 25 = 250$　　　The divisors
　　of 250 are 1, 2, 5, 10, 25, 50, 125, 250.
　　$1 \times 375 = 375,\ 3 \times 125 = 375,\ 5 \times 75 = 375,\ 15 \times 25 = 375$　　　The divisors
　　of 375 are 1, 3, 5, 15, 25, 75, 125, 375.
　　$1 \times 625 = 625,\ 5 \times 125 = 625,\ 25 \times 25 = 625$　　　The divisors of 625 are 1,
　　5, 25, 125, 625.
　　The common divisors of 250, 375, and 625 are 1, 5, 25, and 125.
　　GCD (250, 375, 625) = 125.

When a number is a divisor of a second number, it means that there is a counting number such that the product of it and the divisor equals the second number. However, when the first number is not a divisor of the second, you cannot find a counting number that will yield the second. In this case, you try to get as close as you can and stay less than the second number. To make them equal, you add the missing amount, called the *remainder*.

If a is a divisor of b, then there is a counting number c such that $a \times c = b$. If a is not a divisor of b, then there exist counting numbers q and r such that $a \times q + r = b$, where $0 < r < a$.

Prime Numbers

A **prime number** is a counting number greater than 1 such that its only counting number divisors are 1 and itself. Since a prime number is greater than 1, clearly 0 and 1 are not prime numbers.

A **composite number** is a counting number greater than 1 such that it has at least three divisors. A counting number greater than 1 is either prime or composite. No counting number is both prime and composite.

The **prime factorization** of a number is a set of prime numbers such that the product of these prime factors will yield the given number. A prime factor may be used more than once in the product. The prime factorization of 6 is $6 = 2 \times 3$, and the prime factorization of 8 is $8 = 2 \times 2 \times 2$, or $8 = 2^3$.

Exercise

Find the prime factorization of each number.
A. 24　　　　　B. 50　　　　　C. 72　　　　　D. 23　　　　　E. 39

Solution

A.　$24 = 2 \times 12 = 2 \times 2 \times 6 = 2 \times 2 \times 2 \times 3 = 2^3 \times 3$
B.　$50 = 2 \times 25 = 2 \times 5 \times 5 = 2 \times 5^2$
C.　$72 = 2 \times 36 = 2 \times 2 \times 18 = 2 \times 2 \times 2 \times 9 = 2 \times 2 \times 2 \times 3 \times 3 = 2^3 \times 3^2$
D.　$23 = 23$
E.　$39 = 3 \times 13$

In finding the prime factorization of a counting number, look for divisors (or factors) of the number that are prime. Thus, it is helpful to know some prime numbers. The prime numbers less than 100 are 2, 3, 5, 7, 11, 13, 17, 19, 23, 29, 31, 37, 41, 43, 47, 53, 59, 61, 67, 71, 73, 79, 83, 89, and 97. It is important to notice that 2 is the only even number that is prime, since for a number to be even means that it is divisible by 2.

Example 29

Find the prime factorization of each number.
A. 54   B. 150   C. 168   D. 500   E. 144

Solution

A. $54 = 2 \times 27 = 2 \times 3 \times 9 = 2 \times 3 \times 3 \times 3 = 2 \times 3^3$
B. $150 = 2 \times 75 = 2 \times 3 \times 25 = 2 \times 3 \times 5 \times 5 = 2 \times 3 \times 5^2$
C. $168 = 2 \times 84 = 2 \times 2 \times 42 = 2 \times 2 \times 2 \times 21 = 2 \times 2 \times 2 \times 3 \times 7 = 2^3 \times 3 \times 7$
D. $500 = 2 \times 250 = 2 \times 2 \times 125 = 2 \times 2 \times 5 \times 25 = 2 \times 2 \times 5 \times 5 \times 5 = 2^2 \times 5^3$
E. $144 = 2 \times 72 = 2 \times 2 \times 36 = 2 \times 2 \times 2 \times 18 = 2 \times 2 \times 2 \times 2 \times 9 = 2 \times 2 \times 2 \times 2 \times 3 \times 3 = 2^4 \times 3^2$

Finding the prime factorization of a number requires you to divide the number by primes until you find one that is a divisor; then you use that same prime to see if it is a divisor of the second factor. You continue to work on the factor that is not known to be a prime until you have reduced it to a prime. You check your work by multiplying all the prime factors together to get the original number.

DIVISIBILITY TESTS

One thing that will help you to find the prime factorization of a number is a quick way to tell if a number is divisible by smaller numbers.

- A counting number is divisible by 2 if its units digit is an even number. Thus, if the rightmost digit of a counting number is 0, 2, 4, 6, or 8, the number is divisible by 2.
- A counting number is divisible by 3 if the sum of its digits is divisible by 3.
- A counting number is divisible by 5 if its units digit is 0 or 5.
- A counting number is divisible by 4 if the two-digit number formed by the tens and units digits is divisible by 4.
- A counting number is divisible by 6 if it is divisible by 2 and also by 3. Thus, if the units digit is even and the sum of all digits is divisible by 3, then the number is divisible by 6.
- A counting number is divisible by 9 if the sum of its digits is divisible by 9.
- A counting number is divisible by 10 if the units digit is 0.

Exercise

Which of these numbers are divisible by 2 or 4?
A. 68,532   B. 384,670   C. 165,501   D. 483,000   E. 759,258

Solution

A. Since the units digit is 2, which is even, 68,532 is divisible by 2.
    Since the last two digits are 32, which is divisible by 4, the number 68,532 is divisible by 4.
B. Since the units digits is 0, which is even, 384,670 is divisible by 2.
    Since the last two digits are 70, which is not divisible by 4, the number 384,670 is not divisible by 4.
C. Since the units digit is 1, which is odd, 165,501 is not divisible by 2 or by 4.
D. Since the units digit is 0, which is even, 483,000 is divisible by 2.
    Since the last two digits are 00, which is divisible by 4, the number 483,000 is divisible by 4.
E. Since the units digit is 8, which is even, 759,258 is divisible by 2.
    Since the last two digits are 58, which is not divisible by 4, the number 759,258 is not divisible by 4.

A number can be divisible by 2 and not divisible by 4. However, as you can see in part C above, if a number is not divisible by 2, it is never divisible by 4.

Example 30

Which of these numbers are divisible by 3, 6, or 9?
A. 68,532   B. 384,670   C. 163,521   D. 483,000   E. 759,258

Solution

A. $6 + 8 + 5 + 3 + 2 = 24$
    Since the sum of the digits is 24, which is divisible by 3, the number 68,532 is divisible by 3.
    Since the units digit is 2, the number is divisible by 2. Thus, since 68,532 is divisible by both 2 and 3, it is divisible by 6.
    Since the sum of the digits is 24, which is not divisible by 9, the number 68,532 is not divisible by 9.
B. $3 + 8 + 4 + 6 + 7 + 0 = 28$
    Since the sum of the digits is 28, which is not divisible by 3, the number 384,670 is not divisible by 3.
    Since 384,670 is not divisible by 3, it is not divisible by either 6 or 9.
C. $1 + 6 + 3 + 5 + 2 + 1 = 18$
    Since the sum of the digits is divisible by 3, the number 163,521 is divisible by 3.
    Since the units digit is 1, which is odd, 163,521 is not divisible by 2; therefore, it is not divisible by 6.
    Since the sum of the digits is divisible by 9, the number 163,521 is divisible by 9.
D. $4 + 8 + 3 + 0 + 0 + 0 = 15$
    Since the sum of the digits is divisible by 3, the number 483,000 is divisible by 3.
    Since the units digit is even and the number is divisible by 3, the number 483,000 is divisible by 6.
    Since the sum of the digits is not divisible by 9, the number 483,000 is not divisible by 9.
E. $7 + 5 + 9 + 2 + 5 + 8 = 36$
    Since the sum of the digits is divisible by 3, the number 759,258 is divisible by 3.
    Since the units digit is even and the number is divisible by 3, the number 759,258 is divisible by 6.
    Since the sum of the digits is divisible by 9, the number 759,258 is divisible by 9.

A number can be divisible by 3 and still not be divisible by 6 or 9. It is possible for a number to be divisible by 3, 6, and 9, by just 3 and 6, or by just 3 and 9. However, if a number is not divisible by 3, it is never divisible by 6 or 9.

Exercise

Which of these numbers are divisible by 5 or 10?
A. 68,535   B. 384,670   C. 561,501   D. 483,000   E. 759,205

Solution

A. Since the units digit is 5, the number 68,535 is divisible by 5.
    Since the units digit is not 0, the number 68,535 is not divisible by 10.
B. Since the units digit is 0, the number 384,670 is divisible by 5.
    Since the units digit is 0, the number 384,670 is divisible by 10.
C. Since the units digit is 1, the number 561,501 is not divisible by 5 or by 10.
D. Since the units digit is 0, the number 483,000 is divisible by 5.
    Since the units digit is 0, the number 483,000 is divisible by 10.
E. Since the units digit is 5, the number 759,205 is divisible by 5.
    Since the units digit is not 0, the number 759,205 is not divisible by 10.

A number that has a units digit of 5 is divisible by 5, but not by 10. Also, when the units digit of a number is 0, it will always be divisible by both 5 and 10.

GCD AND LCM REVISITED

A second way to find the GCD and LCM of a number is to use prime factorization. When you are finding the divisors of numbers with many factors, it is easy to overlook a factor that may be a common divisor. Similarly, in listing the multiples of a number, any error in finding one could cause other numbers to be wrong. It could also take a long time to find the common multiple if it is large.

To find the least common multiple (LCM) by using the prime factorization, you must first find the prime factorization of each number. Then you need to find the greatest power each different factor of the number has. The least common multiple will be the product of each different factor to the greatest power at which it occurs.

Exercise

Find the least common multiple of these sets of numbers.
A. 150 and 225   B. 63 and 84   C. 24, 60, and 96

Solution

A. $150 = 2 \cdot 75 = 2 \cdot 3 \cdot 25 = 2 \cdot 3 \cdot 5 \cdot 5 = 2 \cdot 3 \cdot 5^2$
    $225 = 3 \cdot 75 = 3 \cdot 3 \cdot 25 = 3 \cdot 3 \cdot 5 \cdot 5 = 3^2 \cdot 5^2$
    The different prime factors are 2, 3, and 5. The greatest power of 2 is 1, the greatest power of 3 is 2, and the greatest power of 5 is 2.
    LCM $(150, 225) = 2^1 \cdot 3^2 \cdot 5^2 = 2 \cdot 9 \cdot 25 = 450$
B. $63 = 3 \cdot 21 = 3 \cdot 3 \cdot 7 = 3^2 \cdot 7$
    $84 = 2 \cdot 42 = 2 \cdot 2 \cdot 21 = 2 \cdot 2 \cdot 3 \cdot 7 = 2^2 \cdot 3 \cdot 7$
    The greatest power of 2 is 2, the greatest power of 3 is 2, and the greatest power for 7 is 1.
    LCM $(63, 84) = 2^2 \cdot 3^2 \cdot 7 = 4 \cdot 9 \cdot 7 = 252$
C. $24 = 2 \cdot 12 = 2 \cdot 2 \cdot 6 = 2 \cdot 2 \cdot 2 \cdot 3 = 2^3 \cdot 3$
    $60 = 2 \cdot 30 = 2 \cdot 2 \cdot 15 = 2 \cdot 2 \cdot 3 \cdot 5 = 2^2 \cdot 3 \cdot 5$
    $96 = 2 \cdot 48 = 2 \cdot 2 \cdot 24 = 2 \cdot 2 \cdot 2 \cdot 12 = 2 \cdot 2 \cdot 2 \cdot 2 \cdot 6 = 2 \cdot 2 \cdot 2 \cdot 2 \cdot 2 \cdot 3 = 2^5 \cdot 3$
    The greatest occurring power of 2 is 5; the greatest power of 3 is 1, and the greatest power of 5 is 1.
    LCM $(24, 60, 96) = 2^5 \cdot 3 \cdot 5 = 32 \cdot 3 \cdot 5 = 480$

To find the greatest common divisor (GCD) of a set of numbers, first find the prime factorization of each number. Next identify the primes that are common to all the numbers and then the greatest common power that these primes have. The greatest common divisor of the numbers is the product of these common divisors to their greatest common powers.

Exercise

Find the greatest common divisor for these sets of numbers.

A. 32 and 104   B. 120 and 216   C. 225, 375, and 825

Solution

A. $32 = 2 \cdot 16 = 2 \cdot 2 \cdot 8 = 2 \cdot 2 \cdot 2 \cdot 4 = 2 \cdot 2 \cdot 2 \cdot 2 \cdot 2 = 2^5$

$104 = 2 \cdot 52 = 2 \cdot 2 \cdot 26 = 2 \cdot 2 \cdot 2 \cdot 13 = 2^3 \cdot 13$

The only common prime factor for the numbers is 2, and 3 is the greatest common power of 2.

GCD $(32, 104) = 2^3 = 8$

B. $120 = 2 \cdot 60 = 2 \cdot 2 \cdot 30 = 2 \cdot 2 \cdot 2 \cdot 15 = 2 \cdot 2 \cdot 2 \cdot 3 \cdot 5 = 2^3 \cdot 3 \cdot 5$

$216 = 2 \cdot 108 = 2 \cdot 2 \cdot 54 = 2 \cdot 2 \cdot 2 \cdot 27 = 2 \cdot 2 \cdot 2 \cdot 3 \cdot 9 = 2 \cdot 2 \cdot 2 \cdot 3 \cdot 3 \cdot 3 = 2^3 \cdot 3^3$

The common prime divisors are 2 and 3. The greatest common power of 2 is 3, and the greatest common power of 3 is 1.

GCD $(120, 216) = 2^3 \cdot 3^1 = 8 \cdot 3 = 24$

C. $225 = 3 \cdot 75 = 3 \cdot 3 \cdot 25 = 3 \cdot 3 \cdot 5 \cdot 5 = 3^2 \cdot 5^2$

$375 = 3 \cdot 125 = 3 \cdot 5 \cdot 25 = 3 \cdot 5 \cdot 5 \cdot 5 = 3 \cdot 5^3$

$825 = 3 \cdot 275 = 3 \cdot 5 \cdot 55 = 3 \cdot 5 \cdot 5 \cdot 11 = 3 \cdot 5^2 \cdot 11$

The common divisors are 3 and 5. The greatest common power of 3 is 1, and of 5 is 2.

GCD $(225, 375, 825) = 3^1 \cdot 5^2 = 3 \cdot 25 = 75$

PRACTICE PROBLEMS

1. Which of these are odd numbers?
    A. $4 + 3$ B. $3 - 1$ C. 4×3
    D. 5×7 E. $5 + 11$ F. $12 - 5$
    G. $3 + 7$ H. $6 - 4$

2. Which of these numbers are even?
    A. $7 + 2$ B. $8 - 3$ C. 5×2
    D. 6×4 E. $11 + 9$ F. 3×5
    G. $8 - 4$ H. $7 + 3$

3. Find the least common multiple.
    A. 20 and 24   B. 15 and 10
    C. 8 and 24   D. 14 and 10

4. Find the greatest common divisor.
    A. 20 and 24   B. 15 and 28
    C. 8 and 48   D. 14 and 10

5. Which of these numbers are prime?
    A. 14   B. 23   C. 79
    D. 51   E. 117

6. Which of these numbers are composite?
    A. 81   B. 18   C. 43
    D. 19   E. 91

7. Find the prime factorization of each number.
    A. 400   B. 98   C. 54
    D. 96   E. 150

8. Which of these numbers are divisible by 2 or 4?
    A. 4,794   B. 727   C. 9,244   D. 1,812

9. Which of these numbers are divisible by 3, 6, or 9?
    A. 6,858   B. 5,706   C. 7,415   D. 2,853

10. Which of these numbers are divisible by 5 or 10?
    A. 1,565   B. 8,970   C. 2,105   D. 7,283

11. Find the least common multiple.
    A. 252 and 588   B. 54 and 144
    C. 56, 140, and 168

12. Find the greatest common divisor.
    A. 252 and 588   B. 54 and 144
    C. 56, 140, and 168

SOLUTIONS

1. A. even + odd = odd   4 + 3 is odd
   B. odd − odd = even   3 − 1 is NOT odd
   C. even × odd = even   4 × 3 is NOT odd
   D. odd × odd = odd   5 × 7 is odd
   E. odd + odd = even   5 + 11 is NOT odd
   F. even − odd = odd   12 − 5 is odd
   G. odd + odd = even   3 + 7 is NOT odd
   H. even − even = even   6 − 4 is NOT odd

2. A. odd + even = odd   7 + 2 is NOT even
   B. even − odd = odd   8 − 3 is NOT even
   C. odd × even = even   5 × 2 is even
   D. even × even = even   6 × 4 is even
   E. odd + odd = even   11 + 9 is even
   F. odd × odd = odd   3 × 5 is NOT even
   G. even − even = even   8 − 4 is even
   H. odd + odd = even   7 + 3 is even

3. A. The multiples of 20 are 20, 40, 60, 80, 100, 120, 140, 160, ...
      The multiples of 24 are 24, 48, 72, 96, 120, 144, 180, ...
      LCM (20, 24) = 120
   B. The multiples of 15 are 15, 30, 45, 60, 75, 90, 105, ...
      The multiples of 10 are 10, 20, 30, 40, 50, ...
      LCM (15, 10) = 30
   C. The multiples of 8 are 8, 16, 24, 32, 40, 48, 56, ...
      The multiples of 24 are 24, 48, 72, 96, ...
      LCM (8, 24) = 24
   D. The multiples of 14 are 14, 28, 42, 56, 70, 84, ...
      The multiples of 10 are 10, 20, 30, 40, 50, 60, 70, ...
      LCM (14, 10) = 70

4. A. $1 \times 20 = 20, 2 \times 10 = 20, 4 \times 5 = 20$
      The divisors of 20 are 1, 2, 4, 5, 10, 20.
      $1 \times 24 = 24, 2 \times 12 = 24, 3 \times 8 = 24, 4 \times 6 = 24$
      The divisors of 24 are 1, 2, 3, 4, 6, 8, 12, 24.
      GCD (20, 24) = 4
   B. $1 \times 15 = 15, 3 \times 5 = 15$
      The divisors of 15 are 1, 3, 5, 15.
      $1 \times 28 = 28, 2 \times 14 = 28, 4 \times 7 = 28$
      The divisors of 28 are 1, 2, 4, 7, 14, 28.
      GCD (15, 28) = 1

   C. $1 \times 8 = 8, 2 \times 4 = 8$
      The divisors of 8 are 1, 2, 4, 8.
      $1 \times 48 = 48, 2 \times 24 = 48, 3 \times 16 = 48, 4 \times 12 = 48, 6 \times 8 = 48$ The divisors of 48 are 1, 2, 3, 4, 6, 8, 12, 16, 24, 48.
      GCD (8, 48) = 8
   D. $1 \times 14 = 14, 2 \times 7 = 14$
      The divisors of 14 are 1, 2, 7, 14.
      $1 \times 10 = 10, 2 \times 5 = 10$
      The divisors of 10 are 1, 2, 5, 10.
      GCD (14, 10) = 2

5. A. $14 = 2 \cdot 7$ 14 is NOT prime
   B. $23 = 23$ 23 is prime
   C. $79 = 79$ 79 is prime
   D. $51 = 3 \cdot 17$ 51 is NOT prime
   E. $117 = 3 \cdot 39$ 117 is NOT prime

6. A. $81 = 3 \cdot 27$ 81 is composite
   B. $18 = 2 \cdot 9$ 18 is composite
   C. $43 = 43$ 43 is NOT composite
   D. $19 = 19$ 19 is NOT composite
   E. $91 = 7 \cdot 13$ 91 is composite

7. A. $400 = 2 \cdot 200 = 2 \cdot 2 \cdot 100 = 2 \cdot 2 \cdot 2 \cdot 50 = 2 \cdot 2 \cdot 2 \cdot 2 \cdot 25 = 2 \cdot 2 \cdot 2 \cdot 2 \cdot 5 \cdot 5 = 2^4 \cdot 5^2$
   B. $98 = 2 \cdot 49 = 2 \cdot 7 \cdot 7 = 2 \cdot 7^2$
   C. $54 = 2 \cdot 27 = 2 \cdot 3 \cdot 9 = 2 \cdot 3 \cdot 3 \cdot 3 = 2 \cdot 3^3$
   D. $96 = 2 \cdot 48 = 2 \cdot 2 \cdot 24 = 2 \cdot 2 \cdot 2 \cdot 12 = 2 \cdot 2 \cdot 2 \cdot 2 \cdot 6 = 2 \cdot 2 \cdot 2 \cdot 2 \cdot 2 \cdot 3 = 2^5 \cdot 3$
   E. $150 = 2 \cdot 75 = 2 \cdot 3 \cdot 25 = 2 \cdot 3 \cdot 5 \cdot 5 = 2 \cdot 3 \cdot 5^2$

8. A. The units digit is even, so 4,794 is divisible by 2.
      The last two digits are 94, which is not divisible by 4, so 4,794 is not divisible by 4.
   B. The units digit is odd, so 727 is not divisible by either 2 or 4.
   C. The units digit is even, so 9,244 is divisible by 2.
      The last two digits are 44, which is divisible by 4, so 9,244 is divisible by 4.
   D. The units digit is 2, so 1,812 is divisible by 2.
      The last two digits are 12, which is divisible by 4, so 1,812 is divisible by 4.

9. A. $6+8+5+8=27$

Since the sum of the digits is divisible by 3, the number 6,858 is divisible by 3.

Since the units digit is even and the number is divisible by 3, the number 6,858 is divisible by 6.

Since the sum of the digits is 27, which is divisible by 9, the number 6,858 is divisible by 9.

B. $5+7+0+6=18$

Since the sum of the digits is divisible by 3, the number 5,706 is divisible by 3.

Since the units digit is even and the number is divisible by 3, the number 5,706 is divisible by 6.

Since the sum of the digits is divisible by 9, the number 5,706 is divisible by 9.

C. $7+4+1+5=17$

Since the sum of the digits is not divisible by 3, the number 7,415 is not divisible by 3. Because it is not divisible by 3, the number 7,415 is not divisible by 6 or 9.

D. $2+8+5+3=18$

Since the sum of the digits is divisible by 3, the number 2,853 is divisible by 3.

Since the units digit is odd, 2,853 is not divisible by 6.

Since the sum of the digits is divisible by 9, the number 2,853 is divisible by 9.

10. A. Since the units digit is 5, the number 1,565 is divisible by 5.

Since the units digit is not 0, the number 1,565 is not divisible by 10.

B. Since the units digit is 0, the number 8,970 is divisible by 5 and by 10.

C. Since the units digit is 5, the number 2,105 is divisible by 5.

Since the units digit is not 0, the number 2,105 is not divisible by 10.

D. Since the units digit is not 5 or 0, the number 7,283 is not divisible by 5 or by 10.

11. A. $252 = 2 \cdot 126 = 2 \cdot 2 \cdot 63 = 2 \cdot 2 \cdot 3 \cdot 21 = 2 \cdot 2 \cdot 3 \cdot 3 \cdot 7 = 2^2 \cdot 3^2 \cdot 7$

$588 = 2 \cdot 294 = 2 \cdot 2 \cdot 147 = 2 \cdot 2 \cdot 3 \cdot 49 = 2 \cdot 2 \cdot 3 \cdot 7 \cdot 7 = 2^2 \cdot 3 \cdot 7^2$

LCM $(252, 588) = 2^2 \cdot 3^2 \cdot 7^2 = 4 \cdot 9 \cdot 49 = 1{,}764$

B. $54 = 2 \cdot 27 = 2 \cdot 3 \cdot 9 = 2 \cdot 3 \cdot 3 \cdot 3 = 2 \cdot 3^3$

$144 = 2 \cdot 72 = 2 \cdot 2 \cdot 36 = 2 \cdot 2 \cdot 2 \cdot 18 = 2 \cdot 2 \cdot 2 \cdot 2 \cdot 9 = 2 \cdot 2 \cdot 2 \cdot 2 \cdot 3 \cdot 3 = 2^4 \cdot 3^2$

LCM $(54, 144) = 2^4 \cdot 3^3 = 16 \cdot 27 = 432$

C. $56 = 2 \cdot 28 = 2 \cdot 2 \cdot 14 = 2 \cdot 2 \cdot 2 \cdot 7 = 2^3 \cdot 7$

$140 = 2 \cdot 70 = 2 \cdot 2 \cdot 35 = 2 \cdot 2 \cdot 5 \cdot 7 = 2^2 \cdot 5 \cdot 7$

$168 = 2 \cdot 84 = 2 \cdot 2 \cdot 42 = 2 \cdot 2 \cdot 2 \cdot 21 = 2 \cdot 2 \cdot 2 \cdot 3 \cdot 7 = 2^3 \cdot 3 \cdot 7$

LCM $(56, 140, 168) = 2^3 \cdot 3 \cdot 5 \cdot 7 = 8 \cdot 3 \cdot 5 \cdot 7 = 840$

12. The numbers in these exercises are the same as in the above exercise, so the prime factorization from that problem can be used here.

A. $252 = 2^2 \cdot 3^2 \cdot 7$, $588 = 2^2 \cdot 3 \cdot 7^2$.

GCD $(252, 588) = 2^2 \cdot 3 \cdot 7 = 4 \cdot 3 \cdot 7 = 84$

B. $54 = 2 \cdot 3^3$, $144 = 2^4 \cdot 3^2$

GCD $(54, 144) = 2 \cdot 3^2 = 2 \cdot 9 = 18$

C. $56 = 2^3 \cdot 7$, $140 = 2^2 \cdot 5 \cdot 7$, $168 = 2^3 \cdot 3 \cdot 7$

GCD $(56, 140, 168) = 2^2 \cdot 7 = 4 \cdot 7 = 28$

NUMBER PROPERTIES TEST

Use the following test to assess how well you have mastered the material in this chapter. Mark your answer for each question by blackening the corresponding answer oval. An answer key and solutions are provided at the end of the test.

1. What is the coordinate of point *P*?

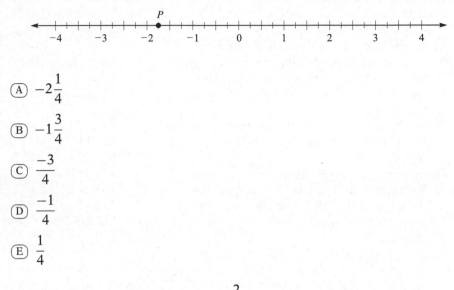

   (A) $-2\frac{1}{4}$

   (B) $-1\frac{3}{4}$

   (C) $\frac{-3}{4}$

   (D) $\frac{-1}{4}$

   (E) $\frac{1}{4}$

2. Which point has a coordinate of $3\frac{2}{5}$?

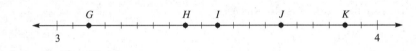

   (A) Point *G*
   (B) Point *H*
   (C) Point *I*
   (D) Point *J*
   (E) Point *K*

3. Which point on the number line represents the smallest number?

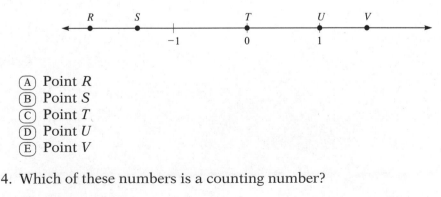

   (A) Point *R*
   (B) Point *S*
   (C) Point *T*
   (D) Point *U*
   (E) Point *V*

4. Which of these numbers is a counting number?

   (A) -4
   (B) 0
   (C) $0.223344\cdots$
   (D) $\sqrt{3}$
   (E) 5

5. Which of these numbers is a whole number?

   (A) -3
   (B) 0
   (C) $0.1212\cdots$
   (D) $\dfrac{1}{2}$
   (E) $\sqrt{10}$

6. Which of these numbers is an irrational number?

   (A) $-\dfrac{2}{3}$
   (B) 0
   (C) $1\dfrac{1}{2}$
   (D) 3
   (E) π

7. Which is a FALSE statement?

   (A) A whole number is an integer.
   (B) An irrational number is a real number.
   (C) A whole number is a rational number.
   (D) A counting number is a whole number.
   (E) An integer is an irrational number.

8. Which shows 3.15 rounded to tenths?

   (A) 3.05
   (B) 3.1
   (C) 3.15
   (D) 3.2
   (E) 3.25

9. In which number would the hundredths digit round up?

   (A) 3.1724
   (B) 5.6149
   (C) 5.6351
   (D) 5.6843
   (E) 5.8134

10. In which number would the thousandths digit NOT round up?

    (A) 2.34647
    (B) 2.48762
    (C) 2.76251
    (D) 3.10093
    (E) 5.92185

11. Which number shows 1,684 rounded to hundreds?

    (A) 16
    (B) 17
    (C) 1,600
    (D) 1,680
    (E) 1,700

12. Which number shows 286,435 rounded to the ten-thousands place?

    (A) 270,000
    (B) 280,000
    (C) 286,430
    (D) 286,440
    (E) 290,000

13. Which number shows 4,316.4725 rounded to the nearest hundredth?

    (A) 4,300
    (B) 4,300.4725
    (C) 4,316.47
    (D) 4,316.48
    (E) 4,320

14. Which is the expanded notation for 43.5?

    (A) $4 + 3 + 5$
    (B) $4 \times 10^3 + 3 \times 10^2 + 5 \times 10^1$
    (C) $4 \times 10^2 + 3 \times 10^1 + 5 \times 10^{-1}$
    (D) $4 \times 10^1 + 3 \times 10^0 + 5 \times 10^{-1}$
    (E) $4 \times 10^3 + 3 \times 10^2 + 5 \times 10^0$

15. Which is the expanded notation for 2,065?

    (A) $2 \times 10^5 + 6 \times 10^3 + 5 \times 10^1$
    (B) $2 \times 10^4 + 6 \times 10^3 + 5 \times 10^2$
    (C) $2 \times 10^3 + 6 \times 10^1 + 5 \times 10^0$
    (D) $2 \times 10^2 + 6 \times 10^1 + 5 \times 10^0$
    (E) $2 \times 10^3 + 6 \times 10^2 + 5 \times 10^1$

16. Which is the standard number for $3 \times 10^5 + 5 \times 10^3 + 7 \times 10^1$?

    (A) 357
    (B) 3,057
    (C) 3,507
    (D) 35,070
    (E) 305,070

17. Which is the expanded notation for 0.2841?

    (A) $2 \times 10^{-4} + 8 \times 10^{-3} + 4 \times 10^{-2} + 1 \times 10^{-1}$
    (B) $2 \times 10^0 + 8 \times 10^{-1} + 4 \times 10^{-2} + 1 \times 10^{-3}$
    (C) $2 \times 10^3 + 8 \times 10^2 + 4 \times 10^1 + 1 \times 10^0$
    (D) $2 \times 10^{-1} + 8 \times 10^{-2} + 4 \times 10^{-3} + 1 \times 10^{-4}$
    (E) $2 \times 10^{-3} + 8 \times 10^{-2} + 4 \times 10^{-1} + 1 \times 10^0$

18. Which of these is the smallest number?

    (A) -5
    (B) -2
    (C) 0
    (D) 3
    (E) 11

19. Which is the greatest number?

    (A) |−10|
    (B) |−5|
    (C) |0|
    (D) −2
    (E) 8

20. Which is the answer to (−7) + (−3)?

    (A) +10
    (B) +4
    (C) +3
    (D) −1
    (E) −10

21. What is the answer to (−6) + (+5)?

    (A) +11
    (B) +1
    (C) 0
    (D) −1
    (E) −11

22. Which is the answer to (+8) + (−5)?

    (A) +13
    (B) +5
    (C) +3
    (D) −3
    (E) −13

23. Which is the answer to (−7) − (+4)?

    (A) −11
    (B) −4
    (C) −3
    (D) +3
    (E) +11

24. What is the answer to (+6) − (+5)?

    (A) +11
    (B) +1
    (C) 0
    (D) −1
    (E) −11

25. What is the answer to (−4) − (−4)?

    (A) −8
    (B) −4
    (C) 0
    (D) +4
    (E) +8

26. What is the answer to $(-5) \times (-2)$?

(A) -10
(B) -7
(C) -3
(D) $+7$
(E) $+10$

27. What is the answer to $(-6) \times (+4)$?

(A) -24
(B) -10
(C) -2
(D) 2
(E) $+24$

28. What is the answer to $(-6) \times (+6)$?

(A) -36
(B) -12
(C) 0
(D) 12
(E) 36

29. What is the answer to $(-6) \div (-3)$?

(A) -9
(B) -2
(C) $-\dfrac{1}{2}$
(D) $+\dfrac{1}{2}$
(E) 2

30. What is the answer to $(-28) \div (+7)$?

(A) -21
(B) -4
(C) $-\dfrac{1}{4}$
(D) $\dfrac{1}{4}$
(E) 4

31. What is the answer to $(+5) + (-3) + (-8) + (+4) + (+1)$?

(A) -480
(B) -21
(C) -1
(D) 1
(E) 480

32. What is the answer to $(-3) \times (-1) \times (+2) \times (+3) \times (-2)$?

    (A) -36
    (B) -1
    (C) 1
    (D) 36
    (E) 48

33. What is the answer to $(-3) \times (-4) \times (-5) \times (0) \times (-2)$?

    (A) -120
    (B) -14
    (C) 0
    (D) $+14$
    (E) 120

34. Which of these is an odd number?

    (A) even + even
    (B) odd + odd
    (C) even × odd
    (D) odd × odd
    (E) odd − odd

35. Which of these is an even number?

    (A) $7 - 4$
    (B) $0 - 5$
    (C) $6 + 3$
    (D) $5 - 11$
    (E) 11×5

36. Which is NOT a multiple of 7?

    (A) 1
    (B) 49
    (C) 56
    (D) 84
    (E) 140

37. Which is a divisor of 96?

    (A) 36
    (B) 32
    (C) 18
    (D) 9
    (E) 5

38. Which is the least common multiple of 15 and 10?

    (A) 300
    (B) 150
    (C) 90
    (D) 30
    (E) 5

39. Which is the least common multiple of 24 and 36?

    (A) 72
    (B) 48
    (C) 12
    (D) 6
    (E) 2

40. Which is the greatest common divisor of 8 and 40?

    (A) 2
    (B) 5
    (C) 8
    (D) 40
    (E) 320

41. Which is the greatest common divisor of 80 and 144?

    (A) 1
    (B) 8
    (C) 16
    (D) 720
    (E) 11,520

42. Which is the greatest common divisor of 8 and 15?

    (A) 120
    (B) 60
    (C) 40
    (D) 1
    (E) 0

43. Which is a prime number?

    (A) 9
    (B) 4
    (C) 2
    (D) 1
    (E) 0

44. Which is a prime number?

    (A) 17
    (B) 57
    (C) 63
    (D) 82
    (E) 91

45. Which is a composite number?

    (A) 0
    (B) 1
    (C) 2
    (D) 29
    (E) 51

46. Which is the prime factorization of 180?

  (A) $2 \cdot 3 \cdot 5$
  (B) $12 \cdot 15$
  (C) $10 \cdot 18$
  (D) $2^2 \cdot 3^2 \cdot 5$
  (E) $2^2 \cdot 3^2 \cdot 5^2$

47. Which is the prime factorization of 588?

  (A) $2 \cdot 3 \cdot 7$
  (B) $2^2 \cdot 3^2 \cdot 7^2$
  (C) $2^2 \cdot 3 \cdot 7^2$
  (D) $2^2 \cdot 3 \cdot 49$
  (E) $2^2 \cdot 147$

48. Which number is divisible by both 2 and 4?

  (A) 2,372
  (B) 2,403
  (C) 5,622
  (D) 7,153
  (E) 9,418

49. Which number is divisible by 5 but is not divisible by 10?

  (A) 3,472
  (B) 3,790
  (C) 4,865
  (D) 5,002
  (E) 6,450

50. Which number is divisible by 3 and divisible by 9, but is not divisible by 6?

  (A) 1,743
  (B) 3,528
  (C) 4,608
  (D) 6,201
  (E) 7,212

ANSWER KEY

1. B	11. E	21. D	31. C	41. C
2. B	12. E	22. C	32. A	42. D
3. A	13. C	23. A	33. C	43. C
4. E	14. D	24. B	34. D	44. A
5. B	15. C	25. C	35. D	45. E
6. E	16. E	26. E	36. A	46. D
7. E	17. D	27. A	37. B	47. C
8. D	18. A	28. A	38. D	48. A
9. C	19. A	29. E	39. A	49. C
10. A	20. E	30. B	40. C	50. D

SOLUTIONS

1. **B** $-1\frac{3}{4}$

   The point P is between -1 and -2. The units are divided into quarter units, so P is at $-1\frac{3}{4}$.

2. **B** Point H

   The unit between 3 and 4 is divided into twentieths, with darker lines at each fifth. Thus H is located at $3\frac{2}{5}$.

3. **A** Point R

   The point R is farthest left on the number line, so it represents the smallest value of the labeled points.

4. **E** 5

   The counting numbers are 1, 2, 3, 4, ... The only counting number listed is 5.

5. **B** 0

   The whole numbers are 0, 1, 2, 3, ... The only whole number listed is 0.

6. **E** π

   Since $3, -\frac{2}{3}, 1\frac{1}{2}$, and 0 are all rational numbers, the only irrational number is π.

7. **E** An integer is an irrational number.

   Since the integers are rational numbers, they cannot also be irrational numbers. The false statement is that "An integer is an irrational number."

8. **D** 3.2

   There is a 1 in the tenths place, and the digit to the right is 5. You increase the tenths digit by 1 to get 2, and you drop the digits to the right of the tenths place.

9. **C** 5.6351

   To round up, the digit to the right of the hundredths place must be 5 or greater, and this is only true of 5.6351.

10. **A** 2.34647

The thousandths digit will not round up if the digit to the right of the thousandths place is 4 or less. This is only true of 2.34647.

11. **E** 1,700

The hundreds digit is 6, and the digit to the right is an 8, so you add 1 to 6 to get 7. Drop the digits to the right of the hundreds, but to maintain the place value of the thousands and hundreds digits, you must add zeros in the tens place and the ones place.

12. **E** 290,000

The digit in the ten-thousands place is an 8, and the digit to the right is a 6. Add 1 to the 8 to get 9 and drop the digits to the right of the ten-thousands. You must replace the dropped digits between the ten-thousands digit and the decimal point with zeros.

13. **C** 4,316.47

There is a 7 in the hundredths place, and to the right of the hundredths place the digit is 4 or less. You drop all the digits to the right of the hundredths place.

14. **D** $4 \times 10^1 + 3 \times 10^0 + 5 \times 10^{-1}$

$$43.5 = 40 + 3 + \frac{5}{10} = 4 \times 10^1 + 3 \times 10^0 + 5 \times 10^{-1}$$

15. **C** $2 \times 10^3 + 6 \times 10^1 + 5 \times 10^0$

$$2{,}065 = 2{,}000 + 60 + 5 = 2 \times 10^3 + 6 \times 10^1 + 5 \times 10^0$$

16. **E** 305,070

$$3 \times 10^5 + 5 \times 10^3 + 7 \times 10^1 = 3 \times 100{,}000 + 5 \times 1{,}000 + 7 \times 10$$
$$= 300{,}000 + 5{,}000 + 70 = 305{,}070$$

17. **D** $2 \times 10^{-1} + 8 \times 10^{-2} + 4 \times 10^{-3} + 1 \times 10^{-4}$

$$0.2841 = 0.2 + 0.08 + 0.004 + 0.0001$$
$$= 2 \times 10^{-1} + 8 \times 10^{-2} + 4 \times 10^{-3} + 1 \times 10^{-4}$$

18. **A** −5

Since negative numbers are less than any positive numbers, −5 and −2 are the lesser numbers. −5 is to the left of −2 on the number line, so −5 is the smallest number.

19. **A** $|-10|$

$|-10| = 10$, $|-5| = 5$, $|0| = 0$, so 10 is the greatest number.

20. **E** −10

$(-7) + (-3)$ is the sum of two numbers with the same sign. $|-7| = 7$, $|-3| = 3$. $7 + 3 = 10$, and the sign is negative, so the answer is −10.

21. **D** −1

$(-6) + (+5)$ is the sum of two numbers with unlike signs. $|-6| = 6$, $|+5| = 5$. $6 - 5 = 1$, and $6 > 5$, so the sign is negative. The answer is −1.

22. **C** +3

    (+8) + (−5) is the sum of two numbers with unlike signs. |+8| = 8, |−5| = 5. 8 − 5 = 3, and 8 > 5, so the sign is positive. The answer is +3.

23. **A** −11

    (−7) − (+4) is the subtraction of +4 from −7. You add the opposite of +4, which is −4, to −7. This is the sum of two numbers with like signs. |−7| = 7, |−4| = 4. 7 + 4 = 11, and the sign is negative. The answer is −11.

24. **B** +1

    (+6) − (+5) is the subtraction of +5 from +6. We add the opposite of +5, which is −5, to +6. This is the sum of two numbers with unlike signs. |+6| = 6, |−5| = 5. 6 − 5 = 1, and 6 > 5, so the sign is positive. The answer is +1.

25. **C** 0

    Since you are subtracting a number from itself, the answer is zero.

26. **E** +10

    Since you are multiplying two numbers with like signs, the answer is positive. |−5| = 5, |−2| = 2, and 5 × 2 = 10. The answer is +10.

27. **A** −24

    Since you are multiplying two numbers with unlike signs, the answer is negative. |−6| = 6, |+4| = 4, and 6 × 4 = 24. The answer is −24.

28. **A** −36

    Since you are multiplying two numbers with unlike signs, the answer is negative. |−6| = 6, |+6| = 6, and 6 × 6 = 36. The answer is −36.

29. **E** +2

    Since you are dividing two numbers with like signs, the answer is positive. |−6| = 6, |−3| = 3, and 6 ÷ 3 = 2. The answer is +2.

30. **B** −4

    Since you are dividing two numbers with unlike signs, the answer is negative. |−28| = 28, |+7| = 7, and 28 ÷ 7 = 4. The answer is −4.

31. **C** −1

$$(+5) + (−3) + (−8) + (+4) + (+1) = [(+5) + (+4) + (+1)] + [(−3) + (−8)]$$
$$= (+10) + (−11) = −(11 − 10) = −1$$

32. **A** −36

    (−3) × (−1) × (+2) × (+3) × (−2) is a product of more than two signed numbers. Since there are an odd number of negative factors, the product is negative. −(3 × 1 × 2 × 3 × 2) = −36

33. **C** 0

    Since one factor in the product is 0, the product is 0.

34. **D** odd × odd

    even + even = even, odd + odd = even, even × odd = even, odd × odd

$$= odd, odd − odd = even$$

35. **D** $5 - 11$

$7 - 4 = 3$, $0 - 5 = -5$, $6 + 3 = 9$, $5 - 11 = -6$, $11 \times 5 = 55$.
-6 is even, so the answer is $5 - 11$.

36. **A** 1

The multiples of 7 are 7, 14, 21, 28, 35, 42, 49, 56, 63, 70, 77, 84, 91, 98, 105, 112, 119, 126, 133, 140, ...
84, 49, 140, and 56 are all in the list of multiples of 7. The number 1 is not in the list, so it is not a multiple of 7.

37. **B** 32

$1 \times 96 = 96$, $2 \times 48 = 96$, $3 \times 32 = 96$, $4 \times 24 = 96$, $6 \times 16 = 96$, $8 \times 12 = 96$.
The divisors of 96 are 1, 2, 3, 4, 6, 8, 12, 16, 24, 32, 48, and 96. Only 32 is listed in the divisors of 96.

38. **D** 30

The multiples of 15 are 15, 30, 45, 60, ...
The multiples of 10 are 10, 20, 30, 40, 50, ...
LCM (10, 15) = 30

39. **A** 72

$24 = 2 \cdot 12 = 2 \cdot 2 \cdot 6 = 2 \cdot 2 \cdot 2 \cdot 3 = 2^3 \cdot 3$
$36 = 2 \cdot 18 = 2 \cdot 2 \cdot 9 = 2 \cdot 2 \cdot 3 \cdot 3 = 2^2 \cdot 3^2$
LCM $(24, 36) = 2^3 \cdot 3^2 = 8 \cdot 9 = 72$

40. **C** 8

$1 \times 8 = 8$, $2 \times 4 = 8$. The divisors of 8 are 1, 2, 4, 8.
$1 \times 40 = 40$, $2 \times 20 = 40$, $4 \times 10 = 40$, $5 \times 8 = 40$. The divisors of 40 are 1, 2, 4, 5, 8, 10, 20, 40.
GCD (8, 40) = 8

41. **C** 16

$80 = 2 \cdot 40 = 2 \cdot 2 \cdot 20 = 2 \cdot 2 \cdot 2 \cdot 10 = 2 \cdot 2 \cdot 2 \cdot 2 \cdot 5 = 2^4 \cdot 5$
$144 = 2 \cdot 72 = 2 \cdot 2 \cdot 36 = 2 \cdot 2 \cdot 2 \cdot 18 = 2 \cdot 2 \cdot 2 \cdot 2 \cdot 9 = 2 \cdot 2 \cdot 2 \cdot 2 \cdot 3 \cdot 3 = 2^4 \cdot 3^2$
GCD $(80, 144) = 2^4 = 16$

42. **D** 1

$8 = 2 \cdot 4 = 2 \cdot 2 \cdot 2 = 2^3$
$15 = 3 \cdot 5$
Since they have no common prime factors, their only common factor is 1, which is a divisor of all counting numbers. GCD (8, 15) = 1

43. **C** 2

$9 = 3 \cdot 3$, and $4 = 2 \cdot 2$. The number 2 is prime, and 0 and 1 are not greater than 1, so are not primes.

44. **A** 17

$17 = 1 \cdot 17$, $82 = 2 \cdot 41$, $63 = 3 \cdot 21$, $57 = 3 \cdot 19$, $91 = 7 \cdot 13$

All the choices but 17 have a counting number divisor that is greater than 1 but less than the number.

45. **E** 51

0 and 1 are not greater than 1, so they are not composite. 2 and 29 are primes. $51 = 3 \cdot 17$, so 51 is a composite number.

46. **D** $2^2 \cdot 3^2 \cdot 5$

    $180 = 2 \cdot 90 = 2 \cdot 2 \cdot 45 = 2 \cdot 2 \cdot 3 \cdot 15 = 2 \cdot 2 \cdot 3 \cdot 3 \cdot 5 = 2^2 \cdot 3^2 \cdot 5$

47. **C** $2^2 \cdot 3 \cdot 7^2$

    $588 = 2 \cdot 294 = 2 \cdot 2 \cdot 147 = 2 \cdot 2 \cdot 3 \cdot 49 = 2 \cdot 2 \cdot 3 \cdot 7 \cdot 7 = 2^2 \cdot 3 \cdot 7^2$

48. **A** 2,372

    Only 2,372, 5,622, and 9,418 have units digits that are even, so they are the only choices divisible by 2.
    Looking at the last two digits of each of these numbers, you see that only 2,372 has the last two digits making a number divisible by 4.
    2,372 is divisible by 2 and 4.

49. **C** 4,865

    To be divisible by 5, the units digit must be 5 or 0, so 6,450, 3,790, and 4,865 are divisible by 5.
    To be divisible by 10, the units digit must be 0. Thus, only 4,865 is divisible by 5 and NOT divisible by 10.

50. **D** 6,201

    To be divisible by 6, the units digit must be even, so 1,743 and 6,201 are NOT divisible by 6.
    $1 + 7 + 4 + 3 = 15$, which is divisible by 3, but not divisible by 9.
    $6 + 2 + 0 + 1 = 9$, which is divisible by 3 and by 9. So 6,201 is the only answer choice that is divisible by 3 and by 9, but not divisible by 6.

GMAT SOLVED PROBLEMS

For each question, select the best answer.

1. **Which number is the least common multiple (LCM) of 48 and 84?**

   A. 4,032
   B. 672
   C. 336
   D. 12
   E. 2

2. **Which expression shows 4,287.3 written in expanded notation?**

   A. $4 \times 10^3 + 2 \times 10^2 + 8 \times 10^1 + 7 \times 10^0 + 3 \times 10^{-1}$

   B. $4 \times 10^3 + 2 \times 10^2 + 8 \times 10^1 + 7 \times 10^{-1} + 3 \times 10^{-2}$

   C. $4 \times 10^4 + 2 \times 10^3 + 8 \times 10^2 + 7 \times 10^1 + 3 \times 10^0$

   D. $4 \times 10^4 + 2 \times 10^3 + 8 \times 10^2 + 7 \times 10^1 + 3 \times 10^{-1}$

   E. $4 \times 10^5 + 2 \times 10^4 + 8 \times 10^3 + 7 \times 10^2 + 3 \times 10^1$

3. **Which is the best answer for $(-23) \div 0$?**

   A. −230
   B. −23
   C. 1
   D. 0
   E. Undefined

4. **Which is the greatest prime factor of 60?**

   A. 2
   B. 5
   C. 20
   D. 30
   E. 57

5. **Which number is NOT equal to $\dfrac{3}{4}$?**

   A. $-\left(\dfrac{-21}{28}\right)$

   B. $\sqrt{\dfrac{9}{16}}$

   C. $3\left(\dfrac{1}{2}\right)^2$

   D. 0.34

   E. $\left(\dfrac{\sqrt{3}}{2}\right)^2$

6. **Which number is equivalent to $|3| - |-1|$?**

   A. 4
   B. 3
   C. 2
   D. 1
   E. 0

7. **It is given that $g, h, i, j,$ and k are consecutive counting numbers. Is $i + j + k < 20$?**
   1. g is prime.
   2. g is less than 7.

   A. Statement 1 ALONE is sufficient, but statement 2 is not sufficient.
   B. Statement 2 ALONE is sufficient, but statement 1 is not sufficient.
   C. BOTH statements TOGETHER are sufficient, but NEITHER statement ALONE is sufficient.
   D. EACH statement ALONE is sufficient.
   E. Statements 1 and 2 TOGETHER are NOT sufficient.

8. **What is the value of $x + y$?**
   1. $x = y$
   2. $y = 3 - x$

   A. Statement 1 ALONE is sufficient, but statement 2 is not sufficient.
   B. Statement 2 ALONE is sufficient, but statement 1 is not sufficient.
   C. BOTH statements TOGETHER are sufficient, but NEITHER statement ALONE is sufficient.
   D. EACH statement ALONE is sufficient.
   E. Statements 1 and 2 TOGETHER are NOT sufficient.

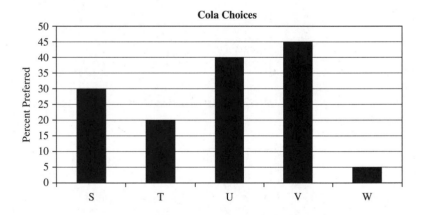

9. **If 10,000 people took part in the Cola Choice experiment, how many people chose Cola T?**

   A. 200,000
   B. 20,000
   C. 10,000
   D. 2,000
   E. 1,000

10. **What percent of the group preferred colas S and U?**

    A. 30%
    B. 40%
    C. 50%
    D. 60%
    E. 70%

SOLUTIONS

1. **C** The least common multiple has to be at least as large as the larger number, so you can eliminate answers D and E. Break both numbers down. $48 = 2 \times 24 = 2 \times 2 \times 12 = 2 \times 2 \times 2 \times 6 = 2 \times 2 \times 2 \times 2 \times 3 = 2^4 \times 3$. And $84 = 2 \times 42 = 2 \times 2 \times 21 = 2 \times 2 \times 3 \times 7 = 2^2 \times 3 \times 7$. The least common multiple is, therefore, $2^4 \times 3 \times 7$. $2^4 \times 3 \times 7 = 336$. Thus, the answer is C.

2. **A** Since all the answers have the digits in the same order, you need to see whether the expanded notation has the correct place value. In 4,287.3, the 4 means 4,000, or 4×10^3; thus, answers A and B are the only possible correct answers. These answers match until you get to the digit 7. Since the 7 means 7 ones, 7×10^0 is needed, which is part of answer A, but not of answer B. Thus, the answer is A.

3. **E** Division by 0 is not defined, so the answer is undefined. The answer is E.

4. **B** First, look for prime factors in 60. $60 = 2 \cdot 2 \cdot 3 \cdot 5$. Thus, the largest prime factor is 5, and the answer is B.

5. **D** Look at the answers and check the easier ones first. In this case, answer D is the only decimal. Try dividing 3 by 4 and you get $3 \div 4 = 0.75$, so the decimal 0.34 is wrong. Thus, the answer is D.

6. **C** Compute: $|3| - |-1| = 3 - 1 = 2$. Thus, the answer is C.

7. **E** Since g, h, i, j, and k are consecutive counting numbers, they can be represented as $g, g+1, g+2, g+3,$ and $g+4$. Therefore, $i+j+k = (g+2) + (g+3) + (g+4) = 3g+9$. If $g = 3$, then $i = 5, j = 6, k = 7$. So $i+j+k = 18$ and $i+j+k < 20$.

   Statement 1 says g is prime. If $g = 3$, then $i = 5$, $j = 6$, $k = 7$. So $i+j+k = 18$ and $i+j+k < 20$. But if $g = 11$, then $i = 13$, $j = 14$, and $k = 15$, so $i+j+k = 42$, which exceeds 20. Thus, g being prime is not enough to tell whether $i+j+k < 20$. Statement 1 alone is not sufficient.

   Statement 2 says $g < 7$, so g could be 6. If $g = 6$, then $i = 8, j = 9, k = 10$, and $i+j+k = 27$ and $i+j+k > 20$. If $g = 3$, then $i = 5, j = 6, k = 7$. So $i+j+k = 18$ and $i+j+k < 20$. Statement 2 alone is also not sufficient.

   When you consider statements 1 and 2 together, g is a prime number less than 7; so g could be 3 or 5. If $g = 3$, then $i = 5, j = 6, k = 7$. So $i+j+k = 18$ and $i+j+k < 20$. If $g = 5$, then $i+j+k = 7+8+9 = 24$ and $i+j+k > 20$. Thus, taken together, there is still not enough information to know whether $i+j+k < 20$. Since statements 1 and 2 taken together are not sufficient, the answer is E.

8. **B** From statement 1, you have $x = y$, but this just lets you say that $x + y = 2x$. You still do not know the value of $x + y$. So statement 1 is not sufficient.

   From statement 2, you have $y = 3 - x$, which can be written as $x + y = 3$. Thus, statement 2 is sufficient. Since statement 2 is sufficient and statement 1 is not sufficient, the answer is B.

9. **D** According to the graph, cola T is selected by 20% of the people responding. If there were 10,000 people involved in the Cola Choice experiment, then cola T was chosen by 20% of 10,000 people, or $0.20 \times 10,000 = 2,000$ people who chose cola T. Thus, the answer is D.

10. **E** Cola S was chosen by 30% of the participants, and cola U was chosen by 40%. $30\% + 40\% = 70\%$. Thus, the answer is E.

▨ GMAT PRACTICE PROBLEMS

For each question, select the best answer.

1. **Which number is the greatest common divisor (GCD) of 45 and 75?**

   A. 3,375
   B. 225
   C. 15
   D. 5
   E. 3

2. **Which number is the same as 5 tenths, 4 hundreds, 3 tens, and 8 ones?**

   A. 43.85
   B. 45.83
   C. 438.5
   D. 458.3
   E. 5,438

3. **Which number is a rational number that is NOT a whole number?**

   A. $\dfrac{-12}{-3}$
   B. $2\dfrac{2}{3} - \dfrac{1}{2} - \dfrac{1}{6}$
   C. 0
   D. $\sqrt{9}$
   E. $5(-2)$

4. **Which is the quotient for $281.68 \div 28$?**

   A. 1.6
   B. 16
   C. 10.06
   D. 10.6
   E. 100.6

5. **Which number is divisible by 4 but not divisible by 8?**

   A. 256
   B. 201
   C. 122
   D. 104
   E. 68

6. **Which is the smallest of the prime factors of 161?**

   A. 3
   B. 5
   C. 7
   D. 11
   E. 37

7. **Is *n* less than 2.6?**
   1. *n* < 2.7
   2. *n* < 2.5

   A. Statement 1 ALONE is sufficient, but statement 2 is not sufficient.
   B. Statement 2 ALONE is sufficient, but statement 1 is not sufficient.
   C. BOTH statements TOGETHER are sufficient, but NEITHER statement ALONE is sufficient.
   D. EACH statement ALONE is sufficient.
   E. Statements 1 and 2 TOGETHER are NOT sufficient.

8. **If *n* is a member of the set {30, 32, 35, 38, 39, 40} what is the value of *n*?**
   1. *n* is odd
   2. *n* is a multiple of 5

   A. Statement 1 ALONE is sufficient, but statement 2 is not sufficient.
   B. Statement 2 ALONE is sufficient, but statement 1 is not sufficient.
   C. BOTH statements TOGETHER are sufficient, but NEITHER statement ALONE is sufficient.
   D. EACH statement ALONE is sufficient.
   E. Statements 1 and 2 TOGETHER are NOT sufficient.

Household Budget

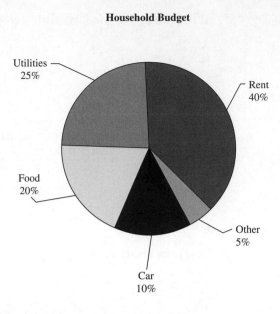

9. **Which expense in the household budget is 5 times another expense?**

    A. Car
    B. Food
    C. Rent
    D. Utilities
    E. Other

10. **Which expense is equal to the sum of the two expense categories Other and Food?**

    A. Rent
    B. Utilities
    C. Food
    D. Car
    E. Other

ANSWER KEY

1.	B
2.	C
3.	E
4.	C
5.	E
6.	C
7.	B
8.	C
9.	D
10.	B

CHAPTER 6
ARITHMETIC COMPUTATION

SYMBOLS

$=$	equals
$>$	is greater than
$<$	is less than
$\geq$	is greater than or equal to
$\leq$	is less than or equal to
$\neq$	is not equal to
x^2	x squared
x^3	x cubed
$\sqrt{x}$	square root of x
$|x|$	absolute value of x
$+$	addition, plus
$-$	subtraction, minus
$a \times b$	a times b, multiplication
$a \cdot b$	a times b, multiplication
$a * b$	a times b, multiplication
ab	a times b, multiplication
$a \div b$	a divided by b, division
$\dfrac{a}{b}$	a divided by b, division
$a : b$	the ratio of a to b
$\%$	percent

ORDER OF OPERATIONS

When there is more than one operation in an expression, you have to use the standard order of operations to do the computation in order to get a consistent, correct, result. You use the order PEMDAS, which stands for *parentheses, exponents, multiplication and division, and addition and subtraction.*

The first step is to work within each set of parentheses or brackets. A fraction bar means that the numerator and denominator are worked separately as though each were enclosed by parentheses. The work inside parentheses follows these rules also.

The second level is exponents, which means that you simplify all powers and roots before trying to use them in computing.

The next level is multiplication and division. These operations are done in the order that they occur from left to right in the problem. In $6 \times 5 \div 2 \times 4$, you multiply 6×5 first to get $30 \div 2 \times 4$, then you divide 30 by 2 and get 15×4. Finally, you multiply 15 by 4 to get 60. Multiplication and division are of equal rank in the order of operations.

The last step is to do the addition and subtraction in the order in which they occur from left to right. In $15 - 7 + 4$, you subtract first, then add: $15 - 7 + 4 = 8 + 4 = 12$. Addition and subtraction are of equal rank in the order of operations.

To help you remember the order of operations, PEMDAS, you can create a sentence based on these letters: **P**lease **E**xcuse **M**e, **D**ear **A**unt **S**ally. The memory device helps you keep the letters in the correct sequence.

Example 1

Evaluate each expression.

A. $7^2 - (-5) + 12$ B. $[5(-7) - 8] \times 2$ C. $-2 * 5 + 15 \div 5$

D. $6(-2) - (-2)(-5)^3$ E. $-(-5)^2 - (-5)^3$ F. $(8 - 2^4)(-3 + \sqrt{49})$

Solution

A. $7^2 - (-5) + 12 = 49 - (-5) + 12 = 54 + 12 = 66$

B. $[5(-7) - 8] \times 2 = [-35 - 8] \times 2 = [-43] \times 2 = -86$

C. $-2 * 5 + 15 \div 5 = -10 + 15 \div 5 = -10 + 3 = -7$

D. $6(-2) - (-2)(-5)^3 = 6(-2) - (-2)(-125) = -12 - 250 = -262$

E. $-(-5)^2 - (-5)^3 = -25 - (-125) = -25 + 125 = 100$

F. $(8 - 2^4)(-3 + \sqrt{49}) = (8 - 16)(-3 + 7) = (-8)(4) = -32$

Example 2

If $a = 2$, $b = 8$, and $c = -10$, evaluate each expression.

A. $\dfrac{a}{b} + \dfrac{5}{c}$ B. $2a - 5b + c^2$ C. $-a^3 + 2b - c$ D. $\dfrac{b+c}{a+b}$

Solution

A. $\dfrac{a}{b} + \dfrac{5}{c} = \dfrac{2}{8} + \dfrac{5}{-10} = \dfrac{1}{4} - \dfrac{1}{2} = \dfrac{1}{4} - \dfrac{2}{4} = -\dfrac{1}{4}$

B. $2a - 5b + c^2 = 2(2) - 5(8) + (-10)^2 = 4 - 40 + 100 = 64$

C. $-a^3 + 2b - c = -(2)^3 + 2(8) - (-10) = -8 + 16 + 10 = 18$

D. $\dfrac{b+c}{a+b} = \dfrac{8 + (-10)}{2 + 8} = \dfrac{-2}{10} = -\dfrac{1}{5}$

PROPERTIES OF OPERATIONS

Commutative Properties

If a and b are real numbers, then $a + b = b + a$ and $ab = ba$. The commutative properties say that $4 + 6$ and $6 + 4$ have the same answer. Also, $-3 * 12$ and $12 * (-3)$ have the same answer.

It is important to note that the commutative properties are not valid for subtraction and division. $4 - 2 = 2$, but $2 - 4 = -2$ and $2 \neq -2$. Also, $8 \div 2 = 4$, but $2 \div 8 = \dfrac{1}{4}$ and $4 \neq \dfrac{1}{4}$.

Note: A single example can show a statement is false, but one example does not show that a statement is true.

Associative Properties

If a, b, and c are real numbers, then $a + (b + c) = (a + b) + c$ and $a(bc) = (ab)c$. The **associative properties** say that $a + b + c$ and abc have meaning, and the value is the same whichever way you compute the values. $(5 + 2) + (-3)$ can be evaluated as $(5 + 2) + (-3)$ or as $5 + [2 + (-3)]$. $(5 + 2) + (-3) = 7 + (-3) = 4$, and $5 + [2 + (-3)] = 5 + (-1) = 4$, so you say $5 + 2 + (-3) = 4$. Similarly, $(-3) * 2 * (-2)$ can be evaluated as $[(-3) * 2] * (-2)$ or as $(-3) * [2 * (-2)]$. $[(-3) * 2] * (-2) = (-6) * (-2) = 12$, and $(-3) * [2 * (-2)] = (-3) * (-4) = 12$, so you can say $(-3) * 2 * (-2) = 12$.

Distributive Property

If a, b, and c are real numbers, then $a * (b + c) = ab + ac$. The **distributive property** allows you to change the order of the operations from addition and then multiplication to multiplication and then addition, or the reverse. $3 * (-7 + 5) = 3 * (-7) + 3 * 5 = -21 + 15 = -6$, and $(-8) * 5 + (-8) * 2 = -8(5 + 2) = -8(7) = -56$. Since subtraction is the same as addition of the opposite, you can convert $a * (b - c) = a * [b + (-c)] = a * b + a * (-c) = ab - ac$.

Identity Properties

For any real number a, $a + 0 = 0 + a = a$, and $a * 1 = 1 * a = a$. The **identity for addition** is 0 and the **identity for multiplication** is 1.

Inverse Properties

For any real number a, there is a real number that is the opposite of a, $-a$, such that $a + (-a) = (-a) + a = 0$. For any nonzero real number b, there is a real number that is the reciprocal of b, $\frac{1}{b}$, such that $b \times \frac{1}{b} = \frac{1}{b} \times b = 1$. For 6, the opposite is -6, and the reciprocal is $\frac{1}{6}$. Thus $6 + (-6) = (-6) + 6 = 0$, and $6 \times \frac{1}{6} = \frac{1}{6} \times 6 = 1$. The **additive inverse** of 6 is -6, and the **multiplicative inverse** of 6 is $\frac{1}{6}$.

Example 3

State the property illustrated by each statement.

A. $5 + (6 + 8) = (5 + 6) + 8$
B. $-7 + 0 = -7$
C. $3 * 1 = 3$
D. $4 * (3 * 9) = (4 * 3) * 9$
E. $(8 + 5) * 3 = 3 * (8 + 5)$
F. $-5 + 5 = 0$

Solution

A. Since the numbers are in the same order and only the grouping has changed, the property is the associative property for addition.
B. Since 0 is added to the number, the property is the addition identity property.

C. Since 1 is multiplied by the number, the property is the multiplication identity property.
D. Since the order of the numbers is unchanged and only the grouping has changed, the property is the associative property for multiplication.
E. Since the order of the factors has been changed, the property is the commutative property of multiplication. You treat $8 + 5$ as a single number here.
F. Since you have added a number and its opposite, this is the addition inverse property.

PRACTICE PROBLEMS

1. Use the order of operations to evaluate each expression.
   A. $6^2 - 4(9 - 1)$
   B. $(-3)(-2) - [7 + (8 - 12)]$
   C. $\dfrac{(-8 + 5) - (4 + 7)}{15 - 17}$
   D. $(-4 - 1)(-3 - 5) - 3^2$
   E. $\dfrac{8(-3) - 2^3(-3)^2}{-3[4 - (-8)]}$

2. Evaluate each expression when $x = -1$, $y = -2$, and $z = 4$.
   A. $-z(2x - 5y)$
   B. $(x - 2) \div 5y + z$
   C. $9x + 2y - 5z$
   D. $-7x + 2y + 3z$

3. Find the addition inverse of each number.
   A. 6   B. −7   C. 0   D. −3   E. $\dfrac{1}{2}$

4. Find the multiplication inverse of each number.
   A. 5   B. −3   C. $\dfrac{1}{2}$ D. $-\dfrac{2}{3}$ E. 1   F. −1

5. Which property is illustrated by each statement?
   A. $(9 + 3) + 0 = 9 + 3$
   B. $5 * (6 * -2) = (5 * 6) * (-2)$
   C. $5 * (3 + 8) = (3 + 8) * 5$
   D. $5 * -7 + 5 * 4 = 5 * (-7 + 4)$
   E. $-3 + 3 = 0$
   F. $3 + (4 + 2) = (3 + 4) + 2$
   G. $-2 * (8 + (-3)) = -2 * 8 + (-2) * (-3)$
   H. $-1/4 * (-4) = 1$
   I. $7 * 1 = 7$
   J. $-5 * (-6) = -6 * (-5)$
   K. $5 + 2 = 2 + 5$

SOLUTIONS

1. A. $6^2 - 4(9 - 1) = 6^2 - 4(8) = 36 - 4 * 8 = 36 - 32 = 4$
   B. $(-3)(-2) - [7 + (8 - 12)] = (-3)(-2) - [7 + (-4)] = 6 - (+3) = 6 - 3 = 3$
   C. $\dfrac{(-8 + 5) - (4 + 7)}{15 - 17} = \dfrac{(-3) - 11}{-2} = \dfrac{-14}{-2} = 7$
   D. $(-4 - 1)(-3 - 5) - 3^2 = (-5)(-8) - 9 = 40 - 9 = 31$
   E. $\dfrac{8(-3) - 2^3(-3)^2}{-3[4 - (-8)]} = \dfrac{-24 - 8(9)}{-3(4 + 8)} = \dfrac{-24 - 72}{-3(12)} = \dfrac{-96}{-36} = +\dfrac{16}{6} = \dfrac{8}{3}$ or $2\dfrac{2}{3}$

2. A. $-z(2x - 5y) = -4[2(-1) - 5(-2)] = -4(-2 + 10) = -4(8) = -32$
   B. $(x - 2) \div 5y + z = (-1 - 2) \div 5(-2) + 4 = -3 \div 5(-2) + 4 = -\dfrac{3}{5} * -2 + 4 = \dfrac{6}{5} + 4 = \dfrac{6}{5} + \dfrac{20}{5} = \dfrac{26}{5} = 5\dfrac{1}{5}$
   C. $9x + 2y - 5z = 9(-1) + 2(-2) - 5(4) = -9 - 4 - 20 = -33$
   D. $-7x + 2y + 3z = -7(-1) + 2(-2) + 3(4) = 7 - 4 + 12 = 3 + 12 = 15$

3. A. Because $6 + (-6) = 0$ and $-6 + 6 = 0$, -6 is the addition inverse of 6.
   B. Because $-7 + 7 = 0$ and $7 + (-7) = 0$, 7 is the addition inverse of -7.
   C. Because $0 + 0 = 0$, 0 is the addition inverse of 0.
   D. Because $-3 + (+3) = 0$ and $+3 + (-3) = 0$, $+3$ is the addition inverse of -3.
   E. Because $\frac{1}{2} + \left(-\frac{1}{2}\right) = 0$ and $-\frac{1}{2} + \frac{1}{2} = 0$, $-\frac{1}{2}$ is the addition inverse of $\frac{1}{2}$.

4. A. Because $5 * \frac{1}{5} = 1$ and $\frac{1}{5} * 5 = 1$, $\frac{1}{5}$ is the multiplication inverse of 5.
   B. Because $-3 * \left(-\frac{1}{3}\right) = 1$ and $-\frac{1}{3} * (-3) = 1$, $-\frac{1}{3}$ is the multiplication inverse of -3.
   C. Because $\frac{1}{2} * 2 = 1$ and $2 * \frac{1}{2} = 1$, 2 is the multiplication inverse of $\frac{1}{2}$.
   D. Because $-\frac{2}{3} * \left(-\frac{3}{2}\right) = 1$ and $-\frac{3}{2} * \left(-\frac{2}{3}\right) = 1$, $-\frac{3}{2}$ is the multiplication inverse of $-\frac{2}{3}$.
   E. Because $1 * 1 = 1$, 1 is the multiplication inverse of 1.
   F. Because $-1 * (-1) = 1$, -1 is the multiplication inverse of -1.

5. A. Because 0 was added to $(9 + 3)$, this shows the addition identity property.
   B. Because all that we changed was the grouping, this shows the associative property for multiplication.
   C. Because the order of the factors 5 and $3 + 8$ is all that has been changed, the property is commutative for multiplication.
   D. The common factor of 5 has been taken out of the two terms, so it is the distributive property.
   E. Opposites are being added, so this is the addition inverse property.
   F. The grouping is changed, so this is the associative property for addition.
   G. Since the -2 has been distributed over the sum, this is the distributive property.
   H. You are multiplying reciprocals, so this is the multiplication inverse.
   I. You are multiplying by 1, so this is the multiplication identity.
   J. The order of the factors has changed, so this is the commutative property of multiplication.
   K. The order of the addends has changed, so this is the commutative property of addition.

FRACTIONS

A fraction is made up of three parts: the **numerator,** the **fraction bar,** and the **denominator.** The numerator tells you how many parts you have, and the denominator tells you how many parts the whole was divided into. The fraction bar is read as "out of." Otherwise it is used as a grouping indicator to remind you to simplify the numerator and denominator separately before doing the division.

A fraction can tell you what part of a whole unit you have, or even that you have more parts than are needed for one whole.

The fraction $\frac{3}{4}$ means that you have 3 of the 4 parts that the whole is divided into, while $\frac{5}{4}$ means that you have all 4 parts of the one whole, plus 1 part of another whole that is divided into 4 equal parts.

In a fraction $\frac{a}{b}$ where a and b are whole numbers and b is not zero, $\frac{a}{b}$ is a **proper fraction** when $a < b$. If $a = b$ or $a > b$, it is an **improper fraction.**

You can use fractions to express the ratio of two quantities. If there are units with the numbers, then they need to be the same units. When the units are different, you convert to a common unit.

A fraction can be used to indicate division; $a \div b = \dfrac{a}{b}$. This use of fractions is especially helpful when you are dividing a smaller counting number by a larger one.

When you have an improper fraction such as $\dfrac{4}{4}$, $\dfrac{7}{5}$, or $\dfrac{11}{2}$, you can change them so that the number of whole units involved is clear. For $\dfrac{4}{4}$, you have all 4 parts for 1 unit, and $\dfrac{4}{4} = 1$. With $\dfrac{7}{5}$, you have 2 more parts than needed to make a whole unit, and you say that $\dfrac{7}{5} = 1\dfrac{2}{5}$. It is understood that $1\dfrac{2}{5} = 1 + \dfrac{2}{5}$. With $\dfrac{11}{2}$, you see that $11 \div 2$ yields 5 with a remainder of 1. The remainder is 1 of 2 parts needed to make the next whole, so it represents $\dfrac{1}{2}$. Thus, $\dfrac{11}{2} = 5\dfrac{1}{2}$. It is very helpful to be able to convert between improper fractions and mixed numbers.

Example 4

Convert these improper fractions to mixed numbers.

A. $\dfrac{7}{3}$　　B. $\dfrac{5}{2}$　　C. $\dfrac{8}{5}$　　D. $\dfrac{14}{5}$　　E. $\dfrac{13}{8}$

Solution

A. $\dfrac{7}{3} = 7 \div 3 = 2$ with remainder 1　　$\dfrac{7}{3} = 2\dfrac{1}{3}$

B. $\dfrac{5}{2} = 5 \div 2 = 2$ with remainder 1　　$\dfrac{5}{2} = 2\dfrac{1}{2}$

C. $\dfrac{8}{5} = 8 \div 5 = 1$ with remainder 3　　$\dfrac{8}{5} = 1\dfrac{3}{5}$

D. $\dfrac{14}{5} = 14 \div 5 = 2$ with remainder 4　　$\dfrac{14}{5} = 2\dfrac{4}{5}$

E. $\dfrac{13}{8} = 13 \div 8 = 1$ with remainder 5　　$\dfrac{13}{8} = 1\dfrac{5}{8}$

Note that in each case, the remainder tells you how many parts of the next unit you have, but the denominator is needed to show how many parts are needed to make the whole.

A **complex fraction** has fractions in the numerator, the denominator, or both. Examples of complex fractions are $\dfrac{1/2}{5}$, $\dfrac{3}{5/6}$, $\dfrac{2/3}{1/5}$, and $\dfrac{1 + (3/4)}{3/10}$.

One way to simplify complex fractions is to find the least common multiple of all the fractions in the numerator and denominator and then multiply the numerator and denominator by this number.

Example 5

Simplify each complex fraction.

A. $\dfrac{1/2}{5}$ 　　　　 B. $\dfrac{3}{5/6}$ 　　　　 C. $\dfrac{2/3}{1/5}$ 　　　　 D. $\dfrac{1+(3/4)}{3/10}$

Solution

A. The only fraction is $\dfrac{1}{2}$, so you need to multiply by 2. $\dfrac{1/2}{5} = \dfrac{1/2*2}{5*2} = \dfrac{1}{10}$

B. The only fraction is $\dfrac{5}{6}$, so you need to multiply by 6. $\dfrac{3}{5/6} = \dfrac{3*6}{5/6*6} = \dfrac{18}{5}$

C. The fractions are $\dfrac{2}{3}$ and $\dfrac{1}{5}$. You find LCM(3, 5), which is 15.

$$\frac{2/3}{1/5} = \frac{2/3*15}{1/5*15} = \frac{2*5}{1*3} = \frac{10}{3}$$

D. The fractions are $\dfrac{3}{4}$ and $\dfrac{3}{10}$. You find LCM(4,10), which is 20.

$$\frac{1+3/4}{3/10} = \frac{[1+(3/4)]20}{3/10*20} = \frac{1*20+3/4*20}{3*2} = \frac{20+3*5}{6} = \frac{20+15}{6} = \frac{35}{6}$$

Equivalent fractions are fractions that are different representations of the same ratio. For example, in this set, there are six objects, and two are *s: $**####$. So the fraction that shows the ratio of *s to all objects in the set is $\dfrac{2}{6}$. In the set $****########$ there are 4 *s and 12 objects, so the fraction representing *s to objects is $\dfrac{4}{12}$. However, in each case, there is 1 * out of every 3 objects. The ratio of objects in each set is $\dfrac{1}{3}$. So $\dfrac{2}{6} = \dfrac{2*1}{2*3} = \dfrac{1}{3}$, and $\dfrac{4}{12} = \dfrac{4*1}{4*3} = \dfrac{1}{3}$. Thus, $\dfrac{1}{3}, \dfrac{2}{6}$, and $\dfrac{4}{12}$ are equivalent fractions.

You use equivalent fractions when you put a fraction in lowest terms and when you want to add or subtract fractions. You can also use equivalent fractions to compare fractions, although other ways are faster.

Example 6

Write each fraction as an equivalent fraction whose denominator is the number given.

A. $\dfrac{2}{3}$, 30 　　　　 B. $\dfrac{5}{7}$, 28 　　　　 C. $\dfrac{11}{12}$, 24 　　　　 D. $\dfrac{3}{5}$, 40

Solution

A. To write $\frac{2}{3}$ as an equivalent fraction with a denominator of 30, you need to find what number times 3 equals 30. $30 \div 3 = 10$, so $3 \times 10 = 30$.

$$\frac{2}{3} = \frac{2}{3} * 1 = \frac{2}{3} * \frac{10}{10} = \frac{2 * 10}{3 * 10} = \frac{20}{30}$$

B. $28 \div 7 = 4$, so $7 \times 4 = 28$.

$$\frac{5}{7} = \frac{5}{7} * 1 = \frac{5}{7} * \frac{4}{4} = \frac{5 * 4}{7 * 4} = \frac{20}{28}$$

C. $24 \div 12 = 2$, so $12 \times 2 = 24$.

$$\frac{11}{12} = \frac{11}{12} * 1 = \frac{11}{12} * \frac{2}{2} = \frac{11 * 2}{12 * 2} = \frac{22}{24}$$

D. $40 \div 5 = 8$, so $5 \times 8 = 40$.

$$\frac{3}{5} = \frac{3}{5} * 1 = \frac{3}{5} * \frac{8}{8} = \frac{3 * 8}{5 * 8} = \frac{24}{40}$$

To reduce a fraction to its lowest terms, find the greatest common divisor between the numerator and the denominator and divide out that common factor. $\frac{20}{36}$ can be reduced because $\text{GCD}(20, 36) = 4$. $\frac{20}{36} = \frac{5 * 4}{9 * 4} = \frac{5}{9} * \frac{4}{4} = \frac{5}{9} * 1 = \frac{5}{9}$ or $\frac{20}{36} = \frac{20 \div 4}{36 \div 4} = \frac{5}{9}$.

Example 7

Reduce each fraction to its lowest terms.

A. $\frac{14}{16}$ B. $\frac{28}{400}$ C. $\frac{21}{28}$ D. $\frac{18}{24}$ E. $\frac{42}{60}$ F. $\frac{40}{200}$

Solution

A. $\text{GCD}(14, 16) = 2$

$$\frac{14}{16} = \frac{7 * 2}{8 * 2} = \frac{7}{8} * \frac{2}{2} = \frac{7}{8} * 1 = \frac{7}{8} \text{ or } \frac{14}{16} = \frac{14 \div 2}{16 \div 2} = \frac{7}{8}$$

B. $\text{GCD}(28, 400) = 4$

$$\frac{28}{400} = \frac{28 \div 4}{400 \div 4} = \frac{7}{100}$$

C. $\text{GCD}(21, 28) = 7$

$$\frac{21}{28} = \frac{21 \div 7}{28 \div 7} = \frac{3}{4}$$

D. GCD(18, 24) = 6

$$\frac{18}{24} = \frac{18 \div 6}{24 \div 6} = \frac{3}{4}$$

E. GCD(42, 60) = 6

$$\frac{42}{60} = \frac{42 \div 6}{60 \div 6} = \frac{7}{10}$$

F. GCD(40, 200) = 40

$$\frac{40}{200} = \frac{40 \div 40}{200 \div 40} = \frac{1}{5}$$

Comparing fractions allows you to determine whether the two fractions are equal or whether one of the fractions is greater than the other. There are many ways to make the comparisons, and you need to decide which procedure works best for you.

When you compare fractions with equal denominators, the fraction with the greater numerator is the greater fraction.

To compare $\frac{11}{25}$ and $\frac{15}{25}$, for example, since 15 > 11, $\frac{15}{25} > \frac{11}{25}$.

This procedure can be used to compare $\frac{3}{8}$ and $\frac{4}{7}$ if you change them to equivalent fractions. The easiest denominator to use is the product of the given denominators (even though the least common multiple of them might be much smaller). $7 \times 8 = 56$, so change each fraction to an equivalent one with a denominator of 56. $\frac{3}{8} = \frac{3*7}{8*7} = \frac{21}{56}$, and $\frac{4}{7} = \frac{4*8}{7*8} = \frac{32}{56}$. Since $32 > 21$, $\frac{32}{56} > \frac{21}{56}$ and $\frac{4}{7} > \frac{3}{8}$.

Occasionally, the fractions you want to compare will have equal numerators. In this case, the fraction with the smallest denominator will be the greater fraction. Compare $\frac{11}{7}$ and $\frac{11}{5}$. Since with sevenths the whole is divided into 7 parts and with fifths the whole is divided into 5 parts, the fifths are larger pieces than the sevenths, so 11 fifths is greater than 11 sevenths, or $\frac{11}{5} > \frac{11}{7}$.

Another procedure that can be helpful is to make a mental comparison to another number. For example, $\frac{1}{3}$ is less than $\frac{1}{2}$, and $\frac{3}{5}$ is more than $\frac{1}{2}$, so $\frac{3}{5} > \frac{1}{2}$. The comparison value needs to be such that one fraction is greater than this value and the other is less than it.

The cross-multiplication procedure is a relatively easy method to use. To compare $\frac{a}{b}$ and $\frac{c}{d}$, cross-multiply to get ad and bc. If $ad > bc$, then $\frac{a}{b} > \frac{c}{d}$. If $ad = bc$, then $\frac{a}{b} = \frac{c}{d}$, and if $ad < bc$, then $\frac{a}{b} < \frac{c}{d}$. To compare $\frac{3}{8}$ and $\frac{4}{7}$, cross-multiply to get 21 and 32. $21 < 32$, so $\frac{3}{8} < \frac{4}{7}$.

Example 8

Compare each pair of fractions.

A. $\dfrac{7}{8}, \dfrac{7}{10}$ B. $\dfrac{3}{17}, \dfrac{5}{17}$ C. $\dfrac{4}{5}, \dfrac{3}{4}$ D. $\dfrac{8}{9}, \dfrac{3}{4}$ E. $\dfrac{3}{5}, \dfrac{5}{12}$

Solution

A. Since the numerators are the same, the fraction with the smaller denominator is the greater fraction. Since $8 < 10$, $\dfrac{7}{8} > \dfrac{7}{10}$.

B. Since the fractions have the same denominators, the fraction with the greater numerator is the greater fraction. Since $5 > 3$, $\dfrac{5}{17} > \dfrac{3}{17}$.

C. Cross-multiply the fractions. $16 > 15$, so $\dfrac{4}{5} > \dfrac{3}{4}$.

D. Cross-multiply the fractions. $32 > 27$, so $\dfrac{8}{9} > \dfrac{3}{4}$.

E. $\dfrac{3}{5}$ is more than $\dfrac{1}{2}$, and $\dfrac{5}{12}$ is less than $\dfrac{1}{2}$, so $\dfrac{3}{5} > \dfrac{5}{12}$.

PRACTICE PROBLEMS

1. Write these mixed numbers as improper fractions.

   A. $1\dfrac{2}{3}$ B. $7\dfrac{1}{3}$ C. $5\dfrac{3}{4}$ D. $2\dfrac{1}{4}$ E. $3\dfrac{1}{7}$

2. Write these improper fractions as mixed numbers.

   A. $\dfrac{11}{6}$ B. $\dfrac{17}{5}$ C. $\dfrac{32}{7}$ D. $\dfrac{15}{8}$ E. $\dfrac{17}{10}$

3. Simplify each of these complex fractions.

   A. $\dfrac{5/6}{8}$ B. $\dfrac{5}{2/3}$ C. $\dfrac{4/5}{5/8}$

   D. $\dfrac{2/3 + 1/4}{3/5}$ E. $\dfrac{1/2 + 5/6}{4}$

4. Write each fraction as an equivalent fraction with the given denominator.

   A. $\dfrac{3}{5}$, 35 B. $\dfrac{2}{7}$, 42 C. $\dfrac{3}{8}$, 40 D. $\dfrac{2}{9}$, 18 E. $\dfrac{3}{4}$, 24

5. Reduce each fraction to lowest terms.

   A. $\dfrac{16}{20}$ B. $\dfrac{15}{18}$ C. $\dfrac{48}{60}$ D. $\dfrac{9}{12}$ E. $\dfrac{15}{60}$

6. Compare these fractions.

   A. $\dfrac{12}{16}, \dfrac{7}{8}$ B. $\dfrac{5}{9}, \dfrac{5}{7}$ C. $\dfrac{10}{15}, \dfrac{14}{21}$ D. $\dfrac{3}{4}, \dfrac{7}{12}$ E. $\dfrac{2}{3}, \dfrac{7}{8}$

SOLUTIONS

1. A. $1\dfrac{2}{3} = 1 + \dfrac{2}{3} = \dfrac{3}{3} + \dfrac{2}{3} = \dfrac{5}{3}$

   B. $7\dfrac{1}{3} = 7 + \dfrac{1}{3} = \dfrac{21}{3} + \dfrac{1}{3} = \dfrac{22}{3}$

   C. $5\dfrac{3}{4} = 5 + \dfrac{3}{4} = \dfrac{20}{4} + \dfrac{3}{4} = \dfrac{23}{4}$

   D. $2\dfrac{1}{4} = 2 + \dfrac{1}{4} = \dfrac{8}{4} + \dfrac{1}{4} = \dfrac{9}{4}$

   E. $3\dfrac{1}{7} = 3 + \dfrac{1}{7} = \dfrac{21}{7} + \dfrac{1}{7} = \dfrac{22}{7}$

2. A. $\dfrac{11}{6} = 11 \div 6 = 1$ with remainder $5 = 1\dfrac{5}{6}$

   B. $\dfrac{17}{5} = 17 \div 5 = 3$ with remainder $2 = 3\dfrac{2}{5}$

   C. $\dfrac{32}{7} = 32 \div 7 = 4$ with remainder $4 = 4\dfrac{4}{7}$

   D. $\dfrac{15}{8} = 15 \div 8 = 1$ with remainder $7 = 1\dfrac{7}{8}$

   E. $\dfrac{17}{10} = 17 \div 10 = 1$ with remainder $7 = 1\dfrac{7}{10}$

3. A. The only fraction has a denominator of 6.

$$\frac{5/6}{8} = \frac{5/6 * 6}{8 * 6} = \frac{5}{48}$$

   B. The only fraction has a denominator of 3.

$$\frac{5}{2/3} = \frac{5 * 3}{2/3 * 3} = \frac{15}{2}$$

   C. The denominators are 5 and 8. LCM(5, 8) = 40.

$$\frac{4/5}{5/8} = \frac{4/5 * 40}{5/8 * 40} = \frac{4 * 8}{5 * 5} = \frac{32}{25}$$

   D. The denominators are 3, 4, and 5. LCM(3, 4, 5) = 60.

$$\frac{2/3 + 1/4}{3/5} = \frac{(2/3 + 1/4) * 60}{3/5 * 60}$$

$$= \frac{2/3 * 60 + 1/4 * 60}{3 * 12}$$

$$= \frac{2 * 20 + 1 * 15}{36} = \frac{40 + 15}{36} = \frac{55}{36}$$

   E. The denominators are 2 and 6. LCM(2, 6) = 6.

$$\frac{1/2 + 5/6}{4} = \frac{(1/2 + 5/6) * 6}{4 * 6}$$

$$= \frac{1/2 * 6 + 5/6 * 6}{24}$$

$$= \frac{1 * 3 + 5 * 1}{24} = \frac{3 + 5}{24}$$

$$= \frac{8}{24} = \frac{8 * 1}{8 * 3} = \frac{1}{3}$$

4. A. $35 \div 5 = 7$, $\quad \dfrac{3}{5} = \dfrac{3 * 7}{5 * 7} = \dfrac{21}{35}$

   B. $42 \div 7 = 6$, $\quad \dfrac{2}{7} = \dfrac{2 * 6}{7 * 6} = \dfrac{12}{42}$

   C. $40 \div 8 = 5$, $\quad \dfrac{3}{8} = \dfrac{3 * 5}{8 * 5} = \dfrac{15}{40}$

   D. $18 \div 9 = 2$, $\quad \dfrac{2}{9} = \dfrac{2 * 2}{9 * 2} = \dfrac{4}{18}$

   E. $24 \div 4 = 6$, $\quad \dfrac{3}{4} = \dfrac{3 * 6}{4 * 6} = \dfrac{18}{24}$

5. A. GCD(16, 20) = 4, $\quad \dfrac{16}{20} = \dfrac{16 \div 4}{20 \div 4} = \dfrac{4}{5}$

   B. GCD(15, 18) = 3, $\quad \dfrac{15}{18} = \dfrac{15 \div 3}{18 \div 3} = \dfrac{5}{6}$

   C. GCD(48, 60) = 12, $\quad \dfrac{48}{60} = \dfrac{48 \div 12}{60 \div 12} = \dfrac{4}{5}$

   D. GCD(9, 12) = 3, $\quad \dfrac{9}{12} = \dfrac{9 \div 3}{12 \div 3} = \dfrac{3}{4}$

   E. GCD(15, 60) = 15, $\quad \dfrac{15}{60} = \dfrac{15 \div 15}{60 \div 15} = \dfrac{1}{4}$

6. A. Cross multiply. $8 * 12 = 96; 16 * 7 = 112$. Since $96 < 112$, $\dfrac{12}{16} < \dfrac{7}{8}$.

   B. Cross-multiply. $5 * 7 = 35, 9 * 5 = 45$. Since $35 < 45$, $\dfrac{5}{9} < \dfrac{5}{7}$.

   C. Cross-multiply. $10 * 21 = 210, 15 * 14 = 210$. Since $210 = 210$, $\dfrac{10}{15} = \dfrac{14}{21}$.

   D. Cross-multiply. $3 * 12 = 36, 4 * 7 = 28$. Since $36 > 28$, $\dfrac{3}{4} > \dfrac{7}{12}$.

   E. Cross-multiply. $2 * 8 = 16, 3 * 7 = 21$. Since $16 < 21$, $\dfrac{2}{3} < \dfrac{7}{8}$.

OPERATIONS WITH FRACTIONS

Adding Fractions

To add two fractions, the fractions must have a common denominator. You add the numerators to get the numerator of the sum, and the denominator of the sum is the common denominator.

$$\frac{3}{5} + \frac{1}{5} = 3 \text{ fifths} + 1 \text{ fifth} = 4 \text{ fifths} = \frac{4}{5}$$

$$\frac{7}{11} + \frac{2}{11} = \frac{7 + 2}{11} = \frac{9}{11}$$

If the fractions do not have a common denominator, you can create one by finding the least common multiple of the denominators, or you can use the product of the denominators. The product of the denominators is quicker to find, but it can be much larger than the LCM, which could make computation more difficult.

Example 9

A. $\dfrac{1}{2} + \dfrac{1}{4}$ B. $\dfrac{2}{9} + \dfrac{5}{9}$ C. $\dfrac{2}{5} + \dfrac{5}{6}$ D. $\dfrac{5}{8} + \dfrac{5}{12}$ E. $\dfrac{3}{10} + \dfrac{1}{6}$

Solution

A. $2 * 4 = 8$ $\dfrac{1}{2} + \dfrac{1}{4} = \dfrac{1 * 4}{2 * 4} + \dfrac{1 * 2}{4 * 2} = \dfrac{4}{8} + \dfrac{2}{8} = \dfrac{6}{8} = \dfrac{6 \div 2}{8 \div 2} = \dfrac{3}{4}$

or LCM$(2, 4) = 4$ $\dfrac{1}{2} + \dfrac{1}{4} = \dfrac{1 * 2}{2 * 2} + \dfrac{1}{4} = \dfrac{2}{4} + \dfrac{1}{4} = \dfrac{3}{4}$

B. $\dfrac{2}{9} + \dfrac{5}{9} = \dfrac{2 + 5}{9} = \dfrac{7}{9}$

C. $5 * 6 = 30$ $\dfrac{2}{5} + \dfrac{5}{6} = \dfrac{2 * 6}{5 * 6} + \dfrac{5 * 5}{6 * 5} = \dfrac{12}{30} + \dfrac{25}{30} = \dfrac{12 + 25}{30} = \dfrac{37}{30}$

or LCM$(5, 6) = 30$

D. $8 * 12 = 96$ $\dfrac{5}{8} + \dfrac{5}{12} = \dfrac{5 * 12}{8 * 12} + \dfrac{5 * 8}{12 * 8} = \dfrac{60}{96} + \dfrac{40}{96} = \dfrac{100}{96} = \dfrac{100 \div 4}{96 \div 4} = \dfrac{25}{24}$

or LCM$(8, 12) = 24$ $\dfrac{5}{8} + \dfrac{5}{12} = \dfrac{5 * 3}{8 * 3} + \dfrac{5 * 2}{12 * 2} = \dfrac{15}{24} + \dfrac{10}{24} = \dfrac{25}{24}$

E. $10 * 6 = 60$ $\dfrac{3}{10} + \dfrac{1}{6} = \dfrac{3 * 6}{10 * 6} + \dfrac{1 * 10}{6 * 10} = \dfrac{18}{60} + \dfrac{10}{60} = \dfrac{28}{60} = \dfrac{28 \div 4}{60 \div 4} = \dfrac{7}{15}$

or LCM$(10, 6) = 30$ $\dfrac{3}{10} + \dfrac{1}{6} = \dfrac{3 * 3}{10 * 3} + \dfrac{1 * 5}{6 * 5} = \dfrac{9}{30} + \dfrac{5}{30} = \dfrac{14}{30} =$

$\dfrac{14 \div 2}{30 \div 2} = \dfrac{7}{15}$

Subtracting Fractions

Subtraction of fractions also requires that the fractions have a common denominator. Once the fractions have a common denominator, you can subtract the numerators, and the result goes over the common denominator.

Order is important in subtraction.

$$\dfrac{3}{4} - \dfrac{3}{5} = \dfrac{3 * 5}{4 * 5} - \dfrac{3 * 4}{5 * 4} = \dfrac{15}{20} - \dfrac{12}{20} = \dfrac{15 - 12}{20} = \dfrac{3}{20}$$

$$\dfrac{3}{5} - \dfrac{3}{4} = \dfrac{3 * 4}{5 * 4} - \dfrac{3 * 5}{4 * 5} = \dfrac{12}{20} - \dfrac{15}{20} = \dfrac{12 - 15}{20} = \dfrac{-3}{20}$$

You can write $\dfrac{-3}{20}$ as $-\dfrac{3}{20}$ with the entire fraction being negative rather than the numerator being negative.

Example 10

A. $\dfrac{5}{8} - \dfrac{1}{4}$ B. $\dfrac{1}{2} - \dfrac{1}{3}$ C. $\dfrac{7}{10} - \dfrac{3}{10}$ D. $\dfrac{3}{5} - \dfrac{7}{20}$ E. $\dfrac{5}{8} - \dfrac{1}{12}$

Solution

A. $\dfrac{5}{8} - \dfrac{1}{4} = \dfrac{5}{8} - \dfrac{1*2}{4*2} = \dfrac{5}{8} - \dfrac{2}{8} = \dfrac{3}{8}$

B. $\dfrac{1}{2} - \dfrac{1}{3} = \dfrac{1*3}{2*3} - \dfrac{1*2}{3*2} = \dfrac{3}{6} - \dfrac{2}{6} = \dfrac{1}{6}$

C. $\dfrac{7}{10} - \dfrac{3}{10} = \dfrac{4}{10} = \dfrac{4 \div 2}{10 \div 2} = \dfrac{2}{5}$

D. $\dfrac{3}{5} - \dfrac{7}{20} = \dfrac{3*4}{5*4} - \dfrac{7}{20} = \dfrac{12}{20} - \dfrac{7}{20} = \dfrac{5}{20} = \dfrac{5 \div 5}{20 \div 5} = \dfrac{1}{4}$

E. $\dfrac{5}{8} - \dfrac{1}{12} = \dfrac{5*3}{8*3} - \dfrac{1*2}{12*2} = \dfrac{15}{24} - \dfrac{2}{24} = \dfrac{13}{24}$

Addition and subtraction of mixed numbers are similar to the procedures for fractions.

$$5\tfrac{2}{3} = \quad 5\tfrac{8}{12} \qquad\qquad 5\tfrac{3}{5} = \quad 5\tfrac{12}{20}$$
$$\underline{+1\tfrac{1}{4}} = \underline{+1\tfrac{3}{12}} \qquad \underline{+2\tfrac{11}{20}} = \underline{+2\tfrac{11}{20}}$$
$$6\tfrac{11}{12} \qquad\qquad 7\tfrac{23}{20} = 7 + \tfrac{23}{20} = 7 + 1 + \tfrac{3}{20} = 8\tfrac{3}{20}$$

Example 11

Add these mixed numbers.

A. $\begin{array}{r} \tfrac{3}{4} \\ +5\tfrac{2}{5} \\ \hline \end{array}$ B. $\begin{array}{r} 2 \\ +3\tfrac{1}{5} \\ \hline \end{array}$ C. $\begin{array}{r} 10\tfrac{1}{2} \\ +9\tfrac{3}{8} \\ \hline \end{array}$ D. $\begin{array}{r} 6\tfrac{3}{4} \\ +16\tfrac{7}{8} \\ \hline \end{array}$

Solution

A. $\begin{array}{r} \tfrac{3}{4} = \tfrac{15}{20} \\ +5\tfrac{2}{5} = 5\tfrac{8}{20} \\ \hline 5\tfrac{23}{20} = 5 + 1 + \tfrac{3}{20} = 6\tfrac{3}{20} \end{array}$

B.
$$\begin{array}{r} 2 \\ +3\frac{1}{5} \\ \hline 5\frac{1}{5} \end{array}$$

C.
$$\begin{array}{r} 10\frac{1}{2} = 10\frac{4}{8} \\ +\ 9\frac{3}{8} = +9\frac{3}{8} \\ \hline 19\frac{7}{8} \end{array}$$

D.
$$\begin{array}{r} 6\frac{3}{4} = 6\frac{6}{8} \\ +16\frac{7}{8} = +16\frac{7}{8} \\ \hline 22\frac{13}{8} = 22+1+\frac{5}{8} = 23\frac{5}{8} \end{array}$$

When you subtract mixed numbers, you may have a fraction to subtract that is the greater fraction.

$$\begin{array}{r} 12\frac{1}{2} = 12\frac{4}{8} = 11\frac{12}{8} \\ -9\frac{7}{8} = -9\frac{7}{8} = -9\frac{7}{8} \\ \hline 2\frac{5}{8} \end{array}$$

Example 12

Subtract these mixed numbers.

A.
$$\begin{array}{r} 8\frac{3}{4} \\ -5\frac{1}{6} \\ \hline \end{array}$$

B.
$$\begin{array}{r} 3\frac{7}{12} \\ -1\frac{3}{8} \\ \hline \end{array}$$

C.
$$\begin{array}{r} 9\frac{1}{6} \\ -2\frac{3}{5} \\ \hline \end{array}$$

D.
$$\begin{array}{r} 13 \\ -9\frac{3}{4} \\ \hline \end{array}$$

Solution

A.
$$\begin{array}{r} 8\frac{3}{4} = 8\frac{9}{12} \\ -5\frac{1}{6} = -5\frac{2}{12} \\ \hline 3\frac{7}{12} \end{array}$$

$$\begin{array}{r} 3\frac{7}{12} = 3\frac{14}{24} \\ \text{B.} \quad -1\frac{3}{8} = -1\frac{9}{24} \\ \hline 2\frac{5}{24} \end{array}$$

$$\begin{array}{r} 9\frac{1}{6} = 9\frac{5}{30} = 8 + \frac{30}{30} + \frac{5}{30} = 8\frac{35}{30} \\ \text{C.} \quad -2\frac{3}{5} = -2\frac{18}{30} = -2\frac{18}{30} \qquad\qquad = -2\frac{18}{30} \\ \hline 6\frac{17}{30} \end{array}$$

$$\begin{array}{r} 13 = 12 + 1 = 12\frac{4}{4} \\ \text{D.} \quad -9\frac{3}{4} = -9\frac{3}{4} = -9\frac{3}{4} \\ \hline 3\frac{1}{4} \end{array}$$

Multiplying Fractions

Multiplication of fractions does not require that the fractions have common denominators.

$$\frac{2}{3} * \frac{3}{4} = \frac{2 * 3}{3 * 4} = \frac{6}{12} = \frac{6 \div 6}{12 \div 6} = \frac{1}{2}$$

You can multiply the numerators together and place the product over the product of the denominators. The next step is to reduce the fraction to lowest terms.

A second way is to divide a numerator and a denominator by a common factor. The second approach is most helpful when the numbers are large or when several fractions are being multiplied.

$$\frac{2}{3} * \frac{3}{4} = \frac{{}^{1}\cancel{2}}{{}_{1}\cancel{3}} * \frac{\cancel{3}^{1}}{\cancel{4}_{2}} = \frac{1 * 1}{1 * 2} = \frac{1}{2}$$

Example 13

Multiply these fractions.

A. $\frac{7}{8} * \frac{4}{5}$ B. $\frac{4}{5} * \frac{15}{16}$ C. $\frac{9}{16} * \frac{5}{6}$ D. $\frac{3}{10} * \frac{5}{9}$

Solution

A. $\frac{7}{8} * \frac{4}{5} = \frac{7 * 4}{8 * 5} = \frac{28}{40} = \frac{28 \div 4}{40 \div 4} = \frac{7}{10}$, or

$$\frac{7}{8} * \frac{4}{5} = \frac{7}{{}_{2}\cancel{8}} * \frac{\cancel{4}^{1}}{5} = \frac{7 * 1}{2 * 5} = \frac{7}{10}$$

B. $\dfrac{4}{5} * \dfrac{15}{16} = \dfrac{4*15}{5*16} = \dfrac{60}{80} = \dfrac{60 \div 20}{80 \div 20} = \dfrac{3}{4}$, or

$$\dfrac{4}{5} * \dfrac{15}{16} = \dfrac{{}^1\cancel{4}}{{}_1\cancel{5}} * \dfrac{\cancel{15}^3}{\cancel{16}_4} = \dfrac{1*3}{1*4} = \dfrac{3}{4}$$

C. $\dfrac{9}{16} * \dfrac{5}{6} = \dfrac{9*5}{16*6} = \dfrac{45}{96} = \dfrac{45 \div 3}{96 \div 3} = \dfrac{15}{32}$, or

$$\dfrac{9}{16} * \dfrac{5}{6} = \dfrac{{}^3\cancel{9}}{16} * \dfrac{5}{\cancel{6}_2} = \dfrac{3*5}{16*2} = \dfrac{15}{32}$$

D. $\dfrac{3}{10} * \dfrac{5}{9} = \dfrac{3*5}{10*9} = \dfrac{15}{90} = \dfrac{15 \div 15}{90 \div 15} = \dfrac{1}{6}$, or

$$\dfrac{3}{10} * \dfrac{5}{9} = \dfrac{{}^1\cancel{3}}{{}_2\cancel{10}} * \dfrac{\cancel{5}^1}{\cancel{9}_3} = \dfrac{1*1}{2*3} = \dfrac{1}{6}$$

Dividing Fractions

To divide fractions, simply multiply by the reciprocal of the divisor. As in all other division, the divisor fraction cannot be zero.

$$\dfrac{1}{3} \div \dfrac{3}{4} = \dfrac{1}{3} * \dfrac{4}{3} = \dfrac{4}{9} \quad \text{and} \quad \dfrac{3}{4} \div \dfrac{3}{8} = \dfrac{3}{4} * \dfrac{8}{3} = \dfrac{24}{12} = 2$$

Example 14

Divide these fractions.

A. $\dfrac{3}{5} \div \dfrac{9}{10}$ B. $\dfrac{5}{6} \div \dfrac{7}{12}$ C. $\dfrac{9}{16} \div \dfrac{3}{8}$ D. $\dfrac{2}{3} \div \dfrac{5}{6}$

Solution

A. $\dfrac{3}{5} \div \dfrac{9}{10} = \dfrac{3}{5} * \dfrac{10}{9} = \dfrac{\cancel{3}^1}{\cancel{5}_1} * \dfrac{\cancel{10}^2}{\cancel{9}_3} = \dfrac{1}{1} * \dfrac{2}{3} = \dfrac{2}{3}$

B. $\dfrac{5}{6} \div \dfrac{7}{12} = \dfrac{5}{6} * \dfrac{12}{7} = \dfrac{5}{\cancel{6}_1} * \dfrac{\cancel{12}^2}{7} = \dfrac{10}{7}$

C. $\dfrac{9}{16} \div \dfrac{3}{8} = \dfrac{9}{16} * \dfrac{8}{3} = \dfrac{\cancel{9}^3}{\cancel{16}_2} * \dfrac{\cancel{8}^1}{\cancel{3}_1} = \dfrac{3}{2} * \dfrac{1}{1} = \dfrac{3}{2}$

D. $\dfrac{2}{3} \div \dfrac{5}{6} = \dfrac{2}{3} * \dfrac{6}{5} = \dfrac{2}{\cancel{3}_1} * \dfrac{\cancel{6}^2}{5} = \dfrac{4}{5}$

When you multiply or divide fractions and whole numbers, write the whole number over 1 before you do the computation, so that, for example, 2 becomes $\dfrac{2}{1}$.

Example 15

Do the indicated multiplications and divisions.

A. $\dfrac{3}{4} * 2$ B. $12 * \dfrac{5}{24}$ C. $\dfrac{2}{3} \div 4$ D. $4 \div \dfrac{3}{5}$

Solution

A. $\dfrac{3}{4} * 2 = \dfrac{3}{4} * \dfrac{2}{1} = \dfrac{3*2}{4*1} = \dfrac{6}{4} = \dfrac{6 \div 2}{4 \div 2} = \dfrac{3}{2}$

B. $12 * \dfrac{5}{24} = \dfrac{12}{1} * \dfrac{5}{24} = \dfrac{12*5}{24*1} = \dfrac{60}{24} = \dfrac{60 \div 12}{24 \div 12} = \dfrac{5}{2}$

C. $\dfrac{2}{3} \div 4 = \dfrac{2}{3} \div \dfrac{4}{1} = \dfrac{2}{3} * \dfrac{1}{4} = \dfrac{2*1}{3*4} = \dfrac{2}{12} = \dfrac{2 \div 2}{12 \div 2} = \dfrac{1}{6}$

D. $4 \div \dfrac{3}{5} = \dfrac{4}{1} \div \dfrac{3}{5} = \dfrac{4}{1} * \dfrac{5}{3} = \dfrac{4*5}{1*3} = \dfrac{20}{3}$

When you perform multiplication or division with mixed numbers, first replace each mixed number with the equivalent improper fraction, then do the computation.

Example 16

Multiply these mixed numbers.

A. $2\dfrac{3}{4} \times \dfrac{9}{11}$ B. $3\dfrac{2}{5} \times 1\dfrac{1}{4}$ C. $4 \times 2\dfrac{7}{8}$ D. $4\dfrac{3}{8} \times 3\dfrac{1}{5}$

Solution

A. $2\dfrac{3}{4} \times \dfrac{9}{11} = \dfrac{11}{4} \times \dfrac{9}{11} = \dfrac{11*9}{4*11} = \dfrac{11}{11} * \dfrac{9}{4} = 1 \times \dfrac{9}{4} = \dfrac{9}{4} = 2\dfrac{1}{4}$

B. $3\dfrac{2}{5} \times 1\dfrac{1}{4} = \dfrac{17}{5} \times \dfrac{5}{4} = \dfrac{17 \times 5}{5 \times 4} = \dfrac{5}{5} \times \dfrac{17}{4} = 1 \times \dfrac{17}{4} = \dfrac{17}{4} = 4\dfrac{1}{4}$

C. $4 \times 2\dfrac{7}{8} = \dfrac{4}{1} \times \dfrac{23}{8} = \dfrac{4 \times 23}{1 \times 8} = \dfrac{4}{4} \times \dfrac{23}{2} = 1 \times \dfrac{23}{2} = \dfrac{23}{2} = 11\dfrac{1}{2}$

D. $4\dfrac{3}{8} \times 3\dfrac{1}{5} = \dfrac{35}{8} \times \dfrac{16}{5} = \dfrac{35 \times 16}{8 \times 5} = \dfrac{5}{5} \times \dfrac{8}{8} \times \dfrac{7 \times 2}{1} = 1 \times 1 \times \dfrac{14}{1} = 14$

Example 17

Divide these mixed numbers.

A. $15 \div 1\dfrac{7}{8}$ B. $11\dfrac{1}{3} \div 2\dfrac{5}{6}$ C. $3\dfrac{3}{16} \div 2\dfrac{1}{8}$ D. $8\dfrac{2}{3} \div 2$

Solution

A. $15 \div 1\dfrac{7}{8} = \dfrac{15}{1} \div \dfrac{15}{8} = \dfrac{15}{1} \times \dfrac{8}{15} = \dfrac{15}{15} \times \dfrac{8}{1} = 1 \times 8 = 8$

B. $11\dfrac{1}{3} \div 2\dfrac{5}{6} = \dfrac{34}{3} \div \dfrac{17}{6} = \dfrac{34}{3} \times \dfrac{6}{17} = \dfrac{17}{17} \times \dfrac{3}{3} \times \dfrac{2 \times 2}{1 \times 1} = 1 \times 1 \times \dfrac{4}{1} = 4$

C. $3\frac{3}{16} \div 2\frac{1}{8} = \frac{51}{16} \div \frac{17}{8} = \frac{51}{16} \times \frac{8}{17} = \frac{17}{17} \times \frac{8}{8} \times \frac{3 \times 1}{1 \times 2} = 1 \times 1 \times \frac{3}{2} = \frac{3}{2} = 1\frac{1}{2}$

D. $8\frac{2}{3} \div 2 = \frac{26}{3} \div \frac{2}{1} = \frac{26}{3} \times \frac{1}{2} = \frac{2}{2} \times \frac{13}{3} = 1 \times \frac{13}{3} = \frac{13}{3} = 4\frac{1}{3}$

PRACTICE PROBLEMS

1. Add these fractions.

   A. $\frac{2}{3}$ B. $\frac{3}{4}$ C. $\frac{7}{8}$ D. $\frac{5}{11}$ E. $\frac{7}{15}$
   $+\frac{1}{4}$ $+\frac{2}{5}$ $+\frac{8}{15}$ $+\frac{3}{7}$ $+\frac{3}{5}$

   F. $\frac{2}{5}$ G. $\frac{1}{12}$ H. $\frac{13}{15}$ I. $\frac{5}{12}$ J. $\frac{19}{24}$
   $+\frac{3}{20}$ $+\frac{13}{16}$ $+\frac{1}{10}$ $+\frac{7}{18}$ $+\frac{13}{18}$

2. Subtract these fractions.

   A. $\frac{5}{6}$ B. $\frac{2}{3}$ C. $\frac{15}{16}$ D. $\frac{3}{4}$ E. $\frac{5}{14}$
   $-\frac{2}{5}$ $-\frac{1}{4}$ $-\frac{1}{6}$ $-\frac{7}{10}$ $-\frac{1}{4}$

   F. $\frac{5}{6}$ G. $\frac{3}{5}$ H. $\frac{3}{4}$ I. $\frac{1}{6}$ J. $\frac{1}{4}$
   $-\frac{7}{18}$ $-\frac{5}{12}$ $-\frac{7}{8}$ $-\frac{2}{3}$ $-\frac{1}{6}$

3. Multiply these fractions.

   A. $\frac{2}{3} \times \frac{9}{10}$ B. $\frac{2}{5} \times \frac{5}{6}$ C. $\frac{7}{8} \times \frac{5}{6}$

   D. $\frac{1}{6} \times \frac{15}{16}$ E. $\frac{1}{10} \times \frac{5}{32}$ F. $\frac{9}{20} \times \frac{5}{12}$

   G. $\frac{7}{24} \times \frac{18}{35}$ H. $\frac{3}{5} \times \frac{10}{27}$ I. $\frac{3}{8} \times \frac{13}{24}$

   J. $\frac{3}{10} \times \frac{5}{8}$

4. Divide these fractions.

   A. $\frac{3}{5} \div \frac{9}{10}$ B. $\frac{1}{4} \div \frac{9}{10}$ C. $\frac{17}{20} \div \frac{4}{5}$ D. $\frac{5}{6} \div \frac{3}{4}$

   E. $\frac{1}{4} \div \frac{2}{3}$ F. $\frac{5}{6} \div \frac{7}{12}$ G. $\frac{8}{9} \div \frac{3}{4}$ H. $\frac{1}{4} \div \frac{5}{14}$

   I. $\frac{3}{4} \div \frac{6}{7}$ J. $\frac{11}{12} \div \frac{11}{15}$

5. Add these mixed numbers.

   A. $7\frac{2}{5} + 9\frac{4}{5}$ B. $4\frac{2}{3} + 6\frac{1}{2}$ C. $12\frac{2}{3} + 5\frac{1}{4}$

   D. $5\frac{2}{3} + 6\frac{5}{6}$ E. $8\frac{1}{12} + 6\frac{1}{6}$

6. Subtract these mixed numbers.

   A. $5\frac{5}{6} - 3\frac{1}{10}$ B. $3\frac{1}{5} - 1\frac{1}{2}$ C. $8\frac{1}{6} - 3\frac{1}{12}$

   D. $8 - 2\frac{4}{7}$ E. $11\frac{3}{4} - 5$

7. Multiply these mixed numbers.

   A. $4\frac{1}{2} \times 2\frac{1}{4}$ B. $6\frac{1}{4} \times \frac{3}{4}$ C. $2 \times 1\frac{9}{16}$

   D. $5\frac{1}{3} \times 1\frac{1}{8}$ E. $2\frac{5}{8} \times 2\frac{2}{5}$

8. Divide these mixed numbers.

   A. $3\frac{1}{7} \div \frac{3}{4}$ B. $14\frac{1}{2} \div 3\frac{5}{8}$ C. $8 \div 1\frac{4}{5}$

   D. $11\frac{7}{8} \div 5$ E. $2\frac{1}{16} \div 1\frac{3}{8}$

9. Compute the value of each of these expressions.

   A. $4\frac{2}{16} + 2\frac{7}{8} + 5\frac{1}{2}$ B. $7\frac{2}{3} + 5\frac{1}{6} + 3\frac{1}{12}$

   C. $\frac{2}{3} + \frac{5}{6} + \frac{5}{8}$ D. $\frac{9}{16} + \frac{3}{8} + \frac{1}{2}$

   E. $2\frac{3}{4} \times 1\frac{1}{8} \times 3\frac{5}{6}$ F. $3\frac{1}{5} \times 1\frac{1}{4} \times 1\frac{1}{3}$

   G. $\frac{2}{5} \times \frac{3}{4} \times \frac{15}{16}$ H. $\frac{2}{3} \times \frac{5}{8} \times \frac{3}{10}$

10. Compute these values, using the order of operations.

    A. $\dfrac{1}{2} + \dfrac{2}{3} - \dfrac{1}{4} \times \dfrac{1}{3} \div \dfrac{1}{6}$ B. $\dfrac{2}{3} + \dfrac{3}{5} - \dfrac{1}{2} + \dfrac{2}{3} - \dfrac{5}{6}$

    C. $\dfrac{3}{4} \times \dfrac{1}{2} + \dfrac{3}{5} \div \dfrac{6}{35}$ D. $\dfrac{3}{4} \div \dfrac{5}{8} - \dfrac{4}{5} \times \dfrac{3}{8}$

    E. $\dfrac{3}{10} \times \dfrac{5}{9} \div \dfrac{3}{4} \times \dfrac{2}{3}$

SOLUTIONS

1. A. $\dfrac{2}{3} + \dfrac{1}{4}$ LCM(3, 4) = 12

   $\dfrac{2 \times 4}{3 \times 4} = \dfrac{8}{12}$ $\dfrac{1 \times 3}{4 \times 3} = \dfrac{3}{12}$

   $\dfrac{8}{12} + \dfrac{3}{12} = \dfrac{11}{12}$

   B. $\dfrac{3}{4} + \dfrac{2}{5}$ LCM(4, 5) = 20

   $\dfrac{3 \times 5}{4 \times 5} = \dfrac{15}{20}$ $\dfrac{2 \times 4}{5 \times 4} = \dfrac{8}{20}$

   $\dfrac{15}{20} + \dfrac{8}{20} = \dfrac{23}{20} = 1\dfrac{3}{20}$

   C. $\dfrac{7}{8} + \dfrac{8}{15} = \dfrac{105}{120} + \dfrac{64}{120} = \dfrac{169}{120} = 1\dfrac{49}{120}$

   D. $\dfrac{5}{11} + \dfrac{3}{7} = \dfrac{35}{77} + \dfrac{33}{77} = \dfrac{68}{77}$

   E. $\dfrac{7}{15} + \dfrac{3}{5} = \dfrac{7}{15} + \dfrac{9}{15} = \dfrac{16}{15} = 1\dfrac{1}{15}$

   F. $\dfrac{2}{5} + \dfrac{3}{20} = \dfrac{8}{20} + \dfrac{3}{20} = \dfrac{11}{20}$

   G. $\dfrac{1}{12} + \dfrac{13}{16} = \dfrac{4}{48} + \dfrac{39}{48} = \dfrac{43}{48}$

   H. $\dfrac{13}{15} + \dfrac{1}{10} = \dfrac{26}{30} + \dfrac{3}{30} = \dfrac{29}{30}$

   I. $\dfrac{5}{12} + \dfrac{7}{18} = \dfrac{15}{36} + \dfrac{14}{36} = \dfrac{29}{36}$

   J. $\dfrac{19}{24} + \dfrac{13}{18} = \dfrac{57}{72} + \dfrac{52}{72} = \dfrac{109}{72} = 1\dfrac{37}{72}$

2. A. $\dfrac{5}{6} - \dfrac{2}{5}$ LCM(6, 5) = 30

   $\dfrac{5 \times 5}{6 \times 5} = \dfrac{25}{30}$ $\dfrac{2 \times 6}{5 \times 6} = \dfrac{12}{30}$

   $\dfrac{25}{30} - \dfrac{12}{30} = \dfrac{13}{30}$

   B. $\dfrac{2}{3} - \dfrac{1}{4}$ LCM(3, 4) = 12

   $\dfrac{2 \times 4}{3 \times 4} = \dfrac{8}{12}$ $\dfrac{1 \times 3}{4 \times 3} = \dfrac{3}{12}$

   $\dfrac{8}{12} - \dfrac{3}{12} = \dfrac{5}{12}$

   C. $\dfrac{15}{16} - \dfrac{1}{6} = \dfrac{45}{48} - \dfrac{8}{48} = \dfrac{37}{48}$

   D. $\dfrac{3}{4} - \dfrac{7}{10} = \dfrac{15}{20} - \dfrac{14}{20} = \dfrac{1}{20}$

   E. $\dfrac{5}{14} - \dfrac{1}{4} = \dfrac{10}{28} - \dfrac{7}{28} = \dfrac{3}{28}$

   F. $\dfrac{5}{6} - \dfrac{7}{18} = \dfrac{15}{18} - \dfrac{7}{18} = \dfrac{8}{18} = \dfrac{4}{9}$

   G. $\dfrac{3}{5} - \dfrac{5}{12} = \dfrac{36}{60} - \dfrac{25}{60} = \dfrac{11}{60}$

   H. $\dfrac{3}{4} - \dfrac{7}{8} = \dfrac{6}{8} - \dfrac{7}{8} = -\dfrac{1}{8}$

   I. $\dfrac{1}{6} - \dfrac{2}{3} = \dfrac{1}{6} - \dfrac{4}{6} = -\dfrac{3}{6} = -\dfrac{1}{2}$

   J. $\dfrac{1}{4} - \dfrac{1}{6} = \dfrac{3}{12} - \dfrac{2}{12} = \dfrac{1}{12}$

3. A. $\frac{2}{3} \times \frac{9}{10} = \frac{2 \times 9}{3 \times 10} = \frac{2}{2} \times \frac{3}{3} \times \frac{3}{5} = 1 \times 1 \times \frac{3}{5} = \frac{3}{5}$

B. $\frac{2}{5} \times \frac{5}{6} = \frac{2 \times 5}{5 \times 6} = \frac{2}{2} \times \frac{5}{5} \times \frac{1}{3} = 1 \times 1 \times \frac{1}{3} = \frac{1}{3}$

C. $\frac{7}{8} \times \frac{5}{6} = \frac{7 \times 5}{8 \times 6} = \frac{35}{48}$

D. $\frac{1}{6} \times \frac{15}{16} = \frac{1 \times 15}{6 \times 16} = \frac{3}{3} \times \frac{1 \times 5}{2 \times 16} = 1 \times \frac{5}{32}$
   $= \frac{5}{32}$

E. $\frac{1}{10} \times \frac{5}{32} = \frac{1 \times 5}{10 \times 32} = \frac{5}{5} \times \frac{1}{2 \times 32} = 1 \times \frac{1}{64}$
   $= \frac{1}{64}$

F. $\frac{9}{20} \times \frac{5}{12} = \frac{9 \times 5}{20 \times 12} = \frac{3}{3} \times \frac{5}{5} \times \frac{3}{4 \times 4}$
   $= 1 \times 1 \times \frac{3}{16} = \frac{3}{16}$

G. $\frac{7}{24} \times \frac{18}{35} = \frac{7 \times 18}{24 \times 35} = \frac{7}{7} \times \frac{6}{6} \times \frac{3}{4 \times 5}$
   $= 1 \times 1 \times \frac{3}{20} = \frac{3}{20}$

H. $\frac{3}{5} \times \frac{10}{27} = \frac{3 \times 10}{5 \times 27} = \frac{3}{3} \times \frac{5}{5} \times \frac{2}{9} = 1 \times 1 \times \frac{2}{9} = \frac{2}{9}$

I. $\frac{3}{8} \times \frac{13}{24} = \frac{3 \times 13}{8 \times 24} = \frac{3}{3} \times \frac{13}{8 \times 8} = 1 \times \frac{13}{64} = \frac{13}{64}$

J. $\frac{3}{10} \times \frac{5}{8} = \frac{3 \times 5}{10 \times 8} = \frac{5}{5} \times \frac{3}{2 \times 8} = 1 \times \frac{3}{16} = \frac{3}{16}$

4. A. $\frac{3}{5} \div \frac{9}{10} = \frac{3}{5} \times \frac{10}{9} = \frac{3 \times 10}{5 \times 9} = \frac{3}{3} \times \frac{5}{5} \times \frac{2}{3}$
   $= 1 \times 1 \times \frac{2}{3} = \frac{2}{3}$

B. $\frac{1}{4} \div \frac{9}{10} = \frac{1}{4} \times \frac{10}{9} = \frac{1 \times 10}{4 \times 9} = \frac{2}{2} \times \frac{1 \times 5}{2 \times 9}$
   $= 1 \times \frac{5}{18} = \frac{5}{18}$

C. $\frac{17}{20} \div \frac{4}{5} = \frac{17}{20} \times \frac{5}{4} = \frac{17 * 5}{20 * 4} = \frac{5}{5} \times \frac{17 \times 1}{4 \times 4}$
   $= 1 \times \frac{17}{16} = \frac{17}{16} = 1\frac{1}{16}$

D. $\frac{5}{6} \div \frac{3}{4} = \frac{5}{6} \times \frac{4}{3} = \frac{5 \times 4}{6 \times 3} = \frac{2}{2} \times \frac{5 \times 2}{3 \times 3} = 1 \times \frac{10}{9}$
   $= \frac{10}{9} = 1\frac{1}{9}$

E. $\frac{1}{4} \div \frac{2}{3} = \frac{1}{4} \times \frac{3}{2} = \frac{1 \times 3}{4 \times 2} = \frac{3}{8}$

F. $\frac{5}{6} \div \frac{7}{12} = \frac{5}{6} \times \frac{12}{7} = \frac{5 \times 12}{6 \times 7} = \frac{6}{6} \times \frac{5 \times 2}{1 \times 7}$
   $= 1 \times \frac{10}{7} = \frac{10}{7} = 1\frac{3}{7}$

G. $\frac{8}{9} \div \frac{3}{4} = \frac{8}{9} \times \frac{4}{3} = \frac{8 \times 4}{9 \times 3} = \frac{32}{27} = 1\frac{5}{27}$

H. $\frac{1}{4} \div \frac{5}{14} = \frac{1}{4} \times \frac{14}{5} = \frac{1 \times 14}{4 \times 5} = \frac{2}{2} \times \frac{1 \times 7}{2 \times 5}$
   $= 1 \times \frac{7}{10} = \frac{7}{10}$

I. $\frac{3}{4} \div \frac{6}{7} = \frac{3}{4} \times \frac{7}{6} = \frac{3 \times 7}{4 \times 6} = \frac{3}{3} \times \frac{1 \times 7}{4 \times 2}$
   $= 1 \times \frac{7}{8} = \frac{7}{8}$

J. $\frac{11}{12} \div \frac{11}{15} = \frac{11}{12} \times \frac{15}{11} = \frac{11 \times 15}{12 \times 11} = \frac{11}{11} \times \frac{3}{3} \times \frac{5}{4}$
   $= 1 \times 1 \times \frac{5}{4} = \frac{5}{4} = 1\frac{1}{4}$

5. A. $7\frac{2}{5} + 9\frac{4}{5} = (7+9) + \left(\frac{2}{5} + \frac{4}{5}\right) = 16 + \frac{6}{5}$
   $= 16 + 1\frac{1}{5} = 17\frac{1}{5}$

B. $4\frac{2}{3} + 6\frac{1}{2} = (4+6) + \left(\frac{2}{3} + \frac{1}{2}\right) = 10 +$
   $\left(\frac{4}{6} + \frac{3}{6}\right) = 10 + \frac{7}{6} = 10 + 1\frac{1}{6} = 11\frac{1}{6}$

C. $12\frac{2}{3} + 5\frac{1}{4} = (12+5) + \left(\frac{2}{3} + \frac{1}{4}\right) = 17 +$
   $\left(\frac{8}{12} + \frac{3}{12}\right) = 17 + \frac{11}{12} = 17\frac{11}{12}$

D. $5\frac{2}{3} + 6\frac{5}{6} = 5 + 6 + \frac{4}{6} + \frac{5}{6} = 11 + \frac{9}{6} = 11 +$
   $1\frac{3}{6} = 12\frac{1}{2}$

E. $8\frac{1}{12} + 6\frac{1}{6} = 8 + 6 + \frac{1}{12} + \frac{2}{12} = 14 + \frac{3}{12} =$
   $14 + \frac{1}{4} = 14\frac{1}{4}$

6. A. $5\frac{5}{6} - 3\frac{1}{10} = (5-3) + \left(\frac{5}{6} - \frac{1}{10}\right) = 2 +$

$\left(\frac{25}{30} - \frac{3}{30}\right) = 2 + \frac{22}{30} = 2 + \frac{11}{15} = 2\frac{11}{15}$

B. $3\frac{1}{5} - 1\frac{1}{2} = (3-1) + \left(\frac{1}{5} - \frac{1}{2}\right) = 2 +$

$\left(\frac{2}{10} - \frac{5}{10}\right) = 2 + \left(-\frac{3}{10}\right) = 1\frac{7}{10}$

C. $8\frac{1}{6} - 3\frac{1}{12} = (8-3) + \left(\frac{1}{6} - \frac{1}{12}\right) = 5 +$

$\left(\frac{2}{12} - \frac{1}{12}\right) = 5 + \frac{1}{12} = 5\frac{1}{12}$

D. $8 - 2\frac{4}{7} = (8-2) + \left(0 - \frac{4}{7}\right) = 6 + \left(-\frac{4}{7}\right) =$

$5\frac{3}{7}$

E. $11\frac{3}{4} - 5 = (11-5) + \left(\frac{3}{4} - 0\right) = 6 + \frac{3}{4} = 6\frac{3}{4}$

7. A. $4\frac{1}{2} \times 2\frac{1}{4} = \frac{9}{2} \times \frac{9}{4} = \frac{9 \times 9}{2 \times 4} = \frac{81}{8} = 10\frac{1}{8}$

B. $6\frac{1}{4} \times \frac{3}{4} = \frac{25}{4} \times \frac{3}{4} = \frac{25 \times 3}{4 \times 4} = \frac{75}{16} = 4\frac{11}{16}$

C. $2 \times 1\frac{9}{16} = \frac{2}{1} \times \frac{25}{16} = \frac{2 \times 25}{1 \times 16} = \frac{2}{2} \times \frac{25}{8} =$

$1 \times \frac{25}{8} = \frac{25}{8} = 3\frac{1}{8}$

D. $5\frac{1}{3} \times 1\frac{1}{8} = \frac{16}{3} \times \frac{9}{8} = \frac{16 \times 9}{3 \times 8} = \frac{8}{8} \times \frac{3}{3} \times$

$\frac{2 \times 3}{1} = 1 \times 1 \times \frac{6}{1} = 6$

E. $2\frac{5}{8} \times 2\frac{2}{5} = \frac{21}{8} \times \frac{12}{5} = \frac{21 \times 12}{8 \times 5} =$

$\frac{4}{4} \times \frac{21 \times 3}{2 \times 5} = 1 \times \frac{63}{10} = \frac{63}{10} = 6\frac{3}{10}$

8. A. $3\frac{1}{7} \div \frac{3}{4} = \frac{22}{7} \div \frac{3}{4} = \frac{22}{7} \times \frac{4}{3} = \frac{22 \times 4}{7 \times 3} =$

$\frac{88}{21} = 4\frac{4}{21}$

B. $14\frac{1}{2} \div 3\frac{5}{8} = \frac{29}{2} \div \frac{29}{8} = \frac{29}{2} \times \frac{8}{29} = \frac{29 \times 8}{2 \times 29} =$

$\frac{29}{29} \times \frac{2}{2} \times \frac{4}{1} = 1 \times 1 \times 4 = 4$

C. $8 \div 1\frac{4}{5} = \frac{8}{1} \div \frac{9}{5} = \frac{8}{1} \times \frac{5}{9} = \frac{8 \times 5}{1 \times 9} = \frac{40}{9} = 4\frac{4}{9}$

D. $11\frac{7}{8} \div 5 = \frac{95}{8} \div \frac{5}{1} = \frac{95}{8} \times \frac{1}{5} = \frac{95 \times 1}{8 \times 5} =$

$\frac{5}{5} \times \frac{19}{8} = 1 \times \frac{19}{8} = \frac{19}{8} = 2\frac{3}{8}$

E. $2\frac{1}{16} \div 1\frac{3}{8} = \frac{33}{16} \div \frac{11}{8} = \frac{33}{16} \times \frac{8}{11} =$

$\frac{33 \times 8}{16 \times 11} = \frac{11}{11} \times \frac{8}{8} \times \frac{3}{2} = 1 \times 1 \times \frac{3}{2} = 1\frac{1}{2}$

9. A. $4\frac{2}{16} + 2\frac{7}{8} + 5\frac{1}{2} = (4 + 2 + 5) +$

$\left(\frac{2}{16} + \frac{14}{16} + \frac{8}{16}\right) = 11 + \frac{24}{16} = 11 + 1\frac{8}{16} =$

$12\frac{1}{2}$

B. $7\frac{2}{3} + 5\frac{1}{6} + 3\frac{1}{12} = (7 + 5 + 3) +$

$\left(\frac{8}{12} + \frac{2}{12} + \frac{1}{12}\right) = 15 + \left(\frac{11}{12}\right) = 15\frac{11}{12}$

C. $\frac{2}{3} + \frac{5}{6} + \frac{5}{8} = \frac{16}{24} + \frac{20}{24} + \frac{15}{24} = \frac{51}{24} = \frac{17}{8} = 2\frac{1}{8}$

D. $\frac{9}{16} + \frac{3}{8} + \frac{1}{2} = \frac{9}{16} + \frac{6}{16} + \frac{8}{16} = \frac{23}{16} = 1\frac{7}{16}$

E. $2\frac{3}{4} \times 1\frac{1}{8} \times 3\frac{5}{6} = \frac{11}{4} \times \frac{9}{8} \times \frac{23}{6} =$

$\frac{11 \times 9 \times 23}{4 \times 8 \times 6} = \frac{3}{3} \times \frac{11 \times 3 \times 23}{4 \times 8 \times 2} =$

$1 \times \frac{759}{64} = \frac{759}{64} = 11\frac{55}{64}$

F. $3\frac{1}{5} \times 1\frac{1}{4} \times 1\frac{1}{3} = \frac{16}{5} \times \frac{5}{4} \times \frac{4}{3} = \frac{16 \times 5 \times 4}{5 \times 4 \times 3} =$

$\frac{5}{5} \times \frac{4}{4} \times \frac{16}{3} = 1 \times 1 \times \frac{16}{3} = \frac{16}{3} = 5\frac{1}{3}$

G. $\frac{2}{5} \times \frac{3}{4} \times \frac{15}{16} = \frac{2 \times 3 \times 15}{5 \times 4 \times 16} = \frac{2}{2} \times \frac{5}{5} \times$

$\frac{3 \times 3}{2 \times 16} = 1 \times 1 \times \frac{9}{32} = \frac{9}{32}$

H. $\frac{2}{3} \times \frac{5}{8} \times \frac{3}{10} = \frac{2 \times 5 \times 3}{3 \times 8 \times 10} = \frac{2}{2} \times \frac{5}{5} \times \frac{3}{3} \times \frac{1}{8} =$

$1 \times 1 \times 1 \times \frac{1}{8} = \frac{1}{8}$

10. A. $\frac{1}{2}+\frac{2}{3}-\frac{1}{4}\times\frac{1}{3}\div\frac{1}{6}=\frac{1}{2}+\frac{2}{3}-\frac{1}{12}\times\frac{6}{1}=\frac{1}{2}+$

$\frac{2}{3}-\frac{1}{2}=\frac{2}{3}$

B. $\frac{2}{3}+\frac{3}{5}-\frac{1}{2}+\frac{2}{3}-\frac{5}{6}=\frac{20}{30}+\frac{18}{30}-\frac{15}{30}+\frac{20}{30}-\frac{25}{30}=$

$\frac{58}{30}-\frac{40}{30}=\frac{18}{30}=\frac{3}{5}$

C. $\frac{3}{4}\times\frac{1}{2}+\frac{3}{5}\div\frac{6}{35}=\frac{3}{8}+\frac{3}{5}\times\frac{35}{6}=\frac{3}{8}+\frac{3\times35}{5\times6}=$

$\frac{3}{8}+\frac{7}{2}=\frac{3}{8}+\frac{28}{8}=\frac{31}{8}=3\frac{7}{8}$

D. $\frac{3}{4}\div\frac{5}{8}-\frac{4}{5}\times\frac{3}{8}=\frac{3}{4}\times\frac{8}{5}-\frac{4\times3}{5\times8}=\frac{3\times8}{4\times5}-$

$\frac{3}{10}=\frac{12}{10}-\frac{3}{10}=\frac{9}{10}$

E. $\frac{3}{10}\times\frac{5}{9}\div\frac{3}{4}\times\frac{2}{3}=\frac{3\times5}{10\times9}\div\frac{3}{4}\times\frac{2}{3}=$

$\frac{1}{6}\times\frac{4}{3}\times\frac{2}{3}=\frac{4}{18}\times\frac{2}{3}=\frac{8}{54}=\frac{4}{27}$

DECIMALS

A decimal is made up of a **whole number** part (which can be zero), a **decimal point**, and a **decimal fraction**. For example, 2.1345, 720.864913, 0.4823, 0.222$\cdots$, and 0.9090090009$\cdots$ are all examples of decimals.

In 0.631579824, the 6 is in the tenths place, 3 is in the hundredths place, 1 is in the thousandths place, 5 is in the ten-thousandths place, 7 is in the hundred-thousandths place, 9 is in the millionths place, 8 is in the ten-millionths place, 2 is in the hundred-millionths place, and 4 is in the billionths place. You can continue naming decimal places indefinitely, but the ones already named go far beyond what you will need for the GMAT.

When you compare decimal fractions, start at the decimal and compare the digits one by one until you find a difference in the digits. The one with the greater number in this place is the greater number.

Example 18

Which decimal is greater?

A. 0.7 or 0.074   B. 0.9086 or 0.908   C. 0.608 or 0.64

Solution

A. 0.7 has a 7 in the tenths place, while 0.074 has a 0 in the tenths place, so 0.7 > 0.074.
B. 0.9086 has 9 in the tenths place, and 0.908 has a 9 in the tenths place. 0.9086 has a 0 in the hundredths place, and 0.908 has a 0 in the hundredths place. 0.9086 has an 8 in the thousandths place, and 0.908 has an 8 in the thousandths place. 0.9086 has an additional digit in the ten-thousandths place, so 0.9086 > 0.908.
C. Both numbers have a 6 in the tenths place. 0.608 has a 0 in the hundredths place, while 0.64 has a 4 in the hundredths place. 0.64 > 0.608.

When you convert decimals to fractions, look at two different situations: one in which the decimal is finite and one in which the decimal is infinite and repeating.

Example 19

Write each decimal as a fraction.

A. 0.265   B. 0.41   C. 0.25   D. 0.65   E. 0.104

Solution

A. 0.265 is 265 thousandths, so $0.265 = \dfrac{265}{1,000} = \dfrac{53}{200}$.

B. 0.41 is 41 hundredths, so $0.41 = \dfrac{41}{100}$.

C. 0.25 is 25 hundredths, so $0.25 = \dfrac{25}{100} = \dfrac{1}{4}$.

D. 0.65 is 65 hundredths, so $0.65 = \dfrac{65}{100} = \dfrac{13}{20}$.

E. 0.104 is 104 thousandths, so $0.104 = \dfrac{104}{1,000} = \dfrac{13}{125}$.

Note that you write the digits in the decimal over a 1 followed by zeros. The number of zeros is equal to the number of digits in the decimal.

When a decimal has all its digits in repeating groups, you can write it as a fraction by writing one repeating group over the same number of 9s as there are digits in the repeating group.

Example 20

Change these repeating decimals to fractions.

A. 0.333···   B. 0.252525···   C. 0.090909···   D. 0.123123123···

Solution

A. 0.333··· has one digit that repeats, 3. You write this repeating value over a 9 since only one digit repeats. So $0.333 \cdots = \dfrac{3}{9} = \dfrac{1}{3}$.

B. 0.252525··· has two digits that repeat, 25. You write the repeating value over two 9s, since two digits repeat. So $0.252525 \cdots = \dfrac{25}{99}$.

C. 0.090909··· has two digits that repeat, 09. So $0.090909 \cdots = \dfrac{09}{99} = \dfrac{9}{99} = \dfrac{1}{11}$.

D. 0.123123123··· has three digits that repeat, 123. So $0.123123123 \cdots = \dfrac{123}{999} = \dfrac{41}{333}$.

If a decimal has some digits between the decimal point and the start of the first repeating group, you have to modify the procedure above. In this case, you write the nonrepeating digits and one repeating group minus the nonrepeating digits over a group of 9s followed by a group of 0s. The number of 9s is the same as the number of digits in the repeating group, and the number of 0s is equal to the number of digits that do not repeat. Thus,

$$0.12453453453 \cdots = \frac{12,453 - 12}{99,900} = \frac{12,441}{99,900} = \frac{4,147}{33,300}.$$

Example 21

Change these decimals to fractions.

A. 0.4353535···   B. 0.142333···   C. 0.12373737···

Solution

A. $0.4353535\cdots = \dfrac{435-4}{990} = \dfrac{431}{990}$

B. $0.142333\cdots = \dfrac{1{,}423-142}{9{,}000} = \dfrac{1{,}281}{9{,}000} = \dfrac{427}{3{,}000}$

C. $0.12373737\cdots = \dfrac{1{,}237-12}{9{,}900} = \dfrac{1{,}225}{9{,}900} = \dfrac{49}{396}$

You can also change fractions to decimals. The easiest fractions to change to decimals are those whose denominators are powers of 10, such as 10, 100, or 1,000. $\dfrac{17}{100} = 0.17$, $\dfrac{263}{1{,}000} = 0.263$, $\dfrac{9}{100} = 0.09$.

In each case, the numerator is written as a whole number so the decimal point is at the right, and then you count to the left of that decimal point the same number of places as there are 0s in the power of 10.

For all other fractions, you do the indicated division until the division terminates with a remainder of zero, or until it repeats a remainder. If the division terminates, you have a finite decimal with the decimal in the quotient as the answer. If you get a repeated remainder, you get a repeating decimal. The repeating group is the part of the quotient found from the first time the remainder occurred to the second time it occurred.

Note that a fraction in lowest terms will terminate only when 2 and 5 are the only prime divisors of the denominator. If the denominator has any prime divisor other than 2 or 5, that fraction will yield a repeating decimal.

Example 22

Change these fractions to decimals.

A. $\dfrac{19}{100}$ B. $\dfrac{7}{1{,}000}$ C. $\dfrac{3}{10}$ D. $\dfrac{7}{100}$ E. $\dfrac{263}{1{,}000}$

Solution

A. $\dfrac{19}{100}$ is 19 hundredths, so $\dfrac{19}{100} = 0.19$.

B. $\dfrac{7}{1{,}000}$ is 7 thousandths, so $\dfrac{7}{1{,}000} = 0.007$.

C. $\dfrac{3}{10}$ is 3 tenths, so $\dfrac{3}{10} = 0.3$.

D. $\dfrac{7}{100}$ is 7 hundredths, so $\dfrac{7}{100} = 0.07$.

E. $\dfrac{263}{1{,}000}$ is 263 thousandths, so $\dfrac{263}{1{,}000} = 0.263$.

Example 23

Change these fractions to decimals.

A. $\dfrac{3}{4}$ B. $\dfrac{2}{5}$ C. $\dfrac{11}{25}$ D. $\dfrac{17}{250}$ E. $\dfrac{9}{125}$

Solution

A. $\dfrac{3}{4} = 3 \div 4 = 0.75$

$$
\begin{array}{r}
0.75 \\
4\overline{)3.00} \\
\underline{28} \\
20 \\
\underline{20} \\
0
\end{array}
$$

B. $\dfrac{2}{5} = 2 \div 5 = 0.4$

$$
\begin{array}{r}
0.4 \\
5\overline{)2.0} \\
\underline{20} \\
0
\end{array}
$$

C. $\dfrac{11}{25} = 11 \div 25 = 0.44$

$$
\begin{array}{r}
0.44 \\
25\overline{)11.00} \\
\underline{100} \\
100 \\
\underline{100} \\
0
\end{array}
$$

D. $\dfrac{17}{250} = 17 \div 250 = 0.068$

$$
\begin{array}{r}
0.068 \\
250\overline{)17.000} \\
\underline{0} \\
170 \\
\underline{0} \\
1{,}700 \\
\underline{1{,}500} \\
2{,}000 \\
\underline{2{,}000} \\
0
\end{array}
$$

E. $\dfrac{9}{125} = 9 \div 125 = 0.072$

$$
\begin{array}{r}
0.072 \\
125\overline{)9.000} \\
\underline{0} \\
90 \\
\underline{0} \\
900 \\
\underline{875} \\
250 \\
\underline{250} \\
0
\end{array}
$$

Example 24

Change these fractions to decimals.

A. $\dfrac{2}{9}$ B. $\dfrac{5}{6}$ C. $\dfrac{7}{12}$ D. $\dfrac{7}{11}$ E. $\dfrac{2}{15}$

Solution

A. $\dfrac{2}{9} = 2 \div 9 = 0.222\cdots$

$$
\begin{array}{r}
0.22 \\
9\overline{)2.00} \\
\underline{18} \\
20 \\
\underline{18} \\
2
\end{array}
$$

        remainder 2

        remainder 2

B. $\dfrac{5}{6} = 5 \div 6 = 0.8333\cdots$

$$
\begin{array}{r}
0.833 \\
6\overline{)5.000} \\
\underline{48} \\
20 \\
\underline{18} \\
20 \\
\underline{18} \\
2
\end{array}
$$

        remainder 2

        remainder 2

        remainder 2

C. $\dfrac{7}{12} = 7 \div 12 = 0.58333\cdots$

$$
\begin{array}{r}
0.5833 \\
12\overline{)7.0000} \\
\underline{60} \\
100 \\
\underline{96} \\
40 \\
\underline{36} \\
40 \\
\underline{36} \\
4
\end{array}
$$

        remainder 4

        remainder 4

        remainder 4

D. $\dfrac{7}{11} = 7 \div 11 = 0.636363\cdots$

$$
\begin{array}{r}
0.6363 \\
11\overline{)7.0000} \\
\underline{66} \\
40 \\
\underline{33} \\
70 \\
\underline{66} \\
40 \\
\underline{33} \\
7
\end{array}
$$

        remainder 7

        remainder 7

E. $\dfrac{2}{15} = 2 \div 15 = 0.1333\cdots$

$$\begin{array}{r} 0.133 \\ 15\overline{\smash{)}2.000} \\ 15 \end{array}$$

$$\begin{array}{rl} 50 & \text{remainder } 5 \\ 45 & \\ \hline 50 & \text{remainder } 5 \\ 45 & \\ \hline 5 & \text{remainder } 5 \end{array}$$

Table of Equivalents

Fraction	Decimal	Fraction	Decimal
1/20	0.05	1/2	0.5
1/16	0.625	3/5	0.6
1/12	0.08333···	5/8	0.625
1/10	0.1	2/3	0.666···
1/8	0.125	7/10	0.7
1/6	0.1666···	3/4	0.75
1/5	0.2	4/5	0.8
1/4	0.25	5/6	0.8333···
3/10	0.3	7/8	0.875
1/3	0.333···	9/10	0.9
3/8	0.375	15/16	0.9375
2/5	0.40	19/20	0.95

PRACTICE PROBLEMS

1. Arrange these decimals in order with the largest first.

   A. 0.01, 0.001, 0.1, 0.0001

   B. 2.25, 0.253, 0.2485, 2.249

   C. 0.38, 1.5, 0.475, 0.0506

   D. 0.006, 5.02, 0.503, 0.1987

   E. 0.92, 0.89, 0.103, 0.098

2. Change each decimal to a fraction.

   A. 0.75   B. 0.08   C. 0.12   D. 0.35
   E. 0.165   F. 0.83   G. 0.248   H. 0.56
   I. 0.625   J. 0.05

3. Change each decimal to a fraction.

   A. 0.888···   B. 0.666···
   C. 0.272727···   D. 0.353535···
   E. 0.145145145···   F. 0.060606···
   G. 0.140140140···   H. 0.909090···

4. Change each decimal to a fraction.

   A. 0.8666···   B. 0.1555···
   C. 0.14252525···   D. 0.5313131···
   E. 0.2666···   F. 0.0545454···
   G. 0.25111···   H. 0.3125125125···

5. Change each fraction to a decimal.

   A. $\dfrac{15}{100}$ B. $\dfrac{85}{1,000}$ C. $\dfrac{37}{100}$ D. $\dfrac{265}{1,000}$

   E. $\dfrac{9}{10,000}$ F. $\dfrac{2}{100}$ G. $\dfrac{7}{10}$ H. $\dfrac{11}{100}$

   I. $\dfrac{5}{10}$ J. $\dfrac{25}{100}$

6. Change each fraction to a decimal.

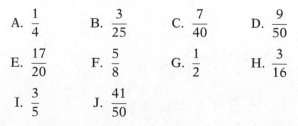

   A. $\dfrac{1}{4}$ B. $\dfrac{3}{25}$ C. $\dfrac{7}{40}$ D. $\dfrac{9}{50}$

   E. $\dfrac{17}{20}$ F. $\dfrac{5}{8}$ G. $\dfrac{1}{2}$ H. $\dfrac{3}{16}$

   I. $\dfrac{3}{5}$ J. $\dfrac{41}{50}$

7. Change each fraction to a decimal.

    A. $\dfrac{2}{3}$ B. $\dfrac{1}{6}$ C. $\dfrac{5}{9}$ D. $\dfrac{7}{90}$

    E. $\dfrac{1}{12}$ F. $\dfrac{7}{45}$ G. $\dfrac{13}{15}$ H. $\dfrac{5}{11}$

    I. $\dfrac{7}{30}$ J. $\dfrac{4}{15}$

▦ SOLUTIONS

1. A. 0.1, 0.01, 0.001, 0.0001
   B. 2.25, 2.249, 0.253, 0.2485
   C. 1.5, 0.475, 0.38, 0.0506
   D. 5.02, 0.503, 0.1987, 0.006
   E. 0.92, 0.89, 0.103, 0.098

2. A. $0.75 = \dfrac{75}{100} = \dfrac{3}{4}$

   B. $0.08 = \dfrac{08}{100} = \dfrac{8}{100} = \dfrac{2}{25}$

   C. $0.12 = \dfrac{12}{100} = \dfrac{3}{25}$

   D. $0.35 = \dfrac{35}{100} = \dfrac{7}{20}$

   E. $0.165 = \dfrac{165}{1,000} = \dfrac{33}{200}$

   F. $0.83 = \dfrac{83}{100}$

   G. $0.248 = \dfrac{248}{1,000} = \dfrac{31}{125}$

   H. $0.56 = \dfrac{56}{100} = \dfrac{14}{25}$

   I. $0.625 = \dfrac{625}{1,000} = \dfrac{5}{8}$

   J. $0.05 = \dfrac{05}{100} = \dfrac{5}{100} = \dfrac{1}{20}$

3. A. $0.888\cdots = \dfrac{8}{9}$

   B. $0.666\cdots = \dfrac{6}{9} = \dfrac{2}{3}$

   C. $0.272727\cdots = \dfrac{27}{99} = \dfrac{3}{11}$

   D. $0.353535\cdots = \dfrac{35}{99}$

   E. $0.145145145\cdots = \dfrac{145}{999}$

   F. $0.060606\cdots = \dfrac{06}{99} = \dfrac{6}{99} = \dfrac{2}{33}$

   G. $0.140140140\cdots = \dfrac{140}{999}$

   H. $0.909090\cdots = \dfrac{90}{99} = \dfrac{10}{11}$

4. A. $0.8666\cdots = \dfrac{86-8}{90} = \dfrac{78}{90} = \dfrac{13}{15}$

   B. $0.1555\cdots = \dfrac{15-1}{90} = \dfrac{14}{90} = \dfrac{7}{45}$

   C. $0.14252525\cdots = \dfrac{1,425-14}{9,900} = \dfrac{1,411}{9,900}$

   D. $0.5313131\cdots = \dfrac{531-5}{990} = \dfrac{526}{990} = \dfrac{263}{495}$

   E. $0.2666\cdots = \dfrac{26-2}{90} = \dfrac{24}{90} = \dfrac{4}{15}$

   F. $0.0545454\cdots = \dfrac{054-0}{990} = \dfrac{54}{990} =$

   $\dfrac{54 \div 18}{990 \div 18} = \dfrac{3}{55}$

   G. $0.25111\cdots = \dfrac{251-25}{900} = \dfrac{226}{900} = \dfrac{113}{450}$

   H. $0.3125125125\cdots = \dfrac{3,125-3}{9,990} = \dfrac{3,122}{9,990} =$

   $\dfrac{1,561}{4,995}$

5. A. $\dfrac{15}{100} = 15$ hundredths $= 0.15$

   B. $\dfrac{85}{1,000} = 85$ thousandths $= 0.085$

   C. $\dfrac{37}{100} = 37$ hundredths $= 0.37$

   D. $\dfrac{265}{1,000} = 265$ thousandths $= 0.265$

   E. $\dfrac{9}{10,000} = 9$ ten-thousandths $= 0.0009$

   F. $\dfrac{2}{100} = 2$ hundredths $= 0.02$

   G. $\dfrac{7}{10} = 7$ tenths $= 0.7$

   H. $\dfrac{11}{100} = 11$ hundredths $= 0.11$

   I. $\dfrac{5}{10} = 5$ tenths $= 0.5$

   J. $\dfrac{25}{100} = 25$ hundredths $= 0.25$

6. A. $\dfrac{1}{4} = 1 \div 4 = 0.25$

   B. $\dfrac{3}{25} = 3 \div 25 = 0.12$

   C. $\dfrac{7}{40} = 7 \div 40 = 0.175$

   D. $\dfrac{9}{50} = 9 \div 50 = 0.18$

   E. $\dfrac{17}{20} = 17 \div 20 = 0.85$

   F. $\dfrac{5}{8} = 5 \div 8 = 0.625$

   G. $\dfrac{1}{2} = 1 \div 2 = 0.5$

   H. $\dfrac{3}{16} = 3 \div 16 = 0.1875$

   I. $\dfrac{3}{5} = 3 \div 5 = 0.6$

   J. $\dfrac{41}{50} = 41 \div 50 = 0.82$

7. A. $\dfrac{2}{3} = 2 \div 3 = 0.666\cdots$

   B. $\dfrac{1}{6} = 1 \div 6 = 0.1666\cdots$

   C. $\dfrac{5}{9} = 5 \div 9 = 0.555\cdots$

   D. $\dfrac{7}{90} = 7 \div 90 = 0.0777\cdots$

   E. $\dfrac{1}{12} = 1 \div 12 = 0.08333\cdots$

   F. $\dfrac{7}{45} = 7 \div 45 = 0.1555\cdots$

   G. $\dfrac{13}{15} = 13 \div 15 = 0.8666\cdots$

   H. $\dfrac{5}{11} = 5 \div 11 = 0.454545\cdots$

   I. $\dfrac{7}{30} = 7 \div 30 = 0.2333\cdots$

   J. $\dfrac{4}{15} = 4 \div 15 = 0.2666\cdots$

COMPUTATION WITH DECIMALS

When you compute with decimals, use terminating decimals only. If a problem has a repeating decimal, either round the decimal or change it to a fraction.

To add or subtract decimals, align the decimal points in the numbers and locate the decimal point in the sum or difference based on this alignment. The numbers can then be added or subtracted as though they were whole numbers.

Example 25

Add these decimals.

A. $0.8 + 0.5$ B. $0.46 + 0.7$ C. $2.9 + 0.12$
D. $0.533 + 4.14 + 0.3 + 2.2$ E. $2.58 + 34.78 + 0.69 + 0.02$

Solution

A. Align the decimal points.

$$\begin{array}{r} 0.8 \\ +\,0.5 \\ \hline 1.3 \end{array}$$

$0.8 + 0.5 = 1.3$

B. Align the decimal points.

$$\begin{array}{r} 0.46 \\ +\,0.7 \\ \hline 1.16 \end{array}$$

$0.46 + 0.7 = 1.16$

C. Align the decimal points.

$$\begin{array}{r} 2.9 \\ +\,0.12 \\ \hline 3.02 \end{array}$$

$2.9 + 0.12 = 3.02$

D. Align the decimal points.

$$\begin{array}{r} 0.533 \\ 4.14 \\ 0.3 \\ +\,2.2 \\ \hline 7.173 \end{array}$$

$0.533 + 4.14 + 0.3 + 2.2 = 7.173$

E. Align the decimal points.

$$\begin{array}{r} 2.58 \\ 34.78 \\ 0.69 \\ +\,0.02 \\ \hline 38.07 \end{array}$$

$2.58 + 34.78 + 0.69 + 0.02 = 38.07$

Example 26

Subtract these decimals.

A. $0.29 - 0.03$ B. $0.73 - 0.32$ C. $8.3 - 5.4$
D. $18.52 - 6.1$ E. $7.86 - 0.215$ F. $2.86 - 0.006$
G. $15 - 3.42$ H. $28.65 - 9$ I. $8 - 7.3$

Solution

A. Align the decimal points.

$$\begin{array}{r} 0.29 \\ -\,0.03 \\ \hline 0.26 \end{array}$$

$0.29 - 0.03 = 0.26$

B. Align the decimal points.

$$\begin{array}{r} 0.73 \\ -\,0.32 \\ \hline 0.41 \end{array}$$

$0.73 - 0.32 = 0.41$

C. Align the decimal points.

$$\begin{array}{r} 8.3 \\ -\,5.4 \\ \hline 2.9 \end{array}$$

$8.3 - 5.4 = 2.9$

D. Align the decimal points.

$$\begin{array}{r} 18.52 \\ -\,6.1 \\ \hline 12.42 \end{array}$$

$18.52 - 6.1 = 12.42$

You can add zeros to the right of the last digit to the right of the decimal point without changing the value of the number. This may aid in subtraction.

E. $7.86 = 7.860$

$$\begin{array}{r} 7.860 \\ - 0.215 \\ \hline 7.645 \end{array}$$

$7.86 - 0.215 = 7.645$

F. $2.86 = 2.860$

$$\begin{array}{r} 2.860 \\ - 0.006 \\ \hline 2.854 \end{array}$$

$2.86 - 0.006 = 2.854$

G. $15 = 15. = 15.00$

$$\begin{array}{r} 15.00 \\ - 3.42 \\ \hline 11.58 \end{array}$$

$15 - 3.42 = 11.58$

H. $9 = 9. = 9.00$

$$\begin{array}{r} 28.65 \\ - 9.00 \\ \hline 19.65 \end{array}$$

$28.65 - 9 = 19.65$

I. $8 = 8. = 8.0$

$$\begin{array}{r} 8.0 \\ - 7.3 \\ \hline 0.7 \end{array}$$

$8 - 7.3 = 0.7$

When you multiply decimals, you do not need to align the decimal points. The decimal placement in the product is determined by the sum of the number of decimal places in the two numbers being multiplied. For example, 1.2×0.34 will have three decimal places in the product. This is so because

$$1.2 \times 0.34 = \frac{12}{10} \times \frac{34}{100} = \frac{12 \times 34}{1,000}$$

Since the denominator is 1,000, you find the product in the numerator and then move the decimal point three places to the left.

$$1.2 \times 0.34 = \frac{12}{10} \times \frac{34}{100} = \frac{12 \times 34}{1,000} = \frac{408}{1,000} = 0.408$$

Example 27

Multiply these decimals.

A. 0.3×8 B. 0.02×0.8 C. 0.5×0.01 D. 2.1×0.04
E. 0.002×0.4 F. 0.12×0.12 G. 0.34×5 H. 0.02×0.003

Solution

A. $0.3 \times 8 = \frac{3}{10} \times \frac{8}{1} = \frac{3 \times 8}{10} = \frac{24}{10} = 2.4$

B. $0.02 \times 0.8 = (2 \times 0.01) \times (8 \times 0.1) = (2 \times 8) \times (0.001 \times 0.1) = 16 \times 0.001 = 0.016$

C.   0.01   Multiply $5 \times 1 = 5$
       $\times$ 0.5   2 decimal places plus 1 decimal place = 3 decimal
       0.005   places. Add a zero on the left to get 0.005 so you have
                       three decimal places.

D.   2.1 $21 \times 4 = 84$
       $\times$ 0.04   Total decimal places are $1 + 2 = 3$.
       0.084   Add a zero to the left to have the needed 3 decimal
                       places.

E.   0.002 $2 \times 4 = 8$
       $\times$ 0.4   Total decimal places are $3 + 1 = 4$.
       0.0008   Add 3 zeros to the left to get 0.0008.

F.   0.12 $12 \times 12 = 144$
       $\times$ 0.12 $2 + 2 = 4$ decimal places
       0.0144   Add 1 zero on the left to get 0.0144.

G.   0.34 34×5
       $\times$ 5 $2 + 0 = 2$ decimal places
       $1.70 = 1.7$ The zero at the right is not needed.

H.   0.02 $2 \times 3 = 6$
       $\times$ 0.003 $2 + 3 = 5$ decimal places
       0.00006   Add 4 zeros on the left to get 0.00006.

When you divide decimals, subtract the number of decimal places in the divisor from the number of decimal places in the dividend to get the number of decimal places in the quotient.

$$0.8 \div 0.004 = \frac{8}{10} \div \frac{4}{1,000} = \frac{8}{10} \times \frac{1,000}{4} = \frac{8}{4} \times \frac{1,000}{10} = 2 \times 100 = 200$$

$$0.048 \div 0.6 = \frac{48}{1,000} \div \frac{6}{10} = \frac{48}{1,000} \times \frac{10}{6} = \frac{48}{6} \times \frac{10}{1,000} = 8 \times \frac{1}{100} = 0.08$$

Example 28

Divide these decimals as indicated.

A. $0.015 \div 5$ B. $0.486 \div 0.2$ C. $0.006 \div 0.012$
D. $2 \div 0.5$ E. $0.2348 \div 0.04$ F. $2,000 \div 0.2$

Solution

A. $0.015 \div 5 = \dfrac{15}{1,000} \div \dfrac{5}{1} = \dfrac{15}{1,000} \times \dfrac{1}{5} = \dfrac{15}{5} \times \dfrac{1}{1,000} = 3 \times \dfrac{1}{1,000} = 0.003$

B. $0.486 \div 0.2 = \dfrac{0.486}{0.2} = \dfrac{0.486}{0.2} \times \dfrac{10}{10} = \dfrac{4.86}{2} = 2.43$

C. $0.006 \div 0.012 = \dfrac{0.006}{0.012} = \dfrac{0.006}{0.012} \times \dfrac{1,000}{1,000} = \dfrac{6}{12} = 0.5$

D. $2 \div 0.5 = \dfrac{2}{0.5} = \dfrac{2}{0.5} \times \dfrac{10}{10} = \dfrac{20}{5} = 4$

E. $0.2348 \div 0.04 = \dfrac{0.2348}{0.04} = \dfrac{0.2348}{0.04} \times \dfrac{100}{100} = \dfrac{23.48}{4} = 5.87$

F. $2,000 \div 0.2 = \dfrac{2,000}{0.2} = \dfrac{2,000}{0.2} \times \dfrac{10}{10} = \dfrac{20,000}{2} = 10,000$

Rather than do the division of decimals by using fractions, you can do the division based on whole-number division. This is based on the fact that with the fractions, the denominators were made into whole numbers by moving the decimal point in the divisor and dividend the same number of places. The end result is that the divisor is a whole number. The decimal placement in the quotient corresponds to the adjusted decimal placement in the quotient.

Example 29

Divide these decimals as indicated.

A. $2 \div 0.8$
B. $9 \div 7.2$
C. $74.898 \div 0.06$
D. $45.54 \div 0.018$
E. $0.4524 \div 0.052$
F. $0.00924 \div 0.231$

Solution

A. $2 \div 0.8 = 2.5$

$$
\begin{array}{r}
2.5 \\
8\overline{)20.0} \\
16 \\
\overline{40} \\
40 \\
\hline
\end{array}
$$

B. $9 \div 7.2 = 1.25$

$$
\begin{array}{r}
1.25 \\
72\overline{)90.00} \\
72 \\
\overline{180} \\
144 \\
\overline{360} \\
360 \\
\hline
\end{array}
$$

C. $74.898 \div 0.06 = 1,248.3$

$$
\begin{array}{r}
1,248.3 \\
6\overline{)7,489.8} \\
6 \\
\overline{14} \\
12 \\
\overline{28} \\
24 \\
\overline{49} \\
48 \\
\overline{18} \\
18 \\
\hline
\end{array}
$$

D. $45.54 \div 0.018 = 2.530$

$$\begin{array}{r} 2.530 \\ 0.018\overline{)45.540} \\ 36 \\ \overline{95} \\ 90 \\ \overline{54} \\ 54 \\ \overline{0} \end{array}$$

E. $0.4524 \div 0.052 = 8.7$

$$\begin{array}{r} 8.7 \\ 52\overline{)452.4} \\ 416 \\ \overline{364} \\ 364 \\ \overline{} \end{array}$$

F. $0.00924 \div 0.231 = 0.04$

$$\begin{array}{r} 0.04 \\ 231\overline{)9.24} \\ 924 \\ \overline{} \end{array}$$

Example 30

Divide these decimals and round as indicated.

A. $825 \div 1.15$ and round to the nearest tenth.
B. $2.9 \div 0.37$ and round to the nearest hundredth.
C. $2.48 \div 0.162$ and round to the nearest thousandth.
D. $\$11.24 \div 0.07$ and round to the nearest cent.

Solution

A.

$$\begin{array}{r} 717.390 \\ 1.15\overline{)825.00\ 00} \\ 805 \\ \overline{200} \\ 115 \\ \overline{850} \\ 805 \\ \overline{450} \\ 345 \\ \overline{1,050} \\ 1,035 \\ \overline{15} \end{array}$$

717.39 rounds to the nearest tenth to 717.4

$825 \div 1.15 = 717.4$ to the nearest tenth

B.

$$\begin{array}{r} 7.837 \\ 0.37\overline{)2.90\ 000} \\ 259 \\ \overline{310} \\ 296 \\ \overline{140} \\ 111 \\ \overline{290} \\ 259 \\ \overline{31} \end{array}$$

7.837 rounds to the nearest hundredth to 7.84

$2.9 \div 0.37 = 7.84$ to the nearest hundredth

C.
$$
\begin{array}{r}
15.3086 \\
0.162\overline{)2.480\ 0000} \\
162 \\
\overline{860} \\
810 \\
\overline{500} \\
486 \\
\overline{140} \\
0 \\
\overline{1,400} \\
1,296 \\
\overline{1,040} \\
972 \\
\overline{68}
\end{array}
$$

15.3086 rounds to the nearest thousandth to 15.309

$2.48 \div 0.162 = 15.309$ to the nearest thousandth

D.
$$
\begin{array}{r}
\$160.571 \\
0.07\overline{)\$11.24\ 000} \\
7 \\
\overline{42} \\
42 \\
\overline{04} \\
0 \\
\overline{40} \\
35 \\
\overline{50} \\
49 \\
\overline{10} \\
7 \\
\overline{3}
\end{array}
$$

$160.571 rounds to the nearest cent (hundredth) to $160.57

$11.24 \div 0.07 = \$160.57$ rounded to the nearest cent

PRACTICE PROBLEMS

1. Add these decimals.

   A. $0.08 + 1.5$ B. $0.9 + 0.62$

   C. $0.0038 + 6.241$ D. $0.95 + 0.3 + 26.1$

   E. $1.6 + 0.28 + 1.31$

   F. $0.021 + 0.0042 + 0.163$

2. Subtract these decimals.

   A. $0.58 - 0.06$ B. $9 - 0.34$

   C. $0.967 - 0.18$ D. $0.835 - 0.124$

   E. $3.621 - 1.03$ F. $5.724 - 5.713$

3. Multiply these decimals.

   A. 0.24×1.4 B. 3.2×0.102

   C. 7×0.21 D. 0.02×0.002

   E. 1.12×2.5 F. 0.051×0.21

4. Divide these decimals.

   A. $0.68 \div 0.004$ B. $0.82563 \div 0.87$

   C. $0.4725 \div 0.75$ D. $39 \div 0.52$

   E. $1.2 \div 1.92$ F. $45.5 \div 0.65$

5. Multiply or divide these decimals and round as indicated.

   A. $8 \times \$0.048$ and round to the nearest cent.

   B. $0.03 \times \$46.92$ and round to the nearest cent.

   C. 3.4×2.41 and round to the nearest tenth.

   D. 5.14×0.02 and round to the nearest tenth.

   E. $8.25 \div 1.24$ and round to the nearest tenth.

   F. $0.844 \div 24$ and round to the nearest thousandth.

SOLUTIONS

1. A.   0.08
      + 1.5
      ———
        1.58

   B.   0.9
      + 0.62
      ———
        1.52

   C.   0.0038
      + 6.241
      ————
        6.2448

   D.   0.95
         0.3
      + 26.1
      ———
        27.35

   E.   1.6
         0.28
      + 1.31
      ———
        3.19

   F.   0.021
         0.0042
      + 0.163
      ————
        0.1882

2. A.   0.58
      − 0.06
      ———
        0.52

   B.   9.00
      − 0.34
      ———
        8.66

   C.   0.967
      − 0.18
      ————
        0.787

   D.   0.835
      − 0.124
      ————
        0.711

   E.   3.621
      − 1.030
      ————
        2.591

   F.   5.724
      − 5.713
      ————
        0.011

3. A.   0.24   2 decimal places
      × 1.4   1 decimal place
      ———
         96
         24
      ————
        0.336   3 decimal places

   B.   3.2   1 decimal place
      × 0.102   3 decimal places
      ————
         64
        320
      ————
        0.3264   4 decimal places

   C.   7   0 decimal places
      × 0.21   2 decimal places
      ———
          7
         14
      ———
        1.47   2 decimal places

   D.   0.02   2 decimal places
      × 0.002   3 decimal places
      ————
        0.00004   5 decimal places

   E.   1.12   2 decimal places
      × 2.5   1 decimal place
      ———
        560
        224
      ————
        2.800   3 decimal places

   The answer is usually written as 2.8.

   F.   0.051   3 decimal places
      × 0.21   2 decimal places
      ———
         51
        102
      ————
        0.01071   5 decimal places

4. A.   170
        0.004)0.680
               4
              ——
              28
              28
              ——
               0
               0
              ——
               0

   B.   0.949
        0.87)0.82563
             783
             ———
             426
             348
             ———
             783
             783
             ———
               0

   C.   0.63
        0.75)0.4725
             450
             ———
             225
             225
             ———
               0

   D.   75.
        0.52)39.00
             364
             ———
             260
             260
             ———
               0

E.
$$
\begin{array}{r}
0.625 \\
1.92\overline{)1.20000} \\
1152 \\
\hline
480 \\
384 \\
\hline
960 \\
960 \\
\hline
\end{array}
$$

F.
$$
\begin{array}{r}
70. \\
0.65\overline{)45.50} \\
455 \\
\hline
0 \\
0 \\
\hline
0
\end{array}
$$

5. A.
$$
\begin{array}{rl}
8 & \text{0 decimal places} \\
\times\ \$0.048 & \text{3 decimal places} \\
\hline
64 & \\
32\ \ & \\
\hline
\$0.384 & \text{3 decimal places}
\end{array}
$$

$8 \times \$0.048 = \$0.38$ rounded to the nearest cent

B.
$$
\begin{array}{rl}
\$46.92 & \text{2 decimal places} \\
\times\ \ 0.03 & \text{2 decimal places} \\
\hline
\$1.4076 & \text{4 decimal places}
\end{array}
$$

$\$46.92 \times 0.03 = \$1.41$ rounded to the nearest cent

C.
$$
\begin{array}{rl}
3.4 & \text{1 decimal place} \\
\times\ 2.41 & \text{2 decimal places} \\
\hline
34 & \\
136\ \ & \\
68\ \ \ & \\
\hline
8.194 & \text{3 decimal places}
\end{array}
$$

$3.4 \times 2.41 = 8.2$ rounded to the nearest tenth

D.
$$
\begin{array}{rl}
5.14 & \text{2 decimal places} \\
\times\ 0.02 & \text{2 decimal places} \\
\hline
0.1028 & \text{4 decimal places}
\end{array}
$$

$5.14 \times 0.02 = 0.1$ rounded to the nearest tenth

E.
$$
\begin{array}{r}
6.65 \\
1.24\overline{)8.25\ 00} \\
744 \\
\hline
810 \\
744 \\
\hline
660 \\
620 \\
\hline
40
\end{array}
$$

$8.25 \div 1.24 = 6.7$ rounded to the nearest tenth

F.
$$
\begin{array}{r}
0.0351 \\
24\overline{)0.8440} \\
72 \\
\hline
124 \\
120 \\
\hline
40 \\
24 \\
\hline
16
\end{array}
$$

$0.844 \div 24 = 0.035$ rounded to the nearest thousandth

WORD PROBLEMS

When you are solving a word problem, the following procedure is quite helpful:

1. **Read** the problem to determine the information that is given and what is to be found.
2. **Plan** how you will solve the problem. This may require the use of a formula or an equation.
3. **Solve** the problem by using the plan created.
4. **Answer** the question asked. Check your answer with all the facts given in the problem.

Word problems often use keywords that indicate the operation to be used in the problem. These common keywords are useful guides, and it pays to watch out for them as you read each problem.

Operation	Keywords
Addition	Sum, total, all together, and, added to, combined, exceeds, increased by, more than, greater than, plus
Subtraction	Minus, difference, decreased by, less, diminished by, reduced by, subtracted from, deducted
Multiplication	Times, twice, doubled, tripled, product, multiplied by, halved
Division	Quotient, divided by, divide

PRACTICE PROBLEMS

1. In a class, 6 students received A's, 12 received B's, 10 C's, 8 D's, and 4 F's. What part of the class received A's?

2. In 36 times at bat, Jones got 8 singles, 3 doubles, 1 triple, and 3 home runs. What part of the time did Jones get a hit?

3. The slope of a roof is the ratio of the rise of the roof to the run of the roof. What is the slope of a roof that rises 6 feet in a run of 24 feet?

4. If four-ninths of a class of 36 students is girls, how many girls are there in the class?

5. If a hydrochloric acid solution has two-thirds water, how much water is used to make 24 ounces of this solution?

6. A book that regularly sold for $19.49 is sold after giving it a $2.98 price reduction. How much did the book sell for?

7. A sales clerk received $218.40 regular pay, $28.50 overtime pay, $36.14 in commissions, and a $25 bonus on a payday. How much money did the clerk receive on that payday?

8. A finance company made a loan of $100 for six monthly payments of $21.55. How much money was repaid to the loan company?

9. Jane drove 331 miles in 6 hours. To the nearest tenth of a mile, what was the average number of miles Jane drove per hour?

10. Harry bought a suit for $194.95 and a shirt for $18.45. How much more than the shirt did the suit cost?

SOLUTIONS

1. **Read:** You know how many students received each grade, so you can add them to find how many students are in the class. $6 + 12 + 10 + 8 + 4 = 40$ students in the class.
Plan: Write the fraction for the number of students receiving A's, 6, divided by the number of students in the class, 40. 6/40
Solve: Simplify the fraction. $6/40 = 3/20$
Answer: Did you find the fraction of students getting A's as a part of the class? Yes, the 6 for the students getting A's is compared to the 40 for the students in the class.

2. 8 singles, 3 doubles, 1 triple, 3 home runs. So $8 + 3 + 1 + 3 = 15$ hits.

 The part of the time Jones got a hit is $\frac{15}{36} = \frac{5}{12}$.

3. $\text{Slope} = \dfrac{\text{rise}}{\text{run}} = \dfrac{6 \text{ ft}}{24 \text{ ft}} = \dfrac{1}{4}$

4. $\dfrac{4}{9}$ girls out of 36 students. $\dfrac{4}{9} \times \dfrac{36}{1} = \dfrac{4 \times 36}{9 \times 1} = \dfrac{4 \times 4}{1} = 16$ girls

5. $\dfrac{2}{3}$ water out of 24 ounces. $\dfrac{2}{3} \times \dfrac{24}{1} = \dfrac{2 \times 24}{3 \times 1} = \dfrac{2 \times 8}{1} = 16$ ounces

6.
$19.49	regular price
− $2.98	price reduction
16.51	selling price

7.
$218.40	regular pay
28.50	overtime pay
36.14	commissions
+ 25	bonus
$308.04	total received

8. $21.55   each payment
   ×   6   payments made
  $129.30   total repaid

10. $194.95 suit
  − 18.45 shirt
  $176.50 difference

9. 331 miles driven in 6 hours

$$6\overline{)331.00} = 55.16$$

$$\begin{array}{r} 30 \\ \hline 31 \\ 30 \\ \hline 10 \\ 6 \\ \hline 40 \\ 36 \\ \hline 4 \end{array}$$

55.16 is 55.2 rounded to the nearest tenth.
Jane averaged 55.2 miles per hour.

RATIO AND PROPORTIONS

A **ratio** is a quotient of two quantities. The ratio of a to b is written as a to b, $\frac{a}{b}$, or $a : b$. When ratios are used to compare numbers that have units of measure, the units need to be the same for both numbers. You can find the ratio of one part to another, such as the ratio of boys to girls in a class, or of the parts to the whole, such as ratio of boys or girls to the whole class.

If there are 12 boys and 18 girls in a class, then there are $12 + 18 = 30$ students in the class. The ratio of boys to girls is $12 : 18$, which simplifies to $2 : 3$. The ratio of girls to the class is $18 : 30$, or $3 : 5$.

If the ratio of yes votes to no votes is $175 : 350$, then the ratio of yes votes to total votes is $175 : (175 + 350) = 175 : 525 = 1 : 3$, and the ratio of no votes to total votes is $350 : (175 + 350) = 350 : 525 = 2 : 3$.

When the ratio is known, you do not necessarily need to know the actual amounts of the quantities compared. The ratio 2 to $3 = 2 : 3 = \frac{2}{3} = \frac{4}{6} = \frac{6}{9} = \frac{2n}{3n} = 2n : 3n$, for all counting numbers n.

Example 31

State the ratios requested.

A. The ratio of a nickel to a quarter
B. The ratio of 3 hours to a day
C. The ratio of boys to students in a class of 40 students with 22 girls
D. The ratio of the short part to the long part of a 10-foot board when the shorter of the two parts is 4 feet

Solution

A. Nickel = 5 cents   quarter = 25 cents

$$\frac{\text{nickel}}{\text{quarter}} = \frac{5}{25} = \frac{1}{5}$$

B. 3 hours   1 day = 24 hours

$$\frac{3 \text{ hours}}{1 \text{ day}} = \frac{3}{24} = \frac{1}{8}$$

C. Girls = 22   class = 40   boys = 40 − 22 = 18

$$\frac{boys}{class} = \frac{18}{40} = \frac{9}{20}$$

D. Shorter part = 4 ft   total = 10 ft   longer part = 10 ft − 4 ft = 6 ft

$$\frac{shorter\ part}{longer\ part} = \frac{4}{6} = \frac{2}{3}$$

An extended ratio can have more than two parts, such as $a : b : c$ or $a : b : c : d$. If a board is 12 feet long and cut into three parts that have a ratio 1 : 2 : 3, the lengths are $1n : 2n : 3n$. Since the total length is 12 feet, the lengths are 2 feet, 4 feet, and 6 feet because 2 ft + 4 ft + 6 ft = 12 ft. You can work this out from the ratio $1n : 2n : 3n$ by using the equation $1n + 2n + 3n = 12$. Thus, $6n = 12$ and $n = 2$. So the parts are $1n = 1(2) = 2$ ft, $2n = 2(2) = 4$ ft, and $3n = 3(2) = 6$ ft.

Example 32

Find the parts for each ratio.

A. A length of cloth is 40 feet long. It is cut into lengths that have the ratio 2 : 3 : 5. What are the lengths of the parts?
B. A banner is 18 feet long and is cut into three parts with the ratio 1 : 3 : 5. What are the lengths of the parts?
C. A board is 48 inches long and is cut into four parts with the ratio 1 : 1 : 3 : 5. Find the lengths of the parts.

Solution

A. 2 : 3 : 5 ratio and the total length is 40 feet
    $2n + 3n + 5n = 40;$ $10n = 40;$ $n = 4$
    $2n = 2(4) = 8$ feet; $3n = 3(4) = 12$ feet; $5n = 5(4) = 20$ feet
    The parts are 8, 12, and 20 feet.
B. 1 : 3 : 5 ratio and the total length is 18 feet
    $1n + 3n + 5n = 18;$ $9n = 18;$ $n = 2$
    $1n = 1(2) = 2$ feet; $3n = 3(2) = 6$ feet; $5n = 5(2) = 10$ feet
    The parts are 2, 6, and 10 feet.
C. 1 : 1 : 3 : 5 ratio and the total length is 48 inches
    $n + n + 3n + 5n = 48;$ $10n = 48;$ $n = 4.8$
    $n = 4.8$ inches; $n = 4.8$ inches; $3n = 3(4.8) = 14.4$ inches; $5n = 5(4.8) = 24$ inches
    The parts are 4.8, 4.8, 14.4, and 24 inches.

A **proportion** is a statement that two ratios are equal. A proportion can be stated as "a is to b as c is to d" and written as $a : b :: c : d$ or $\frac{a}{b} = \frac{c}{d}$. In the proportion, a and d are called the **extremes** and b and c are the **means**. When you want to solve a proportion, you cross-multiply to get the product of the means equal to the product of the extremes.

Example 33

Write each as a proportion.

A. 26 is to 13 is the same as 6 is to 3.
B. 4 is to 12 as 5 is to 15.
C. 45 is to 80 is the same as 18 is to 32.
D. 150 is to 100 as 54 is to 36.

Solution

A. $\dfrac{26}{13} = \dfrac{6}{3}$

B. $\dfrac{4}{12} = \dfrac{5}{15}$

C. $\dfrac{45}{80} = \dfrac{18}{32}$

D. $\dfrac{150}{100} = \dfrac{54}{36}$

Example 34

Solve these proportion problems.

A. If three eggs cost 16 cents, how many eggs can you buy for 80 cents?
B. A recipe calls for 2 cups of flour to 3 tablespoons of shortening. How many cups of flour are needed when you use 15 tablespoons of shortening?
C. If four stamps cost 90 cents, how much would 24 stamps cost?

Solution

A. Let n be the number of eggs you can buy for 80 cents. Then 3 is to 16 as n is to 80.

$$\frac{3}{16} = \frac{n}{80}$$

Cross-multiply $\quad 16(n) = 3(80)$

$$16n = 240$$

$$n = 240 \div 16$$

$$n = 15$$

Fifteen eggs can be bought for 80 cents.

B. Let n be the number of cups of flour needed. Then 2 is to 3 as n is to 15.

$$\frac{2}{3} = \frac{n}{15}$$

Cross-multiply $\quad 3n = 30$

$$n = 10$$

Ten cups of flour are needed when 15 tablespoons of shortening are used.

C. Let n be the number of cents in the cost of 24 stamps. Then 4 is to 90 as 24 is to n.

$$\frac{4}{90} = \frac{24}{n}$$

Cross-multiply $\quad 4n = 90(24)$

$$4n = 2{,}160$$

$$n = 2{,}160 \div 4$$

$$n = 540$$

Twenty-four stamps would cost 540 cents, or \$5.40.

Two quantities are directly proportional when a constant k times one of them gives the other. The distance d that a car travels is directly proportional to the time t that it travels, so $d = kt$. The amount of sales tax t that you pay is proportional to the cost c of the items purchased, so $t = kc$.

Example 35

Write the proportion for each problem.

A. The number of commercials c in a television program is directly proportional to the length of the program m in minutes.
B. The number of miles m that you run in a given time is directly proportional to your rate r of speed.
C. The number of books b that you read in a given time is directly proportional to the number of hours h that you spend reading.

Solution

A. $c = km$
B. $m = kr$
C. $b = kh$

When the product of two quantities is a constant, the quantities are said to be inversely proportional. The number of tickets to a play t that you get for \$100 is inversely proportional to the cost c of a ticket to the play. So $tc = \$100$. The number of workers w needed to finish a job in 6 days is inversely proportional to the rate r of work done per day by a worker. So $wr = 6$.

Example 36

Write the proportion for each problem.

A. The number n of cookies in a box with volume 100 in^3 is inversely proportional to the size s of the cookies.
B. The number n of mowers it takes to mow a field in 10 hours is inversely proportional to the area a that each mower cuts per hour.
C. The number of movie tickets t that you can get for \$50.00 is inversely proportional to the price p of a ticket.

Solution

A. $ns = 100$
B. $na = 10$
C. $tp = 50$

Properties of Proportions

For a proportion $\dfrac{a}{b} = \dfrac{c}{d}$:

1. $ad = bc$
2. $\dfrac{b}{a} = \dfrac{d}{c}$
3. $\dfrac{a}{c} = \dfrac{b}{d}$
4. $\dfrac{a+b}{b} = \dfrac{c+d}{d}$
5. $\dfrac{a-b}{b} = \dfrac{c-d}{d}$
6. $\dfrac{a+b}{a-b} = \dfrac{c+d}{c-d}$

Each of these properties is a transformation of the given proportion.

Even if you do not know the amount of each quantity, sometimes you can still find the ratio of the quantities. If you know that $\frac{1}{3}$ of the students like carrots and $\frac{1}{8}$ of the students like turnips, the ratio of students who like carrots C to students who like turnips T is $\frac{1}{3}$ to $\frac{1}{8}$.

$$\frac{C}{T} = \frac{1/3}{1/8} = \frac{1}{3} \div \frac{1}{8} = \frac{1}{3} \times \frac{8}{1} = \frac{8}{3}$$

Thus, there are 8 students who like carrots for every 3 who like turnips.

■■ PRACTICE PROBLEMS

1. Write the ratio requested.
   A. Ratio of 5 days to a week
   B. Ratio of girls to boys in a class of 35 students with 18 boys
   C. Ratio of a dime to a quarter
   D. Ratio of a foot to a yard

2. Find the values requested.
   A. If a foot-long hotdog was cut into two parts that have a ratio of 1 : 2, how long is each part?
   B. If a collection of 54 coins, only nickels and dimes, has a ratio of nickels to dimes of 4 : 5, how many of each coin are there?
   C. If a collection of 1,000 nickels, dimes, and quarters has a ratio of nickels to dimes to quarters of 5 : 3 : 2, how many of each coin are in the collection?

3. Write each as a proportion.
   A. 50 is to 12 as 150 is to 36.
   B. 14 to 12 is the same as 42 to 36.
   C. 45 is to 90 as 225 is to 450.

4. Solve these proportions.
   A. A recipe calls for 1 cup of flour to 2 cups of sugar. If the next batch uses 3 cups of flour, how much sugar is needed?
   B. A chili recipe calls for 4 cups of beans to 2 cups of tomatoes. If you use 5 cups of tomatoes, how many cups of beans are needed?
   C. If 5 stamps cost $1.95, how much would 20 stamps cost?
   D. If you get 3 oranges for 70 cents, how many oranges can you get for $3.50?

5. Write the proportion.
   A. The number of dollars d in your pay is directly proportional to the number of hours h that you work.
   B. The number of meals m that you eat on a trip is directly proportional to the number of days d in the trip.
   C. The number of pages p copied is directly proportional to the number of minutes m that the copier runs.
   D. The number of lunches l that you get for $50 is inversely proportional to the cost c of a meal.
   E. The number of candy bars c that you can get for $20 is inversely proportional to the price p of the candy bar.

6. Find the ratio of a to b.

   A. In a sentence, $\frac{2}{5}$ of the letters are a's and $\frac{1}{20}$ of the letters are b's.

   B. $\dfrac{a-b}{b} = \dfrac{17}{2}$

   C. $\dfrac{b}{a} = \dfrac{3}{10}$

   D. $\frac{3}{8}$ of a class are girls and $\frac{5}{8}$ of the class are boys and $\dfrac{a}{b} = \dfrac{\text{girls}}{\text{boys}}$

SOLUTIONS

1. A. 1 week = 7 days
   Ratio of 5 days to one week is 5 : 7.
   B. 35 students with 18 boys, so $35 - 18 = 17$ girls.
   Ratio of girls to boys is 17 : 18.
   C. Dime = 10 cents   quarter = 25 cents
   Ratio of dimes to quarters is 10 : 25 or 2 : 5.
   D. One foot = 1 ft   one yard = 3 ft
   Ratio of one foot to one yard is 1 : 3.

2. A. Ratio 1: 2 total length is 12 inches.
   $n + 2n = 12;$ $3n = 12;$ $n = 4$ inches
   The parts are 4 and 8 inches.
   B. Ratio 4 : 5 number of coins is 54.
   $4n + 5n = 54;$ $9n = 5;$ $n = 6$
   $4(6) = 24$ nickels; $5(6) = 30$ dimes
   C. 1,000 coins   ratio 5 : 3 : 2 for nickels to dimes to quarters
   $5n + 3n + 2n = 1,000;$
   $10n = 1,000;$ $n = 100$
   $5(100) = 500$ nickels; $3(100) = 300$ dimes; $2(100) = 200$ quarters

3. A. $50 : 12 : : 150 : 36$ or $\dfrac{50}{12} = \dfrac{150}{36}$
   B. $14 : 12 : : 42 : 36$ or $\dfrac{14}{12} = \dfrac{42}{36}$
   C. $45 : 90 : : 225 : 450$ or $\dfrac{45}{90} = \dfrac{225}{450}$

4. A. 1 cup flour to 2 cups sugar
   $\dfrac{1}{2} = \dfrac{3}{n}$
   $1 \times n = 2 \times 3$
   $n = 6$
   Six cups of sugar are needed.
   B. 4 cups of beans to 2 cups of tomatoes
   $\dfrac{4}{2} = \dfrac{n}{5}$
   $2n = 20$
   $n = 10$
   Ten cups of beans are needed.
   C. 5 stamps for $1.95
   $\dfrac{5}{1.95} = \dfrac{20}{n}$
   $5n = 39.00$
   $n = 7.80$
   Twenty stamps would cost $7.80.

D. 3 oranges for 70¢, $3.50 = 350¢
   $\dfrac{3}{70} = \dfrac{n}{350}$
   $70n = 1,050$
   $n = 15$
   Fifteen oranges can be bought for $3.50.

5. A. $d = kh$
   B. $m = kd$
   C. $p = km$
   D. $lc = 50$
   E. $cp = 20$

6. A. $\dfrac{a}{b} = \dfrac{2}{5} \div \dfrac{1}{20}$
   $\dfrac{a}{b} = \dfrac{2}{5} \times \dfrac{20}{1}$
   $\dfrac{a}{b} = \dfrac{40}{5}$
   $\dfrac{a}{b} = \dfrac{8}{1}$
   B. $\dfrac{a-b}{b} = \dfrac{17}{2}$
   Use proportion property (4).
   $\dfrac{a-b+b}{b} = \dfrac{17+2}{2}$
   $\dfrac{a}{b} = \dfrac{19}{2}$
   C. $\dfrac{b}{a} = \dfrac{3}{10}$
   Use proportion property (2).
   $\dfrac{a}{b} = \dfrac{10}{3}$
   D. $\dfrac{a}{b} = \dfrac{girls}{boys}$
   $\dfrac{a}{b} = \dfrac{3}{8} \div \dfrac{5}{8}$
   $\dfrac{a}{b} = \dfrac{3}{8} \times \dfrac{8}{5}$
   $\dfrac{a}{b} = \dfrac{3}{5}$

■ **MOTION AND WORK PROBLEMS**

The motion formula $d = rt$ states that the distance traveled is equal to the rate of travel multiplied by time traveled. The rate is distance per unit of time and the unit of time used to express the rate must match the unit used to express the time traveled.

$$\text{Distance: } d = rt \qquad \text{rate: } r = \frac{d}{t} \qquad \text{time: } t = \frac{d}{r}$$

If a bicycle travels at 8 miles per hour for 3 hours, then the bicycle has traveled d = 8 miles/hour times 3 hours = 24 miles.

However, if a car traveled 50 miles per hour for 30 minutes, it did NOT travel 50 × 30 miles since 50 is in miles per hour and the time is in minutes. The correct result is found by changing 30 minutes to 0.5 hour. $d = 50$ miles/hour × 0.5 hour = 25 miles.

Example 37

Solve each of these motion problems.

A. A driver drove for 10 hours at the average rate of 53 miles per hour (mph) to get from Memphis to Chicago. How far was it from Memphis to Chicago?
B. A plane traveled the 328 miles from Limestone to Lincoln in 2 hours. What was the plane's average rate of speed?
C. A boat traveled 120 miles from Wabash to Wilson at the average rate of 60 miles per hour. How long did the boat trip take?

Solution

A. $d = rt$
   $d = 53(10)$
   $d = 530$ miles
   It was 530 miles from Memphis to Chicago.
B. $r = \dfrac{d}{t}$
   $r = 328 \div 2$
   $r = 164$ mph
   The average rate of the plane was 164 mph.
C. $t = \dfrac{d}{r}$
   $t = 120 \div 60$
   $t = 2$ hours
   The boat trip took 2 hours.

On the GMAT, you need to be able to convert one unit of measure to another. The units will be in the same measurement system only. Also, only common conversions will be used.

Time	U.S. Customary System or English Units	Metric Units
60 minutes = 1 hour	12 inches = 1 foot	10 millimeters = 1 centimeter
60 seconds = 1 minute	3 feet = 1 yard	100 centimeters = 1 meter
24 hours = 1 day	5,280 feet = 1 mile	1,000 meters = 1 kilometer
7 days = 1 week	1,760 yards = 1 mile	1,000 milligrams = 1 gram
52 weeks = 1 year		1,000 grams = 1 kilogram
12 months = 1 year	16 ounces = 1 pound	1,000 milliliters = 1 liter

Work problems involve individuals or machines working together to accomplish a task when you know how long it takes each to do the work individually. If a person can do a job in 5 hours, then that person can do $\frac{1}{5}$ of the work in 1 hour. Thus, the person can do $\frac{2}{5}$ of the job in 2 hours, $\frac{3}{5}$ in 3 hours, and $\frac{4}{5}$ in 4 hours. There is an assumption that a person always works at a constant rate.

The principle behind work problems is that the time worked t times the rate of work r gives the amount of work w done: $w = tr$. For each person working, calculate the part of the work done and add all the parts together, to get one unit of work completed.

Example 38

Solve these work problems.

A. Sue can paint a room in 4 hours, and Sam can paint the same room in 5 hours. How long would it take them to paint the room together?
B. Abe and Ben, working together, can build a cabinet in 6 days. Abe works twice as fast as Ben. How long would it take each of them to build an identical cabinet on his own?
C. A holding tank can be filled by three pipes (A, B, and C) in 1 hour, 1.5 hours, and 3 hours, respectively. In how many minutes can the tank be filled by the three pipes together?
D. A copy machine makes 40 copies per minute. A second copy machine can make 30 copies per minute. If the two machines work together, how long would it take them to produce 1,400 copies?

Solution

A. Sue paints the room in 4 hours, so she does $\frac{1}{4}$ of the room per hour.

Sam paints the room in 5 hours, so she does $\frac{1}{5}$ of the room per hour.

They work together for t hours.
$$\frac{t}{4} + \frac{t}{5} = 1$$
$$5t + 4t = 20$$
$$9t = 20$$
$$t = 2\frac{2}{9} \text{ hours}$$

It takes Sue and Sam $2\frac{2}{9}$ hours to paint the room together.

B. $t =$ time for Abe and $2t =$ time for Ben.
$$\frac{6}{t} + \frac{6}{2t} = 1$$
$$12 + 6 = 2t$$
$$18 = 2t$$
$$9 = t$$

It would take Abe 9 hours working alone, and it would take Ben 18 hours working alone.

C. t = the time, in minutes, it would take the pipes together to fill the tank.

$$\frac{t}{60} + \frac{t}{90} + \frac{t}{180} = 1$$

$$3t + 2t + t = 180$$

$$6t = 180$$

$$t = 30$$

It takes the three pipes 30 minutes to fill the tank together.

D. t = the number of minutes together

$$40t + 30t = 1,400$$

$$70t = 1,400$$

$$t = 20$$

It takes the two copiers 20 minutes to produce 1,400 copies.

When it takes person A x hours to do a task alone and it takes person B y hours to do the same task alone, then the time it will take them together will be more than one-half of the faster time but less than one-half of the slower time. When you have a multiple-choice question that has two people or machines working together, use the fact that one-half of the faster time < together time < one-half of the slower time to eliminate some of the given answer choices. This is a quick check on the answers to parts A, B, and D in the example above.

▨ PRACTICE PROBLEMS

1. A train left Los Angeles at 8 a.m. headed toward San Francisco. At the same time, another train left San Francisco headed toward Los Angeles. The first train travels at 60 mph and the second train travels at 50 mph. If the distance between Los Angeles and San Francisco is 440 miles, how long will it take the trains to meet?

2. Two planes leave Chicago at the same time, one headed for New York and the other headed in the opposite direction for Denver. The plane headed for New York traveled at 600 mph, while the plane headed for Denver traveled at 150 mph. How long did each plane fly before they were 900 miles apart?

3. Two cars leave Sioux Falls headed toward Fargo. The first car left at 7 a.m., traveling at 60 mph. The second car left at 8 a.m., traveling at 70 mph. How long would it take the second car to overtake the first car?

4. Carlos can run a mile in 6 minutes, and Kevin can run a mile in 8 minutes. If Carlos gives Kevin a 1-minute head start, how far will Kevin run before Carlos passes him?

5. Bev can dig a ditch in 4 hours, and Jan can dig a ditch in 3 hours. If Bev and Jan dig a ditch together, how long would it take?

6. David can type a paper in 5 hours, but when he works with Jim, it takes only 2 hours. How long would it take Jim to type the paper alone?

7. Kim can paint a barn in 5 days, and Alyssa can paint it in 8 days. Kim and Alyssa start painting a barn together, but after 2 days Alyssa gets sick and Kim finishes the work alone. How long did it take Kim to finish painting the barn?

8. Jay can prune an orchard in 50 hours, and Ray can prune the orchard in 40 hours. How long will it take them, working together, to prune the orchard?

SOLUTIONS

1. Los Angeles train: 60 mph, t hours, traveled 60 t miles
San Francisco train: 50 mph, t hours, traveled 50 t miles
Total miles traveled: 440 miles

$$60t + 50t = 440$$
$$110t = 440$$
$$t = 4 \text{ hours}$$

2. New York plane: 600 mph, t hours, traveled 600 t miles
Denver plane: 150 mph, t hours, traveled 150 miles
Total miles traveled: 900 miles

$$600t + 150t = 900$$
$$750t = 900$$
$$t = 1.2 \text{ hours}$$

3. First car: 60 mph, t hours, traveled 60 t miles
Second car: 70 mph, $(t - 1)$ hours, traveled $70(t - 1)$ miles
Second car overtook first car so distances are equal.

$$70(t - 1) = 60t$$
$$70t - 70 = 60t$$
$$10t = 70$$
$$t = 7$$
$$t - 1 = 6 \text{ hours for second car to overtake first car}$$

4. Carlos: 1 mile in 6 minutes, t minutes, $\dfrac{t}{6}$ miles run
Kevin: 1 mile in 8 minutes, $(t + 1)$ minutes, $\dfrac{t+1}{8}$ miles run
Carlos overtakes Kevin, so their distances are equal.

$$\frac{t}{6} = \frac{t+1}{8}$$
$$8(t) = 6(t + 1)$$
$$8t = 6t + 6$$
$$2t = 6$$
$$t = 3 \text{ minutes for Carlos to overtake Kevin}$$

5. Bev: 4 hours, $\dfrac{1}{4}$ of ditch per hour
Jan: 3 hours, $\dfrac{1}{3}$ of ditch per hour
t = hours worked together

$$\frac{t}{4} + \frac{t}{3} = 1$$
$$3t + 4t = 12$$
$$7t = 12$$
$$t = 1\frac{5}{7} \text{ hours together}$$

6. David: 5 hours, $\dfrac{1}{5}$ of paper per hour
Jim: t hours, $\dfrac{1}{t}$ of paper per hour
Together: 2 hours

$$\frac{2}{5} + \frac{2}{t} = 1$$
$$2t + 10 = 5t$$
$$-3t = -10$$
$$t = 3\frac{1}{3} \text{ hours or 3 hours 20 minutes}$$

7. Kim: 5 days, $\dfrac{1}{5}$ of barn per day
Alyssa: 8 days, $\dfrac{1}{8}$ of barn per day
2 days together, x more days for Kim alone

$$\frac{2}{8} + \frac{2+x}{5} = 1$$
$$10 + 16 + 8x = 40$$
$$8x = 14$$
$$x = 1.75 \text{ days}$$

8. Jay: 50 hours, $\dfrac{1}{50}$ of orchard per hour
Ray: 40 hours, $\dfrac{1}{40}$ of orchard per hour
t = time working together

$$\frac{t}{50} + \frac{t}{40} = 1$$
$$4t + 5t = 200$$
$$9t = 200$$
$$t = 22\frac{2}{9} \text{ hours}$$

PERCENTAGES

A **percent** means parts per hundred. The symbol for percent is %. Use percentages to indicate such things as tax rates, discount rates, and interest rates.

To convert from a percent to a decimal, drop the percent sign and move the decimal point two places to the left. When necessary, add zeros on the left of the percent to allow for the correct location of the decimal point.

To convert from a decimal to a percent, move the decimal point to the right, then add the percent. When necessary, add zeros on the right of the decimal to allow for the correct location of the decimal point.

When a percent is to be converted to a fraction, first convert the percent to a decimal, then convert the decimal to a fraction. Similarly, to convert a fraction to a percent, first change the fraction to a decimal, and then change the decimal to a percent.

Example 39

Convert these percentages to decimals.

A. 75%   B. 40.5%   C. 125%   D. 3%
E. 17%   F. 100%   G. 7%   H. 1.25%

Solution

A. $75\% = 0.75$
B. $40.5\% = 0.405$
C. $125\% = 1.25$
D. $3\% = 0.03$
E. $17\% = 0.17$
F. $100\% = 1.00$
G. $7\% = 0.07$
H. $1.25\% = 0.0125$

Example 40

Convert these decimals to percentages.

A. 0.28   B. 0.4   C. 1.2   D. 0.354
E. 0.8   F. 1.32   G. 0.147   H. 0.85

Solution

A. $0.28 = 28\%$
B. $0.4 = 40\%$
C. $1.2 = 120\%$
D. $0.354 = 35.4\%$
E. $0.8 = 80\%$
F. $1.32 = 132\%$
G. $0.147 = 14.7\%$
H. $0.85 = 85\%$

Example 41

Convert these fractions to percentages.

A. $\dfrac{1}{4}$ B. $\dfrac{4}{5}$ C. $\dfrac{2}{3}$ D. $\dfrac{7}{20}$ E. $\dfrac{1}{8}$

Solution

A. $\frac{1}{4} = 0.25 = 25\%$

B. $\frac{4}{5} = 0.8 = 80\%$

C. $\frac{2}{3} = 0.666\cdots = 66.7\%$

D. $\frac{7}{20} = 0.35 = 35\%$

E. $\frac{1}{8} = 0.125 = 12.5\%$

Example 42

Convert these percentages to fractions.

A. 95%   B. 75%   C. 33.3%   D. 16%   E. 50%

Solution

A. $95\% = 0.95 = \frac{95}{100} = \frac{19}{20}$

B. $75\% = 0.75 = \frac{75}{100} = \frac{3}{4}$

C. $33.3\% = 0.333 = \frac{333}{1,000} \left(\text{about } \frac{1}{3}\right)$

D. $16\% = 0.16 = \frac{16}{100} = \frac{4}{25}$

E. $50\% = 0.50 = \frac{50}{100} = \frac{1}{2}$

■ PRACTICE PROBLEMS

1. Change each decimal to a percent.

   A. 0.01 B. 0.28 C. 0.6 D. 1.39 E. 1.2

   F. 0.125 G. 0.08 H. 0.73 I. 1.18 J. 0.8333···

2. Change each fraction to a percent.

   A. $\frac{1}{6}$ B. $\frac{7}{100}$ C. $\frac{27}{50}$ D. $\frac{11}{25}$ E. $\frac{67}{100}$

   F. $\frac{7}{10}$ G. $\frac{3}{5}$ H. $\frac{31}{50}$ I. $\frac{7}{8}$ J. $\frac{13}{10}$

3. Change each percent to a decimal.

   A. 6%   B. 16%   C. 27% D. 40% E. 134%

   F. 4.5% G. 46.4% H. 4%   I. 10% J. 99%

4. Change each percent to a fraction.

   A. 9%   B. 38%   C. 81% D. 148% E. 70%

   F. 6.5% G. 12.5% H. 42% I. 16%   J. 75%

■ SOLUTIONS

1. A. $0.01 = 1\%$
    B. $0.28 = 28\%$
    C. $0.6 = 60\%$
    D. $1.39 = 139\%$
    E. $1.2 = 120\%$
    F. $0.125 = 12.5\%$
    G. $0.08 = 8\%$
    H. $0.73 = 73\%$
    I. $1.18 = 118\%$
    J. $0.8333\cdots = 83.3\%$

2. A. $\dfrac{1}{6} = 0.1666\cdots = 16.7\%$

    B. $\dfrac{7}{100} = 0.07 = 7\%$

    C. $\dfrac{27}{50} = 0.54 = 54\%$

    D. $\dfrac{11}{25} = 0.44 = 44\%$

    E. $\dfrac{67}{100} = 0.67 = 67\%$

    F. $\dfrac{7}{10} = 0.7 = 70\%$

    G. $\dfrac{3}{5} = 0.6 = 60\%$

    H. $\dfrac{31}{50} = 0.62 = 62\%$

    I. $\dfrac{7}{8} = 0.875 = 87.5\%$

    J. $\dfrac{13}{10} = 1.3 = 130\%$

3. A. $6\% = 0.06$
    B. $16\% = 0.16$
    C. $27\% = 0.27$
    D. $40\% = 0.40 = 0.4$
    E. $134\% = 1.34$
    F. $4.5\% = 0.045$
    G. $46.4\% = 0.464$
    H. $4\% = 0.04$
    I. $10\% = 0.10 = 0.1$
    J. $99\% = 0.99$

4. A. $9\% = 0.09 = \dfrac{9}{100}$

    B. $38\% = 0.38 = \dfrac{38}{100} = \dfrac{19}{50}$

    C. $81\% = 0.81 = \dfrac{81}{100}$

    D. $148\% = 1.48 = \dfrac{148}{100} = \dfrac{37}{25}$

    E. $70\% = 0.70 = \dfrac{70}{100} = \dfrac{7}{10}$

    F. $6.5\% = 0.065 = \dfrac{65}{1,000} = \dfrac{13}{200}$

    G. $12.5\% = 0.125 = \dfrac{125}{1,000} = \dfrac{1}{8}$

    H. $42\% = 0.42 = \dfrac{42}{100} = \dfrac{21}{50}$

    I. $16\% = 0.16 = \dfrac{16}{100} = \dfrac{4}{25}$

    J. $75\% = 0.75 = \dfrac{75}{100} = \dfrac{3}{4}$

■ PERCENTAGE WORD PROBLEMS

The basic types of percentage word problems relate these values: the number N, the part of the number W, and the percentage P. You usually change the percentage to a decimal.

Type 1: Find a percent of a number. $P \times N = W$
Type 2: Find what percent one number is of another number. $W \div N = P$
Type 3: Find a number when a percent of it is known. $W \div P = N$

Example 43

Solve these type 1 percentage problems.

A. 3 is what percent of 5?
B. 36 is what percent of 96?
C. What percent of 8 is 5?
D. What percent of 90 is 81?
E. What percent of 24 is 54?

Solution

A. $W \div N = P$ $W = 3$ $N = 5$
    $3 \div 5 = 0.6$ $P = 0.6 = 60\%$
B. $W \div N = P$ $W = 36$ $N = 96$
    $36 \div 96 = 0.375$ $P = 0.375 = 37.5\%$
C. $W \div N = P$ $W = 5$ $N = 8$
    $5 \div 8 = 0.625$ $P = 0.625 = 62.5\%$
D. $W \div N = P$ $W = 81$ $N = 90$
    $81 \div 90 = 0.9$ $P = 0.9 = 90\%$
E. $W \div N = P$ $W = 54$ $N = 24$
    $54 \div 24 = 2.25$ $P = 2.25 = 225\%$

Example 44

Solve these type 2 percentage problems.

A. What number is 24% of 52?
B. What number is 63% of 75?
C. What number is 4% of 462?
D. What number is 120% of 45?
E. What number is 2.5% of 840?

Solution

A. $P \times N = W$ $P = 24\% = 0.24$ $N = 52$
    $0.24 \times 52 = 12.48$ $W = 12.48$
B. $P \times N = W$ $P = 63\% = 0.63$ $N = 75$
    $0.63 \times 75 = 47.25$ $W = 47.25$
C. $P \times N = W$ $P = 4\% = 0.4$ $N = 462$
    $0.04 \times 462 = 18.48$ $W = 18.48$
D. $P \times N = W$ $P = 120\% = 1.2$ $N = 45$
    $1.2 \times 45 = 54.0$ $W = 54$
E. $P \times N = W$ $P = 2.5\% = 0.025$ $N = 840$
    $0.025 \times 840 = 21.000$ $W = 21$

Example 45

Solve these type 3 percentage problems.

A. 45% of what number is 90?
B. 31% of what number is 279?
C. 18 is 60% of what number?
D. 175% of what number is 42?
E. 78 is 156% of what number?

Solution

A. $W \div P = N$ $W = 90$ $P = 45\% = 0.45$
$90 \div 0.45 = 200$ $N = 200$
B. $W \div P = N$ $W = 279$ $P = 31\% = 0.31$
$279 \div 0.31 = 900$ $N = 900$
C. $W \div P = N$ $W = 18$ $P = 60\% = 0.6$
$18 \div 0.6 = 30$ $N = 30$
D. $W \div P = N$ $W = 42$ $P = 175\% = 1.75$
$42 \div 1.75 = 24$ $N = 24$
E. $W \div P = N$ $W = 78$ $P = 156\% = 1.56$
$78 \div 1.56 = 50$ $N = 50$

Many consumer purchases involve an add-on that is a percentage of the price of the purchase. An item that costs $100 when there is a 7% sales tax costs $100 + 0.07($100) = $107. For these types of problems, use this relationship: Price + Add-on = Total Cost. An add-on can be sales tax, a tip, a commission paid, shipping cost, or luxury tax.

Example 46

Solve these percent problems.

A. A store owner paid $60 for a hat and plans to mark up the price by 12%. What will be the selling price for the hat?
B. Jane earns $10.50 per hour. Her boss gave her a 5% raise. What is Jane's new hourly rate of pay?
C. Ralph bought a coat for $39.95 and paid a sales tax of 6% of his purchase. What was the total price of the coat?

Solution

A. $\$60 + 0.12(\$60) = S$
$\$60 + \$7.20 = S$
$\$67.20 = S$
The selling price of the hat will be $67.20.

B. $\$10.50 + 0.05(\$10.50) = S$
$\$10.50 + \$0.525 = S$
$\$11.025 = S$
$\$11.03 = S$ rounded to nearest cent
Jane's new hourly wage is $11.03.

C. $\$39.95 + 0.06(\$39.95) = C$
$\$39.95 + \$2.397 = C$
$\$42.347 = C$
$\$42.35 = C$ rounded to nearest cent
The total cost of the coat was $42.35.

Some problems involve a reduction based on the selling price of an item. These problems are often discount problems in which the selling price is based on the original price reduced by a percentage of itself.

Original Price − Discount = Selling Price

Example 47

Solve these percent problems.

A. A car has a sticker price of $26,410. The customer bargained for 5.5% off. How much did the car sell for?
B. A lamp was usually sold for $60. It was discounted 20%. What was the sale price of the lamp?
C. A table was sold at a 40% discount sale for $150. What was the original price of the table?

Solution

A. Original price − discount = sale price
$$\$26{,}410 - 0.055(\$26{,}410) = S$$
$$\$26{,}410 - \$1{,}452.55 = S$$
$$\$24{,}957.45 = S$$
The selling price of the car was $24,957.45.
B. $\$60 - 0.2(\$60) = S$
$$\$60 - \$12 = S$$
$$\$48 = S$$
The sale price of the lamp was $48.
C. Original price = 100% of P Discount = 40% of P
Sale price = $1.00P - 0.40P$
$$0.6P = \$150$$
$$P = \$150 \div 0.6$$
$$P = \$250$$
The original price of the table was $250.

In some problems, more than one percentage is used. These can be multiple discounts, sales tax and a tip, or a markup and then a discount, among many other possibilities.

Example 48

Solve these percent problems.

A. A vase was purchased at a wholesale warehouse for $120. The vase was marked up 40% in a retail store. The store owner sold the vase at a 25% discount. What was the selling price of the vase?
B. In a restaurant, a meal costs $32.75. There is a 6% tax to be added before you get the bill. If you leave the wait staff a 20% tip, what is the total cost of the meal?
C. The workers at a company took a 15% cut in pay in 1999 and received a 15% pay raise in 2000. If a worker made $19.40 per hour before the 1999 pay cut, how much would this worker be earning after the 2000 pay raise?

Solution

A. Cost = $120
Retail price = $120 + 0.4(\$120) = \$120 + \$48 = \$168$
Sale price = $\$168 - 0.25(\$168) = \$168 - \$42 = \$126$
The selling price of the vase was $126.
B. Cost of meal = $32.75
Meal with tax = $\$32.75 + 0.06(\$32.75) = \$32.75 + \$1.965 = \$34.715 = \$34.72$
Meal with tax and tip: $= \$34.72 + 0.2(\$34.72) = \$34.72 + \$6.944 = \$41.664 = \$41.66$
The total cost of the meal is $41.66.

    C. Original pay rate = $19.40

Pay after 1999 cut = $19.40 − 0.15($19.40) = $19.40 − $2.91 = $16.49

Pay after 2000 raise = $16.49 + 0.15($16.49) = $16.49 + $2.4735 = $18.9635 = $18.96

The worker's pay after the raise in 2000 would be $18.96.

PRACTICE PROBLEMS

1. Solve these percentage problems.
   A. What number is 32% of 65?
   B. What percent of 90 is 27%?
   C. 16 is 40% of what number?
   D. What percent of 1,032 is 645?
   E. What number is 8% of 247?
   F. What number is 120% of 216?
   G. 245% of what number is 98?
   H. 0.4% of what number is 2?
   I. 28 is what percent of 25?
   J. 27 is what percent of 60?

2. A. What would Sharon's salary be after a 4.5% pay raise, if she makes $25,000 per year now?
   B. Jack weighed 65 kg in January and by July he had lost 13 kg. What percent of his body weight did he lose?
   C. In the freshman class at City College, 396 students are from Iowa. If 18% of the freshman class is from Iowa, how large is the freshman class at City College?
   D. A real estate agent receives a 6% commission on the sale price of the property. How much will the real estate agent earn on the sale of a lot for $38,000?
   E. Thrifty Mart marks up the price of greeting cards by 42%. If a card costs Thrifty Mart $2, what will the selling price of the card be?

3. A. Deuce Hardware plans a Fourth of July sale in which all garden tools will be marked down 22%. What will be the sale price of a wheelbarrow that regularly sells for $50?
   B. A paring knife has a wholesale price of $1.20. If it is marked up 30%, what will be the retail price for the knife?
   C. A suit sold for $150 at a 25% off sale. What was the original price of the suit?
   D. You select items with a total price of $38.90. If the sales tax is 5%, what is the total cost of these items?
   E. A table has a list price of $1,200. The store discounted the table by 30%, but it did not sell. At a clearance sale, the store took 20% off the discounted price. What is the price of the table at the clearance sale?
   F. You order a meal with a price of $35. There is a tax of 6% on the meal. If you leave a 20% tip (after tax), what is the total cost of the meal?
   G. Jerry Smith was hired at an annual salary of $26,500. He receives a raise of 11% in January, then another 6% raise in June. What is his salary after the raise in June?

SOLUTIONS

1. A. 32% of 65 = 0.32(65) = 20.8   W = 20.8
   B. 27 ÷ 90 = 0.3   0.3 = 30%   P = 30%
   C. 40% = 0.4   16 ÷ 0.4 = 40   N = 40
   D. 645 ÷ 1,032 = 0.625,   0.625 = 62.5%   P = 62.5%
   E. 0.08(247) = 19.76   W = 19.76
   F. 1.20(216) = 259.2   W = 259.2
   G. 98 ÷ 2.45 = 40   N = 40
   H. 2 ÷ 0.004 = 500   N = 500
   I. 28 ÷ 25 = 1.12   1.12 = 112%   P = 112%
   J. 27 ÷ 60 = 0.45   0.45 = 45%   P = 45%

2. A. $25,000 + 0.45($25,000) = S
       $25,000 + $1,125 = S
       $26,125 = S
   Sharon's salary after the raise would be $26,125.
   B. 13 ÷ 65 = 20%
   Jack lost 20% of his body weight.
   C. 396 ÷ 0.18 = 22
   There are 2,200 freshmen at City College.
   D. 0.06($38,000) = $2,280
   The real estate agent will earn a commission of $2,280.
   E. $2 + 0.42($2) = S
       $2 + $0.84 = S
       $2.84 = S
   Thrifty Mart will sell the card for $2.84.

3. A. $50 - 0.22(\$50) = S$
        $50 - \$11 = S$
        $\$39 = S$
    The sale price of the wheelbarrow will be
    $39.
    B. $\$1.20 + 0.3(\$1.20) = S$
        $\$1.20 + 0.36 = S$
        $\$1.56 = S$
    The paring knife will sell for $1.56.
    C. $100\% - 25\% = 75\%$. The sale price is 75%
    of the original price.
    $\$150 \div 0.75 = \$200$
    The original price of the suit was $200.
    D. $\$38.90 + 0.05(\$38.90) = C$
        $\$38.90 + \$1.945 = C$
        $\$40.845 = C$
        $\$40.85 = C$
    The total cost of the items is $40.85.
    E. List price: $1,200
    Discount price: $\$1,200 - 0.3(\$1,200) =$
    $\$1,200 - \$360 = \$840$
    Clearance price: $\$840 - 0.2(\$840) = \$840 -$
    $\$168 = \$672$
    At the clearance sale, the table has a price
    of $672.

    F. Meal = $35
    Meal plus tax = $\$35 + 0.06(\$35) = \$35 +$
    $\$2.10 = \$37.10$
    Meal plus tax and tip: $\$37.10 +$
    $0.2(\$37.10) = \$37.10 + \$7.42 = \$44.52$
    The total cost of the meal is $44.52.
    G. Starting salary: $26,500
    Salary after first raise: $\$26,500 +$
    $0.11(\$26,500) = \$26,500 + \$2,915 =$
    $\$29,415$
    Salary after second raise: $\$29,415 +$
    $0.06(\$29,415) = \$29,415 + \$1,764.90 =$
    $\$31,179.90$
    His salary after the raise in June is
    $31,179.90.

AVERAGES

The **average**, also called the *arithmetic mean*, is the sum of a set of values
divided by the number of values. The average (arithmetic mean) of the values
8, 16, 4, 12, and 10 is found by finding the SUM $= 8 + 16 + 4 + 12 + 10 =$
50 and dividing by the number of values $N = 5$.

$$\text{AVE} = \text{SUM} \div N$$
$$= 50 \div 5 = 10$$

Example 49

Find the average for each set of data.

A. 104, 114, 124, 134
B. 27, 22, 17, 37, 22
C. 4, 2, 24, 14, 34, 8, 10, 20
D. 5, 1, 7, 3, 1
E. 25, 2, 5, 6, 5, 23, 22, 7, 10, 15, 21, 23

Solution

A. SUM $= 104 + 114 + 124 + 134 = 476$ $N = 4$
    AVE $= \text{SUM} \div N = 476 \div 4 = 119$
B. SUM $= 27 + 22 + 17 + 37 + 22 = 125$ $N = 5$
    AVE $= \text{SUM} \div N = 125 \div 5 = 25$

C. $\text{SUM} = 4 + 2 + 24 + 14 + 34 + 8 + 10 + 20 = 116$ $N = 8$

$\text{AVE} = \text{SUM} \div N = 116 \div 8 = 14.5$

D. $\text{SUM} = 5 + 1 + 7 + 3 + 1 = 17$ $N = 5$

$\text{AVE} = \text{SUM} \div N = 17 \div 5 = 3.4$

E. $\text{SUM} = 25 + 2 + 5 + 6 + 5 + 23 + 22 + 7 + 10 + 15 + 21 + 23 = 164$ $N = 12$

$\text{AVE} = \text{SUM} \div N = 164 \div 12 = 13.666 \cdots = 13.7$

If all values but one are known and the average is also known, then the last value can be determined. Suppose that 8, 16, 4, and 10 are four of five values that have an average of 10. If five values have a mean of 10, then the sum of the values must be $5(10) = 50$. The sum of the four known values is $8 + 16 + 4 + 10 = 38$. The missing value is $50 - 38 = 12$.

Example 50

Find the missing value.

A. If the average of six values is 28 and five of the six values are 29, 19, 23, 20, and 43, what is the sixth value?
B. If the average of five numbers is 41 and the numbers include 46, 35, 38, and 41, what is the missing number?
C. If Sara scored 77, 89, 98, 97, 99, and 91 on the first six tests, what does she need to score on the seventh test to get an average of 93 for the seven tests?
D. If Joe scored 77, 80, and 81 on three quizzes, what does he need to score on the next quiz to have an 82 average?

Solution

A. $6(28) = 168$ $29 + 19 + 23 + 20 + 43 = 134$

$168 - 134 = 34$

The sixth number is 34.
B. $5(41) = 205$ $46 + 35 + 38 + 41 = 160$

$205 - 160 = 45$

The missing number is 45.
C. $7(93) = 651$ $77 + 89 + 98 + 97 + 99 + 91 = 551$

$651 - 551 = 100$

She needs to score 100 on the seventh test.
D. $4(82) = 328$ $77 + 80 + 81 = 238$

$328 - 238 = 90$

He needs to score 90 on the fourth quiz.

To find the average of two or more averages, weight each average with the number of values in the average and then divide the sum of the **weighted averages** by the sum of the numbers for each of the averages. If A is the average of h values, B is the average of i values, and C is the average of j values, then the combined average is the sum of the weighted averages divided by the sum of the weights. $\text{SUM} = hA + iB + jC$ and $N = h + i + j$. $\text{AVE} = (hA + iB + jC) \div (h + i + j)$.

Example 51

Find the weighted averages.

A. The average score on a test for 400 students in Crawford County is 650. The average score on the same test for 600 students in Edwards County is 680. What is the combined average for the students in Crawford and Edwards counties?
B. Miss Jackson has 30 students in first period who averaged 85 on the state algebra test, 24 students in second period averaged a 90 on the algebra test, and 22 students in fifth period averaged an 82 on the algebra test. What was the average for these three classes?
C. The average traffic fine was $90 on Monday for the 18 people ticketed, the average fine was $76 on Tuesday for the 20 people ticketed, and the average fine was $80 on Wednesday for the 24 people ticketed. What was the average fine for the three days?

Solution

A. $\text{SUM} = 400(650) + 600(680) = 260{,}000 + 408{,}000 = 668{,}000$
   $N = 400 + 600 = 1{,}000$
   $\text{AVE} = 668{,}000 \div 1{,}000 = 668$
B. $\text{SUM} = 30(85) + 24(90) + 22(82) = 2{,}550 + 2{,}160 + 1{,}804 = 6{,}514$
   $N = 30 + 24 + 22 = 76$
   $\text{AVE} = 6{,}514 \div 76 = 85.7105 = 85.7$
C. $\text{SUM} = 18(\$90) + 20(\$76) + 24(\$80) = \$1{,}620 + \$1{,}520 + \$1{,}920 = \$5{,}060$
   $N = 18 + 20 + 24 = 62$
   $\text{AVE} = \$5{,}060 \div 62 = \$81.6129 = \$81.61$

When consecutive integers are averaged, the average will always equal the average of the first and last numbers in the sequence. The average of 5, 6, 7, 8, and 9 is $35 \div 5 = 7$ in the traditional way and $(5 + 9) \div 2 = 7$ in the way for consecutive integers.

Example 52

Find the average of these sequences of consecutive integers.

A. 1, 2, 3, 4, 5, 6, 7, 8
B. 7, 8, 9, 10, 11, 12
C. 25, 26, 27, 28, 29

Solution

A. $\text{AVE} = (1 + 8) \div 2 = 9 \div 2 = 4.5$
B. $\text{AVE} = (7 + 12) \div 2 = 19 \div 2 = 9.5$
C. $\text{AVE} = (25 + 29) \div 2 = 54 \div 2 = 27$

The **mode** of a set of values is the value that occurs most often. If all values occur the same number of times, there is no mode. If two or more values occur with the greatest frequency, then each of the values is a mode.

Example 53

Find the mode for the set of values.

A. 2, 8, 7, 6, 4, 3, 8, 5, 1
B. 3, 7, 2, 6, 4, 1, 6, 5, 7, 9
C. 8, 7, 2, 5, 9, 4, 1, 3
D. 8, 7, 6, 9, 4, 18, 6, 3, 2, 6, 7

Solution

A. Since 8 occurs twice and all other values occur once, 8 is the mode.
B. Both 6 and 7 occur twice, so 6 and 7 are both modes.
C. All the values occur once, so there is no mode.
D. Since 6 occurs three times and no other value occurs more than twice, 6 is the mode.

The **median** is the middle value of a set, or the average of the two middle values, when the values are arranged in order from least to greatest. The median of the values 1, 3, 4, 7, 10 is 4 since it is the middle value in the ordered values. The median of the values 1, 3, 4, 7, 10, 20 is the average of the two middle values 4 and 7, or $(4 + 7) \div 2 = 5.5$.

Example 54

Find the median for each set of values.

A. 24, 6, 7, 23, 13, 12, 18
B. 17, 15, 9, 13, 21, 32, 41, 7, 12
C. 147, 159, 132, 181, 174, 253
D. 74, 81, 39, 74, 82, 74, 80, 100, 74, 42
E. 11, 38, 73, 91, 16, 51, 39

Solution

A. The ordered values are 6, 7, 12, 13, 18, 23, 24.
    The middle value of the seven values is 13.
    The median is 13.
B. The ordered values are 7, 9, 12, 13, 15, 17, 21, 32, 41.
    The middle value of the nine values is 15.
    The median is 15.
C. The ordered values are 132, 147, 159, 174, 181, 253.
    The middle two values of the six values are 159 and 174.
    The average of the two middle values is $(159 + 174) \div 2 = 166.5$.
    The median is 166.5.
D. The ordered values are 39, 42, 74, 74, 74, 74, 80, 81, 82, 100.
    The middle two values of the 10 values are 74 and 74.
    The median is 74 since the average of 74 and 74 is 74.
E. The ordered values are 11, 16, 38, 39, 51, 73, 91.
    The middle value of the seven values is 39.
    The median is 39.

The **range** is the easiest way to describe how a set of data spreads out. To compute the range R, subtract the smallest value, the minimum, from the greatest value, the maximum. Thus, $R = \text{Max} - \text{Min}$.

The **standard deviation** is another way to look at how values spread out. It focuses on how much the values differ from the mean. To compute the standard deviation, denoted by SD, find the difference between each score and the mean (AVE) and square the difference. Then compute the sum of all these squared differences (Sum Sq), divide that by the number (NUM) of values, and finally find the square root of that quotient.

$$SD = \sqrt{\frac{\text{Sum Sq}}{\text{NUM}}} = \sqrt{\frac{\text{sum}(X - \text{AVE})^2}{\text{NUM}}}$$

Example 55

Find the range and standard deviation for each set of values.

A. 0, 5, 5, 10   B. 1, 6, 13, 20   C. 12, 12, 12, 12

Solution

A. $R = \text{Max} - \text{Min} = 10 - 0 = 10$

$$AVE = \frac{0 + 5 + 5 + 10}{4} = \frac{20}{4} = 5$$

$$SD = \sqrt{\frac{(0 - 5)^2 + (5 - 5)^2 + (5 - 5)^2 + (10 - 5)^2}{4}} = \sqrt{\frac{25 + 0 + 0 + 25}{4}}$$

$$= \sqrt{\frac{50}{4}} = \frac{\sqrt{50}}{\sqrt{4}} = \frac{\sqrt{50}}{2} \approx \frac{7}{2} = 3.5$$

Note: $7^2 = 49 \approx 50$, so estimate $\sqrt{50} \approx 7$.

B. $R = \text{Max} - \text{Min} = 20 - 1 = 19$

$$AVE = \frac{1 + 6 + 13 + 20}{4} = \frac{40}{4} = 10$$

$$SD = \sqrt{\frac{(1 - 10)^2 + (6 - 10)^2 + (13 - 10)^2 + (20 - 10)^2}{4}}$$

$$= \sqrt{\frac{81 + 16 + 9 + 100}{4}} = \frac{\sqrt{206}}{\sqrt{4}} \approx \frac{14.5}{2} = 7.25$$

Note: $14^2 = 196$ and $15^2 = 225$, so $\sqrt{206} \approx 14.5$.

C. $R = \text{Max} - \text{Min} = 12 - 12 = 0$

$$\text{AVE} = \frac{12 + 12 + 12 + 12}{4} = \frac{48}{4} = 12$$

$$\text{SD} = \sqrt{\frac{(12 - 12)^2 + (12 - 12)^2 + (12 - 12)^2 + (12 - 12)^2}{4}}$$

$$= \sqrt{\frac{0}{4}} = \sqrt{0} = 0$$

Note: Only when all the values are the same will the range and standard deviation be zero.

PRACTICE PROBLEMS

1. Find the average for each set of values. Round approximate answers to the nearest tenth.
   A. 12, 18, 16, 10, 6, 14, 17, 18, 20, 13
   B. 11, 14, 28, 36, 10, 16, 20
   C. 40, 32, 17, 38, 16, 40, 53, 70
   D. 22, 29, 30, 21, 20, 24, 25, 20, 22
   E. 120, 130, 70, 90, 50

2. Find the weighted average.
   A. Class A had 40 students with an average of 78. Class B had 25 students with an average of 72. What is the average for these two classes together?
   B. In January, 32 people bought car tags at an average cost of $97.40, and in February, 48 people bought car tags at an average cost of $87.20. What was the average cost of car tags for these two months?
   C. Last month, Paul's 5 grocery bills averaged $52.70. This month, Paul's 4 grocery bills averaged $67.50. What was Paul's average grocery bill for the last two months?

3. Find the median for each set of values.
   A. 7, 18, 26, 43, 76, 10, 26, 40
   B. 9, 36, 24, 85, 72, 500
   C. 29, 37, 14, 65, 71, 13, 24
   D. 48, 10, 17, 46, 97, 3, 5, 81, 140

4. Find the missing value.
   A. John is trying to average 300 miles each day on his trip. If he traveled 306 miles the first day, 284 miles the second day, and 292 miles the third day, how many miles must he travel the next day to reach his average for the four days?
   B. Larry has to have an average bowling score of 240 to maintain his rank on the bowling team. If he has scores of 260, 210, 250, and 230, what must he score on his next game to be able to keep his rank?
   C. Susan has scored 90, 78, 96, 94, 88, and 100 on her first 6 tests of the semester. If she wants to earn a 90 average for the 7 tests in the semester, what does she need to score on the last test?

5. Find the average of these sequences of consecutive integers.
   A. 1, 2, 3, 4, 5, 6, 7, 8, 9
   B. 501, 502, 503, 504, 505, 506
   C. 298, 299, 300, 301, 302, 303, 304, 305, 306
   D. 37, 38, 39, 40, 41, 42, 43, 44, 45, 46
   E. 632, 633, 634, 635, 636, 637, 638

SOLUTIONS

1. A. $\text{SUM} = 144 \quad N = 10$
      $\text{AVE} = 144 \div 10 = 14.4$
   B. $\text{SUM} = 135 \quad N = 7$
      $\text{AVE} = 135 \div 7 = 19.2857 = 19.3$
   C. $\text{SUM} = 306 \quad N = 8$
      $\text{AVE} = 306 \div 8 = 38.25 = 38.3$

   D. $\text{SUM} = 213 \quad N = 9$
      $\text{AVE} = 213 \div 9 = 23.666 = 23.7$
   E. $\text{SUM} = 460 \quad N = 5$
      $\text{AVE} = 460 \div 5 = 92$

2. A. Class A: 40, AVE $= 78$ Class B: 25,
   AVE $= 72$
   SUM $= 40(78) + 25(72) = 3{,}120 + 1{,}800 =$
   $4{,}920$
   $N = 40 + 25 = 65$
   AVE $= 4{,}920 \div 65 = 75.6923 = 75.7$

   B. January: 32, AVE $= \$97.40$ February:
   48, AVE $= \$87.20$
   SUM $= 32(\$97.40) + 48(\$87.20) =$
   $\$3{,}116.80 + \$4{,}185.60 = \$7{,}302.40$
   $N = 32 + 48 = 80$
   AVE $= \$7{,}302.40 \div 80 = \$91.28$

   C. Last month: 5, AVE $= \$52.70$ This
   month: 4, AVE $= \$67.50$
   SUM $= 5(\$52.70) + 4(\$67.50) = \$263.50 +$
   $\$270.00 = \$533.50$
   $N = 5 + 4 = 9$
   AVE $= \$533.50 \div 9 = \$59.27777 = \$59.28$

3. A. Ordered values: 7, 10, 18, 26, 26, 40, 43, 76
   The middle two values of the eight values
   are 26 and 26.
   The median is 26.

   B. Ordered values: 9, 24, 36, 72, 85, 500
   The middle two values are 36 and 72.
   $(36 + 72) \div 2 = 54$
   The median is 54.

C. Ordered values: 13, 14, 24, 29, 37, 65, 71
   The middle value of the seven values is 29.
   The median is 29.

D. Ordered values: 3, 5, 10, 17, 46, 48, 81,
   97, 140
   The middle value of the nine values is 46.
   The median is 46.

4. A. AVE $= 300$ $N = 4$
   SUM $= 300(4) = 1{,}200$. Given values:
   $306 + 284 + 292 = 882$
   Missing value $= 1{,}200 - 882 = 318$
   John needs to travel 318 miles on day 4.

   B. AVE $= 240$ $N = 5$
   SUM $= 240(5) = 1{,}200$. Given values:
   $260 + 210 + 250 + 230 = 950$
   Missing value $= 1{,}200 - 950 = 250$
   Larry needs to bowl a 250 on his next game.

   C. AVE $= 90$ $N = 7$
   SUM $= 90(7) = 630$. Given values: $90 + 78 +$
   $96 + 94 + 88 + 100 = 546$
   Missing value $= 630 - 546 = 84$
   She needs to score an 84 on the last test.

5. A. AVE $= (1 + 9) \div 2 = 5$
   B. AVE $= (501 + 506) \div 2 = 503.5$
   C. AVE $= (298 + 306) \div 2 = 302$
   D. AVE $= (37 + 46) \div 2 = 41.5$
   E. AVE $= (632 + 638) \div 2 = 635$

POWERS AND ROOTS

A term such as $5x^2$ has three parts: 5 is the **coefficient** of x^2; x is the **base**; and 2 is the **exponent**. The coefficient 5 means that five x^2's have been added together. The 2 means that two factors of x were multiplied to get the x^2.

$$x^3 = x \cdot x \cdot x, \qquad 5^4 = 5 \cdot 5 \cdot 5 \cdot 5, \qquad 5x^2 = 5 \cdot x \cdot x, \qquad x^3 y^2 = x \cdot x \cdot x \cdot y \cdot y$$

When the exponent is 1, you do not write it, so $3x^1 = 3x$. Also, when the coefficient is 1, you do not write it, so $1x^5 = x^5$. You read x^2 as "x squared," x^3 as "x cubed," x^4 as "x to the fourth," x^5 as "x to the fifth," etc. When you write $nx = x + x + x + \cdots + x$, there are n terms of x added together. When you write $x^n = x \cdot x \cdot x \cdots x$, there are n factors of x multiplied together.

Laws of Exponents

If x, a, and b are real numbers, then the following laws hold:

1. $x^a \cdot x^b = x^{a+b}$
2. $(x^a)^b = x^{ab}$
3. $\dfrac{x^a}{x^b} = x^{a-b} \qquad x \neq 0$
4. $(xy)^a = x^a \times y^a$
5. $\left(\dfrac{x}{y}\right)^a = \dfrac{x^a}{y^a} \qquad y \neq 0$

6. $x^{-a} = \dfrac{1}{x^a}$ $a > 0,\ x \neq 0$

7. $x^0 = 1$ $x \neq 0$

Example 56

Use the laws of exponents to simplify each expression.

A. $(3x)^2$ B. $(-4y)^2$ C. 2^4 D. 5^0 E. $\left(\dfrac{2}{3}\right)^3$

F. $x^{-2} \cdot x^5$ G. $x^2 \cdot x^5$ H. $3^4 \cdot 3^9$ I. 2^{-2} J. $(x^2)^3$

Solution

A. $(3x)^2 = 3x \cdot 3x = 3 \cdot 3 \cdot x \cdot x = 9x^2$ or $(3x)^2 = 3^2 x^2 = 9x^2$

B. $(-4y)^2 = (-4y)(-4y) = (-4)(-4)y\,y = 16y^2$

C. $2^4 = 2 \cdot 2 \cdot 2 \cdot 2 = 16$

D. $5^0 = 1$

E. $\left(\dfrac{2}{3}\right)^3 = \dfrac{2^3}{3^3} = \dfrac{8}{27}$

F. $x^{-2} \cdot x^5 = x^{-2+5} = x^3$

G. $x^2 \cdot x^5 = x^{2+5} = x^7$

H. $3^4 \cdot 3^9 = 3^{4+9} = 3^{13}$

I. $(2)^{-2} = \dfrac{1}{2^2} = \dfrac{1}{4}$

J. $(x^2)^3 = x^{2 \cdot 3} = x^6$ or $(x^2)^3 = x^2 \cdot x^2 \cdot x^2 = x^6$

Scientific notation is a way to write very large or very small numbers by rewriting them as numbers between 1 and 10, times a power of 10. The number 265,000 is written as 2.65×10^5, and 0.000148 is written as 1.48×10^{-4}.

Example 57

Write each number in scientific notation.

A. 2,541,000   B. 360,000   C. 0.00045   D. 0.0000157

Solution

A. $2{,}541{,}000 = 2_{\wedge}541000 = 2.541 \times 10^6$

B. $360{,}000 = 3_{\wedge}60000 = 3.6 \times 10^5$

C. $0.00045 = 0.0004_{\wedge}5 = 4.5 \times 10^{-4}$

D. $0.0000157 = 0.00001_{\wedge}57 = 1.57 \times 10^{-5}$

Use exponents to write numbers in expanded notation. $265 = 2 \times 10^2 + 6 \times 10^1 + 5 \times 10^0$, $0.45 = 4 \times 10^{-1} + 5 \times 10^{-2}$, and $24.3 = 2 \times 10^1 + 4 \times 10^0 + 3 \times 10^{-1}$.

Example 58

Write each number in expanded notation.

A. 3,472   B. 0.742   C. 21.45   D. 3.568

Solution

A. $3{,}472 = 3 \times 10^3 + 4 \times 10^2 + 7 \times 10^1 + 2 \times 10^0$
B. $0.742 = 7 \times 10^{-1} + 4 \times 10^{-2} + 2 \times 10^{-3}$
C. $21.45 = 2 \times 10^1 + 1 \times 10^0 + 4 \times 10^{-1} + 5 \times 10^{-2}$
D. $3.568 = 3 \times 10^0 + 5 \times 10^{-1} + 6 \times 10^{-2} + 8 \times 10^{-3}$

If n is a positive integer and if a and b are such that $a^n = b$, then a is the nth root of b. You write $\sqrt[n]{b} = a$. Also $\sqrt{a}$ is the square root of a and $\sqrt[3]{a}$ is the cube root of a. You can also use fractional exponents to indicate roots: $\sqrt{a} = a^{1/2}$, $\sqrt[3]{a} = a^{1/3}$, $\sqrt[n]{a} = a^{1/n}$.

Example 59

Simplify these radicals.

A. $\sqrt{x^2}$ B. $\sqrt{16}$ C. $\sqrt{16x^2}$ D. $\sqrt[3]{x^6}$ E. $\sqrt[3]{125}$

Solution

A. $\sqrt{x^2} = x$
B. $\sqrt{16} = 4$
C. $\sqrt{16x^2} = \sqrt{4^2 x^2} = \sqrt{(4x)^2} = 4x$
D. $\sqrt[3]{x^6} = \sqrt[3]{(x^2)^3} = x^2$
E. $\sqrt[3]{125}\,\sqrt[3]{5 \cdot 5 \cdot 5} = 5$

Table of Squares and Cubes

Number	Square	Cube
1	1	1
2	4	8
3	9	27
4	16	64
5	25	125
6	36	216
7	49	343
8	64	512
9	81	729
10	100	1,000
11	121	
12	144	
13	169	
14	196	
15	225	
16	256	
17	289	
18	324	
19	361	
20	400	

In $\sqrt[n]{a}$, n is the **index**, a is the **radicand**, and $\sqrt{}$ is the **radical sign**. When radical expressions are to be added, they must have the same index and the same radicand. Radical expressions with the same index and the same radicand are said to be like expressions and can be added or subtracted by adding or subtracting their coefficients.

Example 60

Add or subtract as indicated.

A. $3\sqrt{5} + 7\sqrt{5}$

B. $\sqrt{x} + 7\sqrt{x}$

C. $8\sqrt{3x} + 5\sqrt{3x}$

D. $28\sqrt{x} - 2\sqrt{x}$

E. $11\sqrt{5x} - 15\sqrt{5x}$

F. $7\sqrt{5} - 3\sqrt{5}$

Solution

A. $3\sqrt{5} + 7\sqrt{5} = (3+7)\sqrt{5} = 10\sqrt{5}$

B. $\sqrt{x} + 7\sqrt{x} = 1\sqrt{x} + 7\sqrt{x} = (1+7)\sqrt{x} = 8\sqrt{x}$

C. $8\sqrt{3x} + 5\sqrt{3x} = (8+5)\sqrt{3x} = 13\sqrt{3x}$

D. $28\sqrt{x} - 2\sqrt{x} = (28-2)\sqrt{x} = 26\sqrt{x}$

E. $11\sqrt{5x} - 15\sqrt{5x} = (11-15)\sqrt{5x} = -4\sqrt{5x}$

F. $7\sqrt{5} - 3\sqrt{5} = (7-3)\sqrt{5} = 4\sqrt{5}$

You can multiply radicals if they have the same index $\sqrt[n]{a} \cdot \sqrt[n]{b} = \sqrt[n]{a \cdot b}$ when a and b are positive. $\sqrt{2} \times \sqrt{5} = \sqrt{10}$, $\sqrt{a} \times \sqrt{a} = a$ if $a > 0$, $\sqrt{2} \times \sqrt{2} = 2$.

$$\sqrt[n]{a} \div \sqrt[n]{b} = \frac{\sqrt[n]{a}}{\sqrt[n]{b}} = \sqrt[n]{\frac{a}{b}} \qquad \text{if } a > 0 \text{ and } b > 0$$

$$\sqrt{15} \div \sqrt{3} = \frac{\sqrt{15}}{\sqrt{3}} = \sqrt{\frac{15}{3}} = \sqrt{5}$$

Example 61

Multiply or divide these radicals.

A. $\sqrt{5x} \cdot \sqrt{7y}$

B. $\sqrt{3xy} \cdot \sqrt{10z}$

C. $\sqrt{7a} \cdot \sqrt{15b}$

D. $\sqrt{21} \div \sqrt{7}$

E. $\sqrt{10x} \div \sqrt{2x}$

F. $\sqrt{3xy} \div \sqrt{3y}$

Solution

A. $\sqrt{5x} \cdot \sqrt{7y} = \sqrt{5x \cdot 7y} = \sqrt{35xy}$

B. $\sqrt{3xy} \cdot \sqrt{10z} = \sqrt{3xy \cdot 10z} = \sqrt{30xyz}$

C. $\sqrt{7a} \cdot \sqrt{15b} = \sqrt{7a \cdot 15b} = \sqrt{105ab}$

D. $\sqrt{21} \div \sqrt{7} = \frac{\sqrt{21}}{\sqrt{7}} = \sqrt{\frac{21}{7}} = \sqrt{3}$

E. $\sqrt{10x} \div \sqrt{2x} = \frac{\sqrt{10x}}{\sqrt{2x}} = \sqrt{\frac{10x}{2x}} = \sqrt{5}$

F. $\sqrt{3xy} \div \sqrt{3y} = \frac{\sqrt{3xy}}{\sqrt{3y}} = \sqrt{\frac{3xy}{3y}} = \sqrt{x}$

Radical expressions can be simplified by finding the roots of factors.

$$\sqrt{12} = \sqrt{4 \cdot 3} = \sqrt{4} \cdot \sqrt{3} = 2\sqrt{3}$$
$$\sqrt{x^5 y^4 z^3} = \sqrt{x^4 x y^4 z^2 z} = \sqrt{x^4 y^4 z^2}\sqrt{xz} = x^2 y^2 z\sqrt{xz}$$

In square roots, look for the greatest factor that is a perfect square, and then rewrite the radicand as the product of the perfect-square factor and the non-perfect-square factor.

Example 62

Simplify these radicals.

A. $\sqrt{18}$ B. $\sqrt{80}$ C. $\sqrt{81a^3}$ D. $\sqrt{x^3y}$ E. $\sqrt{x^7}$
F. $\sqrt{9b^4c^3}$ G. $\sqrt{32}$ H. $\sqrt{169a^5}$ I. $\sqrt{36x^2}$ J. $\sqrt{125a^2b^2}$

Solution

A. $\sqrt{18} = \sqrt{9\cdot2} = \sqrt{9}\cdot\sqrt{2} = 3\sqrt{2}$

B. $\sqrt{80} = \sqrt{16\cdot5} = \sqrt{16}\cdot\sqrt{5} = 4\sqrt{5}$

C. $\sqrt{81a^3} = \sqrt{81a^2\cdot a} = \sqrt{81a^2}\cdot\sqrt{a} = 9a\sqrt{a}$

D. $\sqrt{x^3y} = \sqrt{x^2\cdot xy} = \sqrt{x^2}\cdot\sqrt{xy} = x\sqrt{xy}$

E. $\sqrt{x^7} = \sqrt{x^6\cdot x} = \sqrt{x^6}\cdot\sqrt{x} = x^3\sqrt{x}$

F. $\sqrt{9b^4c^3} = \sqrt{9b^4c^2\cdot c} = \sqrt{9b^4c^2}\cdot\sqrt{c} = 3b^2c\sqrt{c}$

G. $\sqrt{32} = \sqrt{16\cdot2} = \sqrt{16}\cdot\sqrt{2} = 4\sqrt{2}$

H. $\sqrt{169a^5} = \sqrt{13^2a^4\cdot a} = \sqrt{13^2a^4}\cdot\sqrt{a} = 13a^2\sqrt{a}$

I. $\sqrt{36x^2} = \sqrt{6^2x^2} = 6x$

J. $\sqrt{125a^2b^2} = \sqrt{5^2a^2b^2\cdot5} = \sqrt{5^2a^2b^2}\cdot\sqrt{5} = 5ab\sqrt{5}$

A radical is simplified if it does not contain any perfect-square factors or any factors that are fractions or decimals. To eliminate a fraction under the radical sign, make the denominator a perfect square. $\sqrt{\frac{1}{2}} = \sqrt{\frac{1}{2}\cdot\frac{2}{2}} = \sqrt{\frac{2}{4}} = \frac{\sqrt{2}}{\sqrt{4}} = \frac{\sqrt{2}}{2}$.

Example 63

Simplify each radical expression.

A. $\sqrt{\frac{9}{16}}$ B. $\sqrt{\frac{2}{3}}$ C. $\sqrt{\frac{5}{6}}$ D. $\sqrt{\frac{3}{8}}$ E. $\sqrt{\frac{12}{5}}$ F. $\sqrt{\frac{6}{50}}$

Solution

A. $\sqrt{\frac{9}{16}} = \frac{\sqrt{9}}{\sqrt{16}} = \frac{3}{4}$

B. $\sqrt{\frac{2}{3}} = \sqrt{\frac{2}{3}\cdot\frac{3}{3}} = \sqrt{\frac{6}{9}} = \frac{\sqrt{6}}{\sqrt{9}} = \frac{\sqrt{6}}{3}$

C. $\sqrt{\frac{5}{6}} = \sqrt{\frac{5}{6}\cdot\frac{6}{6}} = \sqrt{\frac{30}{36}} = \frac{\sqrt{30}}{\sqrt{36}} = \frac{\sqrt{30}}{6}$

D. $\sqrt{\dfrac{3}{8}} = \sqrt{\dfrac{3}{8} \cdot \dfrac{2}{2}} = \sqrt{\dfrac{6}{16}} = \dfrac{\sqrt{6}}{\sqrt{16}} = \dfrac{\sqrt{6}}{4}$

E. $\sqrt{\dfrac{12}{5}} = \sqrt{\dfrac{12}{5} \cdot \dfrac{5}{5}} = \sqrt{\dfrac{60}{25}} = \dfrac{\sqrt{4 \cdot 15}}{\sqrt{25}} = \dfrac{\sqrt{4} \cdot \sqrt{15}}{5} = \dfrac{2\sqrt{15}}{5}$

F. $\sqrt{\dfrac{6}{50}} = \sqrt{\dfrac{3}{25}} = \dfrac{\sqrt{3}}{\sqrt{25}} = \dfrac{\sqrt{3}}{5}$

Example 64

Simplify and combine like terms.

A. $\sqrt{27} + \sqrt{48} - \sqrt{12}$ B. $5\sqrt{8} - 3\sqrt{18}$ C. $2\sqrt{150} - 4\sqrt{54} + 6\sqrt{48}$

Solution

A. $\sqrt{27} + \sqrt{48} - \sqrt{12} = \sqrt{9}\sqrt{3} + \sqrt{16}\sqrt{3} - \sqrt{4}\sqrt{3} = 3\sqrt{3} + 4\sqrt{3} -$
$2\sqrt{3} = 5\sqrt{3}$

B. $5\sqrt{8} - 3\sqrt{18} = 5\sqrt{4}\sqrt{2} - 3\sqrt{9}\sqrt{2} = 5 \cdot 2 \cdot \sqrt{2} - 3 \cdot 3 \cdot \sqrt{2} = 10\sqrt{2} -$
$9\sqrt{2} = \sqrt{2}$

C. $2\sqrt{150} - 4\sqrt{54} + 6\sqrt{48} = 2\sqrt{25}\sqrt{6} - 4\sqrt{9}\sqrt{6} + 6\sqrt{16}\sqrt{3} = 2 \cdot 5 \cdot \sqrt{6} -$
$4 \cdot 3 \cdot \sqrt{6} + 6 \cdot 4 \cdot \sqrt{3} = 10\sqrt{6} - 12\sqrt{6} + 24\sqrt{3} = -2\sqrt{6} + 24\sqrt{3}$

PRACTICE PROBLEMS

1. Simplify these exponential expressions.

   A. $x^5 \cdot x^7$ B. $4^3 \cdot 4^5$

   C. 11^0 D. $x^{-5} \cdot x^{11}$

   E. $(xy)^7$ F. $(5x)^2$

   G. $(2ab)(5a^2b^3)$ H. $(-3x)^2$

   I. $-3(x)^2$ J. $(x^3)^4$

2. Write each number in scientific notation.

   A. 26,150,000   B. 1,768   C. 0.00247

   D. 0.0286   E. 12.14

3. Write each number in expanded notation.

   A. 384   B. 12.4   C. 1,050   D. 0.014

   E. 0.15

4. Simplify these radicals.

   A. $\sqrt{x^6}$ B. $\sqrt{64}$ C. $\sqrt{25x^2}$

   D. $\sqrt[4]{16}$ E. $\sqrt[3]{x^{12}}$ F. $\sqrt[3]{64}$

5. Add or subtract as indicated.

   A. $\sqrt{45} + \sqrt{80}$ B. $\sqrt{4x} + \sqrt{49x}$

   C. $\sqrt{192x} - \sqrt{48x}$ D. $\sqrt{605x} - \sqrt{45x}$

   E. $\sqrt{8ab} + \sqrt{50ab}$ F. $\sqrt{245} - \sqrt{500}$

6. Multiply or divide as indicated.

   A. $\sqrt{10x} \cdot \sqrt{6x}$ B. $\sqrt{5xy} \cdot \sqrt{2xy}$

   C. $\sqrt{7a} \cdot \sqrt{14ab}$ D. $\sqrt{48} \div \sqrt{27}$

   E. $\sqrt{125x^3} \div \sqrt{5x}$ F. $\sqrt{8a^3} \div \sqrt{2ab^2}$

7. Simplify these radicals.

   A. $\sqrt{\dfrac{5}{9}}$ B. $\sqrt{\dfrac{16}{3}}$ C. $\sqrt{\dfrac{25}{20}}$

   D. $\sqrt{\dfrac{5}{8}}$ E. $\sqrt{\dfrac{3}{5}}$ F. $\sqrt{\dfrac{4}{15}}$

▒▒▒ SOLUTIONS

1. A. $x^5 \cdot x^7 = x^{5+7} = x^{12}$
    B. $4^3 \cdot 4^5 = 4^{3+5} = 4^8$
    C. $11^0 = 1$
    D. $x^{-5} \cdot x^{11} = x^{-5+11} = x^6$
    E. $(xy)^7 = x^7 y^7$
    F. $(5x)^2 = 5^2 x^2 = 25x^2$
    G. $(2ab)(5a^2 b^3) = 2 \cdot 5 \cdot a \cdot a^2 \cdot b \cdot b^3 = 10a^3 b^4$
    H. $(-3x)^2 = (-3)^2 x^2 = 9x^2$
    I. $-3(x)^2 = -3x^2$
    J. $(x^3)^4 = x^{3 \cdot 4} = 3^{12}$

2. A. $26{,}150{,}000 = 2_\wedge 6150000 = 2.615 \times 10^7$
    B. $1{,}768 = 1_\wedge 768 = 1.768 \times 10^3$
    C. $0.00247 = 0.002_\wedge 47 = 2.47 \times 10^{-3}$
    D. $0.0286 = 0.02_\wedge 86 = 2.86 \times 10^{-2}$
    E. $12.14 = 1_\wedge 2.14 = 1.214 \times 10^1$

3. A. $384 = 3 \times 10^2 + 8 \times 10^1 + 4 \times 10^0$
    B. $12.4 = 1 \times 10^1 + 2 \times 10^0 + 4 \times 10^{-1}$
    C. $1{,}050 = 1 \times 10^3 + 5 \times 10^1$
    D. $0.014 = 1 \times 10^{-2} + 4 \times 10^{-3}$
    E. $0.15 = 1 \times 10^{-1} + 5 \times 10^{-2}$

4. A. $\sqrt{x^6} = \sqrt{(x^3)^2} = x^3$
    B. $\sqrt{64} = \sqrt{(8)^2} = 8$
    C. $\sqrt{25x^2} = \sqrt{(5x)^2} = 5x$
    D. $\sqrt[4]{16} = \sqrt[4]{2^4} = 2$
    E. $\sqrt[3]{x^{12}} = \sqrt[3]{(x^4)^3} = x^4$
    F. $\sqrt[3]{64} = \sqrt[3]{4^3} = 4$

5. A. $\sqrt{45} + \sqrt{80} = \sqrt{9}\sqrt{5} + \sqrt{16}\sqrt{5} = 3\sqrt{5} + 4\sqrt{5} = 7\sqrt{5}$
    B. $\sqrt{4x} + \sqrt{49x} = \sqrt{4}\sqrt{x} + \sqrt{49}\sqrt{x} = 2\sqrt{x} + 7\sqrt{x} = 9\sqrt{x}$
    C. $\sqrt{192x} - \sqrt{48x} = \sqrt{64}\sqrt{3x} - \sqrt{16}\sqrt{3x} = 8\sqrt{3x} - 4\sqrt{3x} = 4\sqrt{3x}$
    D. $\sqrt{605x} - \sqrt{45x} = \sqrt{121}\sqrt{5x} - \sqrt{9}\sqrt{5x} = 11\sqrt{5x} - 3\sqrt{5x} = 8\sqrt{5x}$
    E. $\sqrt{8ab} + \sqrt{50ab} = \sqrt{4}\sqrt{2ab} + \sqrt{25}\sqrt{2ab} = 2\sqrt{2ab} + 5\sqrt{2ab} = 7\sqrt{2ab}$
    F. $\sqrt{245} - \sqrt{500} = \sqrt{49}\sqrt{5} - \sqrt{100}\sqrt{5} = 7\sqrt{5} - 10\sqrt{5} = -3\sqrt{5}$

6. A. $\sqrt{10x} \cdot \sqrt{6x} = \sqrt{10x \cdot 6x} = \sqrt{60x^2} = \sqrt{4x^2}\sqrt{15} = 2x\sqrt{15}$
    B. $\sqrt{5xy} \cdot \sqrt{2xy} = \sqrt{10x^2 y^2} = \sqrt{x^2 y^2}\sqrt{10} = xy\sqrt{10}$
    C. $\sqrt{7a} \cdot \sqrt{14ab} = \sqrt{98a^2 b} = \sqrt{49a^2}\sqrt{2b} = 7a\sqrt{2b}$
    D. $\sqrt{48} \div \sqrt{27} = \dfrac{\sqrt{48}}{\sqrt{27}} = \sqrt{\dfrac{48}{27}} = \sqrt{\dfrac{16}{9}} = \dfrac{\sqrt{16}}{\sqrt{9}} = \dfrac{4}{3}$
    E. $\sqrt{125x^3} \div \sqrt{5x} = \dfrac{\sqrt{125x^3}}{\sqrt{5x}} = \sqrt{\dfrac{125x^3}{5x}} = \sqrt{25x^2} = 5x$
    F. $\sqrt{8a^3} \div \sqrt{2ab^2} = \dfrac{\sqrt{8a^3}}{\sqrt{2ab^2}} = \sqrt{\dfrac{8a^3}{2ab^2}} = \sqrt{\dfrac{4a^2}{b^2}} = \dfrac{2a}{b}$

7. A. $\sqrt{\dfrac{5}{9}} = \dfrac{\sqrt{5}}{\sqrt{9}} = \dfrac{\sqrt{5}}{3}$
    B. $\sqrt{\dfrac{16}{3}} = \sqrt{\dfrac{16}{3} \cdot \dfrac{3}{3}} = \sqrt{\dfrac{48}{9}} = \dfrac{\sqrt{48}}{\sqrt{9}} = \dfrac{\sqrt{16}\sqrt{3}}{3} = \dfrac{4\sqrt{3}}{3}$
    C. $\sqrt{\dfrac{25}{20}} = \sqrt{\dfrac{5}{4}} = \dfrac{\sqrt{5}}{\sqrt{4}} = \dfrac{\sqrt{5}}{2}$
    D. $\sqrt{\dfrac{5}{8}} = \sqrt{\dfrac{5}{8} \cdot \dfrac{2}{2}} = \sqrt{\dfrac{10}{16}} = \dfrac{\sqrt{10}}{\sqrt{16}} = \dfrac{\sqrt{10}}{4}$
    E. $\sqrt{\dfrac{3}{5}} = \sqrt{\dfrac{3}{5} \cdot \dfrac{5}{5}} = \sqrt{\dfrac{15}{25}} = \dfrac{\sqrt{15}}{\sqrt{25}} = \dfrac{\sqrt{15}}{5}$
    F. $\sqrt{\dfrac{4}{15}} = \sqrt{\dfrac{4}{15} \cdot \dfrac{15}{15}} = \sqrt{\dfrac{60}{225}} = \dfrac{\sqrt{60}}{\sqrt{225}} = \dfrac{\sqrt{4}\sqrt{15}}{15} = \dfrac{2\sqrt{15}}{15}$

ARITHMETIC COMPUTATION TEST

Use the following test to assess how well you have mastered the material in this chapter. For each question, mark your answer by blackening the corresponding answer oval. An answer key and solutions are provided at the end of the test.

1. Which is equal to $5 - 3[6 - (-2)] \div 4$?

   (A) -1
   (B) 0
   (C) 1
   (D) 2
   (E) 4

2. Which is the value of $-x(2z - 5y)$ when $x = -2$, $y = 4$, and $z = 3$?

   (A) 28
   (B) 14
   (C) 8
   (D) -8
   (E) -28

3. Which property is illustrated by $(9 + 3) + 0 = 0 + (9 + 3)$?

   (A) Associative property
   (B) Commutative property
   (C) Identity property
   (D) Inverse property
   (E) Distributive property

4. Which is an example of the associative property of addition?

   (A) $3 \cdot (4 + 5) = 3 \cdot 4 + 3 \cdot 5$
   (B) $13 + 8 = 8 + 13$
   (C) $(8 + 4) + 2 = (4 + 8) + 2$
   (D) $(5 \cdot 3) \cdot 7 = 5 \cdot (3 \cdot 7)$
   (E) $3 + (8 + 7) = (3 + 8) + 7$

5. Which mixed number is equal to $\dfrac{17}{5}$?

   (A) 3, remainder 2

   (B) $\dfrac{5}{17}$

   (C) $3\dfrac{2}{5}$

   (D) 3.4

   (E) $3\dfrac{1}{5}$

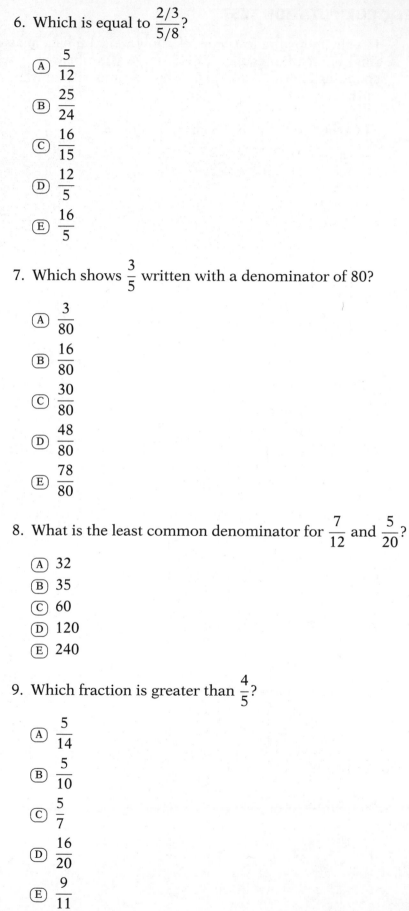

6. Which is equal to $\dfrac{2/3}{5/8}$?

   (A) $\dfrac{5}{12}$

   (B) $\dfrac{25}{24}$

   (C) $\dfrac{16}{15}$

   (D) $\dfrac{12}{5}$

   (E) $\dfrac{16}{5}$

7. Which shows $\dfrac{3}{5}$ written with a denominator of 80?

   (A) $\dfrac{3}{80}$

   (B) $\dfrac{16}{80}$

   (C) $\dfrac{30}{80}$

   (D) $\dfrac{48}{80}$

   (E) $\dfrac{78}{80}$

8. What is the least common denominator for $\dfrac{7}{12}$ and $\dfrac{5}{20}$?

   (A) 32

   (B) 35

   (C) 60

   (D) 120

   (E) 240

9. Which fraction is greater than $\dfrac{4}{5}$?

   (A) $\dfrac{5}{14}$

   (B) $\dfrac{5}{10}$

   (C) $\dfrac{5}{7}$

   (D) $\dfrac{16}{20}$

   (E) $\dfrac{9}{11}$

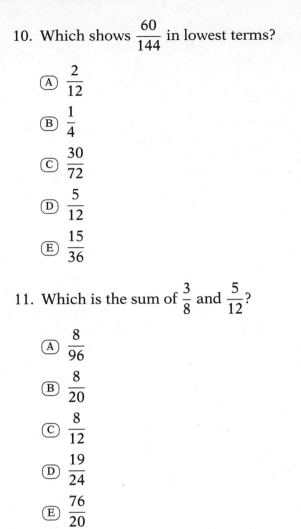

10. Which shows $\frac{60}{144}$ in lowest terms?

(A) $\frac{2}{12}$

(B) $\frac{1}{4}$

(C) $\frac{30}{72}$

(D) $\frac{5}{12}$

(E) $\frac{15}{36}$

11. Which is the sum of $\frac{3}{8}$ and $\frac{5}{12}$?

(A) $\frac{8}{96}$

(B) $\frac{8}{20}$

(C) $\frac{8}{12}$

(D) $\frac{19}{24}$

(E) $\frac{76}{20}$

12. Which is equal to $5\frac{1}{3} + 2\frac{3}{4}$?

(A) $7\frac{1}{12}$

(B) $7\frac{4}{7}$

(C) $7\frac{12}{13}$

(D) $8\frac{1}{12}$

(E) $10\frac{1}{4}$

13. Which is equal to $\frac{11}{15} - \frac{5}{12}$?

    (A) 2

    (B) $\frac{69}{60}$

    (C) $\frac{16}{27}$

    (D) $\frac{2}{5}$

    (E) $\frac{19}{60}$

14. Which is equal to $15 - 8\frac{1}{4}$?

    (A) $6\frac{1}{4}$

    (B) $6\frac{3}{4}$

    (C) $7\frac{1}{4}$

    (D) $7\frac{3}{4}$

    (E) $23\frac{1}{4}$

15. Which is equal to $\frac{2}{3} + \frac{3}{4} - \frac{1}{2} + \frac{5}{12}$?

    (A) $\frac{9}{17}$

    (B) $\frac{3}{4}$

    (C) $\frac{4}{3}$

    (D) $\frac{11}{6}$

    (E) $\frac{7}{3}$

16. Which is equal to $\frac{5}{6} \times \frac{8}{15}$?

    (A) $\frac{4}{9}$

    (B) $\frac{13}{21}$

    (C) $\frac{41}{30}$

    (D) $\frac{13}{90}$

    (E) $\frac{25}{16}$

17. Which is equal to $2\frac{3}{4} \times 3\frac{1}{11}$?

    Ⓐ $8\frac{1}{2}$

    Ⓑ $6\frac{3}{44}$

    Ⓒ $5\frac{4}{15}$

    Ⓓ $5\frac{3}{44}$

    Ⓔ $1\frac{1}{44}$

18. Which is equal to $\frac{5}{6} \div \frac{3}{5}$?

    Ⓐ $\frac{7}{30}$

    Ⓑ $\frac{4}{25}$

    Ⓒ $\frac{1}{2}$

    Ⓓ $\frac{25}{18}$

    Ⓔ $\frac{43}{30}$

19. Which is equal to $4 \times \frac{3}{5}$?

    Ⓐ $\frac{3}{20}$

    Ⓑ $\frac{12}{20}$

    Ⓒ $\frac{12}{5}$

    Ⓓ $\frac{23}{5}$

    Ⓔ $\frac{43}{5}$

20. Which is equal to $6 \div \dfrac{8}{15}$?

    (A) $\dfrac{4}{45}$

    (B) $\dfrac{5}{16}$

    (C) $\dfrac{16}{5}$

    (D) $6\dfrac{8}{15}$

    (E) $\dfrac{45}{4}$

21. Which is equal to $\dfrac{2}{3} - \dfrac{1}{2} + \dfrac{1}{4} \times \dfrac{5}{6} \div \dfrac{1}{5}$?

    (A) $\dfrac{25}{54}$

    (B) $\dfrac{1}{72}$

    (C) $-\dfrac{5}{24}$

    (D) $\dfrac{29}{24}$

    (E) $\dfrac{125}{72}$

22. Which is the greatest value: 12.59, 1.27, 0.56, 9.47, or 0.098?

    (A) 12.59
    (B) 9.47
    (C) 1.27
    (D) 0.56
    (E) 0.098

23. Which is the least value: 1.20, 4.81, 0.39, 0.082, or 1.0003?

    (A) 1.20
    (B) 4.81
    (C) 0.39
    (D) 0.082
    (E) 1.0003

24. Which digit is in the hundredths place in 273.8941?

    (A) 2
    (B) 3
    (C) 7
    (D) 8
    (E) 9

25. Which digit is in the tenths place in 367.4958?

    (A) 4
    (B) 5
    (C) 6
    (D) 7
    (E) 9

26. Which is 0.328 written as a fraction?

    (A) $\dfrac{164}{5}$

    (B) $\dfrac{328}{100}$

    (C) $\dfrac{82}{25}$

    (D) $\dfrac{41}{125}$

    (E) $\dfrac{41}{1250}$

27. Which fraction is equal to $0.060606\cdots$?

    (A) $\dfrac{2}{3}$

    (B) $\dfrac{2}{30}$

    (C) $\dfrac{2}{33}$

    (D) $\dfrac{2}{330}$

    (E) $\dfrac{2}{333}$

28. Which fraction is equal to $0.1232323\cdots$?

    (A) $\dfrac{123}{1000}$

    (B) $\dfrac{123}{999}$

    (C) $\dfrac{61}{495}$

    (D) $\dfrac{123}{990}$

    (E) $\dfrac{23}{99}$

29. Which is $\dfrac{4}{25}$ written as a decimal?

    (A) 0.04
    (B) 0.16
    (C) 0.4
    (D) 0.625
    (E) 6.25

30. What is the sum of 2.9, 1.002, 0.39, and 0.007?

    (A) 1.077
    (B) 1.4802
    (C) 3.9417
    (D) 4.299
    (E) 14.802

31. What is the sum of 5.2, 0.414, 0.03, and 0.22?

    (A) 0.476
    (B) 0.491
    (C) 1.034
    (D) 5.864
    (E) 14.54

32. Which shows the correct placement of the decimal point when 6.285 and 13.94 are multiplied?

    (A) 0.876129
    (B) 8.76129
    (C) 87.6129
    (D) 876.129
    (E) 8761.29

33. Which shows the correct decimal placement for the result of 0.93888 ÷ 0.18?

    (A) 52.16
    (B) 5.216
    (C) 0.5216
    (D) 0.05216
    (E) 0.005216

34. Which shows 281.3576 rounded to the nearest tenth?

    (A) 280
    (B) 281.3
    (C) 281.36
    (D) 281.4
    (E) 290

35. If two-thirds of a class is boys, how many girls are in the class of 48 students?

    (A) 72
    (B) 48
    (C) 32
    (D) 24
    (E) 16

36. A book that regularly sold for $36.29 was given a $3.55 reduction. How much did the book sell for after the price reduction?

    (A) $3.55
    (B) $10.22
    (C) $32.74
    (D) $39.84
    (E) $139.48

37. The angles of a triangle have a sum of 180°. If the angles have a ratio of 1 : 2 : 6, what is the measure of the largest angle?

    (A) 20°
    (B) 40°
    (C) 80°
    (D) 90°
    (E) 120°

38. Which ratio is NOT the same as 45 to 80?

    (A) 9 to 16
    (B) 63 to 112
    (C) 99 to 176
    (D) 90 to 180
    (E) 108 to 192

39. If 3 oranges sell for 80 cents, what would 12 oranges cost?

    (A) $9.60
    (B) $4.80
    (C) $3.20
    (D) $2.40
    (E) $1.60

40. A car traveled 60 mph from Belnap to Lincoln and 50 mph from Lincoln to Belnap. If the whole trip was 660 miles, how long did the round trip take?

    (A) 6 hours
    (B) 11 hours
    (C) 12.1 hours
    (D) 13.2 hours
    (E) 24.2 hours

41. One copy machine can make 20 copies a minute, and a second copy machine makes 15 copies a minute. If the two copiers work together, how long would it take them to make 2,100 copies?

    (A) 60 minutes
    (B) 105 minutes
    (C) 122.5 minutes
    (D) 140 minutes
    (E) 225 minutes

42. What number is 60% of 45?

    (A) 2.7
    (B) 7.5
    (C) 18
    (D) 27
    (E) 75

43. James bought a sweater for $29.95 and paid 7% tax on it. What was the total cost of the sweater?

    (A) $2.10
    (B) $20.97
    (C) $27.85
    (D) $32.05
    (E) $50.92

44. What is the average of 8, 6, 12, 9, 16, 14, 20, and 3?

    (A) 8
    (B) 9
    (C) 9.5
    (D) 11
    (E) 12

45. What is the median of 6, 9, 4, 21, 27, 8, 3, and 2?

    (A) 6
    (B) 7
    (C) 8
    (D) 21
    (E) 24

46. Which shows 2,540,000 written in scientific notation?

    (A) 0.254×10^7
    (B) 2.54×10^6
    (C) 25.4×10^5
    (D) 25.4×10^{-5}
    (E) 2.54×10^{-6}

47. Which is equal to $(-4x^3)^2$?

   (A) $-16x^6$
   (B) $-4x^6$
   (C) $-8x^5$
   (D) $4x^6$
   (E) $16x^6$

48. Which shows $\sqrt{96a^3b^4c^9}$ simplified completely?

   (A) $4ab^2c^4\sqrt{6ac}$
   (B) $2ab^2c^4\sqrt{6ac}$
   (C) $4ab^2c^3\sqrt{6a}$
   (D) $2ab^2c^4\sqrt{24ac}$
   (E) $4b^2\sqrt{6a^3c^9}$

49. Which shows $\sqrt{\dfrac{7}{12}}$ simplified completely?

   (A) $\dfrac{\sqrt{7}}{12}$
   (B) $\dfrac{\sqrt{14}}{12}$
   (C) $\dfrac{\sqrt{21}}{12}$
   (D) $\dfrac{\sqrt{21}}{6}$
   (E) $\dfrac{\sqrt{11}}{4}$

50. Which shows $\sqrt{45}+\sqrt{245}-\sqrt{320}$ simplified completely?

   (A) $-12\sqrt{5}$
   (B) $-12\sqrt{2}$
   (C) $2\sqrt{5}$
   (D) $5\sqrt{2}$
   (E) $18\sqrt{5}$

![bar] **ANSWER KEY**

1. A	11. D	21. D	31. D	41. A
2. E	12. D	22. A	32. C	42. D
3. B	13. E	23. D	33. B	43. D
4. E	14. B	24. E	34. D	44. D
5. C	15. C	25. A	35. E	45. B
6. C	16. A	26. D	36. C	46. B
7. D	17. A	27. C	37. E	47. E
8. C	18. D	28. C	38. D	48. A
9. E	19. C	29. B	39. C	49. D
10. D	20. E	30. D	40. C	50. C

![bar] **SOLUTIONS**

1. **A** -1

   $$5 - 3[6 - (-2)] \div 4 = 5 - 3(8) \div 4 = 5 - 24 \div 4 = 5 - 6 = -1$$

2. **E** -28

   $$-x(2z - 5y) = -(-2)[2(3) - 5(4)] = 2(6 - 20) = 2(-14) = -28$$

3. **B** Commutative property
   $(9 + 3) + 0 = 0 + (9 + 3)$ has the order of $(9 + 3)$ and 0 reversed, so this is an example of the commutative property.

4. **E** $3 + (8 + 7) = (3 + 8) + 7$
   $3 + (8 + 7) = (3 + 8) + 7$ has the grouping changed in the addition, so the associative property of addition has been used.

5. **C** $3\dfrac{2}{5}$

   $$\frac{17}{5} = \frac{15}{5} + \frac{2}{5} = 3 + \frac{2}{5} = 3\frac{2}{5}$$

6. **C** $\dfrac{16}{15}$

   $$\frac{2/3}{5/8} = \frac{2}{3} \div \frac{5}{8} = \frac{2}{3} \times \frac{8}{5} = \frac{16}{15}$$

7. **D** $\dfrac{48}{80}$

   $$80 \div 5 = 16 \qquad \frac{3}{5} = \frac{3}{5} \times \frac{16}{16} = \frac{48}{80}$$

8. **C** 60
   LCM$(12, 20) = 60$, so the least common denominator is 60.

9. **E** $\dfrac{9}{11}$

$\dfrac{4}{5}, \dfrac{9}{11}$ $\quad 4 \times 11 = 44 < 45 = 5 \times 9 \quad$ so $\dfrac{4}{5} < \dfrac{9}{11}$

10. **D** $\dfrac{5}{12}$

$\dfrac{60}{144} = \dfrac{60 \div 12}{144 \div 12} = \dfrac{5}{12}$

11. **D** $\dfrac{19}{24}$

$\dfrac{3}{8} + \dfrac{5}{12} = \dfrac{9}{24} + \dfrac{10}{24} = \dfrac{19}{24}$

12. **D** $8\dfrac{1}{12}$

$5\dfrac{1}{3} + 2\dfrac{3}{4} = 5 + 2 + \dfrac{1}{3} + \dfrac{3}{4} = 7 + \dfrac{4}{12} + \dfrac{9}{12} = 7 + \dfrac{13}{12} = 7 + 1\dfrac{1}{12} = 8\dfrac{1}{12}$

13. **E** $\dfrac{19}{60}$

$\dfrac{11}{15} - \dfrac{5}{12} = \dfrac{44}{60} - \dfrac{25}{60} = \dfrac{19}{60}$

14. **B** $6\dfrac{3}{4}$

$15 - 8\dfrac{1}{4} = 15 - 8 - \dfrac{1}{4} = 7 - \dfrac{1}{4} = 6\dfrac{3}{4}$

15. **C** $\dfrac{4}{3}$

$\dfrac{2}{3} + \dfrac{3}{4} - \dfrac{1}{2} + \dfrac{5}{12} = \dfrac{8}{12} + \dfrac{9}{12} - \dfrac{6}{12} + \dfrac{5}{12} = \dfrac{16}{12} = \dfrac{4}{3}$

16. **A** $\dfrac{4}{9}$

$\dfrac{5}{6} \times \dfrac{8}{15} = \dfrac{40}{90} = \dfrac{4}{9}$

17. **A** $8\dfrac{1}{2}$

$2\dfrac{3}{4} \times 3\dfrac{1}{11} = \dfrac{11}{4} \times \dfrac{34}{11} = \dfrac{34}{4} = \dfrac{17}{2} = 8\dfrac{1}{2}$

18. **D** $\dfrac{25}{18}$

$$\dfrac{5}{6} \div \dfrac{3}{5} = \dfrac{5}{6} \times \dfrac{5}{3} = \dfrac{25}{18}$$

19. **C** $\dfrac{12}{5}$

$$4 \times \dfrac{3}{5} = \dfrac{4}{1} \times \dfrac{3}{5} = \dfrac{12}{5}$$

20. **E** $\dfrac{45}{4}$

$$6 \div \dfrac{8}{15} = \dfrac{6}{1} \div \dfrac{8}{15} = \dfrac{6}{1} \times \dfrac{15}{8} = \dfrac{90}{8} = \dfrac{45}{4}$$

21. **D** $\dfrac{29}{24}$

$$\dfrac{2}{3} - \dfrac{1}{2} + \dfrac{1}{4} \times \dfrac{5}{6} \div \dfrac{1}{5} = \dfrac{2}{3} - \dfrac{1}{2} + \dfrac{5}{24} \times \dfrac{5}{1} = \dfrac{16}{24} - \dfrac{12}{24} + \dfrac{25}{24} = \dfrac{29}{24}$$

22. **A** 12.59
12.59 is the greatest.

23. **D** 0.082
0.082 is the least.

24. **E** 9
The digit in the hundredths place is 9.

25. **A** 4
The digit in the tenths place is 4.

26. **D** $\dfrac{41}{125}$

$$0.328 = \dfrac{328}{1,000} = \dfrac{41}{125}$$

27. **C** $\dfrac{2}{33}$

$$0.060606\cdots = \dfrac{6}{99} = \dfrac{2}{33}$$

28. **C** $\dfrac{61}{495}$

$$0.1232323\cdots = \dfrac{123 - 1}{990} = \dfrac{122}{990} = \dfrac{61}{495}$$

29. **B** 0.16

$$\frac{4}{25} = \frac{16}{100} = 0.16$$

30. **D** 4.299

$$2.9 + 1.002 + 0.39 + 0.007 = 4.299$$

31. **D** 5.864

$$5.2 + 0.414 + 0.03 + 0.22 = 5.864$$

32. **C** 87.6129

$$6.285 \times 13.94 = 87.61290 = 87.6129$$

33. **B** 5.216

$$0.93888 \div 0.18 = 93.888 \div 18 = 5.216$$

34. **D** 281.4
281.3576 rounded to the nearest tenth is 281.4.

35. **E** 16

$$\text{Boys} = \frac{2}{3} - \frac{2}{3} = \frac{1}{3} \qquad \frac{1}{3}(48) = 16 \text{ girls}$$

36. **C** $32.74

$$\$36.29 - \$3.55 = \$32.74$$

37. **E** 120°
1 : 2 : 6 and sum 180° $n + 2n + 6n = 180°$ $9n = 180°$ $n = 20°$
The angles are 20°, 40°, and 120°, so the largest is 120°.

38. **D** 90 to 180

$$\frac{45}{80} = \frac{63}{112} = \frac{99}{176} = \frac{108}{192} = \frac{9}{16} \neq \frac{90}{180} = \frac{1}{2}$$

39. **C** $3.20
3 for 80 cents 12 = 4 × 3   12 for 4 × 80 = 320 cents = $3.20

40. **C** 12.1 hours
330 miles at each rate $330 \div 50 = 6.6$ hours $330 \div 60 = 5.5$ hours
5.5 hours + 6.6 hours = 12.1 hours

41. **A** 60 minutes
$20t + 15t = 2,100$ $35t = 2,100$ $t = $ minutes

42. **D** 27
60% of $45 = 0.6 \times 45 = 27.0 = 27$

43. **D** $32.05
$29.95 + 0.07(\$29.95) = \$29.95 + \$2.0965 = \$32.0465 = \$32.05$ to the nearest cent

44. **D** 11
$\text{SUM} = 8 + 6 + 12 + 9 + 16 + 14 + 20 + 3 = 88, \qquad N = 8$
$\text{AVE} = \text{SUM} \div N = 88 \div 8 = 11$

45. **B** 7
Ordered values are 2, 3, 4, 6, 8, 9, 21, 27.
The middle values of the eight values are 6 and 8. $(6+8) \div 2 = 14 \div 2 = 7$
The median is 7.

46. **B** 2.54×10^6

$2{,}540{,}000 = 2.54 \times 10^6$

47. **E** $16x^6$

$(-4x^3)^2 = (-4)^2(x^3)^2 = 16x^6$

48. **A** $4ab^2c^4\sqrt{6ac}$

$$\sqrt{96a^3b^4c^9} = \sqrt{16 \cdot 6 \cdot a^2 \cdot a \cdot b^4 \cdot c^8 \cdot c} = \sqrt{16a^2b^4c^8}\sqrt{6ac} = 4ab^2c^4\sqrt{6ac}$$

49. **D** $\dfrac{\sqrt{21}}{6}$

$$\sqrt{\frac{7}{12}} = \sqrt{\frac{7}{12} \cdot \frac{3}{3}} = \sqrt{\frac{21}{36}} = \frac{\sqrt{21}}{\sqrt{36}} = \frac{\sqrt{21}}{6}$$

50. **C** $2\sqrt{5}$

$$\sqrt{45} + \sqrt{245} - \sqrt{320} = \sqrt{9}\sqrt{5} + \sqrt{49}\sqrt{5} - \sqrt{64}\sqrt{5}$$
$$= 3\sqrt{5} + 7\sqrt{5} - 8\sqrt{5} = 2\sqrt{5}$$

▬▬ GMAT SOLVED PROBLEMS

For each question, select the best answer.

1. **Which property of operations is illustrated by $2 + (3 \cdot 7) = 2 + (7 \cdot 3)$?**

    A. Associative property of addition
    B. Associative property of multiplication
    C. Commutative property of addition
    D. Commutative property of multiplication
    E. Distributive property

2. **Which number is the result for $3\frac{1}{4} + 2\frac{1}{3}$?**

    A. $5\frac{1}{12}$

    B. $5\frac{2}{7}$

    C. $5\frac{7}{12}$

    D. $6\frac{2}{7}$

    E. $6\frac{1}{12}$

3. **Which number is the result for $\frac{5}{6} \div \frac{3}{8}$?**

    A. $\frac{5}{16}$

    B. $\frac{9}{20}$

    C. $\frac{4}{7}$

    D. $\frac{20}{9}$

    E. $\frac{16}{5}$

4. **Which fraction is equivalent to the decimal $0.3282828\cdots$?**

    A. $\frac{3}{28}$

    B. $\frac{325}{999}$

    C. $\frac{325}{990}$

    D. $\frac{328}{999}$

    E. $\frac{328}{990}$

5. **Which number is equal to 1.68 × 4.5?**

   A. 0.756
   B. 7.56
   C. 75.6
   D. 756
   E. 756.000

6. **Elena's bread recipe calls for 3 ounces of butter for each 4 cups of flour used. She needs to make 4 times the original recipe. If 12 ounces of butter is used, then how many cups of flour are needed?**

   A. 1
   B. 4
   C. 9
   D. 13
   E. 16

7. **A room is to be painted by Jane and Sally working together. How long will it take them to paint the room together?**

   1. **Jane can paint the room in 16 hours, working alone.**
   2. **Sally can paint the room in 12 hours, working alone.**

   A. Statement 1 ALONE is sufficient, but statement 2 is not sufficient.
   B. Statement 2 ALONE is sufficient, but statement 1 is not sufficient.
   C. BOTH statements TOGETHER are sufficient, but NEITHER statement ALONE is sufficient.
   D. EACH statement ALONE is sufficient.
   E. Statements 1 and 2 TOGETHER are NOT sufficient.

8. **A table was purchased for $100 by the owner of Bella Home Furnishings. What is the selling price of the table?**

   1. **Bella Home Furnishings marks up merchandise by 40%.**
   2. **Bella Home Furnishings has a 25% discount sale every Tuesday.**

   A. Statement 1 ALONE is sufficient, but statement 2 is not sufficient.
   B. Statement 2 ALONE is sufficient, but statement 1 is not sufficient.
   C. BOTH statements TOGETHER are sufficient, but NEITHER statement ALONE is sufficient.
   D. EACH statement ALONE is sufficient.
   E. Statements 1 and 2 TOGETHER are NOT sufficient.

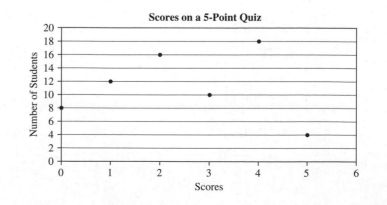

9. **What was the median for the scores on the quiz?**

    A. 1
    B. 2
    C. 3
    D. 4
    E. 5

10. **What was the mode for the scores on the quiz?**

    A. 1
    B. 2
    C. 3
    D. 4
    E. 5

SOLUTIONS

1. **D** The parentheses still contain the same numbers, so it is not an example of an associative property. Since the order of the two numbers inside the parentheses has been changed, it is an example of a commutative property, and the operation between the numbers is multiplication. Thus, the answer is D.

2. **C**

$$3\frac{1}{4} + 2\frac{1}{3} = 3 + 2 + \frac{1}{4} + \frac{1}{3} = 5 + \frac{3}{12} + \frac{4}{12} = 5 + \frac{7}{12} = 5\frac{7}{12}$$

   Thus, the answer is C.

3. **D**

$$\frac{5}{6} \div \frac{3}{8} = \frac{5}{6} \cdot \frac{8}{3} = \frac{40}{18} = \frac{20}{9}$$

   Thus, the answer is D.

4. **E** $0.3282828\cdots$ has one digit in the decimal part that does not repeat and two digits in the repeating group. To write the fraction for the given decimal, the numerator will be the digits from the decimal part to the end of one repeating group, 328, minus the nonrepeating digit 3 or $328 - 3 = 325$. The denominator will be two 9s followed by one 0, since there are two digits in the repeating group and one nonrepeating digit, so the denominator is 990. Therefore, $0.3282828\cdots = \frac{328}{990}$, and the answer is E.

5. **B** $168 \times 45 = 7,560$. In 1.68×4.5, there are two decimal places in 1.68 and one decimal place in 4.5, so the product should have three decimal places. $1.68 \times 4.5 = 7.560 = 7.56$. Thus, the answer is B.

6. **E** The recipe calls for 3 ounces of butter for each 4 cups of flour. Elena is using 12 ounces of butter, so let n represent the number of cups of flour she needs. Write the proportion $\frac{3}{4} = \frac{12}{n}$. From this proportion, $3n = 48$, and $n = 16$. Thus, the answer is E.

7. **C** Neither statement 1 nor statement 2 provides any information about them working together. Thus, you need to consider the statements together. Let n be the number of hours for them to do the job together, and write the equation $\frac{n}{16} + \frac{n}{12} = 1$, which has a unique solution.

   Both statements taken together are sufficient to answer the question, but neither is sufficient alone. The answer is C.

8. **A** Statement 1 says that the table will be marked up 40% for a price of $140. Thus, it is sufficient to answer the question.

   Statement 2 says that on Tuesdays there is a sale, but does not provide any information about the selling price.

   Only statement 1 is sufficient, so the answer is A.

9. **B** The median is the value for which one-half the data is below and one-half is above.

Score	0	1	2	3	4	5
Students	8	12	16	10	18	4
Cumulative	8	20	36	46	64	68

There are 68 values, so the middle value would be the average of the 34th and 35th values, both of which are 2 since the 21st through the 36th values are all 2. The median is 2, and the answer is B.

10. **D** The mode is the most frequent value. Since 4 was scored 18 times, it is the mode. The answer is D.

GMAT PRACTICE PROBLEMS

For each question, select the best answer.

1. **Which number is equivalent to $2\frac{5}{8}$?**

    A. $\frac{10}{16}$

    B. $\frac{7}{8}$

    C. $\frac{10}{8}$

D. $\dfrac{21}{8}$

E. $\dfrac{25}{8}$

2. **Which number is the result of $10\dfrac{1}{6} - 3\dfrac{3}{5}$?**

   A. $-30\dfrac{3}{30}$

   B. $6\dfrac{13}{30}$

   C. $6\dfrac{17}{30}$

   D. $7\dfrac{13}{30}$

   E. $7\dfrac{17}{30}$

3. **Which number is the result of $12\dfrac{2}{3} \times 5\dfrac{1}{4}$?**

   A. 10

   B. $17\dfrac{1}{6}$

   C. $17\dfrac{11}{12}$

   D. $60\dfrac{1}{6}$

   E. $66\dfrac{1}{2}$

4. **Which decimal is equivalent to $\dfrac{5}{6}$?**

   A. 0.56
   B. 0.5666⋯
   C. 0.8333⋯
   D. 0.875
   E. 0.565656⋯

5. **Which number is the sum of $0.633 + 7.25 + 0.4 + 3.5$?**

   A. 0.0001397
   B. 1.397
   C. 11.7
   D. 11.783
   E. 17.48

6. **In Mrs. Webster's algebra class, 8 students received A's, 14 received B's, 12 received C's, 10 received D's, and 6 received F's. Which number represents the ratio of B's to D's for the class?**

    A. $7:25$
    B. $2:3$
    C. $5:7$
    D. $7:5$
    E. $3:2$

7. **How much money was donated to The Hanks Foundation?**

    1. **Individuals donated 35% of all money The Hanks Foundation received.**
    2. **Community groups donated 25% of all the money The Hanks Foundation received.**

    A. Statement 1 ALONE is sufficient, but statement 2 is not sufficient.
    B. Statement 2 ALONE is sufficient, but statement 1 is not sufficient.
    C. BOTH statements TOGETHER are sufficient, but NEITHER statement ALONE is sufficient.
    D. EACH statement ALONE is sufficient.
    E. Statements 1 and 2 TOGETHER are NOT sufficient.

8. **A number w with two digits to the right of the decimal point is multiplied by the number n. How many decimal places are there in the product $w \cdot n$?**

    1. **The number n has three digits to the right of the decimal point.**
    2. **Neither the hundredths digit in w nor the thousandths digit in n is a multiple of 10.**

    A. Statement 1 ALONE is sufficient, but statement 2 is not sufficient.
    B. Statement 2 ALONE is sufficient, but statement 1 is not sufficient.
    C. BOTH statements TOGETHER are sufficient, but NEITHER statement ALONE is sufficient.
    D. EACH statement ALONE is sufficient.
    E. Statements 1 and 2 TOGETHER are NOT sufficient.

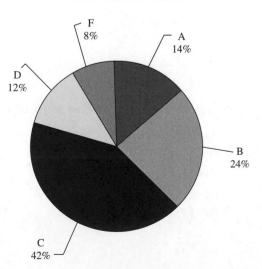

Class Grade Distribution

9. **If there were 150 students in the class, how many students received an A?**

    A. 35
    B. 28
    C. 21
    D. 14
    E. 7

10. **What percentage of the class received a grade lower than a C?**

    A. 24%
    B. 20%
    C. 16%
    D. 12%
    E. 8%

ANSWER KEY

1. D
2. C
3. E
4. C
5. D
6. D
7. E
8. C
9. C
10. B

CHAPTER 7
ALGEBRA

ALGEBRAIC EXPRESSIONS

An **algebraic expression** is a combination of letters and numbers that are used to represent numbers; thus,

$$x^3 - 5xy + 2x - 3y^4, \quad 2ab^2c^5, \quad \text{and} \quad \frac{5xy + 2ab}{5x^2 - 2a^3}$$

are algebraic expressions.

A **term** consists of products and quotients of letters and numbers. Thus, $2xy, 5x^2/3y^3$, and $-4a^5$ are terms. The algebraic expression $3x^2y - 4xy$ consists of two terms.

A **monomial** is a one-term algebraic expression. Example of monomials are $3x, x^2/y$, and $7y$.

A **binomial** is a two-term algebraic expression. Examples of binomials are $x + 2, 5x + 3y$, and $7x^2y^2 + 3ab$.

A **trinomial** is a three-term algebraic expression. Examples of trinomials are $3x + 2y + 3, x^2 + 5xy - y^2$, and $x^3 - ab + xy$.

The term **polynomial** is used when talking about an algebraic expression without stating a specific number of terms.

In the term $7x^2y^3$, the 7 is the **coefficient** of x^2y^3. **Like terms** are terms that have the same variable parts. For example, $7x^2y^3$ and $-2x^2y^3$ are like terms, but $7x^2y^3$ and $3xy^3$ are unlike terms. You combine like terms by adding their coefficients. Unlike terms cannot be combined.

Example 1

Simplify each expression by combining like terms.

A. $7x + 3y^3 - 3x + xy + 5y^3$
B. $3x - 2y^3 + 7xy + 2xy - 5x - 6y^3$

Solution

A. $7x + 3y^3 - 3x + xy + 5y^3 = 7x - 3x + 3y^3 + 5y^3 + xy = 4x + 8y^3 + xy$
B. $3x - 2y^3 + 7xy + 2xy - 5x - 6y^3 = 3x - 5x - 2y^3 - 6y^3 + 7xy + 2xy = -2x - 8y^3 + 9xy$

EXPONENTS REVISITED

If n is a positive integer, then a^n represents the product of n factors of a.

Thus, $a^5 = a \cdot a \cdot a \cdot a \cdot a$ and $b^3 = b \cdot b \cdot b$. In a^n, a is the **base** and n is the **exponent**.

If $n = 2$, then a^2 is read "a squared," and if $n = 3$, then a^3 is read "a cubed." And a^n is read "a to the nth power."

Example 2

Show the meaning of each expression.

A. x^3 B. 3^4 C. $(-2)^5$

Solution

A. $x^3 = x \cdot x \cdot x$
B. $3^4 = 3 \cdot 3 \cdot 3 \cdot 3 = 81$
C. $(-2)^5 = (-2) \cdot (-2) \cdot (-2) \cdot (-2) \cdot (-2) = -32$

      If n is a positive integer, then $a^{-n} = \dfrac{1}{a^n}$, $a \neq 0$.

Example 3

Show the meaning of each expression.

A. 3^{-4} B. 2^{-3} C. $-5y^{-3}$ D. $(x+y)^{-1}$

Solution

A. $3^{-4} = \dfrac{1}{3^4} = \dfrac{1}{81}$ B. $2^{-3} = \dfrac{1}{2^3} = \dfrac{1}{8}$

C. $-5y^{-3} = \dfrac{-5}{y^3}$ D. $(x+y)^{-1} = \dfrac{1}{x+y}$

ROOTS REVISITED

If n is a positive integer and if a and b are such that $a^n = b$, then n is called the **nth root** of b. If b is positive, there is only one positive number a such that $a^n = b$. You write this positive number as $\sqrt[n]{b}$ and call it the **principal nth root** of b. If b is negative and n is even, there is no real nth root of b. However, if n is odd, there is a real nth root of b.

Example 4

Simplify each of these roots.

A. $\sqrt[3]{27}$ B. $\sqrt{25}$ C. $\sqrt[4]{16}$ D. $\sqrt[3]{-8}$ E. $\sqrt[4]{-16}$

Solution

A. $\sqrt[3]{27} = \sqrt[3]{3^3} = 3$
B. $\sqrt{25} = \sqrt{5^2} = 5$
C. $\sqrt[4]{16} = \sqrt[4]{2^4} = 2$
D. $\sqrt[3]{-8} = \sqrt[3]{(-2)^3} = -2$
E. $\sqrt[4]{-16}$ is not a real number since n is even and b is negative.

GENERAL LAWS OF EXPONENTS

If m and n are real numbers, then the following laws hold:

    1. $a^m \cdot a^n = a^{m+n}$
    2. $(a^m)^n = a^{mn}$

3. $\dfrac{a^m}{a^n} = a^{m-n},$ if $a \neq 0$

4. $(ab)^m = a^m b^m$

5. $\left(\dfrac{a}{b}\right)^m = \dfrac{a^m}{b^m}$ if $b \neq 0$

6. $a^{\frac{m}{n}} = \sqrt[n]{a^m}$ if $a \geq 0$

7. $a^0 = 1$ if $a \neq 0$

Example 5

Simplify these expressions by using the laws of exponents.

A. $x^2 \cdot x^4$

B. $x^6 \div x^4$

C. $(x^2 \cdot y^5)^3$

D. $(2^4)^3$

E. $(x^{1/3})^3$

F. 5^0

G. $(x^{-3})^{-4}$

H. $3^9 \cdot 3^{-2} \cdot 3^{-3}$

I. $(x+15)^{4/3} \div (x+15)^{5/6}$

Solution

A. $x^2 \cdot x^4 = x^{2+4} = x^6$

B. $x^6 \div x^4 = x^{6-4} = x^2$

C. $(x^2 \cdot y^5)^3 = (x^2)^3(y^5)^3 = x^6 y^{15}$

D. $(2^4)^3 = 2^{4 \cdot 3} = 2^{12}$

E. $(x^{1/3})^3 = x^{3/3} = x^1 = x$

F. $5^0 = 1$

G. $(x^{-3})^{-4} = x^{-3(-4)} = x^{12}$

H. $3^9 \cdot 3^{-2} \cdot 3^{-3} = 3^{9-2-3} = 3^4 = 3 \cdot 3 \cdot 3 \cdot 3 = 81$

I. $(x+15)^{4/3} \div (x+15)^{5/6} = (x+15)^{4/3-5/6} = (x+15)^{8/6-5/6} = (x+15)^{3/6} = (x+15)^{1/2} = \sqrt{x+15}$

Example 6

Simplify these expressions, using laws of exponents, for $a \neq 0$.

A. $\dfrac{x^5}{x^8}$

B. $8^{-2/3}$

C. $x^{-5/2}$

D. $\dfrac{\sqrt{x}}{\sqrt[3]{x}}$

E. $(ax)^0$

F. $\sqrt[4]{25}$

G. $4^{3/2}$

H. $(-3)^0$

Solution

A. $\dfrac{x^5}{x^8} = x^{5-8} = x^{-3} = \dfrac{1}{x^3}$

B. $8^{-2/3} = (8^{2/3})^{-1} = (\sqrt[3]{8^2})^{-1} = (\sqrt[3]{64})^{-1} = 4^{-1} = \dfrac{1}{4}$

C. $x^{-5/2} = \dfrac{1}{x^{5/2}}$

D. $\dfrac{\sqrt{x}}{\sqrt[3]{x}} = \dfrac{x^{1/2}}{x^{1/3}} = x^{1/2-1/3} = x^{3/6-2/6} = x^{1/6} = \sqrt[6]{x}$

E. $(ax)^0 = a^0 \cdot x^0 = 1 \cdot 1 = 1$

F. $\sqrt[4]{25} = \sqrt[4]{5^2} = 5^{2/4} = 5^{1/2} = \sqrt{5}$

G. $4^{3/2} = (4^{1/2})^3 = (2)^3 = 8$

H. $(-3)^0 = 1$

PRACTICE PROBLEMS

1. Simplify these algebraic expressions.

    A. $17x - 18y + 2xy - 15x + 11y - 8xy$

    B. $5x^2 - 3x + 6 - 2x^2 + 18x - 1$

    C. $15x^2 - 3y^2 + 4z^2 - 8z^2 + 5y^2 + 6x^2$

2. Simplify these exponential expressions.

    A. x^{-3} B. $(-2)^3$ C. $(3x)^3$ D. $(-2x)^2$

3. Simplify each of the roots.

    A. $\sqrt[3]{8}$ B. $\sqrt[3]{-125}$ C. $\sqrt[4]{625}$

    D. $\sqrt{121}$ E. $\sqrt{81}$

4. Simplify these expressions.

    A. $x^3 \cdot x^5$ B. $(x^{1/4})^8$

    C. $5^3 \cdot 5^4$ D. $(x^3 \cdot y^5)^3$

    E. $7^{-3} \cdot 7^8 \cdot 7^{-2}$ F. $(5^4)^5$

    G. $x^{10} \div x^2$

5. Simplify these expressions.

    A. $\dfrac{x^7}{x^9}$ B. $x^{-2/3}$ C. $\dfrac{x^{1/6}}{x^{1/2}}$ D. $\sqrt[4]{4}$

SOLUTIONS

1. A. $17x - 18y + 2xy - 15x + 11y - 8xy = 17x - 15x - 18y + 11y + 2xy - 8xy = 2x - 7y - 6xy$

    B. $5x^2 - 3x + 6 - 2x^2 + 18x - 1 = 5x^2 - 2x^2 - 3x + 18x + 6 - 1 = 3x^2 + 15x + 5$

    C. $15x^2 - 3y^2 + 4z^2 - 8z^2 + 5y^2 + 6x^2 = 15x^2 + 6x^2 - 3y^2 + 5y^2 + 4z^2 - 8z^2 = 21x^2 + 2y^2 - 4z^2$

2. A. $x^{-3} = \dfrac{1}{x^3}$

    B. $(-2)^3 = (-2)(-2)(-2) = -8$

    C. $(3x)^3 = (3x)(3x)(3x) = 27x^3$

    D. $(-2x)^2 = (-2x)(-2x) = 4x^2$

3. A. $\sqrt[3]{8} = \sqrt[3]{2^3} = 2$

    B. $\sqrt[3]{-125} = \sqrt[3]{(-5)^3} = -5$

    C. $\sqrt[4]{625} = \sqrt[4]{5^4} = 5$

    D. $\sqrt{121} = \sqrt{11^2} = 11$

    E. $\sqrt{81} = \sqrt{9^2} = 9$

4. A. $x^3 \cdot x^5 = x^{3+5} = x^8$

    B. $(x^{1/4})^8 = x^{8/4} = x^2$

    C. $5^3 \cdot 5^4 = 5^{3+4} = 5^7$

    D. $(x^3 \cdot y^5)^3 = (x^3)^3(y^5)^3 = x^{3 \cdot 3}y^{5 \cdot 3} = x^9 y^{15}$

    E. $7^{-3} \cdot 7^8 \cdot 7^{-2} = 7^{-3+8-2} = 7^3 = 7 \cdot 7 \cdot 7 = 343$

    F. $(5^4)^5 = 5^{4 \cdot 5} = 5^{20}$

    G. $x^{10} \div x^2 = x^{10-2} = x^8$

5. A. $\dfrac{x^7}{x^9} = x^{7-9} = x^{-2} = \dfrac{1}{x^2}$

    B. $x^{-2/3} = \dfrac{1}{x^{2/3}} = \dfrac{1}{\sqrt[3]{x^2}}$

    C. $\dfrac{x^{1/6}}{x^{1/2}} = x^{1/6-1/2} = x^{1/6-3/6} = x^{-2/6} = x^{-1/3} = \dfrac{1}{x^{1/3}} = \dfrac{1}{\sqrt[3]{x}}$

    D. $\sqrt[4]{4} = \sqrt[4]{(2)^2} = (2^2)^{1/4} = 2^{2/4} = 2^{1/2} = \sqrt{2}$

TABLES OF POWERS AND ROOTS

Number	Square	Cube	Square Root	Cube Root
1	1	1	1	1
2	4	8	1.414	1.260
3	9	27	1.732	1.442
4	16	64	2	1.587
5	25	125	2.236	1.710
6	36	216	2.449	1.817
7	49	343	2.646	1.913
8	64	512	2.828	2
9	81	729	3	2.080
10	100	1,000	3.16	2.154
11	121	1,331	3.317	2.224

Additional Squares

Number	Square	Number	Square
12	144	19	361
13	169	20	400
14	196	21	441
15	225	22	484
16	256	23	529
17	289	24	576
18	324	25	625

RADICAL EXPRESSIONS

A radical $\sqrt[n]{a}$ has three parts: the **index** n, the **radical sign** $\sqrt{\ }$, and the **radicand** a. When you simplify a radical expression, you want the index to be as small as possible, no factors that are nth powers, no fractions in the radicand, and no radical expressions in the denominator.

Example 7

Which radical expressions need to be simplified?

A. $\sqrt{ab}$ B. $\sqrt[6]{x^2}$ C. $\sqrt{9x}$ D. $\sqrt{3x^5}$

E. $\sqrt{\dfrac{1}{4}}$ F. $\dfrac{3}{\sqrt{x}}$ G. $\sqrt{0.2}$ H. $\sqrt{\dfrac{5}{8}}$

Solution

A. $\sqrt{ab}$ Simplified

B. $\sqrt[6]{x^2}$ Common factor between index and exponent of radical $= \sqrt[3]{x}$

C. $\sqrt{9x}$ Has a perfect square factor of $9 = \sqrt[3]{x}$

D. $\sqrt{3x^5}$ Has a perfect square factor of $x^4 = x^2\sqrt{3x}$

E. $\sqrt{\dfrac{1}{4}}$ Has a perfect square factor of $\dfrac{1}{4} = \dfrac{1}{2}$

F. $\dfrac{3}{\sqrt{x}}$ Has a radical in the denominator of the fraction $= 3\dfrac{\sqrt{x}}{x}$

G. $\sqrt{0.2}$ Has a decimal fraction in the radicand $= \sqrt{\dfrac{1}{5}} = \dfrac{\sqrt{5}}{5}$

H. $\sqrt{\dfrac{5}{8}}$ Has a common fraction in the radicand $= \dfrac{\sqrt{10}}{4}$

Reducing the Index

A radical can be written with a fractional exponent, as in $\sqrt[n]{x^a} = x^{\frac{a}{n}}$. Whenever $GCD(a, n) > 1$, you can simplify the index by reducing the fractional exponent. If $GCD(a, n) = 1$, the index is as small as it can get.

Example 8

Reduce the index wherever possible.

A. $\sqrt[4]{a^2}$ B. $\sqrt[6]{a^4b^2}$ C. $\sqrt{a^3}$ D. $\sqrt{a^4}$ E. $\sqrt[5]{a^2b^3}$

Solution

A. $\sqrt[4]{a^2} = a^{2/4} = a^{1/2} = \sqrt{a}$

B. $\sqrt[6]{a^4b^2} = \sqrt[6]{(a^2b)^2} = (a^2b)^{2/6} = (a^2b)^{1/3} = \sqrt[3]{a^2b}$

C. $\sqrt{a^3} = \sqrt{a^3}$, since GCD$(2, 3) = 1$, the index cannot be reduced.

D. $\sqrt{a^4} = a^{4/2} = a^2$, so there is no radical in answer.

E. $\sqrt[5]{a^2b^3} = \sqrt[5]{(a^2b^3)^1}$, since GCD$(1, 5) = 1$, the index cannot be reduced.

Removing the Perfect-Square Factors in the Radicand

If the radicand has a factor with an exponent greater than or equal to the index, then the radicand can be simplified. $\sqrt{a^2b} = \sqrt{a^2}\sqrt{b} = a\sqrt{b}$, and $\sqrt{a^3b} = \sqrt{a^2}\sqrt{ab} = a\sqrt{ab}$.

Example 9

Simplify each radicand.

A. $\sqrt{75}$ B. $\sqrt{27a}$ C. $\sqrt{12xy}$ D. $\sqrt{4xy^2}$ E. $\sqrt{200x^5}$

Solution

A. $\sqrt{75} = \sqrt{3 \cdot 5^2} = \sqrt{5^2}\sqrt{3} = 5\sqrt{3}$

B. $\sqrt{27a} = \sqrt{3^3a} = \sqrt{3^2}\sqrt{3a} = 3\sqrt{3a}$

C. $\sqrt{12xy} = \sqrt{2^2 \cdot 3xy} = \sqrt{2^2}\sqrt{3xy} = 2\sqrt{3xy}$

D. $\sqrt{4xy^2} = \sqrt{2^2xy^2} = \sqrt{2^2y^2}\sqrt{x} = 2y\sqrt{x}$

E. $\sqrt{200x^5} = \sqrt{2 \cdot 10^2 \cdot x^4 \cdot x} = \sqrt{10^2 \cdot x^4}\sqrt{2x} = 10x^2\sqrt{2x}$

Fractions in the Radicand

If there is a decimal in the radicand, write the decimal factor as a common fraction. When there is a common fraction in the radicand, multiply the numerator and denominator by a common factor that makes the denominator a perfect square. For example,

$$\sqrt{\frac{1}{2}} = \sqrt{\frac{1}{2} \cdot \frac{2}{2}} = \sqrt{\frac{2}{4}} = \frac{\sqrt{2}}{\sqrt{4}} = \frac{\sqrt{2}}{2}$$

Example 10

Simplify each radicand.

A. $\sqrt{\dfrac{8}{9}}$ B. $\sqrt{\dfrac{7}{3}}$ C. $\sqrt{\dfrac{1}{4}}$ D. $\sqrt{\dfrac{3}{8}}$ E. $\sqrt{\dfrac{3}{10}}$ F. $\sqrt{0.2}$

Solution

A. $\sqrt{\dfrac{8}{9}} = \dfrac{\sqrt{8}}{\sqrt{9}} = \dfrac{\sqrt{4}\sqrt{2}}{3} = \dfrac{2\sqrt{2}}{3}$

B. $\sqrt{\dfrac{7}{3}} = \sqrt{\dfrac{7}{3} \cdot \dfrac{3}{3}} = \sqrt{\dfrac{21}{9}} = \dfrac{\sqrt{21}}{\sqrt{9}} = \dfrac{\sqrt{21}}{3}$

C. $\sqrt{\dfrac{1}{4}} = \dfrac{\sqrt{1}}{\sqrt{4}} = \dfrac{1}{2}$

D. $\sqrt{\dfrac{3}{8}} = \sqrt{\dfrac{3}{8} \cdot \dfrac{2}{2}} = \sqrt{\dfrac{6}{16}} = \dfrac{\sqrt{6}}{\sqrt{16}} = \dfrac{\sqrt{6}}{4}$

E. $\sqrt{\dfrac{3}{10}} = \sqrt{\dfrac{3}{10} \cdot \dfrac{10}{10}} = \sqrt{\dfrac{30}{100}} = \dfrac{\sqrt{30}}{\sqrt{100}} = \dfrac{\sqrt{30}}{10}$

F. $\sqrt{0.2} = \sqrt{\dfrac{2}{10}} = \sqrt{\dfrac{1}{5}} = \sqrt{\dfrac{1}{5} \cdot \dfrac{5}{5}} = \sqrt{\dfrac{5}{25}} = \dfrac{\sqrt{5}}{\sqrt{25}} = \dfrac{\sqrt{5}}{5}$

Radicals in the Denominator of a Fraction

If a fraction has a radical in the denominator, multiply the numerator and denominator of the fraction by the radical expression that will make the denominator a perfect nth root. For example,

$$\frac{5}{\sqrt{2}} = \frac{5}{\sqrt{2}} \cdot \frac{\sqrt{2}}{\sqrt{2}} = \frac{5\sqrt{2}}{\sqrt{4}} = \frac{5\sqrt{2}}{2}$$

Example 11

Simplify.

A. $\dfrac{4}{\sqrt{7}}$ B. $\dfrac{3}{\sqrt{2}}$ C. $\dfrac{5}{\sqrt{3}}$ D. $\dfrac{\sqrt{2}}{\sqrt{15}}$

Solution

A. $\dfrac{4}{\sqrt{7}} = \dfrac{4}{\sqrt{7}} \cdot \dfrac{\sqrt{7}}{\sqrt{7}} = \dfrac{4\sqrt{7}}{\sqrt{49}} = \dfrac{4\sqrt{7}}{7}$

B. $\dfrac{3}{\sqrt{2}} = \dfrac{3}{\sqrt{2}} \cdot \dfrac{\sqrt{2}}{\sqrt{2}} = \dfrac{3\sqrt{2}}{\sqrt{4}} = \dfrac{3\sqrt{2}}{2}$

C. $\dfrac{5}{\sqrt{3}} = \dfrac{5}{\sqrt{3}} \cdot \dfrac{\sqrt{3}}{\sqrt{3}} = \dfrac{5\sqrt{3}}{\sqrt{9}} = \dfrac{5\sqrt{3}}{3}$

D. $\dfrac{\sqrt{2}}{\sqrt{15}} = \dfrac{\sqrt{2}}{\sqrt{15}} \cdot \dfrac{\sqrt{15}}{\sqrt{15}} = \dfrac{\sqrt{30}}{15}$

PRACTICE PROBLEMS

1. Simplify these radical expressions.

   A. $\sqrt{18}$ B. $\sqrt[3]{40}$ C. $\sqrt[3]{81}$

   D. $\sqrt{648}$

2. Simplify these radical expressions.

   A. $\sqrt[4]{9a^2}$ B. $\sqrt[6]{125a^3b^3}$ C. $\sqrt{a^3}$

   D. $\sqrt[9]{a^3}$

3. Simplify these expressions.

   A. $\sqrt{7a^3y^2}$ B. $\sqrt{8b^4x^3}$ C. $\sqrt{25x^6}$

   D. $\sqrt{8x^5y^7}$

4. Simplify these radical expressions.

   A. $\dfrac{10\sqrt{6}}{5\sqrt{2}}$ B. $\dfrac{3}{\sqrt{5}}$ C. $\sqrt{\dfrac{5}{16}}$ D. $\sqrt{\dfrac{7}{18}}$

SOLUTIONS

1. A. $\sqrt{18} = \sqrt{9}\sqrt{2} = 3\sqrt{2}$

   B. $\sqrt[3]{40} = \sqrt[3]{8} \cdot \sqrt[3]{5} = 2\sqrt[3]{5}\sqrt[3]{5}$

   C. $\sqrt[3]{81} = \sqrt[3]{3^4} = \sqrt[3]{3^3} \cdot \sqrt[3]{3} = 3\sqrt[3]{3}$

   D. $\sqrt{648} = \sqrt{(2^3 \cdot 3^4)} = \sqrt{(2^2 \cdot 3^4)}\sqrt{2} =$
   $2 \cdot 3^2\sqrt{2} = 18\sqrt{2}$

2. A. $\sqrt[4]{9a^2} = \sqrt[4]{(3a)^2} = (3a)^{2/4} = (3a)^{1/2} = \sqrt{3a}$

   B. $\sqrt[6]{125a^3b^3} = \sqrt[6]{(5ab)^3} = (5ab)^{3/6} =$
   $(5ab)^{1/2} = \sqrt{5ab}$

   C. $\sqrt{a^3} = \sqrt{a^2}\sqrt{a} = a\sqrt{a}$

   D. $\sqrt[9]{a^3} = (a)^{3/9} = a^{1/3} = \sqrt[3]{a}$

3. A. $\sqrt{7a^3y^2} = \sqrt{a^2y^2}\sqrt{7a} = ay\sqrt{7a}$

   B. $\sqrt{8b^4x^3} = \sqrt{4b^4x^2}\sqrt{2x} = 2b^2x\sqrt{2x}$

   C. $\sqrt{25x^6} = \sqrt{5^2(x^3)^2} = 5x^3$

   D. $\sqrt{8x^5y^7} = \sqrt{4x^4y^6}\sqrt{2xy} = 2x^2y^3\sqrt{2xy}$

4. A. $\dfrac{10\sqrt{6}}{5\sqrt{2}} = \dfrac{\sqrt{10}}{5} \cdot \dfrac{\sqrt{6}}{\sqrt{2}} = 2 \cdot \sqrt{\dfrac{6}{2}} = 2\sqrt{3}$

   B. $\dfrac{3}{\sqrt{5}} = \dfrac{3}{\sqrt{5}} \cdot \dfrac{\sqrt{5}}{\sqrt{5}} = \dfrac{3\sqrt{5}}{5}$

   C. $\sqrt{\dfrac{5}{16}} = \dfrac{\sqrt{5}}{\sqrt{16}} = \dfrac{\sqrt{5}}{4}$

   D. $\sqrt{\dfrac{7}{18}} = \sqrt{\dfrac{7}{18} \cdot \dfrac{2}{2}} = \sqrt{\dfrac{14}{36}} = \dfrac{\sqrt{14}}{\sqrt{36}} = \dfrac{\sqrt{14}}{6}$

OPERATIONS WITH RADICALS

When adding or subtracting radicals, you can combine them if they are **like radicals**—they have the same index and the same radicand. Like radicals are combined by combining their coefficients.

Example 12

Simplify and combine these radical expressions.

A. $\sqrt{54} - \sqrt{24} + \sqrt{96}$

B. $5\sqrt{40} - 3\sqrt{90}$

C. $15\sqrt{10} - \sqrt{250} + 8\sqrt{90}$

D. $2\sqrt{108y} - \sqrt{27y} + \sqrt{363y}$

E. $\sqrt{p^3} + \sqrt{25p^3} + \sqrt{9p}$

Solution

A. $\sqrt{54} - \sqrt{24} + \sqrt{96} = \sqrt{9}\sqrt{6} - \sqrt{4}\sqrt{6} + \sqrt{16}\sqrt{6} = 3\sqrt{6} - 2\sqrt{6} + 4\sqrt{6} =$
$5\sqrt{6}$

B. $5\sqrt{40} - 3\sqrt{90} = 5\sqrt{4}\sqrt{10} - 3\sqrt{9}\sqrt{10} = 5(2)\sqrt{10} - 3(3)\sqrt{10} =$
$10\sqrt{10} - 9\sqrt{10} = \sqrt{10}$

C. $15\sqrt{10} - \sqrt{250} + 8\sqrt{90} = 15\sqrt{10} - \sqrt{25}\sqrt{10} + 8\sqrt{9}\sqrt{10} =$

$15\sqrt{10} - 5\sqrt{10} + 8(3)\sqrt{10} = 10\sqrt{10} + 24\sqrt{10} = 34\sqrt{10}$

D. $2\sqrt{108y} - \sqrt{27y} + \sqrt{363y} = 2\sqrt{36}\sqrt{3y} - \sqrt{9}\sqrt{3y} + \sqrt{121}\sqrt{3y} =$

$2(6)\sqrt{3y} - 3\sqrt{3y} + 11\sqrt{3y} = 12\sqrt{3y} + 8\sqrt{3y} = 20\sqrt{3y}$

E. $\sqrt{p^3} + \sqrt{25p^3} + \sqrt{9p} = \sqrt{p^2}\sqrt{p} + \sqrt{25p^2}\sqrt{p} + \sqrt{9}\sqrt{p} = p\sqrt{p} +$

$5p\sqrt{p} + 3\sqrt{p} = 6p\sqrt{p} + 3\sqrt{p} = (6p + 3)\sqrt{p}$

When n is a positive integer, and a and b are positive real numbers, $\sqrt[n]{a}\sqrt[n]{b} = \sqrt[n]{ab}$.

For example, $\sqrt{2}\sqrt{3} = \sqrt{2 \cdot 3} = \sqrt{6}$, $\sqrt{2x} \cdot \sqrt{5y} = \sqrt{2x \cdot 5y} = \sqrt{10xy}$

Also, $\dfrac{\sqrt[n]{a}}{\sqrt[n]{b}} = \sqrt[n]{\dfrac{a}{b}}$

Example 13

Multiply these radical expressions.

A. $\sqrt{8} \cdot \sqrt{6}$
B. $(5\sqrt{3})(4\sqrt{5})$
C. $\sqrt{5}(3\sqrt{7} - 2\sqrt{5})$

D. $\sqrt{5}(\sqrt{15} + \sqrt{10})$
E. $(3\sqrt{5x})(5\sqrt{10x})$

Solution

A. $\sqrt{8} \cdot \sqrt{6} = \sqrt{48} = \sqrt{16 \cdot 3} = \sqrt{16}\sqrt{3} = 4\sqrt{3}$

B. $(5\sqrt{3})(4\sqrt{5}) = 5 \cdot 4 \cdot \sqrt{3} \cdot \sqrt{5} = 20\sqrt{15}$

C. $\sqrt{5}(3\sqrt{7} - 2\sqrt{5}) = \sqrt{5}(3\sqrt{7}) + \sqrt{5}(-2\sqrt{5}) = 3\sqrt{35} - 2\sqrt{25} = 3\sqrt{35} - 10$

D. $\sqrt{5}(\sqrt{15} + \sqrt{10}) = \sqrt{5}\sqrt{15} + \sqrt{5}\sqrt{10} = \sqrt{75} + \sqrt{50} = \sqrt{25}\sqrt{3} +$

$\sqrt{25}\sqrt{2} = 5\sqrt{3} + 5\sqrt{2}$

E. $(3\sqrt{5x})(5\sqrt{10x}) = 3 \cdot 5 \cdot \sqrt{5x}\sqrt{10x} = 15\sqrt{50x^2} = 15\sqrt{25x^2}\sqrt{2} =$

$15(5x)\sqrt{2} = 75x\sqrt{2}$

Example 14

Divide the radical expressions.

A. $\dfrac{\sqrt{18}}{\sqrt{2}}$
B. $\dfrac{\sqrt{108y^3}}{\sqrt{3y}}$
C. $\dfrac{\sqrt{3}}{\sqrt{21}}$
D. $\dfrac{\sqrt{5}}{\sqrt{6}}$
E. $\dfrac{8}{3\sqrt{11x}}$

Solution

A. $\dfrac{\sqrt{18}}{\sqrt{2}} = \sqrt{\dfrac{18}{2}} = \sqrt{9} = 3$

B. $\dfrac{\sqrt{108y^3}}{\sqrt{3y}} = \sqrt{\dfrac{108y^3}{3y}} = \sqrt{36y^2} = 6y$

C. $\dfrac{\sqrt{3}}{\sqrt{21}} = \sqrt{\dfrac{3}{21}} = \sqrt{\dfrac{1}{7}} = \sqrt{\dfrac{1}{7} \cdot \dfrac{7}{7}} = \sqrt{\dfrac{7}{49}} = \dfrac{\sqrt{7}}{\sqrt{49}} = \dfrac{\sqrt{7}}{7}$

D. $\dfrac{\sqrt{5}}{\sqrt{6}} = \sqrt{\dfrac{5}{6}} = \sqrt{\dfrac{5}{6} \cdot \dfrac{6}{6}} = \sqrt{\dfrac{30}{36}} = \dfrac{\sqrt{30}}{\sqrt{36}} = \dfrac{\sqrt{30}}{6}$

E. $\dfrac{8}{3\sqrt{11x}} = \dfrac{8}{3\sqrt{11x}} \cdot \dfrac{\sqrt{11x}}{\sqrt{11x}} = \dfrac{8\sqrt{11x}}{3(11x)} = \dfrac{8\sqrt{11x}}{33x}$

PRACTICE PROBLEMS

1. Simplify each expression by combining like terms.

   A. $5\sqrt{11} + 3\sqrt{11}$

   B. $8\sqrt{5} + 2\sqrt{5}$

   C. $7\sqrt{3} - 3\sqrt{3} + 2\sqrt{3}$

   D. $\sqrt{27} + \sqrt{12}$

   E. $3\sqrt{54} + 4\sqrt{6}$

   F. $4\sqrt{72} - 5\sqrt{8} + \sqrt{50}$

   G. $\sqrt{2x^3} + \sqrt{50x^3}$

   H. $\sqrt{75y} - \sqrt{3y} - \sqrt{12y}$

   I. $5\sqrt{108x} - \sqrt{27x}$

2. Find each product and simplify.

   A. $\sqrt{50} \cdot \sqrt{6}$ B. $\sqrt{45} \cdot \sqrt{135}$

   C. $(2\sqrt{7})(5\sqrt{35})$ D. $(2\sqrt{x})(-7\sqrt{y})$

   E. $\sqrt[3]{9}\sqrt[3]{18}$ F. $(\sqrt{x+1})(-3\sqrt{x+1})$

   G. $\sqrt{3}(4 - \sqrt{5})$ H. $\sqrt{6}\sqrt{30}$

   I. $\sqrt{3}(\sqrt{7x} - \sqrt{15y})$

3. Simplify each expression completely.

   A. $\dfrac{3}{\sqrt{6}}$ B. $\dfrac{6}{\sqrt{21}}$ C. $\sqrt{\dfrac{1}{6t}}$ D. $\dfrac{\sqrt{27}}{\sqrt{54}}$

   E. $\dfrac{\sqrt{7}}{\sqrt{27}}$

SOLUTIONS

1. A. $5\sqrt{11} + 3\sqrt{11} = 8\sqrt{11}$

   B. $8\sqrt{5} + 2\sqrt{5} = 10\sqrt{5}$

   C. $7\sqrt{3} - 3\sqrt{3} + 2\sqrt{3} = (7 - 3 + 2)\sqrt{3} = 6\sqrt{3}$

   D. $\sqrt{27} + \sqrt{12} = \sqrt{9}\sqrt{3} + \sqrt{4}\sqrt{3} = 3\sqrt{3} +$
   $2\sqrt{3} = 5\sqrt{3}$

   E. $3\sqrt{54} + 4\sqrt{6} = 3\sqrt{9}\sqrt{6} + 4\sqrt{6} = 3(3)\sqrt{6} +$
   $4\sqrt{6} = 9\sqrt{6} + 4\sqrt{6} = 13\sqrt{6}$

   F. $4\sqrt{72} - 5\sqrt{8} + \sqrt{50} = 4\sqrt{36}\sqrt{2} - 5\sqrt{4}\sqrt{2} +$
   $\sqrt{25}\sqrt{2} = 4(6)\sqrt{2} - 5(2)\sqrt{2} + 5\sqrt{2} =$
   $24\sqrt{2} - 10\sqrt{2} + 5\sqrt{2} = 19\sqrt{2}$

   G. $\sqrt{2x^3} + \sqrt{50x^3} = \sqrt{x^2}\sqrt{2x} + \sqrt{25x^2}\sqrt{2x} =$
   $x\sqrt{2x} + 5x\sqrt{2x} = 6x\sqrt{2x}$

   H. $\sqrt{75y} - \sqrt{3y} - \sqrt{12y} = \sqrt{25}\sqrt{3y} - \sqrt{3y} -$
   $\sqrt{4}\sqrt{3y} = 5\sqrt{3y} - \sqrt{3y} - 2\sqrt{3y} = 2\sqrt{3y}$

   I. $5\sqrt{108x} - \sqrt{27x} = 5\sqrt{36}\sqrt{3x} - \sqrt{9}\sqrt{3x} =$
   $5(6)\sqrt{3x} - 3\sqrt{3x} = 30\sqrt{3x} - 3\sqrt{3x} =$
   $27\sqrt{3x}$

2. A. $\sqrt{50} \cdot \sqrt{6} = \sqrt{300} = \sqrt{100}\sqrt{3} = 10\sqrt{3}$

   B. $\sqrt{45}\sqrt{135} = \sqrt{9}\sqrt{5} \cdot \sqrt{9}\sqrt{15} =$
   $3 \cdot \sqrt{5} \cdot 3\sqrt{15} = 9\sqrt{75} =$
   $9\sqrt{25}\sqrt{3} = 9(5)\sqrt{3} = 45\sqrt{3}$

   C. $(2\sqrt{7})(5\sqrt{35}) = 10\sqrt{245} = 10\sqrt{49}\sqrt{5} =$
   $10(7)\sqrt{5} = 70\sqrt{5}$

   D. $(2\sqrt{x})(-7\sqrt{y}) = -14\sqrt{xy}$

   E. $\sqrt[3]{9}\sqrt[3]{18} = \sqrt[3]{162} = \sqrt[3]{27}\sqrt[3]{6} = 3\sqrt[3]{6}$

   F. $(\sqrt{x+1})(-3\sqrt{x+1}) = -3(x+1) = -3x - 3$

   G. $\sqrt{3}(4 - \sqrt{5}) = 4\sqrt{3} - \sqrt{15}$

   H. $\sqrt{6}\sqrt{30} = \sqrt{180} = \sqrt{36}\sqrt{5} = 6\sqrt{5}$

   I. $\sqrt{3}(\sqrt{7x} - \sqrt{15y}) = \sqrt{21x} - \sqrt{45y} =$
   $\sqrt{21x} - 3\sqrt{5y}$

3. A. $\dfrac{3}{\sqrt{6}} = \dfrac{3}{\sqrt{6}} \cdot \dfrac{\sqrt{6}}{\sqrt{6}} = \dfrac{3\sqrt{6}}{6} = \dfrac{\sqrt{6}}{2}$

 B. $\dfrac{6}{\sqrt{21}} = \dfrac{6}{\sqrt{21}} \cdot \dfrac{\sqrt{21}}{\sqrt{21}} = \dfrac{6\sqrt{21}}{21} = \dfrac{2\sqrt{21}}{7}$

 C. $\sqrt{\dfrac{1}{6t}} = \sqrt{\dfrac{1}{6t} \cdot \dfrac{6t}{6t}} = \sqrt{\dfrac{6t}{(6t)^2}} = \dfrac{\sqrt{6t}}{6t}$

 D. $\dfrac{\sqrt{27}}{\sqrt{54}} = \sqrt{\dfrac{27}{54}} = \sqrt{\dfrac{1}{2}} = \sqrt{\dfrac{1}{2} \cdot \dfrac{2}{2}} = \sqrt{\dfrac{2}{4}} = \dfrac{\sqrt{2}}{2}$

 E. $\dfrac{\sqrt{7}}{\sqrt{27}} = \dfrac{\sqrt{7}}{\sqrt{27}} \cdot \dfrac{\sqrt{3}}{\sqrt{3}} = \dfrac{\sqrt{21}}{\sqrt{81}} = \dfrac{\sqrt{21}}{9}$

▨ TRANSLATING VERBAL EXPRESSIONS INTO ALGEBRAIC EXPRESSIONS

Algebra frequently involves translating English expressions and statements into algebraic expressions and statements.

Keywords for Operations

Operations	Keywords
Addition, +	Sum, total, plus, combined, joined, more than, all together, added to
Subtraction, −	Difference, less than, subtracted from, reduced by, decreased by, minus
Multiplication, ×	Times, product, twice, double, triple, of, multiplied by
Division, ÷	Divided by, ratio of

Example 15

Translate each into an algebraic expression.

A. The sum of x and 2 is less than 10.
B. The product of 3 and x is greater than 15.
C. The sum of 3 times y and 2 is equal to 8.
D. Two less than the product of 10 and x does not equal 100.
E. The product of 5 and y increased by 1 equals 7.
F. Three more than the quotient of w and 4 equals 13.
G. Five-eighths of x is 7.

Solution

A. $x + 2 < 10$
B. $3x > 15$
C. $3y + 2 = 8$
D. $10x - 2 \neq 100$
E. $5y + 1 = 7$
F. $\dfrac{w}{4} + 3 = 13$
G. $\dfrac{5}{8}x = 7$

▨ EVALUATING ALGEBRAIC EXPRESSIONS

You evaluate an algebraic expression by replacing each variable with its value, then using the order of operations to find the value of the expression.

Example 16

Evaluate each expression.

A. $40 - 9x^2$, for $x = -3$

B. $9y - 16y^2$, for $y = 2$

C. $x^2 - 3xy - y + 4$, for $x = 2$ and $y = 3$

D. $5xy - 2x^2y + 7$, for $x = -1$ and $y = -2$

E. $w^3 - w + 8$, for $w = 4$

F. $x^4 - x^3 - 4x + 18$, for $x = 2$

Solution

A. $40 - 9x^2 = 40 - 9(-3)^2 = 40 - 9(9) = 40 - 81 = -41$

B. $9y - 16y^2 = 9(2) - 16(2)^2 = 18 - 16(4) = 18 - 64 = -46$

C. $x^2 - 3xy - y + 4 = (2)^2 - 3(2)(3) - 3 + 4 = 4 - 18 - 3 + 4 = -13$

D. $5xy - 2x^2y + 7 = 5(-1)(-2) - 2(-1)^2(-2) + 7 = 10 + 4 + 7 = 21$

E. $w^3 - w + 8 = 4^3 - 4 + 8 = 64 - 4 + 8 = 68$

F. $x^4 - x^3 - 4x + 18 = 2^4 - 2^3 - 4(2) + 18 = 16 - 8 - 8 + 18 = 18$

EVALUATING FORMULAS

A formula is a special equation in which the left side tells what you are finding, and the right side tells you how to determine the value of the quantity.

To evaluate $C = \dfrac{5}{9}(F - 32)$ when $F = 95$, replace F by 95 to get

$$C = \frac{5}{9}(95 - 32) = \frac{5}{9}(63) = 5(7) = 35$$

Example 17

Evaluate each formula.

A. $P = 2(l + w)$ when $l = 20$ and $w = 15$

B. $S = P(1 + rt)$ when $P = \$4{,}000$, $r = 7\%$, and $t = 5$ years

C. $A = s^2$, when $s = 15$ feet

D. $P = 6s$, when $s = 10$ cm

E. $A = lw$, when $l = 7$ and $w = 5$

F. $V = s^3$, when $s = 7$ inches

G. $S = 6s^2$, when $s = 4$

H. $d = rt$, when $r = 10$ and $t = 3$

Solution

A. $P = 2(l + w) = 2(20 + 15) = 2(35) = 70$

B. $S = P(1 + rt) = \$4{,}000[1 + 0.07(5)] = \$4{,}000(1.35) = \$5{,}400$

C. $A = s^2 = (15 \text{ feet})^2 = 225 \text{ ft}^2$

D. $P = 6s = 6(10 \text{ cm}) = 60 \text{ cm}$

E. $A = lw = 7(5) = 35$

F. $V = s^3 = (7 \text{ inches})^3 = 343 \text{ in}^3$

G. $S = 6s^2 = 6(4)^2 = 6 \cdot 16 = 96$

H. $d = rt = (10)(3) = 30$

PRACTICE PROBLEMS

1. Translate each statement into an algebraic expression.

   A. Twice a number x plus the product of 2 more than the number x and 3 is less than 5.
   B. A number n less 4 times the number is n plus 5.
   C. The difference of x and 8 is less than the product of x and 8.
   D. The cube of a number n less the square of n is 8.
   E. The product of a number x and 7 decreased by 4 is 35
   F. Five times the sum of x and (–4) is equal to 21.
   G. 2 less than a number n is greater than 7.

2. Evaluate each expression when $x = 3$ and $y = -2$.

   A. $5x(2y + 7)$
   B. $2x + 3y - xy$
   C. $x^2 - y^2$
   D. $5(y + 5) - (3 + 2x)$
   E. x^3y^4
   F. $9(x - 2y)$
   G. $x(2y - x)$
   H. $2x - 5y^2$

3. Evaluate each formula.

   A. $I = prt$, for $p = \$8,000, r = 4\%$, and $t = 3$ years
   B. $F = 1.4C + 32$, for $C = 30$
   C. $V = lwh$, for $l = 8, w = 5$, and $h = 6$
   D. $P = 3s$, for $s = 6$
   E. $P = 2l + 2w$, for $l = 16$ feet, $w = 10$ feet
   F. $V = Bh$, for $B = 300$ m$^2, h = 6$ m
   G. $V = s^3$, for $s = 12$ cm

SOLUTIONS

1. A. $2x + (x + 2)3 < 5$
    B. $n - 4n = n + 5$
    C. $x - 8 < 8x$
    D. $n^3 - n^2 = 8$
    E. $7x - 4 = 35$
    F. $5[x + (-4)] = 21$
    G. $n - 2 > 7$

2. A. $5x(2y+7) = 5 \cdot 3[2 \cdot (-2)+7] = 15(-4+7) =$
       $15(3) = 45$
    B. $2x + 3y - xy = 2(3) + 3(-2) - 3(-2) =$
       $6 - 6 + 6 = 6$
    C. $x^2 - y^2 = 3^2 - (-2)^2 = 9 - 4 = 5$
    D. $5(y+5) - (3+2x) = 5(-2+5) - (3+2 \cdot 3) =$
       $5(3) - (3 + 6) = 15 - 9 = 6$
    E. $x^3y^4 = (3)^3(-2)^4 = 27(16) = 432$

    F. $9(x - 2y) = 9[3 - 2(-2)] = 9(3 + 4) =$
       $9(7) = 63$
    G. $x(2y - x) = 3[2(-2) - 3] = 3(-4 - 3) =$
       $3(-7) = -21$
    H. $2x - 5y^2 = 2(3) - 5(-2)^2 = 6 - 5(4) =$
       $6 - 20 = -14$

3. A. $I = prt, (\$8,000)(0.04)(3) = \$960$
    B. $F = 1.4C + 32 = 1.4(30) + 32 = 42 + 32 = 74$
    C. $V = lwh = 8(5)(6) = 240$
    D. $P = 3s = 3(6) = 18$
    E. $P = 2l + 2w = 2(16$ ft$) + 2(10$ ft$) = 32$ ft $+$
       20 ft $= 52$ ft
    F. $V = Bh = (300$ m$^2)(6$ m$) = 1,800$ m^3
    G. $V = s^3 = (12$ cm$)^3 = 1,728$ cm^3

ADDITION AND SUBTRACTION OF ALGEBRAIC EXPRESSIONS

To combine two algebraic expressions by addition or subtraction, you must find the like terms and then add or subtract their coefficients as indicated. Align the problems so that the like terms form a column. When you get the total for a column, write the total and the sign for the term, even if the total has a positive coefficient.

Example 18

Add these expressions.

A. $5x^2 + 3x + 2$
   $+ \underline{3x^2 + 2x + 7}$

B. $2x^2 - 7x + 8$
   $+ \underline{3x^2 - 8x - 12}$

C. $3y^3 - 5y^2 + 6y + 4$
    $2y^3 \qquad + 8y - 7$
   $+ \underline{\qquad 7y^2 - 15y - 5}$

Solution

A. $5x^2 + 3x + 2$ $\qquad 5x^2 + 3x^2 = 8x^2 \qquad 3x + 2x = 5x \qquad 2 + 7 = 9$
   $+ \underline{3x^2 + 2x + 7}$
   $8x^2 + 5x + 9$

B. $2x^2 - 7x + 8$ $\qquad 2x^2 + 3x^2 = 5x^2 \qquad -7x - 8x = -15x \qquad 8 - 12 = -4$
   $+ \underline{3x^2 - 8x - 12}$
   $5x^2 - 15x - 4$

C. $3y^3 - 5y^2 + 6y + 4 \qquad 3y^3 + 2y^3 = 5y^3 \qquad -5y^2 + 7y^2 = 2y^2$
    $2y^3 \qquad + 8y - 7 \qquad 6y + 8y - 15y = -y \qquad 4 - 7 - 5 = -8$
   $+ \underline{7y^2 - 15y - 5}$
   $5y^3 + 2y^2 - y - 8$

Example 19

Subtract these expressions.

A. $-5a^2b + 3ab^2 + 11$
   $- \underline{-7a^2b + 8ab^2 - 18}$

B. $3x^2 - 4x + 6$
   $- \underline{x^2 - 5x + 8}$

C. $9y^3 + 5y^2 - 4$
   $- \underline{4y^3 - 5y + 8}$

Solution

You change the signs of the terms in the subtrahend and add. That is, you change from subtraction to addition of the opposite.

A. $-5a^2b + 3ab^2 + 11$
   $- \underline{-7a^2b + 8ab^2 - 18}$
   $2a^2b - 5ab^2 + 29$

B. $3x^2 - 4x + 6$
   $- \underline{x^2 - 5x + 8}$
   $2x^2 + x - 2$

C. $9y^3 + 5y^2 \qquad - 4$
   $- \underline{4y^3 \qquad - 5y + 8}$
   $5y^3 + 5y^2 + 5y - 12$

MULTIPLICATION OF ALGEBRAIC EXPRESSIONS

When you multiply an algebraic expression by a monomial, you multiply each term in the algebraic expression by the monomial. For example, $3y^2(4y^3 + 7y) = 3y^2(4y^3) + 3y^2(7y) = 3 \cdot 4 \cdot y^2 \cdot y^3 + 3 \cdot 7 \cdot y^2 \cdot y = 12y^{2+3} + 21y^{2+1} = 12y^5 + 21y^3$. Thus, $3y^2(4y^3 + 7y) = 12y^5 + 21y^3$.

Example 20

Find the product of these expressions.

A. $7x(5x - 4)$ $\qquad$ B. $3y^4(y^2 - 5y + 7)$ $\qquad$ C. $-3y^2(-5y^3 - 7y^2 + 12)$

Solution

A. $7x(5x-4) = 7x(5x) + 7x(-4) = 35x^2 - 28x$

B. $3y^4(y^2 - 5y + 7) = 3y^4(y^2) + 3y^4(-5y) + 3y^4(7) = 3y^{4+2} - 15y^{4+1} + 21y^4 = 3y^6 - 15y^5 + 21y^4$

C. $-3y^2(-5y^3 - 7y^2 + 12) = -3y^2(-5y^3) - 3y^2(-7y^2) - 3y^2(12) = 15y^{2+3} + 21y^{2+2} - 36y^2 = 15y^5 + 21y^4 - 36y^2$

When an algebraic expression is multiplied by a binomial, multiply each term in the algebraic expression by each term of the binomial.

Example 21

Find the product of these algebraic expressions.

A. $(3x - 2)(2x + 5)$ 　　　　　　　　　B. $(3x - 5)(2x^2 + 7x - 5)$

Solution

A. $(3x-2)(2x+5) = 3x(2x+5) - 2(2x+5) = 6x^2 + 15x - 4x - 10 = 6x^2 + 11x - 10$

B. $(3x-5)(2x^2+7x-5) = 3x(2x^2) + 3x(7x) + 3x(-5) + (-5)(2x^2) + (-5)(7x) + (-5)(-5) = 6x^3 + 21x^2 - 15x - 10x^2 - 35x + 25 = 6x^3 + 11x^2 - 50x + 25$

Example 22

Multiply these expressions.

A.　$3x^3 - 5xy + 5y^3$ 　　　B.　$2y - 7$ 　　　C.　$x^2 + 2xy - y^2$
　　$\times \quad\quad x - y$ 　　　　　$\times \quad y + 5$ 　　　　$\times \, x - xy + y$

Solution

A.　$3x^3 - 5xy \quad\quad + 5y^3$
　　$\times \underline{\quad\quad\quad\quad x - y \quad\quad\quad\quad}$
　　$3x^4 \quad\quad\quad - 5x^2y + 5xy^3$
　　$\underline{\quad\quad - 3x^3y \quad\quad\quad\quad + 5xy^2 - 5y^4}$
　　$3x^4 - 3x^3y - 5x^2y + 5xy^3 + 5xy^2 - 5y^4$

B.　$2y - 7$
　　$\times \underline{\quad y + 5 \quad}$
　　$2y^2 - \quad 7y$
　　$\underline{\quad\quad + 10y - 35}$
　　$2y^2 + \quad 3y - 35$

C.　$x^2 + 2xy - y^2$
　　$\times \underline{\, x - xy + y \quad}$
　　$x^3 + 2x^2y - xy^2$
　　$\quad\quad\quad\quad - x^3y - 2x^2y^2 + xy^3$
　　$\underline{\quad\quad x^2y + 2xy^2 \quad\quad\quad\quad\quad - y^3}$
　　$x^3 + 3x^2y + xy^2 - x^3y - 2x^2y^2 + xy^3 - y^3$

When you multiply two binomials, you get four terms: $(a + b)(c + d) = ac + ad + bc + bd$, where ac is the product of the **F**irst terms of the binomials;

ad is the product of the **O**uter terms of the two binomials; *bc* is the product of the **I**nner terms of the binomials; and *bd* is the product of the **L**ast terms of the binomials. Because the first letters of the words spell **F O I L**, the method of multiplying binomials is called the FOIL method. Frequently, the outer products and inner products are like terms, and they are combined into a single term.

Using the FOIL method to multiply $(4x - 3y)(x - y)$, you get $4x^2 - 4xy - 3xy + 3y^2 = 4x^2 - 7xy + 3y^2$.

Example 23

Multiply these binomials, using the FOIL method.

A. $(2x + y)(x + 3y)$ B. $(3x - 2y)(2x + 3y)$ C. $(10x - 7)(5x - 8)$

D. $(9x - 7y)(5x - 4y)$ E. $(5x - 7y)(5x + 7y)$ F. $(4x + 9)(4x - 9)$

Solution

A. $(2x+y)(x+3y) = (2x)(x)+(2x)(3y)+y(x)+y(3y) = 2x^2+6xy+xy+3y^2 = 2x^2 + 7xy + 3y^2$

B. $(3x - 2y)(2x + 3y) = (3x)(2x) + (3x)(3y) + (-2y)(2x) + (-2y)(3y) = 6x^2 + 9xy - 4xy - 6y^2 = 6x^2 + 5xy - 6y^2$

C. $(10x - 7)(5x - 8) = 50x^2 - 80x - 35x + 56 = 50x^2 - 115x + 56$

D. $(9x - 7y)(5x - 4y) = 45x^2 - 36xy - 35xy + 28y^2 = 45x^2 - 71xy + 28y^2$

E. $(5x - 7y)(5x + 7y) = 25x^2 + 35xy - 35xy - 49y^2 = 25x^2 - 49y^2$

F. $(4x + 9)(4x - 9) = 16x^2 + 36x - 36x - 81 = 16x^2 - 81$

Some types of binomials are multiplied so often that there are patterns for the way the answer will look. The square of a binomial is one such special product: $(a + b)^2 = a^2 + 2ab + b^2$ and $(a - b)^2 = a^2 - 2ab + b^2$. The product of the sum and difference of two terms is another special product: $(a + b)(a - b) = a^2 - b^2$.

Example 24

Multiply these special products.

A. $(2x - 3y)^2$ B. $(5x + 2y)^2$ C. $(2x + 3y)(2x - 3y)$ D. $(9x - y)(9x + y)$

Solution

A. $(2x - 3y)^2 = (2x)^2 - 2(2x)(3y) + (3y)^2 = 4x^2 - 12xy + 9y^2$

B. $(5x + 2y)^2 = (5x)^2 + 2(5x)(2y) + (2y)^2 = 25x^2 + 20xy + 4y^2$

C. $(2x + 3y)(2x - 3y) = (2x)^2 - (3y)^2 = 4x^2 - 9y^2$

D. $(9x - y)(9x + y) = (9x)^2 - (y)^2 = 81x^2 - y^2$

Sometimes you need to multiply more than two binomials. To do that, use the FOIL method to multiply the first two binomials and then multiply that product by the third binomial. Occasionally, you have the cube of a binomial, which is a special product.

$$(a + b)^3 = a^3 + 3a^2b + 3ab^2 + b^3$$

$$(a - b)^3 = a^3 - 3a^2b + 3ab^2 - b^3$$

Example 25

Multiply these binomials.

A. $(2x - 3y)(x + y)(x - 5y)$

B. $(3x + 2y)(x - y)(2x + y)$

C. $(2x - y)^3$

D. $(3x + 5y)^3$

Solution

A. $(2x - 3y)(x + y)(x - 5y) = (2x^2 - xy - 3y^2)(x - 5y) = 2x^3 - x^2y - 3xy^2 - 10x^2y + 5xy^2 + 15y^3 = 2x^3 - 11x^2y + 2xy^2 + 15y^3$

B. $(3x + 2y)(x - y)(2x + y) = (3x^2 - xy - 2y^2)(2x + y) = 6x^3 - 2x^2y - 4xy^2 + 3x^2y - xy^2 - 2y^3 = 6x^3 + x^2y - 5xy^2 - 2y^3$

C. $(2x - y)^3 = (2x)^3 - 3(2x)^2y + 3(2x)(y)^2 - (y)^3 = 8x^3 - 12x^2y + 6xy^2 - y^3$

D. $(3x + 5y)^3 = (3x)^3 + 3(3x)^2(5y) + 3(3x)(5y)^2 + (5y)^3 = 27x^3 + 3(9x^2)(5y) + 9x(25y^2) + 125y^3 = 27x^3 + 135x^2y + 225xy^2 + 125y^3$

DIVISION OF ALGEBRAIC EXPRESSIONS

When you divide one monomial by another monomial, use integer divisions and the laws of exponents. For example,

$$\frac{6x^2y}{2xy} = \frac{6}{2} \cdot \frac{x^2}{x} \cdot \frac{y}{y} = 3x \cdot 1 = 3x$$

and

$$\frac{12x^6y^7}{-4x^4y^9} = \frac{12}{-4} \cdot \frac{x^6}{x^4} \cdot \frac{y^7}{y^9} = -3 \cdot \frac{x^2}{y^2} = \frac{-3x^2}{y^2}$$

Example 26

Divide these monomials.

A. $14x^3yz \div 7x^5yz^2$ B. $9xy^2 \div -3x^4y$ C. $10y^7 \div 4y^3$ D. $\dfrac{36x^2y^7z^3}{15x^2y^5z^5}$

Solution

A. $\dfrac{14x^3yz}{7x^5yz^2} = \dfrac{14}{7} \cdot \dfrac{x^3}{x^5} \cdot \dfrac{y}{y} \cdot \dfrac{z}{z^2} = 2 \cdot \dfrac{1}{x^2} \cdot 1 \cdot \dfrac{1}{z} = \dfrac{2}{x^2z}$

B. $\dfrac{9xy^2}{-3x^4y} = \dfrac{9}{-3} \cdot \dfrac{x}{x^4} \cdot \dfrac{y^2}{y} = -3 \cdot \dfrac{1}{x^3} \cdot \dfrac{y}{1} = \dfrac{-3y}{x^3}$

C. $\dfrac{10y^7}{4y^3} = \dfrac{10}{4} \cdot \dfrac{y^7}{y^3} = \dfrac{5}{2} \cdot \dfrac{y^4}{1} = \dfrac{5y^4}{2}$

D. $\dfrac{36x^2y^7z^3}{15x^2y^5z^5} = \dfrac{36}{15} \cdot \dfrac{x^2}{x^2} \cdot \dfrac{y^7}{y^5} \cdot \dfrac{z^3}{z^5} = \dfrac{12}{5} \cdot 1 \cdot \dfrac{y^2}{1} \cdot \dfrac{1}{z^2} = \dfrac{12y^2}{5z^2}$

Example 27

Divide the polynomial by the monomial.

A. $(9ab^2 - 6a^2) \div 3a$ B. $(15x^2y^5 - 25x^4y^3) \div (-5xy^2)$

C. $(4x^2y^3 - 16xy^3 + 4xy) \div (2xy)$ D. $[16(a+b)^4 + 12(a+b)^3] \div [2(a+b)]$

Solution

A. $\dfrac{9ab^2 - 6a^2}{3a} = \dfrac{9ab^2}{3a} + \dfrac{-6a^2}{3a} = 3b^2 - 2a$

B. $\dfrac{15x^2y^5 - 25x^4y^3}{-5xy^2} = \dfrac{15x^2y^5}{-5xy^2} + \dfrac{-25x^4y^3}{-5xy^2} = -3xy^3 + 5x^3y$

C. $\dfrac{4x^2y^3 - 16xy^3 + 4xy}{2xy} = \dfrac{4x^2y^3}{2xy} + \dfrac{-16xy^3}{2xy} + \dfrac{4xy}{2xy} = 2xy^2 - 8y^2 + 2$

D. $\dfrac{16(a+b)^4 + 12(a+b)^3}{2(a+b)} = \dfrac{16(a+b)^4}{2(a+b)} + \dfrac{12(a+b)^3}{2(a+b)} = 8(a+b)^3 + 6(a+b)^2$

▮ PRACTICE PROBLEMS

1. Add these algebraic expressions.

    A. $2x^2 + y^2 - x + y$

       $-x^2 + 3y^2 - x$

    $+ x^2 - 4y^2 + x - 2y$

    B. $x^2 - xy + 2yz + 3z^2$

    $+ x^2 + 2xy - 3yz - 8z^2$

    C. $5x^3 - 4x^2 + 7x - 4$

    $+ 3x^3 + 11x^2 - 17x + 12$

2. Subtract these algebraic expressions.

    A. $3xy - 2yz + 4xz$ B. $3x^4 - 7x^2 + 8x$

       $-2xy + yz + 3xz$ $-5x^4 - 7x + 12$

    C. $3x^2 - 5xy - y^2$

      $- x^2 - 5xy + 14y^2$

3. Multiply these algebraic expressions.

    A. $5x^2 + 3xy + y^2$ B. $5x^3 + 2x - 4$

      $\times 2x - y$ $\times 3x - 2$

    C. $3x + 7y$

      $\times \underline{5x - 2y}$

4. Multiply these algebraic expressions.

    A. $(4x^2y^5)(-2xy)$ B. $(a^2b^3c)(abc)(ab^3c^3)$

    C. $(-3x^2y)(3xy)(-4xy)$

5. Multiply these algebraic expressions.

    A. $(3-x-2y)(2x-y)$

    B. $(x^3+x^2y+xy^2+y^3)(2x^2y)$

6. Multiply these binomials.

    A. $(y+3)(y+7)$ B. $(2x+5)(3x-7)$

    C. $(2x-y)(x+5y)$ D. $(2x+3y)(2x-3y)$

    E. $(x+3y)^2$ F. $(5x-4)(5x+4)$

7. Multiply these binomials.

    A. $(x+2)(3x-1)(2x+3)$ B. $(5x-2y)^3$

8. Divide as indicated.

    A. $\dfrac{-12a^4b^7c^3}{3a^2b^4c}$ B. $\dfrac{-16r^{10}s^3t^4}{-4r^7st^3}$

    C. $\dfrac{4ab^3 - 6a^2bc + 12a^3b^2c^4}{-2ab}$

▮▮ SOLUTIONS

1. A. $2x^2 + y^2 - x + y$
         $-x^2 + 3y^2 - x$
     $+ \quad x^2 - 4y^2 + x - 2y$
     $\overline{ 2x^2 \qquad - x - y}$

   B. $x^2 - xy + 2yz + 3z^2$
     $+ \quad x^2 + 2xy - 3yz - 8z^2$
     $\overline{2x^2 + xy - yz - 5z^2}$

   C. $5x^3 - 4x^2 + 7x - 4$
     $+ 3x^3 + 11x^2 - 17x + 12$
     $\overline{8x^3 + 7x^2 - 10x + 8}$

2. A. $3xy - 2yz + 4xz$
     $- \quad 2xy + yz + 3xz$
     $\overline{5xy - 3yz + xz}$

   B. $3x^4 - 7x^2 + 8x$
     $- \quad 5x^4 \qquad - 7x + 12$
     $\overline{-2x^4 - 7x^2 + 15x - 12}$

   C. $3x^2 - 5xy - y^2$
     $- \quad x^2 - 5xy + 14y^2$
     $\overline{2x^2 \qquad - 15y^2}$

3. A. $5x^2 + 3xy + y^2$
     $\times \quad \underline{\qquad 2x - y}$
     $10x^3 + 6x^2y - 2xy^2$
     $\underline{\qquad - 5x^2y - 3xy^2 - y^3}$
     $10x^3 + x^2y - xy^2 - y^3$

   B. $5x^3 + 2x - 4$
     $\times \quad \underline{\qquad 3x - 2}$
     $15x^4 \qquad + 6x^2 - 12x$
     $\underline{\quad - 10x^3 \qquad - 4x + 8}$
     $15x^4 - 10x^3 + 6x^2 - 16x + 8$

   C. $3x + 7y$
     $\times \underline{5x - 2y}$
     $15x^2 + 35xy$
     $\underline{\qquad - 6xy - 14y^2}$
     $15x^2 + 29xy - 14y^2$

4. A. $(4x^2y^5)(-2xy) = -8x^3y^6$

   B. $(a^2b^3c)(abc)(ab^3c^3) = a^4b^7c^5$

   C. $(-3x^2y)(3xy)(-4xy) = 36x^4y^3$

5. A. $(3 - x - 2y)(2x - y) = 6x - 2x^2 - 4xy - 3y + xy + 2y^2 = 6x - 2x^2 - 3xy - 3y + 2y^2$

   B. $(x^3 + x^2y + xy^2 + y^3)(2x^2y) = 2x^5y + 2x^4y^2 + 2x^3y^3 + 2x^2y^4$

6. A. $(y + 3)(y + 7) = y^2 + 7y + 3y + 21 = y^2 + 10y + 21$

   B. $(2x + 5)(3x - 7) = 6x^2 - 14x + 15x - 35 = 6x^2 + x - 35$

   C. $(2x - y)(x + 5y) = 2x^2 + 10xy - xy - 5y^2 = 2x^2 + 9xy - 5y^2$

   D. $(2x + 3y)(2x - 3y) = (2x)^2 - (3y)^2 = 4x^2 - 9y^2$

   E. $(x + 3y)^2 = x^2 + 2(x)(3y) + (3y)^2 = x^2 + 6xy + 9y^2$

   F. $(5x - 4)(5x + 4) = (5x)^2 - (4)^2 = 25x^2 - 16$

7. A. $(x + 2)(3x - 1)(2x + 3) = [3x^2 + 5x - 2](2x + 3) = 6x^3 + 10x^2 - 4x + 9x^2 + 15x - 6 = 6x^3 + 19x^2 + 11x - 6$

   B. $(5x - 2y)^3 = (5x)^3 - 3(5x)^2(2y) + 3(5x)(2y)^2 - (2y)^3 = 125x^3 - 150x^2y + 60xy^2 - 8y^3$

8. A. $\dfrac{-12a^4b^7c^3}{3a^2b^4c} = -\dfrac{12}{3} \cdot \dfrac{a^4}{a^2} \cdot \dfrac{b^7}{b^4} \cdot \dfrac{c^3}{c} = -4a^2b^3c^2$

   B. $\dfrac{-16r^{10}s^3t^4}{-4r^7st^3} = \dfrac{-16}{-4} \cdot \dfrac{r^{10}}{r^7} \cdot \dfrac{s^3}{s} \cdot \dfrac{t^4}{t^3} = 4r^3s^2t$

   C. $\dfrac{4ab^3 - 6a^2bc + 12a^3b^2c^4}{-2ab} = \dfrac{4ab^3}{-2ab} + \dfrac{-6a^2bc}{-2ab} + \dfrac{12a^3b^2c^4}{-2ab} = -2b^2 + 3ac - 6a^2bc^4$

ALGEBRAIC FRACTIONS

One concern with algebraic fractions is that you must be sure that the fraction is defined. Thus, you need to know what values of the variable will result in the denominator becoming zero and then exclude those values.

Example 28

For what values of the variable will the fraction not be defined?

A. $\dfrac{3x}{x-7}$ B. $\dfrac{y+6}{y+10}$ C. $\dfrac{3x-1}{(x+6)(x-5)}$ D. $\dfrac{3y-5}{(y-1)(2y+1)}$

Solution

A. $\dfrac{3x}{x-7}$ Denominator is zero when $x = 7$

B. $\dfrac{y+6}{y+10}$ Denominator is zero when $y = -10$

C. $\dfrac{3x-1}{(x+6)(x-5)}$ Denominator is zero when either factor is zero, so when $x = -6$ or $x = 5$

D. $\dfrac{3y-5}{(y-1)(2y+1)}$ Denominator is zero when $y = 1$ or $-\dfrac{1}{2}$

To simplify algebraic fractions to the lowest terms, use the distributive property to find the common factor between numerator and denominator.

Example 29

Reduce each fraction to lowest terms.

A. $\dfrac{15x}{3x^2}$ B. $\dfrac{25x^2y^5}{45x^3y^2}$ C. $\dfrac{m^2+m}{m^2-m}$ D. $\dfrac{mn}{m^2-5m}$

Solution

A. $\dfrac{15x}{3x^2} = \dfrac{3\cdot5x}{3\cdot x\cdot x} = \dfrac{3x}{3x}\cdot\dfrac{5}{x} = 1\cdot\dfrac{5}{x} = \dfrac{5}{x}$

B. $\dfrac{25x^2y^5}{45x^3y^2} = \dfrac{5x^2y^2\cdot5y^3}{5x^2y^2\cdot9x} = \dfrac{5x^2y^2}{5x^2y^2}\cdot\dfrac{5y^3}{9x} = 1\cdot\dfrac{5y^3}{9x} = \dfrac{5y^3}{9x}$

C. $\dfrac{m^2+m}{m^2-m} = \dfrac{m\cdot m+m\cdot1}{m\cdot m-m\cdot1} = \dfrac{m(m+1)}{m(m-1)} = \dfrac{m+1}{m-1}$

D. $\dfrac{mn}{m^2-5m} = \dfrac{mn}{m(m-5)} = \dfrac{n}{m-5}$

FACTORING ALGEBRAIC EXPRESSIONS

When factoring polynomials, first look for a common monomial factor in each term. For example, $15x + 35 = 5(3x) + 5(7) = 5(3x + 7)$.

Example 30

Factor each polynomial by factoring out the common monomial factor.

A. $2y^3 + 4y^2$ B. $4y^5 + 8y^3$ C. $3x^3y^4 - 9x^2y^3 - 6xy^2$ D. $-2x^2y - 8xy^2$

Solution

A. $2y^3 + 4y^2 = 2y^2(y) + 2y^2(2) = 2y^2(y+2)$

B. $4y^5 + 8y^3 = 4y^3(y^2) + 4y^3(2) = 4y^3(y^2+2)$

C. $3x^3y^4 - 9x^2y^3 - 6xy^2 = 3xy^2(x^2y^2 - 3xy - 2)$

D. $-2x^2y - 8xy^2 = -2xy(x+4y)$

When you have four-term expressions, factor the expression by grouping the terms into two groups of two terms and then factoring out a common monomial factor to get a common quantity. Finally, factor the common quantity out of each term. For example,

$ax + 4x + ay + 4y = (ax + 4x) + (ay + 4y) = x(a+4) + y(a+4) = (a+4)(x+y)$

Example 31

Factor each polynomial by using grouping.

A. $5xy + 5xz + 2y + 2z$ B. $ac - ad - 2c + 2d$

C. $3xm + 3ym - 2x - 2y$ D. $3a^2 + 3ab + a + b$

Solution

A. $5xy + 5xz + 2y + 2z = (5xy + 5xz) + (2y + 2z) = 5x(y+z) + 2(y+z) = (y+z)(5x+2)$

B. $ac - ad - 2c + 2d = (ac-ad) + (-2c+2d) = a(c-d) - 2(c-d) = (c-d)(a-2)$

C. $3xm + 3ym - 2x - 2y = (3xm+3ym) + (-2x-2y) = 3m(x+y) - 2(x+y) = (x+y)(3m-2)$

D. $3a^2 + 3ab + a + b = (3a^2+3ab) + (a+b) = 3a(a+b) + 1(a+b) = (a+b)(3a+1)$

Special products can be used to factor algebraic expressions. Since $(a+b)(a-b) = a^2 - b^2$, you can factor the difference of two squares into the sum and the difference of the square roots of the terms. A perfect-square trinomial has two perfect-square terms, and the third term, usually in the middle, is plus or minus 2 times the square roots of the other terms. Since $(a+b)^2 = a^2 + 2ab + b^2$ and $(a-b)^2 = a^2 - 2ab + b^2$, you have the squares of two terms and twice the products of those terms.

Example 32

Factor these algebraic expressions by using special products.

A. $25a^2 - 9$ B. $x^2 + 4x + 4$ C. $4 - x^2$ D. $4x^2 - 20xy + 25y^2$

Solution

A. $25a^2 - 9 = (5a)^2 - 3^2 = (5a+3)(5a-3)$

B. $x^2 + 4x + 4 = (x)^2 + 2(x)(2) + 2^2 = (x+2)^2$

C. $4 - x^2 = 2^2 - x^2 = (2+x)(2-x)$

D. $4x^2 - 20xy + 25y^2 = (2x)^2 - 2(2x)(5y) + (5y)^2 = (2x-5y)^2$

Other expressions can be factored by using the FOIL method, especially when the first term is just the variable squared. For example, $x^2 + 6x + 5$ can be factored by using the fact that you want factors of 5 that add up to 6: $(x+1)(x+5) = x^2 + 6x + 5$.

Example 33

Factor each trinomial.

A. $x^2 - 9x + 20$ B. $x^2 + 7x + 12$ C. $x^2 - 29x - 30$

Solution

A. $x^2 - 9x + 20$ Since the first term is x^2, each binomial will have a first term of x.

$(x \quad)(x \quad)$ Since the constant term is positive and the middle term
$(x -)(x -)$ is negative, the signs for the binomials are "$-$."

You need two factors of 20 that add together to total 9.
$1(20) = 20, 1 + 20 = 21; 2(10) = 20, 2 + 10 = 12.$
$(x - 5)(x - 4)$ $5(4) = 20, 5 + 4 = 9$

You can check the answer by FOIL.

B. $x^2 + 7x + 12$ Since the first term is x^2, each binomial will have a first term of x.

$(x \quad)(x \quad)$ Since the constant term is positive and the middle term
$(x +)(x +)$ is positive, the signs for the binomials are "$+$."
$(x + 3)(x + 4)$ Two factors of 12 that have a sum of 7 are 3 and 4.

C. $x^2 - 29x - 30$ Since the first term is x^2, each binomial will have a first term of x.

$(x \quad)(x \quad)$ Since the constant term is negative, one binomial has a
$(x +)(x -)$ $+$ sign, and the other has a $-$ sign.

You need two factors of 30 that have a difference of -29.
$(x + 1)(x - 30)$ $1(30) = 30, 1 - 30 = -29.$ Therefore, the 1 is placed with the binomial that has the $+$ sign, and the 30 is placed with the other binomial.

When the trinomial is in the form of $a^2 + bx + c$, you use the "ac" method to find two numbers that add together to yield b. For example, $6m^2 - 11m - 10, a = 6, b = -11, c = -10$, and $ac = -60$. You need two factors of -60, one positive and one negative, that will add together to yield -11. Now $4(15) = 60$ and $4 - 15 = -11$, so you want 4 and -15 as your factors of -60. Thus, $6m^2 - 11m - 10 = 6m^2 + (4 - 15)m - 10 = 6m^2 + 4m - 15m - 10$. Then you use factoring by grouping: $6m^2 + 4m - 15m - 10 = (6m^2 + 4m) + (-15m - 10) = 2m(3m + 2) - 5(3m + 2) = (3m + 2)(2m - 5)$.

Example 34

Factor the trinomials.

A. $12a^2 + 5ab - 3b^2$ B. $6x^2 + 13x + 6$ C. $4x^2 - 35xy - 9y^2$

Solution

A. $12a^2 + 5ab - 3b^2$ $a = 12, b = 5, c = -3, ac = 12(-3) = -36$
$12a^2 + (-4 + 9)ab - 3b^2$ You need two factors of -36 that sum to 5.
$12a^2 - 4ab + 9ab - 3b^2$ $-4(9) = -36$ and $-4 + 9 = 5$.
$(12a^2 - 4ab) + (9ab - 3b^2)$ Group the terms.
$4a(3a - b) + 3b(3a - b)$ Factor each binomial.
$(3a - b)(4a + 3b)$ Factor the binomial out of each term.

Thus, $12a^2 + 5ab - 3b^2 = (3a - b)(4a + 3b)$.

B. $6x^2 + 13x + 6$
$6x^2 + (4 + 9)x + 6$
$6x^2 + 4x + 9x + 6$
$(6x^2 + 4x) + (9x + 6)$
$2x(3x + 2) + 3(3x + 2)$
$(3x + 2)(2x + 3)$

$a = 6, b = 13, c = 6, ac = 6(6) = 36$, so both factors have the same sign. In this case, b is positive, so both factors are positive. $36 = 4(9)$ and $4 + 9 = 13$

So, $6x^2 + 13x + 6 = (3x + 2)(2x + 3)$.

C. $4x^2 - 35xy - 9y^2$
$4x^2 + (1 - 36)xy - 9y^2$
$4x^2 + xy - 36xy - 9y^2$

$a = 4, b = -35, c = -9, ac = -36$, so the factors of ac have opposite signs. You need two factors of -36 that sum to -35.

$(4x^2 + xy) + (-36xy - 9y^2)$ $-36 = 1(-36)$ and $1 - 36 = -35$
$x(4x + y) - 9y(4x + y)$
$(4x + y)(x - 9y)$

So, $4x^2 - 35xy - 9y^2 = (4x + y)(x - 9y)$.

PRACTICE PROBLEMS

1. Reduce these fractions to lowest terms.

A. $\dfrac{35a^5b^4c^5}{7a^2b^8c^4}$ B. $\dfrac{3x - 6}{12x - 15}$ C. $\dfrac{2x + 5xy}{x^2y^2}$

2. Reduce these fractions to lowest terms.

A. $\dfrac{xy - 5y}{5x - 25}$ B. $\dfrac{2x + 4}{7x + 14}$ C. $\dfrac{x^2 - x}{xy - y}$

3. Factor these expressions.

A. $25x^2 - 9y^2$ B. $5x^2 - 10xy + 30y$
C. $x^4 - 1$ D. $ax + bx - ay - by$

E. $12x^2 - 30x^5$ F. $64a^2 - 49b^2$
G. $x^2 - 5xy - 36y^2$ H. $6y^2 - y - 15$
I. $4x^2 - 12x + 9$ J. $2x^2y + 6x^2 + 3a + ay$
K. $3x^2 + 5x - 28$ L. $20x^2 - 31xy + 12y^2$

4. Factor and reduce these fractions.

A. $\dfrac{7x^2 - 5xy}{49x^3 - 25xy^2}$ B. $\dfrac{3x^2 + 7x + 4}{3x^2 + x - 4}$
C. $\dfrac{y^2 + 4y}{y^2 + 6y + 8}$ D. $\dfrac{4x^2 - 9}{6x^2 - 9x}$

SOLUTIONS

1. A. $\dfrac{35a^5b^4c^5}{7a^2b^8c^4} = \dfrac{35}{7} \cdot \dfrac{a^5}{a^2} \cdot \dfrac{b^4}{b^8} \cdot \dfrac{c^5}{c^4} = \dfrac{5}{1} \cdot \dfrac{a^3}{1} \cdot \dfrac{1}{b^4} \cdot \dfrac{c}{1} = \dfrac{5a^3c}{b^4}$

B. $\dfrac{3x - 6}{12x - 15} = \dfrac{3(x - 2)}{3(4x - 5)} = \dfrac{x - 2}{4x - 5}$

C. $\dfrac{2x + 5xy}{x^2y^2} = \dfrac{x(2 + 5y)}{x^2y^2} = \dfrac{2 + 5y}{xy^2}$

2. A. $\dfrac{xy - 5y}{5x - 25} = \dfrac{y(x - 5)}{5(x - 5)} = \dfrac{y}{5}$

B. $\dfrac{2x + 4}{7x + 14} = \dfrac{2(x + 2)}{7(x + 2)} = \dfrac{2}{7}$

C. $\dfrac{x^2 - x}{xy - y} = \dfrac{x(x - 1)}{y(x - 1)} = \dfrac{x}{y}$

3. A. $25x^2 - 9y^2 = (5x)^2 - (3y)^2 = (5x + 3y)(5x - 3y)$

B. $5x^2 - 10xy + 30y = 5(x^2 - 2xy + 6y)$

C. $x^4 - 1 = (x^2) - 1^2 = (x^2 + 1)(x^2 - 1) = (x^2 + 1) \times (x + 1)(x - 1)$

D. $ax + bx - ay - by = (ax + bx) + (-ay - by) = x(a + b) - y(a + b) = (a + b)(x - y)$

E. $12x^2 - 30x^5 = 6x^2(2 - 5x^3)$

F. $64a^2 - 49b^2 = (8a)^2 - (7b)^2 = (8a + 7b)(8a - 7b)$

G. $x^2 - 5xy - 36y^2 = (x + 4y)(x - 9y)$

H. $6y^2 - y - 15 = 6y^2 + 9y - 10y - 15 =$
$(6y^2 + 9y) + (-10y - 15) = 3y(2y + 3) -$
$5(2y + 3) = (2y + 3)(3y - 5)$

I. $4x^2 - 12x + 9 = (2x)^2 - 2(2x)3 + 3^2 = (2x-3)^2$

J. $2x^2y + 6x^2 + 3a + ay = 2x^2(y+3) + a(3+y) =$
$(y + 3)(2x^2 + a)$

K. $3x^2 + 5x - 28 = 3x^2 - 7x + 12x - 28 =$
$x(3x - 7) + 4(3x - 7) = (3x - 7)(x + 4)$

L. $20x^2 - 31xy + 12y^2 = 20x^2 - 15xy - 16xy +$
$12y^2 = 5x(4x - 3y) - 4y(4x - 3y) =$
$(4x - 3y)(5x - 4y)$

4. A. $\dfrac{7x^2 - 5xy}{49x^3 - 25xy^2} = \dfrac{x(7x - 5y)}{x(49x^2 - 25y^2)} =$

$\dfrac{x(7x - 5y)}{x(7x + 5y)(7x - 5y)} = \dfrac{1}{7x + 5y}$

B. $\dfrac{3x^2 + 7x + 4}{3x^2 + x - 4} = \dfrac{(3x + 4)(x + 1)}{(3x + 4)(x - 1)} = \dfrac{x + 1}{x - 1}$

C. $\dfrac{y^2 + 4y}{y^2 + 6y + 8} = \dfrac{y(y + 4)}{(y + 2)(y + 4)} = \dfrac{y}{y + 2}$

D. $\dfrac{4x^2 - 9}{6x^2 - 9x} = \dfrac{(2x + 3)(2x - 3)}{3x(2x - 3)} = \dfrac{2x + 3}{3x}$

OPERATIONS WITH ALGEBRAIC FRACTIONS

In addition and subtraction of algebraic fractions, you use factoring to help find the least common denominator for the fractions and to reduce the answer to the lowest terms.

Example 35

Combine these fractions and reduce to lowest terms.

A. $\dfrac{7}{10x} + \dfrac{8}{15x}$ B. $\dfrac{3}{4a} + \dfrac{5}{6ab}$ C. $\dfrac{5}{x^2y} - \dfrac{3}{xy^3}$

D. $\dfrac{2}{x^2 - x} - \dfrac{5}{x^2 - 1}$ E. $\dfrac{3}{a^2 - 2a - 8} + \dfrac{4}{a^2 + 2a}$ F. $\dfrac{5}{x - 6} - \dfrac{5}{6 - x}$

Solution

A. LCD$(10x, 15x) = 30x$

$\dfrac{7}{10x} + \dfrac{8}{15x} = \dfrac{21}{30x} + \dfrac{16}{30x} = \dfrac{37}{30x}$

B. LCD$(4a, 6ab) = 12ab$

$\dfrac{3}{4a} + \dfrac{5}{6ab} = \dfrac{9b}{12ab} + \dfrac{10}{12ab} = \dfrac{9b + 10}{12ab}$

C. LCD$(x^2y, xy^3) = x^2y^3$

$\dfrac{5}{x^2y} - \dfrac{3}{xy^3} = \dfrac{5y^2}{x^2y^3} - \dfrac{3x}{x^2y^3} = \dfrac{5y^2 - 3x}{x^2y^3}$

D. LCD $= x(x - 1)(x + 1)$

$\dfrac{2}{x^2 - x} - \dfrac{5}{x^2 - 1} = \dfrac{2}{x(x - 1)} - \dfrac{5}{(x + 1)(x - 1)}$

$= \dfrac{2(x + 1)}{x(x + 1)(x - 1)} - \dfrac{5x}{x(x + 1)(x - 1)}$

$= \dfrac{2x + 2 - 5x}{x(x + 1)(x - 1)} = \dfrac{-3x + 2}{x(x + 1)(x - 1)}$

E. $LCD = a(a + 2)(a - 4)$

$$\frac{3}{a^2 - 2a - 8} + \frac{4}{a^2 + 2a} = \frac{3}{(a - 4)(a + 2)} + \frac{4}{a(a + 2)}$$

$$= \frac{3a}{a(a - 4)(a + 2)} + \frac{4(a - 4)}{a(a - 4)(a + 2)}$$

$$= \frac{3a + 4a - 16}{a(a - 4)(a + 2)} = \frac{7a - 16}{a(a - 4)(a + 2)}$$

F. $\dfrac{5}{x - 6} - \dfrac{5}{6 - x}$ Since $6 - x = -1(x - 6)$, change the second fraction.

$$\frac{5}{x - 6} - \frac{5}{-(x - 6)} = \frac{5}{x - 6} + \frac{5}{x - 6} = \frac{5 + 5}{x - 6} = \frac{10}{x - 6}$$

When you multiply and divide fractions, factor the numerator and denominator of each fraction and reduce fractions if possible. Then write the indicated product of the numerator factors over the indicated product of the denominator factors. In a product, you may cancel a numerator factor with a common factor in any denominator.

Example 36

Multiply these fractions.

A. $\dfrac{x^3 y^2}{x^2 y} \cdot \dfrac{x y^3}{x^3 y^2}$ B. $\dfrac{a}{a - 1} \cdot \dfrac{a^2 - 1}{a^3}$ C. $\dfrac{6x - 6}{x^2 + 2x} \cdot \dfrac{x^2 + 4x + 4}{2x^2 + 2x - 4}$

Solution

A. $\dfrac{x^3 y^2}{x^2 y} \cdot \dfrac{x y^3}{x^3 y^2} = \dfrac{x \cdot y}{1 \cdot 1} \cdot \dfrac{1 \cdot y}{x^2 \cdot 1} = \dfrac{x y^2}{x^2} = \dfrac{y^2}{x}$

B. $\dfrac{a}{a - 1} \cdot \dfrac{a^2 - 1}{a^3} = \dfrac{a(a + 1)(a - 1)}{(a - 1)a^3} = \dfrac{a(a - 1)(a + 1)}{a(a - 1)a^2} = \dfrac{a + 1}{a^2}$

C. $\dfrac{6x - 6}{x^2 + 2x} \cdot \dfrac{x^2 + 4x + 4}{2x^2 + 2x - 4} = \dfrac{6(x - 1)}{x(x + 2)} \cdot \dfrac{(x + 2)(x + 2)}{2(x + 2)(x - 1)}$

$$= \frac{6(x - 1)(x + 2)(x + 2)}{2x(x - 1)(x + 2)(x + 2)} = \frac{3}{x}$$

Example 37

Divide these fractions.

A. $\dfrac{3x^2}{5y} \div \dfrac{2x^3}{6y^3}$ B. $\dfrac{a + b}{4} \div \dfrac{(a + b)^3}{12}$ C. $\dfrac{y^2 + 5y + 6}{y^2 - 4} \div \dfrac{y^2 + 4y + 4}{y^2 - 4y + 4}$

Solution

A. $\dfrac{3x^2}{5y} \div \dfrac{2x^3}{6y^3} = \dfrac{3x^2}{5y} \cdot \dfrac{6y^3}{2x^3} = \dfrac{3x^2 \cdot 6y^3}{5y \cdot 2x^3} = \dfrac{2x^2 \cdot y^2 \cdot 3 \cdot 3 \cdot y}{2 \cdot x^2 \cdot y \cdot 5 \cdot x} = \dfrac{9y^2}{5x}$

B. $\dfrac{a+b}{4} \div \dfrac{(a+b)^3}{12} = \dfrac{a+b}{4} \cdot \dfrac{12}{(a+b)^3} = \dfrac{4(a+b)3}{4(a+b)(a+b)^2} = \dfrac{3}{(a+b)^2}$

C. $\dfrac{y^2 + 5y + 6}{y^2 - 4} \div \dfrac{y^2 + 4y + 4}{y^2 - 4y + 4} = \dfrac{(y+2)(y+3)}{(y+2)(y-2)} \cdot \dfrac{(y-2)^2}{(y+2)^2} = \dfrac{(y+3)(y-2)}{(y+2)^2}$

Example 38

Combine these fractions as indicated.

A. $\dfrac{x^2 - x}{y^2 - 1} \cdot \dfrac{y-1}{x^2 y - xy} \div \dfrac{y-1}{y^2}$ B. $\dfrac{2a-1}{2a^2 + 2a} \div \dfrac{6a^2 - 6}{4a^2 + a - 3} \cdot \dfrac{4a^3 - 4a}{8a^2 - 10a + 3}$

Solution

A. $\dfrac{x^2 - x}{y^2 - 1} \cdot \dfrac{y-1}{x^2 y - xy} \div \dfrac{y-1}{y^2} = \dfrac{x(x-1)}{(y+1)(y-1)} \cdot \dfrac{y-1}{xy(x-1)} \cdot \dfrac{y^2}{y-1} =$

$\dfrac{xy^2(x-1)(y-1)}{xy(y+1)(y-1)(x-1)(y-1)} = \dfrac{y}{(y+1)(y-1)}$ or $\dfrac{y}{y^2 - 1}$

B. $\dfrac{2a-1}{2a^2 + 2a} \div \dfrac{6a^2 - 6}{4a^2 + a - 3} \cdot \dfrac{4a^3 - 4a}{8a^2 - 10a + 3}$

$= \dfrac{2a-1}{2a(a+1)} \cdot \dfrac{(4a+3)(a+1)}{6(a+1)(a-1)} \cdot \dfrac{4a(a+1)(a-1)}{(4a-3)(2a-1)}$

$= \dfrac{4a(2a-1)(4a-3)(a+1)(a+1)(a-1)}{12a(2a-1)(4a-3)(a+1)(a+1)(a-1)} = \dfrac{1}{3}$

▨ PRACTICE PROBLEMS

1. Add or subtract as indicated and simplify the results.

A. $\dfrac{11}{18ab} + \dfrac{1}{18ab}$ B. $\dfrac{3x}{x-4} + \dfrac{2}{x+1}$

C. $\dfrac{3}{2a^2 - a - 1} - \dfrac{2}{a^2 - a - 2}$

D. $\dfrac{2y}{2y^2 + 5y + 2} + \dfrac{y}{3y^2 + 5y - 2} - \dfrac{1}{6y^2 + y - 1}$

2. Multiply or divide as indicated and simplify the results.

A. $\dfrac{x^2 + xy}{xy} \cdot \dfrac{5y}{x^2 - y^2}$

B. $\dfrac{3x^2 - 12}{3x^2 - 3} \cdot \dfrac{x-1}{2x+4}$

C. $\dfrac{a^2 + 7a + 10}{a^2 + 10a + 25} \div \dfrac{a+2}{a+5}$

D. $\dfrac{a^3 b^2 - a^2 b^3}{2a} \div \dfrac{a^2 - b^2}{4a}$

E. $\dfrac{12 - 6a}{7a - 21} \div \dfrac{2a - 4}{a^2 - 4}$

F. $\dfrac{x^3}{5x + 10} \div \dfrac{x^4}{x+2}$

G. $\dfrac{x-1}{x^2 - 4} \cdot \dfrac{2x+4}{x^2 - 1} \div \dfrac{2x+2}{x^2 - 4x + 4}$

H. $\dfrac{x-3}{x^2 + 2x - 3} \div \dfrac{x^2 - 9}{x^2 - 1} \cdot \dfrac{x^2 - 2x + 1}{x^2 - 2x - 3}$

SOLUTIONS

1. A. $\dfrac{11}{18ab} + \dfrac{1}{18ab} = \dfrac{12}{18ab} = \dfrac{6\cdot 2}{6\cdot 3ab} = \dfrac{2}{3ab}$

B. $\dfrac{3x}{x-4} + \dfrac{2}{x+1} = \dfrac{3x(x+1)}{(x-4)(x+1)} +$

$\dfrac{2(x-4)}{(x-4)(x+1)} = \dfrac{3x^2+3x+2x-8}{(x-4)(x+1)} =$

$\dfrac{3x^2+5x-8}{(x-4)(x+1)}$

C. $\dfrac{3}{2a^2-a-1} - \dfrac{2}{a^2+a-2} =$

$\dfrac{3}{(2a+1)(a-1)} - \dfrac{2}{(a-1)(a+2)} =$

$\dfrac{3(a+2)}{(2a+1)(a-1)(a+2)} -$

$\dfrac{2(2a+1)}{(2a+1)(a-1)(a+2)} =$

$\dfrac{3a+6-4a-2}{(2a+1)(a-1)(a+2)} =$

$\dfrac{-a+4}{(2a+1)(a-1)(a+2)}$

D. $\dfrac{2y}{2y^2+5y+2} + \dfrac{y}{3y^2+5y-2} - \dfrac{1}{6y^2+y-1}$

$= \dfrac{2y}{(2y+1)(y+2)} + \dfrac{y}{(3y-1)(y+2)} - \dfrac{1}{(3y-1)(2y+1)}$

$= \dfrac{2y(3y-1)+y(2y+1)-1(y+2)}{(3y-1)(2y+1)(y+2)}$

$= \dfrac{6y^2-2y+2y^2+y-y-2}{(3y-1)(2y+1)(y+2)}$

$= \dfrac{8y^2-2y-2}{(3y-1)(2y+1)(y+2)}$

2. A. $\dfrac{x^2+xy}{xy} \cdot \dfrac{5y}{x^2-y^2} = \dfrac{x(x+y)\cdot 5y}{xy(x+y)(x-y)} =$

$\dfrac{5}{x-y}$

B. $\dfrac{3x^2-12}{3x^2-3} \cdot \dfrac{x-1}{2x+4} = \dfrac{3(x^2-4)}{3(x^2-1)} \cdot \dfrac{x-1}{2(x+2)} =$

$\dfrac{3(x+2)(x-2)(x-1)}{6(x+2)(x-1)(x-1)} = \dfrac{x-2}{2(x+1)}$

C. $\dfrac{a^2+7a+10}{a^2+10a+25} \div \dfrac{a+2}{a+5} = \dfrac{(a+2)(a+5)}{(a+5)(a+5)} \cdot$

$\dfrac{a+5}{a+2} = 1$

D. $\dfrac{a^3b^2-a^2b^3}{2a} \div \dfrac{a^2-b^2}{4a} =$

$\dfrac{a^2b^2(a-b)}{2a} \cdot \dfrac{4a}{(a+b)(a-b)} = \dfrac{2a^2b^2}{a+b}$

E. $\dfrac{12-6a}{7a-21} \div \dfrac{2a-4}{a^2-4} = \dfrac{-6(a-2)}{7(a-3)} \cdot$

$\dfrac{(a+2)(a-2)}{2(a-2)} = \dfrac{-3(a-2)(a+2)}{7(a-3)}$

F. $\dfrac{x^3}{5x+10} \div \dfrac{x^4}{x+2} = \dfrac{x^3}{5(x+2)} \cdot \dfrac{x+2}{x^4} =$

$\dfrac{x^3(x+2)}{5x^4(x+2)} = \dfrac{1}{5x}$

G. $\dfrac{x-1}{x^2-4} \cdot \dfrac{2x+4}{x^2-1} \div \dfrac{2x+2}{x^2-4x+4} =$

$\dfrac{x-1}{(x+2)(x-2)} \cdot \dfrac{2(x+2)}{(x+1)(x-1)} \cdot \dfrac{(x-2)(x-2)}{2(x+1)} =$

$\dfrac{2(x-1)(x+2)(x-2)(x-2)}{2(x-1)(x+1)(x+1)(x+2)(x-2)} =$

$\dfrac{x-2}{(x+1)^2}$

H. $\dfrac{x-3}{x^2+2x-3} \div \dfrac{x^2-9}{x^2-1} \cdot \dfrac{x^2-2x+1}{x^2-2x-3} =$

$\dfrac{x-3}{(x+3)(x-1)} \cdot \dfrac{(x+1)(x-1)}{(x+3)(x-3)} \cdot \dfrac{(x-1)(x-1)}{(x-3)(x+1)} =$

$\dfrac{(x-3)(x+1)(x-1)(x-1)(x-1)}{(x-3)(x-3)(x+3)(x+3)(x+1)(x-1)} =$

$\dfrac{(x-1)^2}{(x-3)(x+3)^2}$

LINEAR EQUATIONS

A linear equation in one variable has the form $ax + b = 0$ if $a \neq 0$ and its solution is $x = -\dfrac{b}{a}$. It is linear since the variable is raised to the first power.

The general procedure for solving linear equations is as follows:

1. If there are parentheses in the equation, perform the operations needed to remove them.
2. Combine like terms, if possible, on each side of the equation.
3. Get all terms containing the variables on one side of the equation.
4. If there is a constant term on the variable side of the equation, undo the operation so that the constant is zero.
5. If the coefficient of the variable is not a positive one, divide each side of the equation by the coefficient.
6. Check the solution in the original equation.

$2(x + 3) = 3(x - 1) + 4$	
$2x + 6 = 3x - 3 + 4$	Remove parentheses.
$2x + 6 = 3x + 1$	Combine like terms.
$2x + 6 - 3x = 3x + 1 - 3x$	To get all variable terms on left, add $-3x$.
$-x + 6 = 1$	Combine like terms.
$-x + 6 - 6 = 1 - 6$	To get variable on one side by itself, add -6.
$-x = -5$	Combine like terms.
$\dfrac{-x}{-1} = \dfrac{-5}{-1}$	Divide each side by -1.
$x = 5$	

Check: Left side: $2(x + 3) = 2(5 + 3) = 2(8) = 16$
Right side: $3(x - 1) + 4 = 3(5 - 1) + 4 = 3(4) + 4 = 12 + 4 = 16$
Since $16 = 16$, $x = 5$ is the solution to the equation.

Example 39

Solve each equation for x.

A. $x + 8 - 2(x + 1) = 3x - 6$ B. $3x + 2 = 6x - 4$

C. $2(x + 3) = 5(x - 1) - 7(x - 3)$ D. $3x + 4(x - 2) = x - 5 + 3(2x - 1)$

Solution

A. $x + 8 - 2(x + 1) = 3x - 6$
$x + 8 - 2x - 2 = 3x - 6$
$-x + 6 = 3x - 6$
$-x + 6 - 3x = 3x - 6 - 3x$
$-4x + 6 = -6$
$-4x + 6 - 6 = -6 - 6$
$-4x = -12$
$\dfrac{-4x}{-4} = \dfrac{-12}{-4}$
$x = 3$

B. $3x + 2 = 6x - 4$
$3x + 2 - 6x = 6x - 4 - 6x$
$-3x + 2 = -4$
$-3x + 2 - 2 = -4 - 2$
$-3x = -6$
$\dfrac{-3x}{-3} = \dfrac{-6}{-3}$
$x = 2$

C. $2(x + 3) = 5(x - 1) - 7(x - 3)$
$2x + 6 = 5x - 5 - 7x + 21$
$2x + 6 = -2x + 16$
$4x + 6 = 16$
$4x = 10$
$\dfrac{4x}{4} = \dfrac{10}{4}$
$x = \dfrac{5}{2}$

D. $3x + 4(x - 2) = x - 5 + 3(2x - 1)$
$3x + 4x - 8 = x - 5 + 6x - 3$
$7x - 8 = 7x - 8$
This is an identity equation, so the equation is true for all real numbers.

LITERAL EQUATIONS

Literal equations are equations in which some of the constants are letters, not specific numbers. The literal equations you encounter most often are formulas. For example, $d = rt$ can be solved for r to get $r = \dfrac{d}{t}$.

Example 40

Solve each equation for the letter indicated.

A. $A = 0.5(h + b)$ for h

B. $6k = 3(l + w) - 2h$ for h

C. $\dfrac{2a - 3b}{c} = \dfrac{3a - 2c}{b}$ for a

D. $A = p + irt$ for p

Solution

A. $A = 0.5(h + b)$ for h
$2(A) = 2[0.5(h + b)]$
$2A = 1(h + b)$
$2A = h + b$
$2A - b = h$
$h = 2A - b$

B. $6k = 3(l + w) - 2h$ for h
$6k - 3(l + w) = -2h$
$-6k + 3(l + w) = 2h$
$\dfrac{3(l + w) - 6k}{2} = h$
$h = \dfrac{3(l + w) - 6k}{2}$

C. $\dfrac{2a - 3b}{c} = \dfrac{3a - 2c}{b}$ for a

$b(2a - 3b) = c(3a - 2c)$

$2ab - 3b^2 = 3ac - 2c^2$

$2ab - 3b^2 - 3ac = -2c^2$

$2ab - 3ac = 3b^2 - 2c^2$

$a(2b - 3c) = 3b^2 - 2c^2$

$a = \dfrac{3b^2 - 2c^2}{2b - 3c}$

D. $A = p + irt$ for p

$A - irt = P$

$P = A - irt$

EQUATIONS WITH FRACTIONS

A **fractional equation** is an algebraic equation with the variable in the denominator of a fraction. You have to be sure that any answer that you get will not make a denominator zero, which would cause the problem to be undefined.

For example, $\dfrac{4}{x} = 2$, then $4 = 2x$ and $x = 2$. You have to check to see if $x = 2$ makes a denominator zero, and in this case it does not. So $x = 2$ is the solution.

In $\dfrac{4}{x} = \dfrac{1}{x}$, you get $4x = x$ and $3x = 0$, so $x = 0$. You check to see if $x = 0$ makes the denominator zero, and in this case it does. Thus, $x = 0$ is not a solution.

Example 41

Solve these equations for x.

A. $\dfrac{3}{x} - \dfrac{4}{5x} = \dfrac{1}{10}$

B. $\dfrac{2}{x - 1} + \dfrac{6}{x} = \dfrac{5}{x - 1}$

C. $\dfrac{3}{x - 3} + 4 = \dfrac{x}{x - 3}$

D. $\dfrac{1}{2x} + \dfrac{8}{5} = \dfrac{3}{x}$

Solution

A. $\dfrac{3}{x} - \dfrac{4}{5x} = \dfrac{1}{10}$ LCD $= 10x$

$10x\left(\dfrac{3}{x} - \dfrac{4}{5x}\right) = 10x\left(\dfrac{1}{10}\right)$

$30 - 8 = x$

$22 = x$ Solution, since only $x = 0$ is not allowed.

B. $\dfrac{2}{x-1} + \dfrac{6}{x} = \dfrac{5}{x-1}$ LCD $= x(x-1)$

$$x(x-1)\left(\dfrac{2}{x-1} + \dfrac{6}{x}\right) = x(x-1)\dfrac{5}{x-1}$$

$2x + 6(x-1) = 5x$

$2x + 6x - 6 - 5x = 5x - 5x$

$6x - 6 = 0$

$3x - 6 + 6 = 0 + 6$

$3x = 6$

$\dfrac{3x}{3} = \dfrac{6}{3}$

$x = 2$ Solution, since only $x = 0$ is not allowed.

C. $\dfrac{3}{x-3} + 4 = \dfrac{x}{x-3}$

$$x - 3\left(\dfrac{3}{x-3} + 4\right) = (x-3)\dfrac{x}{x-3}$$

$3 + 4(x-3) = x$

$3 + 4x - 12 - x = x - x$

$3x - 9 = 0$

$3x - 9 + 9 = 0 + 9$

$3x = 9$

$\dfrac{3x}{3} = \dfrac{9}{3}$

$x = 3$ Not a solution, since $x = 3$ is not allowed.

D. $\dfrac{1}{2x} + \dfrac{8}{5} = \dfrac{3}{x}$ LCD $= 10x$

$$10x\left(\dfrac{1}{2x} + \dfrac{8}{5}\right) = 10x \cdot \dfrac{3}{x}$$

$5 + 8(2x) = 10 \cdot 3$

$5 + 16x = 30$

$5 + 16x - 5 = 30 - 5$

$16x = 25$

$\dfrac{16x}{16} = \dfrac{25}{16}$

$x = \dfrac{25}{16}$ Solution, since only $x = 0$ is not allowed.

These equations contain fractions, but they do not have variables in the denominator of the fractions. They are equations containing fractions, but are not fractional equations.

Example 42

Solve for x.

A. $\dfrac{2x}{5} - \dfrac{4}{5} = \dfrac{9}{5}$ B. $\dfrac{x}{6} - \dfrac{1}{2} = \dfrac{2}{3}$ C. $\dfrac{9x+1}{6} = x + \dfrac{1}{3}$ D. $\dfrac{x-4}{3} = \dfrac{x}{5} + 2$

Solution

A. $\dfrac{2x}{5} - \dfrac{4}{5} = \dfrac{9}{5}$ LCD = 5

$5\left(\dfrac{2x}{5} - \dfrac{4}{5}\right) = 5\left(\dfrac{9}{5}\right)$

$2x - 4 = 9$
$2x - 4 + 4 = 9 + 4$
$2x = 9 + 4$
$2x = 13$

$\dfrac{2x}{2} = \dfrac{13}{2}$

$x = \dfrac{13}{2}$

B. $\dfrac{x}{6} - \dfrac{1}{2} = \dfrac{2}{3}$ LCD = 6

$6\left(\dfrac{x}{6} - \dfrac{1}{2}\right) = 6\left(\dfrac{2}{3}\right)$

$x - 3 = 4$
$x - 3 + 3 = 4 + 3$
$x = 7$

C. $\dfrac{9x + 1}{6} = x + \dfrac{1}{3}$ LCD = 6

$6\left(\dfrac{9x + 1}{6}\right) = 6\left(x + \dfrac{1}{3}\right)$

$9x + 1 = 6x + 2$
$9x + 1 - 6x = 6x + 2 - 6x$
$3x + 1 = 2$
$3x + 1 - 1 = 2 - 1$
$3x = 1$

$\dfrac{3x}{3} = \dfrac{1}{3}$

$x = \dfrac{1}{3}$

D. $\dfrac{x - 4}{3} = \dfrac{x}{5} + 2$ LCD = 15

$15\left(\dfrac{x - 4}{3}\right) = 15\left(\dfrac{x}{5} + 2\right)$

$5(x - 4) = 3x + 15(2)$
$5x - 20 = 3x + 30$
$5x - 20 - 3x = 3x + 30 - 3x$
$2x - 20 = 30$

$$2x - 20 + 20 = 30 + 20$$
$$2x = 50$$
$$\frac{2x}{2} = \frac{50}{2}$$
$$x = 25$$

EQUATIONS THAT ARE PROPORTIONS

Proportions are equations with two fractions equal to each other. The equation may or may not have a variable in the denominator of a fraction.

Example 43

Solve for x.

A. $(5 - x) : (x + 1) = 2 : 1$

B. $(x + 3) : 10 = (3x - 2) : 8$

C. $\dfrac{4}{x} = \dfrac{2}{7}$

D. $\dfrac{x + 3}{x - 2} = \dfrac{3}{2}$

Solution

A. $(5 - x) : (x + 1) = 2 : 1$

$$\frac{5 - x}{x + 1} = \frac{2}{1}$$
$$1(5 - x) = 2(x + 1)$$
$$5 - x = 2x + 2$$
$$5 - x + x = 2x + 2 + x$$
$$5 = 3x + 2$$
$$5 - 2 = 3x + 2 - 2$$
$$3 = 3x$$
$$1 = x$$
$$x = 1$$

Solution, since only $x = -1$ is not allowed.

B. $(x + 3) : 10 = (3x - 2) : 8$

$$\frac{x + 3}{10} = \frac{3x - 2}{8}$$
$$8(x + 3) = 10(3x - 2)$$
$$8x + 24 = 30x - 20$$
$$8x + 24 - 8x = 30x - 20 - 8x$$
$$24 = 22x - 20$$
$$24 + 20 = 22x - 20 + 20$$
$$44 = 22x$$
$$2 = x$$

Solution, since all real numbers are allowed.

C. $\dfrac{4}{x} = \dfrac{2}{7}$

$$4(7) = 2(x)$$
$$28 = 2x$$
$$14 = x$$

Solution, since only $x = 0$ is not allowed.

D. $\dfrac{x+3}{x-2} = \dfrac{3}{2}$

$2(x+3) = 3(x-2)$

$2x + 6 = 3x - 6$

$2x + 6 + 6 = 3x - 6 + 6$

$2x + 12 = 3x$

$2x + 12 - 2x = 3x - 2x$

$12 = x$

Solution, since only $x = 2$ is not allowed.

EQUATIONS WITH RADICALS

When an equation contains a radical, you get the radical on one side alone and then you remove the radical by squaring each side of the equation. When there are two radicals, you get one radical on each side of the equation before squaring it.

Example 44

Solve these radical equations for x.

A. $\sqrt{8x} - 7 = 17$ B. $\sqrt{10x} + 10 = 2$ C. $\sqrt{-2x} = 8$

D. $\sqrt{10 - 2x} = \sqrt{3x + 25}$ E. $\sqrt{5x - 1} = \sqrt{2x + 8}$ F. $\sqrt{x} + 11 = 16$

G. $\sqrt{-8x + 1} = \sqrt{17}$ H. $\sqrt{14x} - \sqrt{42} = 0$ I. $\sqrt{7x} + \sqrt{35} = 0$

Solution

A. $\sqrt{8x} - 7 = 17$

$\sqrt{8x} = 24$

$(\sqrt{8x})^2 = (24)^2$

$8x = 576$

$x = 72$

B. $\sqrt{10x} + 10 = 2$

$\sqrt{10x} = -8$

No solution because the principal square root is never a negative number.

C. $\sqrt{-2x} = 8$

$(\sqrt{-2x})^2 = 8^2$

$-2x = 64$

$x = -32$ since $-2(-32) = +64$

D. $\sqrt{10 - 2x} = \sqrt{3x + 25}$

$(\sqrt{10 - 2x})^2 = (\sqrt{3x + 25})^2$

$10 - 2x = 3x + 25$

$10 - 5x = 25$

$-5x = 15$

$x = -3$

You have to check to be sure each radicand is nonnegative.

$10 - 2x = 10 - 2(-3) = 10 + 6 = 16 \geq 0$

$3x + 25 = 3(-3) + 25 = -9 + 25 = 16 \geq 0$

$x = -3$ is a solution.

E. $\sqrt{5x-1} = \sqrt{2x+8}$

$(\sqrt{5x-1})^2 = (\sqrt{2x+8})^2$

$5x - 1 = 2x + 8$

$3x - 1 = 8$

$3x = 9$

$x = 3$

F. $\sqrt{x} + 11 = 16$

$\sqrt{x} = 5$

$(\sqrt{x})^2 = (5)^2$

$x = 25$

G. $\sqrt{-8x+1} = \sqrt{17}$

$(\sqrt{-8x+1})^2 = (\sqrt{17})^2$

$-8x + 1 = 17$

$-8x = 16$

$x = -2$ since $-8(-2) + 1 = 15 + 1 = 17$

H. $\sqrt{14x} - \sqrt{42} = 0$

$\sqrt{14x} = \sqrt{42}$

$(\sqrt{14x})^2 = (\sqrt{42})^2$

$14x = 42$

$x = 3$

I. $\sqrt{7x} + \sqrt{35} = 0$

$\sqrt{7x} = -\sqrt{35}$

$(\sqrt{7x})^2 = (-\sqrt{35})^2$

$7x = 35$

$x = 5$

Check: $\sqrt{7x} + \sqrt{35} = \sqrt{7(5)} + \sqrt{35} = \sqrt{35} + \sqrt{35} = 2\sqrt{35} \neq 0$ thus, $x = 5$ is not a solution.
No solution.

▊ PRACTICE PROBLEMS

1. Solve the equations for x.

   A. $7x + 8 = 1$
   B. $8 - 8x = -16$
   C. $5x - 4 = 21$
   D. $9 - 2x = 15$
   E. $9x - 5x + 13 = 3x + 6$
   F. $2x + 5 - x = 4x - 4$
   G. $27x - 4 = -3x + 7 - 3$
   H. $-8x + 9x - 4 = 6x - 4$

2. Solve these equations for y.

   A. $2(y + 3) = -4(y + 2) + 2$
   B. $3(2y + 1) - 2(y - 2) = 5$
   C. $4(y - 9) = 8(y - 3)$
   D. $2y + 3(y - 4) = 2(y - 3)$
   E. $6y - 3(5y + 2) = 4(1 - y)$
   F. $-2y - 3(4 - 2y) = 2(y - 3)$

3. Solve for the indicated letter.

   A. $P = 2l + 2w$ for l B. $P = a + b + c$ for c

   C. $A = lw$ for w D. $A = \frac{1}{2}(B + b)h$ for B

   E. $C = 2\pi r$ for r F. $I = prt$ for t

4. Solve these equations for x.

   A. $\dfrac{3x}{4} + \dfrac{5x}{2} = 13$

   B. $\dfrac{8x}{3} - \dfrac{2x}{4} = -13$

   C. $\dfrac{x-8}{5} + \dfrac{8}{5} = \dfrac{-x}{3}$

5. Solve these equations for y.

A. $\dfrac{1}{y} + \dfrac{2}{y} = 3 - \dfrac{3}{y}$

B. $\dfrac{3}{4y} - \dfrac{1}{6} = \dfrac{4}{8y} + \dfrac{1}{2}$

C. $\dfrac{1}{y} + \dfrac{1}{y-1} = \dfrac{5}{y-1}$

6. Solve these equations for x.

A. $\dfrac{9}{x} = \dfrac{3}{38}$ 　　 B. $\dfrac{16}{x} = \dfrac{2}{7}$

C. $\dfrac{4}{x-2} = \dfrac{10}{25}$ 　　 D. $\dfrac{x-2}{3} = \dfrac{x+6}{5}$

7. Solve these equations for y.

A. $\sqrt{12y+1} = \sqrt{25-12y}$

B. $\sqrt{7y} - 5 = 23$

C. $\sqrt{y+1} = \sqrt{21+5y}$

D. $\sqrt{3y} + 21 = 33$

E. $\sqrt{5y} + 8 = -2$

F. $\sqrt{5y-20} = \sqrt{3y+30}$

▊ SOLUTIONS

1. A. $7x + 8 = 1$
    $7x = -7$
    $x = -1$
    B. $8 - 8x = -16$
    $-8x = -24$
    $x = 3$
    C. $5x - 4 = 21$
    $5x = 25$
    $x = 5$
    D. $9 - 2x = 15$
    $-2x = 6$
    $x = -3$
    E. $9x - 5x + 13 = 3x + 6$
    $4x + 13 = 3x + 6$
    $x + 13 = 6$
    $x = -7$
    F. $2x + 5 - x = 4x - 4$
    $x + 5 = 4x - 4$
    $-3x + 5 = -4$
    $-3x = -9$
    $x = 3$
    G. $27x - 4 = -3x + 7 - 3$
    $27x - 4 = -3x + 4$
    $30x - 4 = 4$
    $30x = 8$
    $x = \dfrac{8}{30}$
    $x = \dfrac{4}{15}$
    H. $-8x + 9x - 4 = 6x - 4$
    $x - 4 = 6x - 4$
    $-5x - 4 = -4$
    $-5x = 0$
    $x = 0$

2. A. $2(y + 3) = -4(y + 2) + 2$
    $2y + 6 = -4y - 8 + 2$
    $2y + 6 = -4y - 6$
    $6y + 6 = -6$
    $6y = -12$
    $y = -2$
    B. $3(2y + 1) - 2(y - 2) = 5$
    $6y + 3 - 2y + 4 = 5$
    $4y + 7 = 5$
    $4y = -2$
    $y = -\dfrac{1}{2}$
    C. $4(y - 9) = 8(y - 3)$
    $4y - 36 = 8y - 24$
    $-4y - 36 = -24$
    $-4y = 12$
    $y = -3$
    D. $2y + 3(y - 4) = 2(y - 3)$
    $2y + 3y - 12 = 2y - 6$
    $5y - 12 = 2y - 6$
    $3y - 12 = -6$
    $3y = 6$
    $y = 2$
    E. $6y - 3(5y + 2) = 4(1 - y)$
    $6y - 15y - 6 = 4 - 4y$
    $-9y - 6 = 4 - 4y$
    $-5y - 6 = 4$
    $-5y = 10$
    $y = -2$
    F. $-2y - 3(4 - 2y) = 2(y - 3)$
    $-2y - 12 + 6y = 2y - 6$
    $4y - 12 = 2y - 6$
    $2y - 12 = -6$
    $2y = 6$
    $y = 3$

3. A. $P = 2l + 2w$ for l

$P - 2w = 2l$

$$\frac{P - 2w}{2} = l$$

B. $P = a + b + c$ for c

$P - a - b = c$

C. $A = lw$ for w

$$\frac{A}{l} = w$$

D. $A = \frac{1}{2}(B + b)h$ for B

$2A = (B + b)h$

$2A = Bh + bh$

$2A - bh = Bh$

$$\frac{2A - bh}{h} = B$$

E. $C = 2\pi r$ for r

$$\frac{C}{2\pi} = r$$

F. $I = prt$ for t

$$\frac{I}{pr} = t$$

4. A. $\dfrac{3x}{4} + \dfrac{5x}{2} = 13$

$3x + 2(5x) = 4(13)$

$3x + 10x = 52$

$13x = 52$

$x = 4$

B. $\dfrac{8x}{3} - \dfrac{2x}{4} = -13$

$4(8x) + 3(-2x) = 12(-13)$

$32x - 6x = -156$

$26x = -156$

$x = -6$

C. $\dfrac{x - 8}{5} + \dfrac{8}{5} = \dfrac{-x}{3}$

$3(x - 8) + 3(8) = 5(-x)$

$3x - 24 + 24 = -5x$

$3x = -5x$

$8x = 0$

$x = 0$

5. A. $\dfrac{1}{y} + \dfrac{2}{y} = 3 - \dfrac{3}{y}$

$1 + 2 = 3y - 3$

$3 = 3y - 3$

$6 = 3y$

$2 = y$

B. $\dfrac{3}{4y} - \dfrac{1}{6} = \dfrac{4}{8y} + \dfrac{1}{2}$ LCD $= 24y$

$$24y\left(\frac{3}{4y} - \frac{1}{6}\right) = 24y\left(\frac{4}{8y} + \frac{1}{2}\right)$$

$6(3) + 4y(-1) = 3(4) + 12y(1)$

$18 - 4y = 12 + 12y$

$18 = 12 + 16y$

$6 = 16y$

$$\frac{6}{16} = y$$

$$\frac{3}{8} = y$$

C. $\dfrac{1}{y} + \dfrac{1}{y - 1} = \dfrac{5}{y - 1}$ LCD $= y(y - 1)$

$y - 1 + y = 5y$

$2y - 1 = 5y$

$-1 = 3y$

$$-\frac{1}{3} = y$$

6. A. $\dfrac{9}{x} = \dfrac{3}{38}$

$3x = 342$

$x = 114$

B. $\dfrac{16}{x} = \dfrac{2}{7}$

$2x = 112$

$x = 56$

C. $\dfrac{4}{x - 2} = \dfrac{10}{25}$

$10(x - 2) = 25(4)$

$10x - 20 = 100$

$10x = 120$

$x = 12$

D. $\dfrac{x - 2}{3} = \dfrac{x + 6}{5}$

$5(x - 2) = 3(x + 6)$

$5x - 10 = 3x + 18$

$2x - 10 = 18$

$2x = 28$

$x = 14$

7. A. $\sqrt{12y + 1} = \sqrt{25 - 12y}$

$(\sqrt{12y + 1})^2 = (\sqrt{25 - 12y})^2$

$12y + 1 = 25 - 12y$

$24y + 1 = 25$

$24y = 24$

$y = 1$

B. $\sqrt{7y} - 5 = 23$

$\sqrt{7y} = 28$

$(\sqrt{7y})^2 = 28$

$7y = 784$

$y = 112$

C. $\sqrt{y+1} = \sqrt{21 + 5y}$

$(\sqrt{y+1})^2 = (\sqrt{21 + 5y})^2$

$y + 1 = 21 + 5y$

$1 = 21 + 4y$

$-20 = 4y$

$-5 = y$

Since each radicand becomes negative when $y = -5$, -5 is not a solution. No solution.

D. $\sqrt{3y} + 21 = 33$

$\sqrt{3y} = 12$

$(\sqrt{3y})^2 = (12)^2$

$3y = 144$

$y = 48$

E. $\sqrt{5y} + 8 = -2$

$\sqrt{5y} = -10$

No solution, since a principal square root is not negative.

F. $\sqrt{5y - 20} = \sqrt{3y + 30}$

$(\sqrt{5y - 20})^2 = (\sqrt{3y + 30})^2$

$5y - 20 = 3y + 30$

$2y - 20 = 30$

$2y = 50$

$y = 25$

SYSTEMS OF LINEAR EQUATIONS

A system of two linear equations in two variables has a solution when there is a point (x, y) that makes each of the equations a true statement. There are graphical and algebraic methods for finding the point if one exists.

Example 45

Graph each system and find the solution.

A. $2x - y = 4$ and $x + y = 5$

B. $3x - y = -6$ and $2x + 3y = 7$

Solution

A. (1) For $2x - y = 4$

x	-1	0	1
y	-6	-4	-2

(2) For $x + y = 5$

x	-1	0	1
y	6	5	4

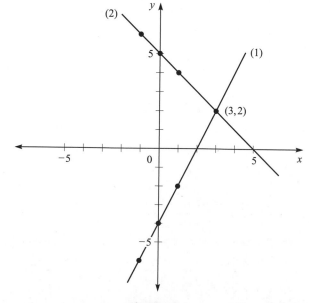

Figure 7.1

B. (1) For $3x - y = -6$

x	-2	-1	0
y	0	3	6

(2) $2x + 3y = 7$

x	-1	2	5
y	3	1	-1

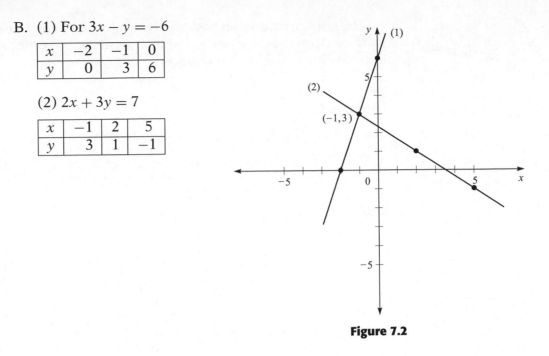

Figure 7.2

To use the **elimination method**, choose a variable to eliminate and multiply each equation as needed so that the variables have the same coefficient but with opposite signs. Then add the equations, and the chosen variable should be eliminated. After that, solve the resulting equation and then substitute into a given equation to find the value of the second variable.

Example 46

Solve these systems of equations by elimination.

A. $5x + 2y = 3$ and $2x + 3y = -1$

B. $2x - 3y = 7$ and $3x + y = 5$

Solution

A.

(1) $5x + 2y = 3$　(2) $2x + 3y = -1$

$2 \times (1)$　　$10x + 4y = 6$

$-5 \times (2)$　$\underline{-10x - 15y = 5}$

　　　　　　$-11y = 11$

　　　　　　　$y = -1$

Eliminate x, LCM $(5, 2) = 10$.
Substitute $y = -1$ into (1).

$5x + 2(-1) = 3$

$5x - 2 = 3$

$5x\ \ = 5$

$x\ \ = 1$

$(x, y) = (1, -1)$

B.

(1) $2x - 3y = 7$　(2) $3x + y = 5$

$1 \times (1)$　$2x - 3y = 7$

$3 \times (2)$　$\underline{9x + 3y = 15}$

　　　　$11x\ \ = 22$

　　　　　$x\ \ = 2$

Eliminate y, LCM $(3, 1) = 3$.
Substitute $x = 2$ into (1).

$2(2) - 3y = 7$

$4 - 3y = 7$

$-3y = 3$

$y = -1$

$(x, y) = (2, -1)$

The **substitution method** of solving a system of equations requires you to solve one equation for one variable in terms of the other and then substitute that value into the other equation.

Example 47

Solve these systems of equations by substitution.

A. $2x + y + 1 = 0$ and $3x - 2y + 5 = 0$ B. $3x + 2y = 13$ and $4x - y = -1$

Solution

A. (1) $2x + y + 1 = 0$

$y = -2x - 1$

(2) $3x - 2y + 5 = 0$

$3x - 2(-2x - 1) + 5 = 0$

$3x + 4x + 2 + 5 = 0$

$7x + 7 = 0$

$7x = -7$

$x = -1$

$(x, y) = (-1, 1)$

(2) $3x - 2y + 5 = 0$ Solve (1) for y.

Substitute $x = -1$ into $y = -2x - 1$.

$y = -2(-1) - 1 = 2 - 1 = 1$

$y = 1$

B. $3x + 2y = 13$ and $4x - y = -1$

(1) $3x + 2y = 13$

(2) $4x - y = -1$

$4x + 1 = y$

(1) $3x + 2y = 13$

$3x + 2(4x + 1) = 13$

$3x + 8x + 2 = 13$

$11x + 2 = 13$

$11x = 11$

$x = 1$

$(x, y) = (1, 5)$

(2) $4x - y = -1$ Solve (2) for y.

Substitute $x = 1$ into $y = 4x + 1$.

$y = 4(1) + 1 = 4 + 1 = 5$

$y = 5$

▨ PRACTICE PROBLEMS

1. Solve these systems by graphing.
   A. $3x + y = 3$ and $x + 2y = -4$
   B. $3x + y = 3$ and $3x - 2y = 3$

2. Solve these systems by elimination.
   A. $2x + 3y = 2$ and $4x - 2y = -12$
   B. $2x + y = 3$ and $2x + 2y = 6$

3. Solve these systems by substitution.
   A. $2x + y = 6$ and $3x - 6y = 24$
   B. $x + y = 3$ and $x - y = 4$

▇▇ SOLUTIONS

1. A. $3x + y = 3$ and $x + 2y = -4$
   (1) $3x + y = 3$

x	-1	0	1
y	6	3	0

   (2) $x + 2y = -4$

x	-2	0	2
y	-1	-2	-3

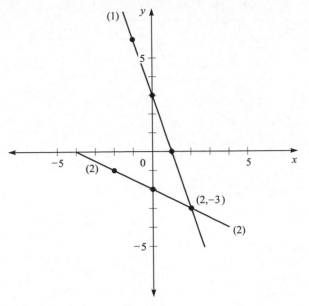

Figure 7.3

B. $3x + y = 3$ and $3x - 2y = 3$
   (1) $3x + y = 3$

x	-1	0	1
y	6	3	0

   (2) $3x - 2y = 3$

x	-1	1	3
y	-3	0	3

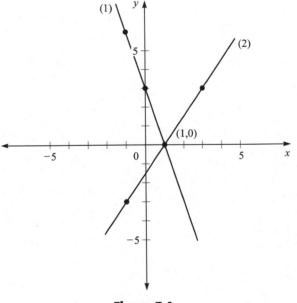

Figure 7.4

2. A. (1) $2x + 3y = 2$
   (2) $4x - 2y = -12$ Eliminate y

   $2 \times (1)$ $4x + 6y = 4$ $2x + 3y = 2$
   $3 \times (2)$ $\underline{12x - 6y = -36}$ $2(-2) + 3y = 2$
            $16x \quad\quad = -32$ $-4 + 3y = 2$
             $x \quad\quad = -2$ $3y = 6$
                          $y = 2$

   $(x, y) = (-2, 2)$

   B. (1) $2x + y = 3$ (2) $2x + 2y = 6$
                                Eliminate x

   (1) $2x + y = 3$ $2x + y = 3$
   $-1 \times (2)$ $\underline{-2x - 2y = -6}$ $2x + 3 = 3$
                      $-y = -3$ $2x = 0$
                         $y = 3$ $x = 0$

   $(x, y) = (0, 3)$

3. A. (1) $2x + y = 6$ (2) $3x - 6y = 24$ B. (1) $x + y = 3$ (2) $x - y = 4$

Solve (1) for y $y = -2x + 6$ Solve (2) for x $x = y + 4$ $x = y + 4$

$y = -2x + 6$ Substitute into (1) $x = -0.5 + 4$

Substitute into (2) $y + 4 + y = 3$

$3x - 6(-2x + 6) = 24$ $y = -2(4) + 6$ $2y = -1$ $x = 3.5$

$3x + 12x - 36 = 24$ $y = -8 + 6$ $y = -0.5$

$15x = 60$ $y = -2$ $(x, y) = (3.5, -0.5)$

$x = 4$

$(x, y) = (4, -2)$

LINEAR INEQUALITIES

An **inequality** is a statement of a relationship between two quantities. The relationship is described as less than ($<$), greater than ($>$), less than or equal to ($\leq$), or greater than or equal to ($\geq$). Linear inequalities in one variable are solved by methods similar to those for linear equations, with one major difference. When multiplying or dividing both sides of an inequality by a negative, you must change the direction of the inequality symbol.

Example 48

Solve these inequalities for x.

A. $x + 2 > 7$ B. $3x < 9$ C. $x - 6 < -5$ D. $-2x > 6$

Solution

A. $x + 2 > 7$ B. $3x < 9$ C. $x - 6 < -5$

    $x + 2 - 2 > 7 - 2$ $\dfrac{3x}{3} < \dfrac{9}{3}$ $x - 6 + 6 < -5 + 6$

    $x > 5$ $x < 3$ $x < 1$

D. $-2x > 6$

    $\dfrac{-2x}{-2} < \dfrac{6}{-2}$ Since you divide by -2, change the direction of the sign.

    $x < -3$

PRACTICE PROBLEMS

Solve each inequality for x.

1. $2x + 7 < 15$

2. $7x - 5 \geq 9$

3. $-6x + 5 < 17$

4. $2x + 13 > -41$

5. $4(3 - x) \geq 2(x - 3)$

6. $0 < 2x + 7 - 9x$

7. $23 - 8x \leq 5 + x$

8. $3x - 4 > 2x - 9$

9. $3x - 2 + x \leq 5x$

10. $4(-x + 2) - (1 - 5x) > -8$

11. $6(10 - x) + 3(7 - 2x) < 45$

SOLUTIONS

1. $2x + 7 < 15$
   $2x + 7 - 7 < 15 - 7$
   $2x < 8$
   $x < 4$

2. $7x - 5 \geq 9$
   $7x \geq 14$
   $x \geq 2$

3. $-6x + 5 < 17$
   $-6x < 12$
   $x > -2$

4. $2x + 13 > -41$
   $2x > -54$
   $x > -27$

5. $4(3 - x) \geq 2(x - 3)$
   $12 - 4x \geq 2x - 6$
   $12 - 6x \geq -6$
   $-6x \geq -18$
   $x \leq 3$

6. $0 < 2x + 7 - 9x$
   $0 < -7x + 7$
   $7x < 7$
   $x < 1$

7. $23 - 8x \leq 5 + x$
   $23 - 9x \leq 5$
   $-9x \leq -18$
   $x \geq 2$

8. $3x - 4 > 2x - 9$
   $x - 4 > -9$
   $x > -5$

9. $3x - 2 + x \leq 5x$
   $4x - 2 \leq 5x$
   $-x - 2 \leq 0$
   $-x \leq 0 + 2$
   $x \geq -2$

10. $4(-x + 2) - (1 - 5x) > -8$
    $-4x + 8 - 1 + 5x > -8$
    $x + 7 > -8$
    $x > -15$

11. $6(10 - x) + 3(7 - 2x) < 45$
    $60 - 6x + 21 - 6x < 45$
    $81 - 12x < 45$
    $-12x < -36$
    $x > 3$

QUADRATIC EQUATIONS AND INEQUALITIES

A **quadratic equation in one variable** is an equation of the form $ax^2 + bx + c = 0$ where a, b, and c are real numbers and $a \neq 0$. Quadratic equations are generally solved by two methods: factoring and using the quadratic formula. Some quadratic equations cannot be factored, but all quadratic equations can be solved by using the quadratic formula.

The zero product principle is the basis for factoring. If a and b are real numbers and $ab = 0$, then $a = 0$ or $b = 0$. To solve a quadratic equation by using this property, one side of the equation must be equal to zero.

Example 49

Solve each equation by factoring.

A. $x^2 + 4x = 21$ B. $2y^2 - y = 1$ C. $5x^2 + 15x = 0$
D. $9y^2 = 7(6y - 7)$ E. $(x + 6)(x - 2) = -7$ F. $4y^2 = 9$

Solution

A. $x^2 + 4x = 21$
   $x^2 + 4x - 21 = 0$
   $(x + 7)(x - 3) = 0$
   $x + 7 = 0$ or $x - 3 = 0$
   $x = -7$ or $x = 3$
   The solutions are -7 and 3.

B. $2y^2 - y = 1$
 $2y^2 - y - 1 = 0$
 $(2y + 1)(y - 1) = 0$
 $2y + 1 = 0$ or $y - 1 = 0$
 $2y = -1$ or $y = 1$
 $y = -\dfrac{1}{2}$

 The solutions are $-\dfrac{1}{2}$ and 1.

C. $5x^2 + 15x = 0$
 $5x(x + 3) = 0$
 $5x = 0$ or $x + 3 = 0$
 $x = 0$ or $x = -3$
 The solutions are 0 and -3.

D. $9y^2 = 7(6y - 7)$
 $9y^2 = 42y - 49$
 $9y^2 - 42y + 49 = 0$
 $(3y - 7)(3y - 7) = 0$
 $3y - 7 = 0$ or $3y - 7 = 0$
 $3y = 7$ or $3y = 7$
 $y = \dfrac{7}{3}$ or $y = \dfrac{7}{3}$

 The solutions are both $\dfrac{7}{3}$.

E. $(x + 6)(x - 2) = -7$ (Note that the equation does not equal zero.
 $x^2 + 4x - 12 + 7 = 0$ Multiply out and get the equation to equal zero.)
 $x^2 + 4x - 5 = 0$
 $(x + 5)(x - 1) = 0$
 $x + 5 = 0$ or $x - 1 = 0$
 $x = -5$ or $x = 1$
 The solutions are -5 and 1.

F. $4y^2 = 9$
 $4y^2 - 9 = 0$
 $(2y + 3)(2y - 3) = 0$
 $2y + 3 = 0$ or $2y - 3 = 0$
 $2y = -3$ or $2y = 3$
 $y = \dfrac{-3}{2}$ or $y = \dfrac{3}{2}$

 The solutions are $\dfrac{-3}{2}$ and $\dfrac{3}{2}$.

When you have $ax^2 + bx + c = 0$ and $a \neq 0$, then $x = \dfrac{-b \pm \sqrt{b^2 - 4ac}}{2a}$.

If $b^2 - 4ac$ is negative, the quadratic equation has no real roots.

Example 50

Solve each equation by using the quadratic formula.

A. $3x^2 + 4x - 4 = 0$
C. $(x - 1)(x + 3) = -5$

B. $y^2 - 4y + 3 = -y^2 + 2y$
D. $4y^2 - 8y + 3 = 0$

Solution

A. $3x^2 + 4x - 4 = 0$
$a = 3, b = 4, c = -4$

$$x = \frac{-4 \pm \sqrt{4^2 - 4(3)(-4)}}{2(3)}$$

$$x = \frac{-4 \pm \sqrt{64}}{6}$$

$$x = \frac{-4 \pm 8}{6}$$

$$x = \frac{-4 + 8}{6} \qquad \text{or} \qquad x = \frac{-4 - 8}{6}$$

$$x = \frac{4}{6} \qquad \text{or} \qquad x = \frac{-12}{6}$$

$$x = \frac{2}{3} \qquad \text{or} \qquad x = -2$$

The solutions are $\frac{2}{3}$ and -2.

B. $y^2 - 4y + 3 = -y^2 + 2y$
$2y^2 - 6y + 3 = 0$
$a = 2, b = -6, c = 3$

$$y = \frac{-(-6) \pm \sqrt{(-6)^2 - 4(2)(3)}}{2(2)}$$

$$y = \frac{6 \pm \sqrt{12}}{4}$$

$$y = \frac{6 \pm 2\sqrt{3}}{4}$$

$$y = \frac{2(3 \pm \sqrt{3})}{4}$$

$$y = \frac{3 \pm \sqrt{3}}{2}$$

The solutions are $\frac{3 + \sqrt{3}}{2}$ and $\frac{3 - \sqrt{3}}{2}$.

C. $(x - 1)(x + 3) = -5$
$x^2 + 2x - 3 = -5$
$x^2 + 2x + 2 = 0$
$a = 1, b = 2, \text{ and } c = 2$

$$x = \frac{-2 \pm \sqrt{2^2 - 4(1)(2)}}{2(1)}$$

$$x = \frac{-2 \pm \sqrt{-4}}{2}$$

Since $b^2 - 4ac < 0$, there are no real solutions.

D. $4y^2 - 8y + 3 = 0$
$a = 4, b = -8, c = 3$

$$y = \frac{-(-8) \pm \sqrt{(-8)^2 - 4(4)(3)}}{2(4)}$$

$$y = \frac{8 \pm \sqrt{16}}{8}$$

$$y = \frac{8 \pm 4}{8}$$

$$y = \frac{8 + 4}{8} \quad \text{or} \quad y = \frac{8 - 4}{8}$$

$$y = \frac{12}{8} \quad \text{or} \quad y = \frac{4}{8}$$

$y = 1.5 \quad \text{or} \quad y = 0.5$
The solutions are 1.5 and 0.5.

Quadratic inequalities that can be factored can be solved by using the properties of the product of signed numbers. If $ab > 0$, then $a > 0$ and $b > 0$, or $a < 0$ and $b < 0$; and if $ab < 0$, then $a > 0$ and $b < 0$, or $a < 0$ and $b > 0$.

Example 51

Solve these quadratic inequalities.

A. $6y^2 - 7y - 5 > 0$ B. $6x^2 - 7x + 2 < 0$
C. $2y^2 - 5y - 3 \geq 0$ D. $6x^2 + x - 5 \leq 0$

Solution

A. $6y^2 - 7y - 5 > 0$
$(3y - 5)(2y + 1) > 0$

Case 1: $3y - 5 > 0$ and $2y + 1 > 0$ or   Case 2: $3y - 5 < 0$ and $2y + 1 < 0$

$3y > 5$ and $2y > -1$ $3y < 5$ and $2y < -1$

$y > \dfrac{5}{3}$ and $y > -\dfrac{1}{2}$ or $y < \dfrac{5}{3}$ and $y < \dfrac{-1}{2}$

$y > \dfrac{5}{3}$ or $y < -\dfrac{1}{2}$

The solution is $y > \dfrac{5}{3}$ or $y < -\dfrac{1}{2}$.

B. $6x^2 - 7x + 2 < 0$
$(3x - 2)(2x - 1) < 0$

Case 1: $3x - 2 < 0$ and $2x - 1 > 0$ or   Case 2: $3x - 2 > 0$ and $2x - 1 < 0$

$3x < 2$ and $2x > 1$ $3x > 2$ and $2x < 1$

$x < \dfrac{2}{3}$ and $x > \dfrac{1}{2}$ $x > \dfrac{2}{3}$ and $x < \dfrac{1}{2}$

$\dfrac{1}{2} < x < \dfrac{2}{3}$ or   No solution

The solution is $\dfrac{1}{2} < x < \dfrac{2}{3}$.

C. $2y^2 - 5y - 3 \geq 0$
$(2y + 1)(y - 3) \geq 0$

Case 1: $2y + 1 \geq 0$ and $y - 3 \geq 0$ or   Case 2: $2y + 1 \leq 0$ and $y - 3 \leq 0$

$2y \geq -1$ and $y \geq 3$ or $2y \leq -1$ and $y \leq 3$

$y \geq -\dfrac{1}{2}$ and $y \geq 3$ or $y \leq \dfrac{-1}{2}$ and $y \leq 3$

$y \geq 3$ or $y \leq -\dfrac{1}{2}$

The solution is $y \geq 3$ or $y \leq -\dfrac{1}{2}$.

D. $6x^2 + x - 5 \leq 0$
$(6x - 5)(x + 1) \leq 0$

Case 1: $6x - 5 \leq 0$ and $x + 1 \geq 0$ or   Case 2: $6x - 5 \geq 0$ and $x + 1 \leq 0$

$6x \leq 5$ and $x \geq -1$ or $6x \geq 5$ and $x \leq -1$

$x \leq \dfrac{5}{6}$ and $x \geq -1$ or $x \geq \dfrac{5}{6}$ and $x \leq -1$

$-1 \leq x \leq \dfrac{5}{6}$ No solution

The solution is $-1 \leq x \leq \dfrac{5}{6}$.

PRACTICE PROBLEMS

1. Solve these equations by factoring.
   A. $x^2 - 5x + 6 = 0$ B. $y^2 = 4y$
   C. $x^2 + 3x = 28$ D. $5y - 2y^2 = 2$
   E. $5x^2 + 40 = 33x$ F. $x^2 = 121$

2. Solve these equations by using the quadratic formula.
   A. $x^2 - 6x + 8 = 0$ B. $y^2 = 4 - 3y$
   C. $3x^2 + 8x + 5 = 0$ D. $x^2 + 4x + 1 = 0$
   E. $2y^2 + 3y = 5$ F. $4x^2 + 5 = 4x$

3. Solve these quadratic inequalities.
   A. $x^2 - 7x > -12$ B. $2y^2 + 2 < 5y$
   C. $9x^2 < 9x - 2$ D. $x^2 + x \leq 6$
   E. $y^2 \geq 5y + 24$ F. $4x - 5x^2 \leq -12$

SOLUTIONS

1. A. $x^2 - 5x + 6 = 0$
      $(x - 3)(x - 2) = 0$
      $x - 3 = 0$ or $x - 2 = 0$
      $x = 3$ or $x = 2$

   B. $y^2 = 4y$
      $y^2 - 4y = 0$
      $y(y - 4) = 0$
      $y = 0$ or $y - 4 = 0$
      $y = 0$ or $y = 4$

   C. $x^2 + 3x = 28$
      $x^2 + 3x - 28 = 0$
      $(x + 7)(x - 4) = 0$
      $x + 7 = 0$ or $x - 4 = 0$
      $x = -7$ or $x = 4$

   D. $5y - 2y^2 = 2$
      $-2y^2 + 5y - 2 = 0$
      $2y^2 - 5y + 2 = 0$
      $(2y - 1)(y - 2) = 0$
      $2y - 1 = 0$ or $y - 2 = 0$
      $2y = 1$ or $y = 2$
      $y = \dfrac{1}{2}$ or $y = 2$

E. $5x^2 + 40 = 33x$
$5x^2 - 33x + 40 = 0$
$(5x - 8)(x - 5) = 0$
$5x - 8 = 0$　or　$x - 5 = 0$
$5x = 8$　or　$x = 5$
$x = 1.6$　or　$x = 5$

F. $x^2 = 121$
$x^2 - 121 = 0$
$(x + 11)(x - 11) = 0$
$x + 11 = 0$　or　$x - 11 = 0$
$x = -11$　or　$x = 11$

2. A. $x^2 - 6x + 8 = 0$
$a = 1, b = -6, c = 8$

$$x = \frac{-(-6) \pm \sqrt{(-6)^2 - 4(1)(8)}}{2(1)}$$

$$x = \frac{6 \pm \sqrt{36 - 32}}{2}$$

$$x = \sqrt{\frac{6 + \sqrt{4}}{2}}$$

$$x = \frac{6 + 2}{2} \quad \text{or} \quad x = \frac{6 - 2}{2}$$

$x = 4$　or　$x = 2$

B. $y^2 = 4 - 3y$
$y^2 + 3y - 4 = 0$
$a = 1, b = 3, c = -4$

$$y = \frac{-3 \pm \sqrt{3^2 - 4(1)(-4)}}{2(1)}$$

$$y = \frac{-3 \pm \sqrt{25}}{2}$$

$$y = \frac{-3 \pm 5}{2}$$

$$y = \frac{-3 + 5}{2} \quad \text{or} \quad y = \frac{-3 - 5}{2}$$

$y = 1$　or　$y = -4$

C. $3x^2 + 8x + 5 = 0$
$a = 3, b = 8, c = 5$

$$x = \frac{-8 \pm \sqrt{(8)^2 - 4(3)(5)}}{2(3)}$$

$$x = \frac{-8 \pm \sqrt{4}}{6}$$

$$x = \frac{-8 \pm 2}{6}$$

$$x = \frac{-8 + 2}{6} \quad \text{or} \quad x = \frac{-8 - 2}{6}$$

$x = -1$　or　$x = -\dfrac{5}{3}$

D. $x^2 + 4x + 1 = 0$
$a = 1, b = 4, c = 1$

$$x = \frac{-4 \pm \sqrt{4^2 - 4(1)(1)}}{2(1)}$$

$$x = \frac{-4 \pm \sqrt{12}}{2}$$

$$x = \frac{-4 \pm 2\sqrt{3}}{2}$$

$x = -2 \pm \sqrt{3}$

E. $2y^2 + 3y = 5$
$2y^2 + 3y - 5 = 0$
$a = 2, b = 3, c = -5$

$$y = \frac{-3 \pm \sqrt{3^2 - 4(2)(-5)}}{2(2)}$$

$$y = \frac{-3 \pm \sqrt{49}}{4}$$

$$y = \frac{-3 \pm 7}{4}$$

$$y = \frac{-3 + 7}{4} \quad \text{or} \quad y = \frac{-3 - 7}{4}$$

$y = 1$　or　$y = -2.5$

F. $4x^2 + 5 = 4x$
$4x^2 - 4x + 5 = 0$
$a = 4, b = -4, c = 5$

$$x = \frac{-(-4) \pm \sqrt{(-4)^2 - 4(4)(5)}}{2(4)}$$

$$x = \frac{4 \pm \sqrt{-64}}{8}$$

Since $b^2 - 4ac < 0$, there are no real solutions.

3. A. $x^2 - 7x > -12$
$x^2 - 7x + 12 > 0$
$(x - 3)(x - 4) > 0$

Case 1: $x - 3 > 0$　and　$x - 4 > 0$
　　　　　 $x > 3$　and　$x > 4$
　　　　　 $x > 4$
or
Case 2: $x - 3 < 0$　and　$x - 4 < 0$
　　　　　 $x < 3$　and　$x < 4$
　　　　　 $x < 3$
The solution is $x > 4$ or $x < 3$.

B. $2y^2 + 2 < 5y$

$2y^2 - 5y + 2 < 0$

$(2y - 1)(y - 2) < 0$

Case 1: $2y - 1 < 0$ and $y - 2 > 0$

$\qquad 2y \quad < 1 \quad$ and $\quad y \qquad > 2$

$\qquad y \quad < \frac{1}{2} \quad$ and $\quad y \qquad > 2$

No solution

or

Case 2: $2y - 1 > 0$ and $y - 2 < 0$

$\qquad 2y \quad > 1 \quad$ and $\quad y \qquad < 2$

$\qquad y \quad > \frac{1}{2} \quad$ and $\quad y \qquad < 2$

$\qquad\qquad \frac{1}{2} < y < 2$

The solution is $\frac{1}{2} < y < 2$.

C. $9x^2 < 9x - 2$

$9x^2 - 9x + 2 < 0$

$(3x - 2)(3x - 1) < 0$

Case 1: $3x - 2 < 0$ and $3x - 1 > 0$

$\qquad 3x \quad < 2 \quad$ and $\quad 3x \qquad > 1$

$\qquad x \quad < \frac{2}{3} \quad$ and $\qquad x > \frac{1}{3}$

$\qquad\qquad \frac{1}{3} < x < \frac{2}{3}$

or

Case 2: $3x - 2 > 0$ and $3x - 1 < 0$

$\qquad 3x \quad > 2 \quad$ and $\quad 3x \qquad < 1$

$\qquad x \quad > \frac{2}{3} \quad$ and $\quad x \qquad < \frac{1}{3}$

No solution

The solution is $\frac{1}{3} < x < \frac{2}{3}$.

D. $x^2 + x \le 6$

$x^2 + x - 6 \le 0$

$(x + 3)(x - 2) \le 0$

Case 1: $x + 3 \le 0$ and $x - 2 \ge 0$

$\qquad x \quad \le -3 \quad$ and $\quad x \qquad \ge 2$

No solution

or

Case 2: $x + 3 \ge 0$ and $x - 2 \le 0$

$\qquad x \ge -3 \quad$ and $\quad x \qquad \le 2$

$\qquad\qquad -3 \le x \le 2$

The solution is $-3 \le x \le 2$.

E. $y^2 \ge 5y + 24$

$y^2 - 5y - 24 \ge 0$

$(y - 8)(y + 3) \ge 0$

Case 1: $y - 8 \ge 0$ and $y + 3 \ge 0$

$\qquad y \quad \ge 8 \quad$ and $\quad y \qquad \ge -3$

$\qquad y \quad \ge 8$

or

Case 2: $y - 8 \le 0$ and $y + 3 \le 0$

$\qquad y \quad \le 8 \quad$ and $\quad y \qquad \le -3$

$\qquad y \quad \le -3$

The solution is $y \ge 8$ or $y \le -3$.

F. $4x - 5x^2 \le -12$

$-5x^2 + 4x + 12 \le 0$

$5x^2 - 4x - 12 \ge 0$

$(5x + 6)(x - 2) \ge 0$

Case 1: $5x + 6 \ge 0$ and $x - 2 \ge 0$

$\qquad 5x \quad \ge -6 \quad$ and $\quad x \qquad \ge 2$

$\qquad x \quad \ge -\frac{6}{5} \quad$ and $\quad x \qquad \ge 2$

$\qquad x \quad \ge 2$

or

Case 2: $5x + 6 \le 0$ and $x - 2 \le 0$

$\qquad 5x \quad \le -6 \quad$ and $\quad x \qquad \le 2$

$\qquad x \quad \le -\frac{6}{5} \quad$ and $\quad x \qquad \le 2$

$\qquad x \quad \le -\frac{6}{5}$

The solution is $x \ge 2$ or $x \le -\frac{6}{5}$.

▨ FUNCTIONS

A **relation** is a set of ordered pairs, an equation, or a rule. In the ordered pair, the first element belongs to the **domain**, and this value is usually represented by x. The second element in the ordered pair belongs to the **range**, and this value is usually represented as y.

A **function** is a relation for which the first element in the ordered pair is paired with exactly one second element. This can be stated that for each x value, there is exactly one y value. You denote a function in the variable x by $f(x)$.

Sometimes a special symbol such as $\diamond$, $\square$, #, or $*$ may denote the rule for a function. For example, $\square$ could be defined so that $3\square = 5(3) - 2$, # could denote $5\# = 5^2 + 3(5)$, and $*$ could be defined so that $x* = x^2 + 3x$.

Example 52

Evaluate each function as indicated.

A. $f(x) = 3x^2 - 2x$ when $x = -2, x = 0, x = 3$
B. $f(x) = 7x - 2$ when $x = -3, x = 0, x = 5$
C. $f(x) = x^3 - 5x$ when $x = -1, x = 0, x = 2$

Solution

A. $f(x) = 3x^2 - 2x$ when $x = -2, x = 0, x = 3$
    $f(-2) = 3(-2)^2 - 2(-2) = 3(4) + 4 = 12 + 4 = 16$
    $f(0) = 3(0)^2 - 2(0) = 3(0) - 0 = 0 - 0 = 0$
    $f(3) = 3(3)^2 - 2(3) = 3(9) - 6 = 27 - 6 = 21$
B. $f(x) = 7x - 2$ when $x = -3, x = 0, x = 5$
    $f(-3) = 7(-3) - 2 = -21 - 2 = -23$
    $f(0) = 7(0) - 2 = 0 - 2 = -2$
    $f(5) = 7(5) - 2 = 35 - 2 = 33$
C. $f(x) = x^3 - 5x$ when $x = -1, x = 0, x = 2$
    $f(-1) = (-1)^3 - 5(-1) = -1 + 5 = 4$
    $f(0) = 0^3 - 5(0) = 0 - 0 = 0$
    $f(2) = 2^3 - 5(2) = 8 - 10 = -2$

Example 53

Evaluate each function as indicated.

A. $x \diamondsuit = 5x^2 - 3x + 10$ when $x = 2, x = -3$
B. $x \square = \dfrac{x^2 - 5x}{x + 2}$ if $x \neq -2$, when $x = 0, x = 3$
C. $x \square y = \dfrac{x^2 + xy - y^2}{xy}$ if $x \neq 0$ and $y \neq 0$, when $x = 2$ and $y = 3$ and when $x = 3$ and $y = -1$

Solution

A. $x \diamondsuit = 5x^2 - 3x + 10$ when $x = 2, x = -3$
    $2 \diamondsuit = 5(2)^2 - 3(2) + 10 = 5(4) - 6 + 10 = 20 - 6 + 10 = 24$
    $-3 \diamondsuit = 5(-3)^2 - 3(-3) + 10 = 5(9) + 9 + 10 = 45 + 9 + 10 = 64$
B. $x \square = \dfrac{x^2 - 5x}{x + 2}$ if $x \neq -2$, when $x = 0, x = 3$
    $0 \square = \dfrac{0^2 - 5(0)}{0 + 2} = \dfrac{0 - 0}{2} = 0$
    $3 \square = \dfrac{3^2 - 5(3)}{3 + 2} = \dfrac{9 - 15}{5} = \dfrac{-6}{5}$
C. $x \square y = \dfrac{x^2 + xy - y^2}{xy}$ if $x \neq 0$ and $y \neq 0$, when $x = 2$ and $y = 3$ and when $x = 3$ and $y = -1$
    $2 \square 3 = \dfrac{2^2 + 2(3) - 3^2}{2(3)} = \dfrac{4 + 6 - 9}{6} = \dfrac{1}{6}$
    $3 \square -1 = \dfrac{3^2 + 3(-1) - (-1)^2}{3(-1)} = \dfrac{9 - 3 - 1}{-3} = \dfrac{5}{-3} = \dfrac{-5}{3}$

▬ PRACTICE PROBLEMS

1. Demonstrate that each expression is not a function by evaluating it for the given x value.

   A. $x^2 + y^2 = 25$ for $x = 3$

   B. $y^2 = 5x + 11$ for $x = 5$

2. Evaluate each function as indicated.

   A. $f(x) = \dfrac{3}{x+4}, x \neq -4$ for $x = -3$

   B. $f(x) = x^2 - 9x$ for $x = 6$

   C. $f(x) = 9 - 2x^2$ for $x = -2$

   D. $f(x) = \dfrac{x^2 - 3}{2x}, x \neq 0$, for $x = 5$

   E. $f(x) = 2(x+5)^2$ for $x = 2$

3. Evaluate each function as indicated.

   A. $x \diamond = 3x^2 - 2x$ for $x = 2$

   B. $x \square = \dfrac{x}{x^2 + 2}$ for $x = 6$

   C. $x \square = \dfrac{5x - 2}{7 - 4x}$ for $x = -3$

   D. $x \square y = 2x^2 - 5y^2$ for $x = 3$ and $y = -2$

   E. $x \square y = y^2 - 5xy$ for $x = 5$ and $y = 3$

▬ SOLUTIONS

1. A. $x^2 + y^2 = 25$ for $x = 3$
      $3^2 + y^2 = 25$
      $9 + y^2 = 25$
      $y^2 = 16$
      $y = \pm 4$
      Since $(3, 4)$ and $(3, -4)$ are values for the expression, it is not a function.

   B. $y^2 = 5x + 11$ for $x = 5$
      $y^2 = 5(5) + 11$
      $y^2 = 25 + 11$
      $y^2 = 36$
      $y = \pm 6$
      Since $(5, 6)$ and $(5, -6)$ are values for the expression, it is not a function.

2. A. $f(x) = \dfrac{3}{x+4}, x \neq -4$, for $x = -3$

      $f(-3) = \dfrac{3}{-3+4} = \dfrac{3}{1} = 3$

   B. $f(x) = x^2 - 9x$ for $x = 6$
      $f(6) = 6^2 - 9(6)$
      $f(6) = 36 - 54 = -18$

   C. $f(x) = 9 - 2x^2$ for $x = -2$
      $f(-2) = 9 - 2(-2)^2 = 9 - 2(4) = 9 - 8 = 1$

   D. $f(x) = \dfrac{x^2 - 3}{2x}, x \neq 0$, for $x = 5$

      $f(x) = \dfrac{5^2 - 3}{2(5)} = \dfrac{25 - 3}{10} = \dfrac{22}{10} = 2.2$

   E. $f(x) = 2(x+5)^2$ for $x = 2$
      $f(x) = 2(2+5)^2 = 2(7)^2 = 2(49) = 98$

3. A. $x \diamond = 3x^2 - 2x$ for $x = 2$
      $2 \diamond = 3(2)^2 - 2(2) = 3(4) - 4 = 12 - 4 = 8$

   B. $x \square = \dfrac{x}{x^2 + 2}$ for $x = 6$

      $6 \square = \dfrac{6}{6^2 + 2} = \dfrac{6}{36 + 2} = \dfrac{6}{38} = \dfrac{3}{19}$

   C. $x \square = \dfrac{5x - 2}{7 - 4x}$ for $x = -3$

      $3 \square = \dfrac{5(-3) - 2}{7 - 4(-3)} = \dfrac{-15 - 2}{7 + 12} = \dfrac{-17}{-19}$

   D. $x \square y = 2x^2 - 5y^2$ for $x = 3$ and $y = -2$
      $3 \square 2 = 2(3)^2 - 5(2)^2 = 2(9) - 5(4) = 18 - 20 = -2$

   E. $x \square y = y^2 - 5xy$ for $x = 5$ and $y = 3$
      $5 \square 3 = 3^2 - 5(5)3 = 9 - 75 = -66$

▬ ALGEBRAIC WORD PROBLEMS

Solving word problems combines two skills: translating word statements into algebraic expressions and solving equations. A general procedure for solving word problems allows you to solve problems over a wide variety of applications.

Solving Word Problems

1. Read the problem carefully, looking for key terms and concepts. Identify the question you must answer. A diagram may help you to interpret the given information.
2. List all the unknown quantities in the problem and represent them in terms of one variable if possible, such as x or x and y.
3. Use the information identified in step 1 to write algebraic relationships among the quantities identified in step 2.
4. Combine the algebraic relationships into equations.
5. Solve the equation or system of equations.
6. Verify your results by checking against the facts in the problem.

Example 54

Solve these numerical word problems.

A. The sum of two numbers is 94, and the larger number is 5 less than twice the smaller number. Find the numbers.
B. Two numbers have a sum of 18. Find the numbers if one number is 8 larger than the other.
C. Find three consecutive integers if their sum is 21.
D. Find three consecutive even integers such that the first plus twice the second plus 4 times the third equals 174.

Solution

A. $x =$ smaller number   Represent the smaller number by using x.

$2x - 5 =$ larger number   Represent the larger number.
$x + 2x - 5 = 94$ Add the two numbers to get the sum.
$3x - 5 = 94$ Combine like terms to simplify.
$x = 33$ Solve the equation.
$2x - 5 = 2(33) - 5 = 66 - 5 = 61.$ Find the larger number.
The two numbers are 33 and 61.   Write an answer to the question asked.

B. $x =$ smaller number
$y =$ larger number
$\quad x + y = 18$
$\quad x + 8 = y$

$\begin{array}{ll} x + y = 18 & x + y = 18 \\ \underline{+ \; x - y = -8} & 5 + y = 18 \\ \quad\; 2x \quad\;\; = 10 & \qquad y = 13 \\ \quad\;\; x \quad\;\; = \;\; 5 & \end{array}$

The two numbers are 5 and 13.

C. $x =$ first integer
$x + 1 =$ second integer
$x + 2 =$ third integer
$x + x + 1 + x + 2 = 21$
$3x + 3 = 21$
$3x = 18$
$x = 6$
$x + 1 = 7$
$x + 2 = 8$
The three consecutive integers are 6, 7, and 8.

D. x = first even integer
$x + 2$ = second even integer
$x + 4$ = third even integer
$x + 2(x + 2) + 4(x + 4) = 174$
$x + 2x + 4 + 4x + 16 = 174$
$7x + 20 = 174$
$7x = 154$
$x = 22$
$x + 2 = 24$
$x + 4 = 26$
The three consecutive even integers are 22, 24, and 26.

Example 55

Solve these age word problems.

A. Carlos is 3 years older than his brother Jose. In 4 years from now, the sum of their ages will be 33 years. How old is each now?
B. Kia is 5 years younger than her sister Yvette. Three years ago, the sum of their ages was 23. How old is each now?

Solution

A. x = age of Jose now   Represent the younger person's age as x.
  $x + 3$ = age of Carlos now   Using x, represent the older person's age.
  $x + 4 + x + 3 + 4 = 33$ Add their ages in 4 years to get that sum.
  $2x + 11 = 33$ Combine like terms to simplify.
  $2x = 22$ Solve the equation.
  $x = 11$ Find the second person's age.
  $x + 3 = 14$ Write an answer to the question asked.
Jose is 11 years old now and Carlos is 14 years old.

B. x = age of Yvette now
  $x - 5$ = age of Kia now
  $x - 3 + x - 5 - 3 = 23$
  $2x - 11 = 23$
  $2x = 34$
  $x = 17$
  $x - 5 = 12$
Kia is 12 years old now and Yvette is 17 years old.

Example 56

Solve these statistical word problems.

A. Ken's percent grades on five tests were 84, 72, 91, 64, and 83. Find the average (arithmetic mean) grade.
B. Von had an average percent score on the first four tests of 84, and his average percent score on the next six tests was 92. What was Von's average score for all the tests?
C. Marie's monthly school expenses were $64, $82, $51, $90, $67, $71, $58, $94, and $63. What is Marie's median monthly school expense?
D. Tim's monthly food costs were $412, $408, $410, $408, $401, $410, and $408. What is the mode for the monthly food costs?

Solution

A. SUM $= 84 + 72 + 91 + 64 + 83 = 394$, $N = 5$
    AVE $=$ SUM $\div N = 394 \div 5 = 78.8$
    Ken's average percent score is 78.8.
B. Average of 4 tests 84, average of 6 tests 92

$$AVE = \frac{4(84) + 6(92)}{4 + 6} = \frac{336 + 552}{10} = \frac{888}{10} = 88.8$$

Von's average score on the 10 tests was 88.8.
C. Sequenced expenses: \$51, \$58, \$63, \$64, \$67, \$71, \$82, \$90, \$94. Since there are an odd number of values, the median is the middle value, the fifth one. The median of Marie's monthly school expense is \$67.
D. Sequenced costs: \$401, \$401, \$408, \$408, \$408, \$410, \$410, \$412, \$420. The most frequent number is \$408. The mode monthly food cost for Tim is \$408.

Example 57

Solve these mixture word problems.

A. Beth has one solution that is 16% acid and a second solution that is 26% acid. How many ounces of each is needed to make 30 ounces of a solution that is 18% acid?
B. Lynn has 100 pounds of candy worth \$4.80 per pound. How many pounds of a second candy worth \$5.20 per pound should she mix with the 100 pounds to obtain a mixture worth \$5.00 per pound?

Solution

A. $x =$ number of ounces of 16%   Represent one quantity.
    acid solution
    $30 - x =$ number of ounces of 26%   Represent second quantity.
    acid solution
    $0.16x + 0.26(30 - x) = 0.18(30)$ Represent the number of
                                                      ounces of acid.

    $0.16x + 7.8 - 0.26x = 5.4$ Simplify the equation.
    $-0.10x + 7.8 = 5.4$
    $-0.10x = -2.4$ Solve the equation.
    $x = 24$
    $30 - x = 6$ Find the second quantity.
    Beth needs to use 24 ounces of the   Write an answer to
    16% acid solution and 6 ounces   the question asked.
    of the 26% acid solution.

B. $x =$ number of pounds of \$5.20 per pound candy needed
    $100(\$4.80) + x(\$5.20) = (100 + x)(\$5.00)$
    $\$480 + \$5.20x = \$500 + \$5.00x$
    $\$480 + \$0.20x = \$500$
    $\$0.20x = \$20$
    $x = 100$
    Lynn needs to use 100 pounds of the \$5.20 candy.

Example 58

Solve these rate word problems.

A. Tyrone rides his bicycle 5 miles from his home to the city bus stop at the rate of 8 miles per hour. He arrives in time to catch the bus to work, which travels at 25 miles per hour. If he spends 1.5 hours traveling from home to work, how far does he travel on the bus?

B. Maria jogs 15 miles to her sister's house to get her bicycle and then bicycles home. The total trip takes 3 hours. If she bicycles twice as fast as she jogs, how fast does she bicycle?

C. Two drivers, Brenda and Julie, are 300 miles apart. Brenda drives at 30 miles per hour, and Julie drives at 45 miles per hour. If they drive toward each other, how far will each have traveled when they meet?

D. At what rate must Eden travel to overtake Rex, who is traveling at a rate 20 miles per hour slower than Eden, if Eden starts 2 hours after Rex and wants to overtake him in 4 hours?

E. Two planes start from Minneapolis at the same time and fly in opposite directions, one averaging 40 miles per hour faster than the other. If they are 2,000 miles apart in 5 hours, what is the average speed for each plane?

Solution

A. $d = rt$ where d is the distance traveled, r is the rate, and t is the time.

$x =$ distance traveled on bus   Represent the quantities.

$\dfrac{5}{8} =$ time spent riding bicycle

$\dfrac{x}{25} =$ time spent riding bus

$\dfrac{5}{8} + \dfrac{x}{25} = \dfrac{3}{2}$ 1.5 hours $= \dfrac{3}{2}$ hours   Add the times to get total time.

$200\left(\dfrac{5}{8}\right) + 200\left(\dfrac{x}{25}\right) = 200\left(\dfrac{3}{2}\right)$

LCM$(8, 25, 2) = 200$ Clear equation of fractions.

$25(5) + 8(x) = 100(3)$ Simplify the equation.

$125 + 8(x) = 300$

$8x = 175$ Solve the equation.

$x = 21.875$

Tyrone traveled 21.875 miles on the bus.   Write the answer to the question.

B. $x =$ miles per hour for jogging
$2x =$ miles per hour for bicycling

$\dfrac{15}{x} + \dfrac{15}{2x} = 3$

$30 + 15 = 6x$
$45 = 6x$
$7.5 = x$
$15 = 2x$

Maria bicycles at the rate of 15 miles per hour.

C. x = time they traveled
   $30x + 45x = 300$
   $75x = 300$
   $x = 4$
   $30x = 120$
   $45x = 180$
   Brenda traveled 120 miles and Julie traveled 180 miles.

D. x = miles per hour for Eden
   $x - 20$ = miles per hour for Rex
   $6(x - 20) = 4x$
   $6x - 120 = 4x$
   $2x - 120 = 0$
   $2x = 120$
   $x = 60$
   Eden needs to travel at 60 miles per hour.

E. x = rate of faster plane
   $x + 40$ = rate of slower plane
   $5x + 5(x + 40) = 2,000$
   $5x + 5x + 200 = 2,000$
   $10x = 1,800$
   $x = 180$
   $x + 40 = 220$
   The planes travel at 180 and 220 miles per hour.

Example 59

Solve these work word problems.

A. Jamal can fill the vending machine in 45 minutes. When his sister, Violet, helps him, it takes them 20 minutes. How long would it take Violet to fill the machine by herself?
B. One pipe can fill a pool in 18 hours. Another pipe can fill it in 24 hours. The drainpipe can empty the tank in 12 hours. With all three pipes open, how long will it take to fill the pool?
C. One work crew can do a job in 8 days. After the first crew worked 3 days, a second crew joins them, and together, the two crews finish the job in 3 more days. How long would it take the second crew to do the job alone?
D. One machine can wrap 200 boxes per hour. A newer machine can wrap 250 boxes per hour. How long would it take the two machines working together to wrap 4,950 boxes?
E. Barbara and Wesley can paint a room together in 6 hours. If Barbara can paint the room alone in 10 hours, how long would it take Wesley working alone to paint the room?

Solution

A. x = number of minutes   Represent each person's time.
   for Violet alone
   $\dfrac{20}{x} + \dfrac{20}{45} = 1$ Add work done by each person.
   $900 + 20x = 45x$ Solve equation.

$$900 = 25x$$
$$36 = x$$

It would take Violet 36 minutes working alone.

Write an answer to the question.

B. x = number of hours together

$$\frac{x}{18} + \frac{x}{24} - \frac{x}{12} = 1 \qquad \text{LCM}(18, 24, 12) = 72$$

$$72 \left(\frac{x}{18} + \frac{x}{24} - \frac{x}{12} \right) = 72(1)$$

$$4x + 3x - 6x = 72$$
$$x = 72$$

With all three pipes open, it would take 72 hours to fill the pool.

C. x = number of days for second crew

$$\frac{6}{8} + \frac{3}{x} = 1$$

$$6x + 24 = 8x$$
$$24 = 2x$$
$$12 = x$$

The second crew could do the job alone in 12 days.

D. x = number of hours together

$$200x + 250x = 4{,}950$$
$$450x = 4{,}950$$
$$x = 11$$

It would take the two machines together 11 hours to do the job.

E. x = number of hours for Wesley

$$\frac{6}{10} + \frac{6}{x} = 1$$

$$6x + 60 = 10x$$
$$60 = 4x$$
$$15 = x$$

Wesley can paint the room alone in 15 hours.

Sometimes you will need to use data from a survey to answer questions. A problem with the data occurs when you allow an object to have multiple attributes. For example, a person might own both a desktop computer and a laptop computer, so that person would belong to two categories.

You use **Venn diagrams** to represent the data in distinct categories while showing relationships among the categories. Overlapping circles allow you to visually analyze the data. For each of the given groups, use one circle. With two groups there are four regions: group 1 only, group 2 only, both groups, and neither group.

Example 60

Solve these problems by using Venn diagrams.

A. One hundred people were asked about the computers that they owned. Laptop computers were owned by 55 people, desktop computers were owned by 68 people, and 28 people owned both a laptop and a desktop computer. How many people did not own a computer? How many people owned just one computer?

B. At a wine-tasting party, 150 people were asked which of the three wines served that they liked.
68 like Boone's Farm Strawberry Hill.
68 like Ripple.
80 like Thunderbird.
35 like Boone's and Thunderbird.
30 like Ripple and Thunderbird.
28 like Boone's and Ripple.
20 like all three.
How many people like exactly two of these wines?
How many people like exactly one of these wines?

Solution

A. Two groups: L = laptops and D = desktops.
Draw a rectangle enclosing two intersecting circles.

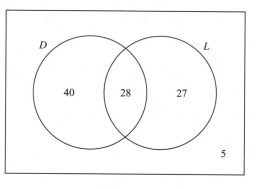

Figure 7.5

Since $N = 100$, the sum of the numbers in the regions must total 100.
Since 28 people owned both a laptop and a desktop, put 28 in the overlap of the circles labeled D and L. There are 55 laptop owners, so $55 - 28 = 27$ goes in the part of L not shared with D. There are 68 desktop owners, so $68 - 28 = 40$ goes in the part of D not in L. You have accounted for $40 + 28 + 27 = 95$ of the 100 people, so 5 are outside the circles for D and L. Thus, there are 5 people who do not own a computer. There are 40 people with desktops only and 27 people with laptops only, so there are $40 + 27 = 67$ people who own one computer.

B. Three groups: B = Boone's, R = Ripple, T = Thunderbird.
Draw a rectangle enclosing three intersecting circles.

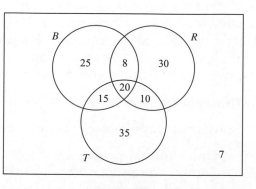

Figure 7.6

Since $N = 150$, the numbers put in the eight regions must total 150. Since 20 people like all three wines, place 20 in the region common to B, R, and T. There are $28 - 20 = 8$ in the overlap of B and R and not in all three, $30 - 20 = 10$ in the overlap of R and T not in all three, and $35 - 20 = 15$ in the overlap of B and T and not in all three. There are $68 - 15 - 20 - 8 = 25$ in B only, $68 - 8 - 20 - 10 = 30$ in R only, and $80 - 15 - 20 - 10 = 35$ in T only. There are $25 + 15 + 20 + 8 + 30 + 10 + 35 = 143$ accounted for by those who like at least one of the wines. There are $150 - 143 = 7$ people who did not like any of the wines.

There are 15 who like Boone's and Thunderbird only, 10 who like Ripple and Thunderbird only, and 8 who like Boone's and Ripple only, so 33 people like exactly two of these wines. There are 25 who like Boone's only, 30 who like Ripple only, and 35 who like Thunderbird only, so 90 people like exactly one of these wines.

Probability is the likelihood that a given event will occur. It is the ratio of the number of favorable outcomes to the total number of outcomes. There are two ways a coin can come up when it is flipped. $P(\text{heads}) = \dfrac{1}{2}$. There are six outcomes for a die when it is rolled: 1, 2, 3, 4, 5, or 6. Thus $P(1) = P(2) = P(3) = P(4) = P(5) = P(6) = \dfrac{1}{6}$.

The probability of an event is $0 \leq P(\text{event}) \leq 1$. There is a probability of 0 only when the event cannot occur, and a probability of 1 when the event is certain to occur. If $P(E)$ is the probability event E will occur, and $P(\text{not } E)$ is the probability event E will not occur, then $P(\text{not } E) = 1 - P(E)$.

Example 61

Find the probability of the event.

A. Two coins are flipped once. What is the probability of getting two tails?
B. A jar contains 3 yellow marbles, 4 green marbles, 2 black marbles, and 1 white marble. One marble is selected without looking. What is the probability that the marble will be green?
C. A box contains 20 light switches, and 3 of them are defective. If you select one switch from the box at random, what is the probability that it will not be defective?
D. What is the probability that a card selected at random from a standard deck of playing cards is a 10?
E. What is the probability that a card selected at random from a standard deck of playing cards will be a 7 or a club?

Solution

A. The possible outcomes are HH, HT, TH, and TT. $P(\text{two tails}) = \dfrac{1}{4}$.

B. $3 + 4 + 2 + 1 = 10$ possible outcomes, 4 outcomes green. $P(\text{green}) = \dfrac{4}{10} = \dfrac{2}{5}$.

C. 20 light switches and 3 are defective. $P(\text{defective}) = \dfrac{3}{20}$, $P(\text{not defective}) = 1 - P(\text{defective})$.

$$P(\text{not defective}) = 1 - \frac{3}{20} = \frac{17}{20}$$

D. There are 52 cards in a standard deck. There are four 10s: 10 of hearts, 10 of clubs, 10 of spades, and 10 of diamonds. $P(10) = \dfrac{4}{52} = \dfrac{1}{13}$.

E. There are 52 cards in a deck. There are 13 each in hearts, clubs, spades, and diamonds. There are four 7s, one each in hearts, clubs, spades, and diamonds. Thus, the 7 of clubs is counted twice, once as a club and once as a 7. There are 13 clubs plus three 7s that are not clubs. $P(7 \text{ or club}) = \dfrac{16}{52} = \dfrac{4}{13}$.

In computing probability, you must find the number of outcomes for the event of interest and the number of outcomes that are possible. In the examples above, you were able to list all the outcomes or reason out how many outcomes there were. This is not always possible, but there are tools that can help you determine the number of outcomes without listing them. The most common of these tools are the multiplication principle, permutations, and combinations.

If an activity consists of distinct parts, then the **multiplication principle** says that the number of ways the activity can be done is the product of the number of ways for all the parts of the activity. If an activity consists of parts A, B, and C and part A can be done in a ways, part B can be done in b ways, and part C can be done in c ways, then the activity can be done in $a \times b \times c$ ways.

Example 62

Find the number of ways each activity can be done.

A. Kim selects a shirt, a pair of slacks, and a jacket to wear to work. She has 7 shirts, 4 pairs of slacks, and 3 jackets in her closet. If she does not worry about which clothes match, how many different outfits can she create?
B. Randy flips a coin and then rolls a six-sided die. How many different outcomes are there?
C. Noah is packing his backpack with toys for a trip to Grandpa Bruce's house. He gets to take 1 car, 1 book, and 1 ball. If Noah has 4 cars, 6 books, and 3 balls, how many different sets of toys can he take?

Solution

A. Kim selects 1 each of her shirts, slacks, and jackets. She has $7 \times 4 \times 3 = 84$ choices. There are 84 different outfits she could create.
B. Randy flips a coin, then rolls a die, so he has $2 \times 6 = 12$ outcomes. There are 12 total outcomes for the activity.
C. Noah packs 1 each of his cars, books, and balls, so he has $4 \times 6 \times 3 = 72$ choices. There are 72 different sets of toys that he could take.

When you select from a collection of objects, the number of ways the selection can be made depends on the number of objects in the collection, the number of objects being selected, and whether the order of selection matters. If the objects selected are all going to be treated exactly the same way, order is not important. However, if the objects will be treated differently based on the sequence of selection, then order is important.

When there are n objects in the collection and you select $r, 0 \leq r \leq n$, objects, and order is important, it is a **permutation**. If order is not important, it is a **combination**. For example, if there are 10 people in a race and the first person to finish gets a trophy, and the second person to finish gets a medal, and the third person to finish gets a ribbon, then you can use permutation to determine in how many different ways the prizes could be awarded. In another race of 10 people, if the first three people to finish go to the next round of competition, then you use combinations to determine the number of ways the group of three people who go on to the next round could turn out. The formulas $_nP_r = \dfrac{n!}{(n-r)!}$ and $_nC_r = \dfrac{n!}{(n-r)! \cdot r!}$ are for computing the number of permutations and combinations, respectively. And $n!$ is defined to be the product of the counting number n and all the counting numbers less than n down to and including 1. Use $0! = 1$ to define $0!$. The ! in these expressions is read as "factorial."

$$7! = 7 \times 6 \times 5 \times 4 \times 3 \times 2 \times 1 = 5,040 \text{ and } 6! = 6 \times 5 \times 4 \times 3 \times 2 \times 1 = 720$$

$$n! = n \times (n-1)! \quad \text{so} \quad 7! = 7 \times 6! = 7 \times 720 = 5,040$$

Example 63

Evaluate each expression.

   A. $_9P_7$ **B.** $_8P_3$ **C.** $_9C_7$ **D.** $_8C_3$

Solution

A. $_9P_7 = \dfrac{9!}{(9-7)!} = \dfrac{9 \times 8 \times 7 \times 6 \times 5 \times 4 \times 3 \times 2!}{2!} = 181,440$

B. $_8P_3 = \dfrac{8!}{(8-3)!} = \dfrac{8 \times 7 \times 6 \times 5!}{5!} = 336$

C. $_9C_7 = \dfrac{9!}{(9-7)! \times 7!} = \dfrac{9 \times 8 \times 7!}{2! \times 7!} = \dfrac{72}{2} = 36$

D. $_8C_3 = \dfrac{8!}{(8-3)! \times 3!} = \dfrac{8 \times 7 \times 6 \times 5!}{5! \times 3!} = \dfrac{336}{6} = 56$

Example 64

1. Café Laura offers a lunch consisting of one of 4 soups, one of 7 sandwiches, one of 5 chips, and one of 3 drinks. How many different lunches can it serve?
2. A sorority has 10 members, and 4 of them are to attend the national convention. In how many ways can the 4 people attending the national convention be selected?
3. There are 20 members on the city council. One is to be selected chairperson, a second person will be selected vice-chairperson, and a third person will be selected secretary. In how many ways can these offices be filled?

Solution

1. Since the activity has four separate parts that can be done in multiple ways, use the multiplication principle. Lunch = soup, sandwich, chips, and drink: $4 \times 7 \times 5 \times 3 = 420$. There are 420 possible lunches that could be served at Café Laura.

2. Since all 4 members selected will go to the convention, order of selection is not important. Use combinations.

$$_{10}C_4 = \frac{10!}{(10-4)! \times 4!} = \frac{10 \times 9 \times 8 \times 7 \times 6!}{6! \times 4!} = \frac{10 \times 9 \times 8 \times 7}{4 \times 3 \times 2 \times 1} = 210$$

3. Since the 3 people selected are given offices based on their order of selection, use permutations.

$$_{20}P_3 = \frac{20!}{(20-3)!} = \frac{20!}{17!} = \frac{20 \times 19 \times 18 \times 17!}{17!} = 20 \times 19 \times 18 = 6,840$$

PRACTICE PROBLEMS

1. Find two numbers such that twice the first plus 5 times the second is 20, and 4 times the first less 3 times the second is 14.

2. Three more than twice a certain number is 57. Find the number.

3. Wendy's mother is 3 times as old as Wendy. In 14 years, she will be twice as old as Wendy is then. How old is each now?

4. Joan is 3 years older than Susan. Eight years ago, Joan was 4 times the age of Susan. How old is each now?

5. Michelle scored 95, 91, 98, 90, 96, and 100. What is her average test score?

6. David weighed himself each week. In May, he weighed himself 5 times with an average weight of 185 pounds. In June, he weighed himself 4 times with an average weight of 180 pounds. What is his average weight?

7. John's cell phone bills were $87, $81, $88, $87, $84, $87, $89, $80, $78, $79, $81, and $82 for the past year. What was the median for his bills? What is the mode for his bills?

8. An 80% acid solution is mixed with a 20% acid solution to get 3 gallons of a solution that is $\frac{1}{3}$ acid. How much of each acid solution was used?

9. A mixture of 40 pounds of mixed nuts worth $1.80 a pound is to be made from peanuts costing $1.35 a pound added to fancy mixed nuts costing $2.55 a pound. How many pounds of each kind of nut should be used?

10. In her motorboat, Ruth can go downstream in 1 hour less time than she can go upstream. If the current is 5 miles per hour, how fast can she travel in still water if it takes her 2 hours to travel upstream the given distance?

11. Two drivers started toward each other from towns 255 miles apart. One driver traveled at 40 miles per hour, and the other traveled at 45 miles per hour. How long did the people drive until they met?

12. Amanda can mow a lawn in 1 hour 20 minutes. Kim can mow the same lawn in 2 hours. How long would it take them, working together, to mow the lawn?

13. One computer can do a payroll in 12 hours. A second computer can do the payroll in 6 hours. How long will it take to do the payroll if both computers work on the payroll at the same time?

14. A survey was taken of 52 students at Macon High School. They were asked which amusement parks they would like to visit on a class trip: Six Flags, Disney World, and Opryland. The data is summarized as follows.

    28 preferred Six Flags.
    25 preferred Disney World.
    26 preferred Opryland.
    10 preferred Opryland and Disney World.
    11 preferred Disney World and Six Flags.
    14 preferred Six Flags and Opryland.
    6 preferred all three.

    How many students prefer both Disney World and Six Flags and did not prefer Opryland? How many did not prefer any of these three sites?

15. Three coins are flipped once. What is the probability that exactly two coins will be heads?

16. A card is selected at random from a standard deck of playing cards. What is the probability that the card selected is a red card or a jack?

17. Chez Vicki makes a lunch special with 3 choices of salad, 4 types of sandwiches, and 2 desserts. One of the types of sandwich is grilled cheese. What is the probability that if you make the lunch special choices at random, you will get a lunch containing a grilled cheese sandwich?

18. If a club has 10 members and 3 are to be chosen to be delegates to a conference, what is the probability that Sara, a member of the club, will be one of the delegates?

SOLUTIONS

1. x = first number
   y = second number
   (1) $2x + 5y = 20$
   (2) $4x - 3y = 14$

(2)	$4x - 3y =$	14		$4x - 3y = 14$
$-2 \times (2) +$	$-4x - 10y =$	-40		$4x - 3(2) = 14$
	$-13y =$	-26		$4x - 6 = 14$
	$y =$	2		$4x = 20$
				$x = 5$

   The first number is 5 and the second number is 2.

2. x = the number
   $2x + 3 = 57$
   $2x = 54$
   $x = 27$
   The number is 27.

3. x = Wendy's age now
   $3x$ = mother's age now
   $3x + 14 = 2(x + 14)$
   $3x + 14 = 2x + 28$
   $x + 14 = 28$
   $x = 14$
   $3x = 42$
   Wendy is 14 years old, and her mother is 42 years old now.

4. x = Susan's age now
   $x + 3$ = Joan's age now
   $x + 3 - 8 = 4(x - 8)$
   $x - 5 = 4x - 32$
   $-3x - 5 = -32$
   $-3x = -27$
   $x = 9$
   $x + 3 = 12$
   Joan's age is 12 years and Susan's age is 9 years now.

5. SUM $= 95 + 91 + 98 + 90 + 96 + 100 = 570$,
   $N = 6$
   AVE = SUM $\div N = 570 \div 6 = 95$
   Michelle's average test score is 95.

6. May: average is $185 - 5$ weighings. June: average is $180 - 4$ weighings.
   $$\text{AVE} = \frac{5(185) + 4(180)}{5 + 4} = \frac{925 + 720}{9} = \frac{1,645}{9} = 182.7777 = 182.8$$

   David's average weight is 182.8 pounds to the nearest tenth of a pound.

7. Sequenced bills: $78, $79, $80, $81, $81, $82, $84, $87, $87, $87, $88, $89. There are 12 bills, and the middle two values are $82 and $84.
   The median is ($82 + $84) $\div 2 = $83.
   The bill of $87 occurred the most, 3 times. The mode is $87.

8. x = gallons of 80% acid used
   $3 - x$ = gallons of 20% acid used
   Since $\frac{1}{3}$ of the 3 gallons is acid, 1 gallon of the solution is acid.
   $0.80x + 0.20(3 - x) = 1$
   $0.80x + 0.60 - 0.20x = 1$
   $0.60x + 0.60 = 1$
   $0.60x = 0.40$
   $x = \dfrac{0.40}{0.60} = \dfrac{2}{3}$
   $3 - x = 2\dfrac{1}{3}$
   So $\frac{2}{3}$ gallon of the 80% acid solution and $2\frac{1}{3}$ gallons of the 20% solution were used.

9. x = number of pounds of peanuts used
$40 - x$ = number of pounds of fancy mixed nuts used
$\$1.35x + \$2.55(40 - x) = \$1.80(40)$
$\$1.35x + \$102.00 - \$2.55x = \$72.00$
$-\$1.20x + \$102.00 = \$72.00$
$-\$1.20x = -\$30.00$
$x = 25$
$40 - x = 15$
So 25 pounds of peanuts and 15 pounds of fancy mixed nuts should be used.

10. x = still water rate of Ruth's boat
$x + 5$ = downstream rate of boat
$x - 5$ = upstream rate of boat
$2(x - 5) = 1(x + 5)$
$2x - 10 = x + 5$
$x = 15$
The still water rate of Ruth's motorboat is 15 miles per hour.

11. x = time each drove until they met
$40x + 45x = 255$
$85x = 255$
$x = 3$
It took the drivers 3 hours to meet.

12. x = number of minutes working together
$\dfrac{x}{80} + \dfrac{x}{120} = 1$
$3x + 2x = 240$
$5x = 240$
$x = 48$
They can mow the lawn together in 48 minutes.

13. x = number of hours for two computers to do payroll together
$\dfrac{x}{12} + \dfrac{x}{6} = 1$
$x + 2x = 12$
$3x = 12$
$x = 4$
It would take the two computers 4 hours to do the payroll together.

14. 3 categories: S = Six Flags, O = Opryland, D = Disney World

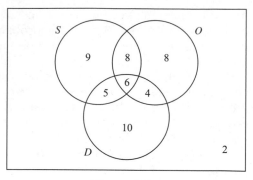

Figure 7.7

Placing the number who prefer all three in the diagram first, determine the regions for two. $10 - 6 = 4$, $11 - 6 = 5$, and $14 - 6 = 8$. From the completed Venn diagram, 5 people prefer Six Flags and Disney World and do not prefer Opryland. Two did not prefer any of the three sites.

15. Three coins are flipped with possible outcomes of HHH, HHT, HTH, HTT, THH, THT, TTH, TTT. Of the 8 outcomes, 3 have exactly 2 heads.
$P(\text{exactly 2 heads}) = \dfrac{3}{8}$

16. There are 52 cards in a standard deck of playing cards, of which 26 are red cards. Of the 4 jacks, 2 are red and 2 are black. Thus, there are $26 + 2$ red cards and nonred jacks.
$P(\text{red or jack}) = \dfrac{28}{52} = \dfrac{7}{13}$

17. $P(\text{lunch special with grilled cheese}) = \dfrac{3 \times 1 \times 2}{3 \times 4 \times 2} = \dfrac{1}{4}$

18. $P(\text{Sara is a delegate}) = \dfrac{{}_9C_2 \times 1}{{}_{10}C_2} = \dfrac{36 \times 1}{120} = \dfrac{36}{120} = \dfrac{3}{10}$

◼◼◼ ALGEBRA TEST

Use the following test to assess how well you have mastered the material in this chapter. For each question, mark your answer by blackening the corresponding answer oval. An answer key and solutions are provided at the end of the test.

1. Which is equal to $(x^2 + 2x + 3) - (2x^2 + x - 5) - (-x^2 - 3x + 1)$?

   (A) $4x + 7$
   (B) $4x - 1$
   (C) $-2x^2 + 4x + 7$
   (D) $2x^2 + 4x - 1$
   (E) $-2x^2 + 9$

2. Which is equal to $(x^3)^2 + 5^3(5^4)$?

   (A) $x^9 + 5^7$
   (B) $x^9 + 25^7$
   (C) $x^6 + 25^7$
   (D) $x^6 + 25^7$
   (E) $x^6 + 5^7$

3. Which is $\sqrt{300x^5y^9}$ completely simplified?

   (A) $10x^2y^4\sqrt{3xy}$
   (B) $10x^2y^2\sqrt{3xy}$
   (C) $10x^2y^3\sqrt{3x}$
   (D) $3x^2y^4\sqrt{10xy}$
   (E) $5xy\sqrt{8x^3y^5}$

4. Which is $2\sqrt{108y} - \sqrt{27y} + \sqrt{363y}$ completely simplified?

   (A) $14\sqrt{3y}$
   (B) $14\sqrt{3}$
   (C) $9\sqrt{3y} + \sqrt{363y}$
   (D) $20\sqrt{3y}$
   (E) $20\sqrt{y}$

5. Which is $9(13) - 7(8 + 2) \div 5$ simplified completely?

   (A) -9
   (B) 61.4
   (C) 103
   (D) 108
   (E) 131

6. Which illustrates the commutative property of multiplication?

   (A) $15 + 17 = 17 + 15$
   (B) $x \cdot (8 + y) = (8 + y) \cdot x$
   (C) $5 \cdot (8 + 2) = 5 \cdot 8 + 5 \cdot 2$
   (D) $8 \cdot (7 \cdot x) = (8 \cdot 7) \cdot x$
   (E) $(3 + x) \cdot 5 = 3 \cdot 5 + x \cdot 5$

7. Which is the algebraic expression that is the translation of "The product of 7 and x decreased by 5 equals 3 subtracted from x"?

   (A) $7x + 5 = 3 - x$
   (B) $7(x - 5) = 3 - x$
   (C) $7x - 5 = 3 - x$
   (D) $7(x - 5) = x - 3$
   (E) $7x - 5 = x - 3$

8. Which is the value of $x^2 - 5y$ when $x = -6$ and $y = 2$?

   (A) -46
   (B) -22
   (C) -12
   (D) 26
   (E) 34

9. Which of these equations has -3 as its solution?

   (A) $y - 6 = 9$
   (B) $-y = -3$
   (C) $y + 5 = 2$
   (D) $4y - 9 = 3$
   (E) $-9x = 3$

10. Which is the value of C when $F = 68$, using the formula $F = 1.8C + 32$?

    (A) 2
    (B) 18
    (C) 20
    (D) 33.8
    (E) 36

11. Which is the value of $\dfrac{a - b}{a + b}$ when $a = 5$ and $b = 10$?

    (A) -3

    (B) $-\dfrac{1}{3}$

    (C) $-\dfrac{1}{2}$

    (D) $\dfrac{1}{3}$?

    (E) 3

12. Which is the value of $3x^2y - 5xy^3$ when $x = -2$ and $y = -3$?

    (A) -306
    (B) -126
    (C) -54
    (D) 234
    (E) 306

13. What is the value of v when $V = 45$, $g = 32$, and $t = 5$ using the formula $v = V + gt$?

   (A) 82
   (B) 205
   (C) 257
   (D) 385
   (E) 7,200

14. $\begin{aligned} & 5x^2 + 3x - 2y^2 \\ + & \underline{-2x^2 - 8x + 2y^2} \end{aligned}$ What is the sum?

   (A) $3x^4 - 5x^2$
   (B) $3x^4 - 5x^2 + y^4$
   (C) $7x^2 + 1x - 4y^2$
   (D) $3x^2 - 5x$
   (E) $3x^2 - 5x + y^2$

15. $\begin{aligned} & 3a^2 - 6ab - 2b^2 \\ - & \underline{-4a^2 + 8ab - 8b^2} \end{aligned}$ What is the difference?

   (A) $-a^2 + 2ab - 10b^2$
   (B) $-a^2 - 14ab - 10b^2$
   (C) $7a^2 - 14ab - 10b^2$
   (D) $7a^2 + 2ab - 10b^2$
   (E) $7a^2 - 14ab + 6b^2$

16. $\begin{aligned} & 3x^4 - 5x^3 \\ \times & \underline{ - 5x + 4} \end{aligned}$ What is the product?

   (A) $-15^5 - 20x^3$
   (B) $25x^3 + 12x^4$
   (C) $-15x^5 + 37x^4 - 20x^3$
   (D) $-15x^5 + 25x^4 + 4$
   (E) $3x^4 - 5x^3 - 5x + 4$

17. $\dfrac{12a^2b^3 - 28a^4b^4}{4ab^2}$ What is the value of the quotient?

   (A) $3ab - 28a^4b^4$
   (B) $12a^2b^3 - 7a^3b^2$
   (C) $3ab - 7a^3b^2$
   (D) $8a^2b - 22a^3b^2$
   (E) $-4a^4b^3$

18. Which is equal to $(3x - 5)^2$?

   (A) $9x^2 + 25$

   (B) $9x^2 - 25$

   (C) $9x^2 - 15x + 25$

   (D) $9x^2 - 30x + 25$

   (E) $9x^2 + 30x + 25$

19. Which expression is not defined when $x = 4$?

   (A) $\dfrac{x - 4}{x + 4}$

   (B) $\dfrac{3}{x^2 + 4}$

   (C) $\dfrac{2x^2}{x^2 - 4}$

   (D) $x - 4$

   (E) $\dfrac{3}{x - 4}$

20. Which is $25x^2 - 49$ factored completely?

   (A) $(25x - 1)(x + 49)$

   (B) $(5x - 7)(5x + 7)$

   (C) $(5x - 7)(7x - 5)$

   (D) $(5x + 7)(5x + 7)$

   (E) $(5x - 7)(5x - 7)$

21. Which is $3x^2 + 10x + 3$ factored completely?

   (A) $(3x + 3)(x + 1)$

   (B) $(3x + 1)(x + 3)$

   (C) $(3x - 1)(x + 3)$

   (D) $(3x + 1)(x - 3)$

   (E) $(3x - 1)(x - 3)$

22. Which is $10x^2 + 11x - 6$ factored completely?

   (A) $(5x + 2)(2x - 3)$

   (B) $(10x - 1)(x + 6)$

   (C) $(5x + 2)(2x + 3)$

   (D) $(10x + 1)(x - 6)$

   (E) $(5x - 2)(2x + 3)$

23. Which is $\dfrac{x^2 + 2x - 8}{x^2 - x - 2}$ reduced to lowest terms?

(A) $\dfrac{x + 4}{x + 1}$

(B) $\dfrac{x - 4}{x - 1}$

(C) $\dfrac{x - 4}{x + 1}$

(D) $\dfrac{x + 4}{x - 1}$

(E) 4

24. Which is equal to $\dfrac{4}{x^2 - x} - \dfrac{2}{x^2 - 1}$?

(A) $\dfrac{x + 2}{x(x - 1)(x + 1)}$

(B) $\dfrac{2}{x(x - 1)}$

(C) $\dfrac{2(x + 2)}{x(x - 1)(x + 1)}$

(D) $\dfrac{2}{x(x + 1)}$

(E) $\dfrac{4}{x}$

25. Which is $\dfrac{a^2}{a + 1} \cdot \dfrac{a^2 - 1}{a^3}$ in simplest form?

(A) $\dfrac{a + 1}{a^2}$

(B) $a(a + 1)$

(C) $\dfrac{a - 1}{a}$

(D) $\dfrac{a + 1}{a}$

(E) $\dfrac{a - 1}{a^2}$

26. Which is the solution of $x - 3 - 2(6 - 2x) = 2(2x - 5)$?

    (A) -2

    (B) -1

    (C) $\dfrac{20}{7}$

    (D) 5

    (E) 10

27. Which is the solution of $(2x + 1)^2 = (x - 4)^2 + 3x(x + 3)$?

    (A) $-\dfrac{17}{3}$

    (B) -5

    (C) 5

    (D) $\dfrac{17}{3}$

    (E) 6

28. If $A = 0.5h(a + b)$ is solved for b, what is the value of b?

    (A) $b = 2A - h - a$

    (B) $b = \dfrac{A - 0.05h}{a}$

    (C) $b = A - 0.5ah$

    (D) $b = A - 0.5h - a$

    (E) $b = \dfrac{2A - ah}{h}$

29. Which is the solution of $\dfrac{2}{x - 3} - \dfrac{4}{x + 3} = \dfrac{16}{x^2 - 9}$?

    (A) 4

    (B) 1

    (C) -0.5

    (D) -6.5

    (E) -8

30. Which is the solution of $\dfrac{5}{6} = \dfrac{n}{30}$?

    (A) 150

    (B) 36

    (C) 29

    (D) 25

    (E) 20

31. Which is the solution of $\sqrt{5x - 3} = 4$?

   (A) 1

   (B) 1.4

   (C) 3.8

   (D) 4.2

   (E) 5

32. Which is a solution for the system of equations $3x - y = -2$ and $x + y = 6$?

   (A) (3, 1)

   (B) (2, 4)

   (C) (−4, −10)

   (D) (1, 5)

   (E) (3, 3)

33. Which is a solution for the system of equations $13x + 11y = 21$ and $7x + 6y = -3$?

   (A) (159, −186)

   (B) (3, −4)

   (C) (−56, 49)

   (D) (−4, 5)

   (E) (−43, 38)

34. Which is the solution for $7(x - 3) \leq 4(x + 5) - 47$?

   (A) $x \leq 2$

   (B) $x \geq -2$

   (C) $x \geq 2$

   (D) $x \leq -2$

   (E) $x \geq 0$

35. Which are the solutions for $9x^2 - 2x - 11 = 0$?

   (A) $\dfrac{11}{9}, -1$

   (B) $-\dfrac{11}{9}, 1$

   (C) $-\dfrac{11}{9}, -1$

   (D) $\dfrac{11}{9}, 1$

   (E) $\dfrac{11}{3}, -\dfrac{1}{3}$

36. Which are the solutions for $(x + 1)(2x - 1) = 2$?

   (A) $\frac{3}{2}, -1$

   (B) $1, 1$

   (C) $\frac{2}{3}, -1$

   (D) $\frac{3}{2}, 0$

   (E) $-\frac{3}{2}, 1$

37. Which are the solutions for $4x^2 = -16x$?

   (A) $0, 4$

   (B) $0, -4$

   (C) $4, -4$

   (D) -4 only

   (E) 4 only

38. Which is the solution for $6x^2 - 8x = 3$?

   (A) $\frac{4 \pm \sqrt{34}}{6}$

   (B) $\frac{-4 \pm \sqrt{34}}{6}$

   (C) $\frac{2 \pm \sqrt{34}}{3}$

   (D) $\frac{4 \pm \sqrt{2}}{6}$

   (E) No real solutions

39. Which is the solution $x^2 + 3x < 28$?

   (A) $x < -7$

   (B) $x > 4$

   (C) $-4 < x < 7$

   (D) $-7 < x < 4$

   (E) No real solutions

40. If $f(x) = 2x^2 - 4x - 3$, what is $f(-2)$?

   (A) -3

   (B) -1

   (C) 11

   (D) 13

   (E) 21

41. Two bicyclists travel in opposite directions. One travels 5 miles per hour faster than the other. In 2 hours they are 50 miles apart. What is the rate of the faster bicyclist?

    (A) 10 mph
    (B) 11.25 mph
    (C) 15 mph
    (D) 20 mph
    (E) 22.5 mph

42. Two sisters were born in consecutive years. How old are they now if the product of their present ages is 1,056?

    (A) 12, 13
    (B) 16, 66
    (C) 31, 36
    (D) 32, 33
    (E) 42, 43

43. A bicycle rider travels 8 miles per hour faster than a jogger. It takes the bicyclist one-half as long as it takes the jogger to travel 16 miles. What is the jogger's speed?

    (A) 8 mph
    (B) 16 mph
    (C) 24 mph
    (D) 32 mph
    (E) 40 mph

44. Anthony and Ben can paint a water tower in 6 days when they work together. If Anthony works twice as fast as Ben, how long would it take Ben to paint the water tower, working alone?

    (A) 1.5 days
    (B) 3 days
    (C) 4.5 days
    (D) 9 days
    (E) 18 days

45. Pipe A can fill a tank in 20 minutes. Pipe B can empty the tank in 30 minutes. Pipe C can fill the tank in 60 minutes. If all three pipes work together, how long will it take to fill the tank?

    (A) 10 minutes
    (B) 20 minutes
    (C) 30 minutes
    (D) 45 minutes
    (E) 60 minutes

46. What is the average (mean) of the values 18, 16, 24, 16, 16, 24?

    (A) 16
    (B) 17
    (C) 18
    (D) 19
    (E) 24

47. What is the median for the set of values 62, 72, 62, 83, 79, 68, 72, 62?

    (A) 62
    (B) 68
    (C) 70
    (D) 72
    (E) 83

48. A survey of 50 people at a shopping center provided the following information:

    25 like country music.
    21 like rap music.
    10 like both country music and rap music.

    How many people in the survey did not like either country music or rap music?

    (A) 4
    (B) 6
    (C) 14
    (D) 16
    (E) 24

49. What is the probability of drawing at random one green marble from a bag containing 24 green marbles and 32 yellow marbles?

    (A) $\dfrac{1}{24}$

    (B) $\dfrac{3}{7}$

    (C) $\dfrac{4}{7}$

    (D) $\dfrac{2}{3}$

    (E) $\dfrac{3}{4}$

50. Two hundred tickets were sold for a charity raffle. You buy 5 tickets. What is the probability that you will not win the raffle?

    (A) 0.02
    (B) 0.025
    (C) 0.5
    (D) 0.975
    (E) 0.98

ANSWER KEY

1. A	11. B	21. B	31. C	41. C
2. E	12. A	22. E	32. D	42. D
3. A	13. B	23. A	33. A	43. A
4. D	14. D	24. C	34. D	44. E
5. C	15. E	25. C	35. A	45. C
6. B	16. C	26. D	36. E	46. D
7. E	17. C	27. C	37. B	47. C
8. D	18. D	28. E	38. A	48. C
9. C	19. E	29. B	39. D	49. B
10. C	20. B	30. D	40. D	50. D

SOLUTIONS

1. **A** $4x + 7$
$(x^2 + 2x + 3) - (2x^2 + x - 5) - (-x^2 - 3x + 1) = x^2 + 2x + 3 - 2x^2 - x + 5 + x^2 + 3x - 1 = 0x^2 + 4x + 7 = 4x + 7$

2. **E** $x^6 + 5^7$
$(x^3)^2 + 5^3 \cdot 5^4 = x^{3 \cdot 2} + 5^{3+4} = x^6 + 5^7$

3. **A** $10x^2y^4\sqrt{3xy}$
$\sqrt{300x^5y^9} = \sqrt{3 \cdot 100 \cdot x^4 \cdot x \cdot y^8 \cdot y} = \sqrt{100x^4y^8}\sqrt{3xy} = 10x^2y^4\sqrt{3xy}$

4. **D** $20\sqrt{3y}$
$2\sqrt{108y} - \sqrt{27y} + \sqrt{363y} = 2\sqrt{36}\sqrt{3y} - \sqrt{9}\sqrt{3y} + \sqrt{121}\sqrt{3y} = 2(6)\sqrt{3y} - 3\sqrt{3y} + 11\sqrt{3y} = 12\sqrt{3y} - 3\sqrt{3y} + 11\sqrt{3y} = 20\sqrt{3y}$

5. **C** 103
$9(13) - 7(8 + 2) \div 5 = 117 - 7(10) \div 5 = 117 - 14 = 103$

6. **B** $x \cdot (8 + y) = (8 + y) \cdot x$
$x \cdot (8 + y) = (8 + y) \cdot x$ is $a \cdot b = b \cdot a$ when $a = x, b = (8 + y)$

7. **E** $7x - 5 = x - 3$

8. **D** 26
$x^2 - 5y = (-6)^2 - 5(2) = 36 - 10 = 26$

9. **C** $y + 5 = 2$
$y + 5 = -3 + 5 = 2$ $y + 5 = 2$ has solution -3

10. **C** 20
$F = 1.8C + 32$, $F = 68$, $68 = 1.8C + 32$, $36 = 1.8C$, $C = 20$

11. **B** $-\dfrac{1}{3}$

$\dfrac{a - b}{a + b} = \dfrac{5 - 10}{5 + 10} = \dfrac{-5}{15} = \dfrac{-1}{3}$

12. **A** -306

$3x^2y - 5xy^3 = 3(-2)^2(-3) - 5(-2)(-3)^3 = -36 - 270 = -306$

13. **B** 205

$v = V + gt, V = 45, g = 32, t = 5, v = 45 + 32(5) = 45 + 160 = 205$

14. **D** $3x^2 - 5x$

$$\begin{array}{r} 5x^2 + 3x - 2y^2 \\ + \underline{-2x^2 - 8x - 2y^2} \\ 3x^2 - 5x \end{array}$$

15. **E** $7a^2 - 14ab + 6b^2$

$$\begin{array}{r} 3a^2 - 6ab - 2b^2 \\ - \underline{-4a^2 + 8ab - 8b^2} \\ 7a^2 - 14ab + 6b^2 \end{array}$$

16. **C** $-15x^5 + 37x^4 - 20x^3$

$$\begin{array}{r} 3x^4 - 5x^3 \\ \times \underline{- 5x + 4} \\ -15x^5 + 25x^4 \\ \underline{+ 12x^4 - 20x^3} \\ -15x^5 + 37x^4 - 20x^3 \end{array}$$

17. **C** $3ab - 7a^3b^2$

$$\frac{12a^2b^3 - 28a^4b^4}{4ab^2} = 3ab - 7a^3b^2$$

18. **D** $9x^2 - 30x + 25$

$(3x - 5)^2 = (3x)^2 - 2(3x)(5) + 5^2 = 9x^2 - 30x + 25$

19. **E** $\dfrac{3}{x - 4}$

$\dfrac{3}{x - 4} = \dfrac{3}{4 - 4} = \dfrac{3}{0}$ Not defined

20. **B** $(5x - 7)(5x + 7)$

$25x^2 - 49 = (5x)^2 - 7^2 = (5 - 7)(5x + 7)$

21. **B** $(3x + 1)(x + 3)$

$3x^2 + 10x + 3 = (3x + 1)(x + 3)$

22. **E** $(5x - 2)(2x + 3)$

$10x^2 + 11x - 6 = 10(-6) = -60, 15(-4) = 60,$ and $+15 - 4 = 11$
$10x^2 + 15x - 4x - 6 = 5x(2x + 3) - 2(2x + 3) = (5x - 2)(2x + 3)$

23. **A** $\dfrac{x + 4}{x + 1}$

$\dfrac{x^2 + 2x - 8}{x^2 - x - 2} = \dfrac{(x + 4)(x - 2)}{(x + 1)(x - 2)} = \dfrac{x + 4}{x + 1}$

24. **C** $\dfrac{2(x+2)}{x(x+1)(x-1)}$

$$\dfrac{4}{x^2-x} - \dfrac{2}{x^2-1} = \dfrac{4}{x(x-1)} - \dfrac{2}{(x+1)(x-1)} = \dfrac{4(x+1)-2x}{x(x+1)(x-1)} =$$

$$\dfrac{2x+4}{x(x+1)(x-1)} = \dfrac{2(x+2)}{x(x-1)(x+1)}$$

25. **C** $\dfrac{a-1}{A}$

$$\dfrac{a^2}{a+1} - \dfrac{a^2-1}{a^3} = \dfrac{a-1}{a}$$

26. **D** 5

$x - 3 - 2(6 - 2x) = 2(2x - 5)$
$x - 3 - 12 + 4x = 4x - 10$
$x - 15 = -10$
$x = 5$

27. **C** 5

$(2x+1)^2 = (x-4)^2 + 3x(x+3)$
$4x^2 + 4x + 1 = x^2 - 8x + 16 + 3x^2 + 9x$
$4x + 1 = -8x + 16 + 9x$
$3x + 1 = 16$
$3x = 15$
$x = 5$

28. **E** $b = \dfrac{2A - ah}{h}$

$A = 0.5h(a + b)$
$2A = h(a + b)$
$2A = ha + hb$
$2A - ha = hb$

$\dfrac{2A - ah}{h} = b$

29. **B** 1

$$\dfrac{2}{x-3} - \dfrac{4}{x+3} = \dfrac{16}{x^2-9}$$

$2(x+3) - 4(x-3) = 16$

$2x + 6 - 4x + 12 = 16$

$-2x + 18 = 16$
$-2x = -2$
$x = 1$

30. **D** 25

$\dfrac{5}{6} = \dfrac{n}{30}, 6n = 150, n = 25$

31. **C** 3.8

$$\sqrt{5x - 3} = 4$$
$$(\sqrt{5x - 3})^2 = (4)^2$$
$$5x - 3 = 16$$
$$5x = 19$$
$$x = 3.8$$

32. **D** (1, 5)

$$
\begin{array}{ll}
3x - y = -2 & 3(1) - y = -2 \\
+\ \underline{x + y = 6} & -y = -5 \\
4x = 4 & y = 5 \\
x = 1 & y = 5
\end{array}
$$

$$(1, 5) = (x, y)$$

33. **A** (159, −186)

$$
\begin{array}{llll}
(1)\ \ 13x + 11y = 21 & 6 \times (1) & 78x + 66y = 126 \\
(2)\ \ 7x + 6y = -3 & -11 \times (2) & +\ \underline{-77x - 66y = 33} \\
& & x = 159
\end{array}
$$

$$7(159) + 6y = -3, 1,113 + 6y = -3, 6y = -1,116, y = -186$$
$$(x, y) = (159, -186)$$

34. **D** $x \le -2$

$$7(x - 3) \le 4(x + 5) - 47$$
$$7x - 21 \le 4x + 20 - 47$$
$$7x - 21 \le 4x - 27$$
$$3x - 21 \le -27$$
$$3x \le -6$$
$$x \le -2$$

35. **A** $\dfrac{11}{9}, -1$

$$9x^2 - 2x - 11 = 0$$
$$(9x - 11)(x + 1) = 0$$
$$9x - 11 = 0 \quad \text{or} \quad x + 1 = 0$$
$$x = \frac{11}{9} \quad \text{or} \quad x = -1$$

36. **E** $-\dfrac{3}{2}, 1$

$$(x + 1)(2x - 1) = 2$$
$$2x^2 + x - 1 = 2$$
$$2x^2 + x - 3 = 0$$
$$(2x + 3)(x - 1) = 0$$
$$2x + 3 = 0 \quad \text{or} \quad x - 1 = 0$$
$$x = -\frac{3}{2} \qquad\qquad x = 1$$

37. **B** 0, −4

$$4x^2 = -16x$$
$$4x^2 + 16x = 0$$
$$4x(x + 4) = 0$$
$$4x = 0 \quad \text{or} \quad x + 4 = 0$$
$$x = 0 \qquad\qquad x \quad = -4$$

38. **A** $\dfrac{4 \pm \sqrt{34}}{6}$

$$6x^2 - 8x = 3$$
$$6x^2 - 8x - 3 = 0$$
$$a = 6, b = -8, c = -3$$

$$x = \frac{-b \pm \sqrt{b^2 - 4ac}}{2a}$$

$$x = \frac{-(-8) \pm \sqrt{(-8)^2 - 4(6)(-3)}}{2(6)}$$

$$x = \frac{8 \pm \sqrt{136}}{12}$$

$$x = \frac{8 \pm 2\sqrt{34}}{12}$$

$$x = \frac{4 \pm \sqrt{34}}{6}$$

39. **D** $-7 < x < 4$

$$x^2 + 3x < 28$$
$$x^2 + 3x - 28 < 0$$
$$(x + 7)(x - 4) < 0$$
Case 1: $x + 7 < 0 \quad$ and $\quad x - 4 > 0$
$$x \quad < -7 \qquad\qquad x \quad > 4$$
No solution
or
Case 2: $x + 7 > 0 \quad$ and $\quad x - 4 < 0$
$$x \quad > -7 \qquad\qquad x \quad < 4$$
$$-7 < x < 4$$
The solution is $-7 < x < 4$.

40. **D** 13

$$f(x) = 2x^2 - 4x - 3$$
$$f(-2) = 2(-2)^2 - 4(-2) - 3 = 8 + 8 - 3 = 13$$

41. **C** 15 mph

$$x = \text{slower rate}$$
$$x + 5 = \text{faster rate}$$
$$2x + 2(x + 5) = 50$$
$$2x + 2x + 10 = 50$$
$$4x = 40$$
$$x = 10$$
$$x + 5 = 15$$

42. **D** 32, 33

    x = first age
    $x + 1$ = second age
    $x(x + 1) = 1,056$
    $x^2 + x - 1,056 = 0$
    $(x + 33)(x - 32) = 0$
    $x + 33 = 0$ or $x - 32 = 0$
    $x \quad\quad = -33$ $x \quad\quad = 32$
    -33 is not a solution. $x = 32, x + 1 = 33$

43. **A** 8 mph

    x = rate for jogger
    $x + 8$ = rate for bicyclist

    $$\frac{16}{x} = 2\frac{16}{x + 8}$$

    $$\frac{16}{x} = \frac{32}{x + 8}$$

    $16(x + 8) = 32x$
    $16x + 128 = 32x$
    $128 = 16x$
    $8 = x$

44. **E** 18 days

    x = time for Anthony alone
    $2x$ = time for Ben alone

    $$\frac{6}{x} + \frac{6}{2x} = 1$$

    $12 + 6 = 2x$
    $18 = 2x$
    $9 = x$

45. **C** 30 minutes

    x = time to complete job together
    LCM(20, 30, 60) = 60

    $$\frac{x}{20} - \frac{x}{30} + \frac{x}{60} = 1$$

    $3x - 2x + x = 60$
    $2x = 60$
    $x = 30$ minutes

46. **D** 19

    SUM $= 18 + 16 + 24 + 16 + 16 + 24 = 114$ $N = 6$
    AVE $=$ SUM $\div N = 114 \div 6 = 19$

47. **C** 70

    Sequential list: 62, 62, 62, 68, 72, 72, 79, 83
    Eight values in list so average of the middle two values is median.
    Median $= (68 + 72) \div 2 = 140 \div 2 = 70$

48. **C** 14

Two categories: C = country music, R = rap music

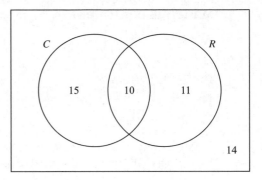

$50 - (15 + 10 + 11) = 50 - 36 = 14$ not in any category.
There are 14 people who do not like either.

49. **B** $\dfrac{3}{7}$

24 green marbles, 32 yellow marbles, $24 + 32 = 56$ marbles
$P(\text{green}) = \dfrac{24}{56} = \dfrac{3}{7}$

50. **D** 0.975

$P(\text{win}) = \dfrac{5}{200} = 0.025$
$P(\text{lose}) = 1 - P(\text{win}) = 1 - 0.025 = 0.975$

GMAT SOLVED PROBLEMS

For each question, select the best answer.

1. **Which is equivalent to $5^6 \cdot 5^8$?**

   A. 5^{14}
   B. 10^{14}
   C. 25^{14}
   D. 5^{48}
   E. 25^{48}

2. **Which expression shows the result when $\sqrt{54} - \sqrt{24} + \sqrt{96}$ has been simplified and combined?**

   A. $-24\sqrt{6}$
   B. $-\sqrt{174}$
   C. $4\sqrt{6}$
   D. $\sqrt{126}$
   E. $5\sqrt{6}$

3. **Which number is equivalent to $4 \cdot 5^3 + 12 \div 3 - 3^2$?**

   A. 58
   B. 495
   C. 498
   D. 7,995
   E. 7,999

4. **Which expression is equivalent to $(5x - 3y)^2$?**

   A. $10x - 6y$
   B. $25x - 9y$
   C. $25x^2 - 9y^2$
   D. $25x^2 - 15xy + 9y^2$
   E. $25x^2 - 30xy + 9y^2$

5. **Which expression is equivalent to $\dfrac{(x+y)^2}{12} \div \dfrac{(x+y)^5}{36}$?**

   A. $\dfrac{(x+y)^3}{3}$

   B. $\dfrac{(x+y)^{10}}{432}$

   C. $\dfrac{(x+y)^7}{48}$

   D. $\dfrac{3}{(x+y)^3}$

   E. $\dfrac{3}{x+y}$

6. Which number is a solution for $\dfrac{x+5}{4} = \dfrac{x}{8} + 3$?

    A. −14
    B. −7
    C. 0
    D. 7
    E. 14

7. $x, y,$ and z are numbers that have a sum of 93. Find the numbers.

    1. **The numbers are primes.**
    2. **The numbers are consecutive integers.**

    A. Statement 1 ALONE is sufficient, but statement 2 is not sufficient.
    B. Statement 2 ALONE is sufficient, but statement 1 is not sufficient.
    C. BOTH statements TOGETHER are sufficient, but NEITHER statement ALONE is sufficient.
    D. EACH statement ALONE is sufficient.
    E. Statements 1 and 2 TOGETHER are NOT sufficient.

8. **Jack is 4 years older than Daniel. What are their ages now?**

    1. **16 years ago, Jack was twice as old as Daniel.**
    2. **18 years ago, Jack was 3 times as old as Daniel.**

    A. Statement 1 ALONE is sufficient, but statement 2 is not sufficient.
    B. Statement 2 ALONE is sufficient, but statement 1 is not sufficient.
    C. BOTH statements TOGETHER are sufficient, but NEITHER statement ALONE is sufficient.
    D. EACH statement ALONE is sufficient.
    E. Statements 1 and 2 TOGETHER are NOT sufficient.

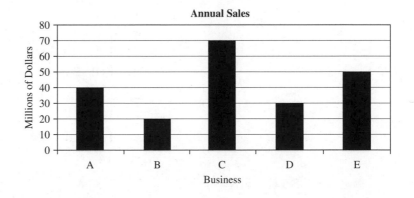

9. **Which two businesses together earned exactly $80 million?**

    A. A and B
    B. B and C
    C. C and D
    D. D and E
    E. A and E

10. **What two businesses together had sales equal to the sales of business E?**

    A. A and B
    B. B and D
    C. A and D
    D. B and E
    E. C and D

SOLUTIONS

1. **A** $5^6 \cdot 5^8 = 5^{6+8} = 5^{14}$

2. **E**

$$\sqrt{54} - \sqrt{24} + \sqrt{96} = \sqrt{9}\sqrt{6} - \sqrt{4}\sqrt{6} + \sqrt{16}\sqrt{6} = 3\sqrt{6} - 2\sqrt{6} + 4\sqrt{6}$$
$$= (3 - 2 + 4)\sqrt{6} = 5\sqrt{6}$$

3. **B** $4 \cdot 5^3 + 12 \div 3 - 3^2 = 4 \cdot 125 + 12 \div 3 - 9 = 500 + 4 - 9 = 504 - 9 = 495$

4. **E** $(5x - 3y)^2 = (5x)^2 + 2(5x)(-3y) + (-3y)^2 = 25x^2 - 30xy + 9y^2$, so the answer is E.

5. **D** $\dfrac{(x+y)^2}{12} \div \dfrac{(x+y)^5}{36} = \dfrac{(x+y)^2}{12} \cdot \dfrac{36}{(x+y)^5} = \dfrac{1}{1} \cdot \dfrac{3}{(x+y)^3} = \dfrac{3}{(x+y)^3}$
   So, the answer is D.

6. **E**

$$\frac{x+5}{4} = \frac{x}{8} + 3$$
$$\frac{8}{1} \cdot \frac{x+5}{4} = \frac{8}{1} \cdot \frac{x}{8} + 8 \cdot 3$$
$$2(x+5) = x + 24$$
$$2x + 10 = x + 24$$
$$2x + 10 - x = x + 24 - x$$
$$x + 10 = 24$$
$$x + 10 - 10 = 24 - 10$$
$$x = 14$$

So the answer is E.

7. **B** For statement 1, you need to find exactly one set of prime numbers, each less than 93, whose sum is 93. Because 3, 43, and 47 are primes and $3 + 43 + 47 = 93$, and 3, 29, and 61 are primes and $3 + 29 + 61 = 93$, statement 1 does not determine x, y, and z uniquely.

   For statement 2, you need to find exactly one set of consecutive integers with a sum of 93. The only set of numbers that meets the criterion is 30, 31, and 32. Thus, statement 2 determines x, y, and z uniquely.
   Since statement 2 alone is sufficient, the correct answer is B.

8. **D** You can construct a table of possible ages.

Daniel's age	1	2	3	4	5	6	7	8	9	10	11	12	13	14	15	16	17	18	19	20
Jack's age	5	6	7	8	9	10	11	12	13	14	15	16	17	18	19	20	21	22	23	24

Statement 1 says that 16 years ago, Jack was twice as old as Daniel. When Jack was 8 and Daniel was 4, Jack was twice as old. Now, 16 years later, Jack is 24 and Daniel is 20. So statement 1 determines their ages.

Statement 2 says that 18 years ago, Jack was 3 times as old as Daniel. According to the table, this was true when Jack was 6 and Daniel was 2. Their current ages, 18 years later, are 24 for Jack and 20 for Daniel. So statement 2 determines their ages.

Thus, both statements alone determine their ages, and the correct answer is D.

9. **D** According to the graph, business D had $30 million in sales and business E had $50 million in sales. So D and E together had $80 million in sales. Thus, the answer is D.

10. **B** Business E has sales of $50 million. Business B has $20 million in sales and business D has $30 million. So B + D = E, and the answer is B.

GMAT PRACTICE PROBLEMS

For each question, select the best answer.

1. **Combine like terms: $5x + 8x^3 - 2x^2 + 3x + 5x^3 - 6x + 4x^2$**

    A. $17x$
    B. $17x^{10}$
    C. $2x + 2x^2 + 13x^3$
    D. $2x^3 + 2x^4 + 13x^6$
    E. $17x^6$

2. **Which number is equal to $27^{-2/3}$?**

    A. -18
    B. -9
    C. $-\dfrac{1}{18}$
    D. $\dfrac{1}{9}$
    E. 9

3. **Evaluate this expression: $6 \times 5 - 18 \div 3 + 6 \times 10$.**

    A. 280
    B. 84
    C. 10
    D. -24
    E. -600

4. **What property is illustrated by $20 + (5 \cdot 4) = 20 + (4 \cdot 5)$?**

   A. Commutative property for multiplication
   B. Commutative property for addition
   C. Distributive property
   D. Associative property for multiplication
   E. Associative property for addition

5. **Which is the product for $(2x - 5)(2x + 5)$?**

   A. $4x$
   B. $4x^2 - 25$
   C. $4x^2 + 25$
   D. $4x^2 - 10x + 25$
   E. $4x^2 + 10x + 25$

6. **Which is the solution of $\dfrac{3}{x-3} + 4 = \dfrac{x}{x-3}$?**

   A. 0
   B. 3
   C. 7
   D. All real numbers are solutions.
   E. There is no solution.

7. **What is the value of x?**

   1. $2(x + y) = x + 2y$
   2. $x^3 + y^3 = (x + y)^3$

   A. Statement (1) ALONE is sufficient, but statement (2) is not sufficient.
   B. Statement (2) ALONE is sufficient, but statement (1) is not sufficient.
   C. BOTH statements TOGETHER are sufficient, but NEITHER statement ALONE is sufficient.
   D. EACH statement ALONE is sufficient.
   E. Statements (1) and (2) TOGETHER are not sufficient.

8. **If $xy = 10$, what is the value of $x + y$?**

   1. **x and y are positive numbers.**
   2. $\dfrac{1}{x} + \dfrac{1}{y} = 3$

   A. Statement 1 ALONE is sufficient, but statement 2 is not sufficient.
   B. Statement 2 ALONE is sufficient, but statement 1 is not sufficient.
   C. BOTH statements TOGETHER are sufficient, but NEITHER statement ALONE is sufficient.
   D. EACH statement ALONE is sufficient.
   E. Statements 1 and 2 TOGETHER are not sufficient.

County	Population, 1990	Population, 2000
Brown	180,500	204,300
Carson	140,300	157,800
Lake	97,300	106,200
Mounds	240,300	272,400
Polk	150,300	175,200

9. **Which county had the greatest increase in population from 1990 to 2000?**

    A. Brown
    B. Carson
    C. Lake
    D. Mounds
    E. Polk

10. **Which county had the greatest percentage increase in population from 1990 to 2000?**

    A. Brown
    B. Carson
    C. Lake
    D. Mounds
    E. Polk

ANSWER KEY

1.	C
2.	D
3.	B
4.	A
5.	B
6.	E
7.	A
8.	B
9.	D
10.	E

CHAPTER 8

GEOMETRY

π	pi (about 3.14)
‖	is parallel to
⊥	is perpendicular to
∠	angle
△	triangle
a°	a degrees
∟	right angle

POINTS, LINES, AND ANGLES

Points are represented with dots and are named by capital letters. A line extends indefinitely in two directions and can be named by naming two points on it. Because a line has infinitely many points, a line can have many names.

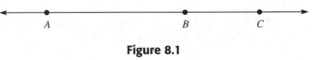

Figure 8.1

The line in Figure 8.1 can be named line *AB*, line *AC*, or line *BC*.

- A **line segment** is a part of a line between two points. The two points are the endpoints of the line segment.

In Figure 8.1, there is a line segment *AB*, a line segment *AC*, and a line segment *BC*. The line segment *AB* and the line segment *BA* are two names for the same segments, *AB* = *BA*.

- A **ray** is a part of a line with exactly one endpoint. Ray *AB* is a ray with endpoint *A* going through point *B*. Ray *BA* is a ray with endpoint *B* going through point *A*. Ray *AB* ≠ ray *BA*.
- An **angle** is the figure formed by two rays with a common endpoint. The common endpoint of the rays is called the **vertex** of the angle, and the rays are called the **sides** of an angle.

The symbol for an angle is ∠. An angle can be named by stating only its vertex if no other angle has the same vertex. In general, an angle is named by naming a point on one side of the angle, then its vertex, and finally a point on the other side of the angle. In Figure 8.2, the angle can be named ∠A, ∠BAC, ∠CAB, ∠BAD, ∠DAB, and ∠EAC, among many other names.

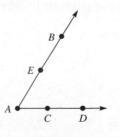

Figure 8.2

253

Angles are measured in degrees. There are 360° about a point and 180° about the point staying on one side of a line through that point.

The measure of an angle is the number of degrees of rotation it takes to get from one side of the angle to the other.

- An **acute angle** is an angle whose measure is greater than 0° but less than 90°.
- A **right angle** is an angle whose measure is exactly 90°.
- An **obtuse angle** is an angle whose measure is greater than 90° but less than 180°.
- A **straight angle** is an angle whose sides are a pair of opposite rays and the measure is exactly 180°.
- A **reflex angle** is an angle whose measure is greater than 180°, but less than 360°.
- **Adjacent angles** are two angles in the same plane that have a common vertex and a common side that separates the two angles.

If the rotation from one side of the angle to the other is 0°, the rays lie on top of each other. Also, if the rotation between the sides of the angle is 360°, the rays lie on top of each other. In both cases, the angle looks like a single ray.

- Two angles are **complementary** if the sum of the measures is 90°.
- Two angles are **supplementary** if the sum of the measures is 180°.

To be complementary or supplementary, the two angles do not have to be adjacent. The sum of the measures of the two angles is all that matters in deciding if the pair of angles is either supplementary or complementary. A way to remember which pair has which sum is to put the terms in alphabetical order, complementary then supplementary, and put the sums in numerical order, 90° then 180°. The results match up in the orders shown.

Example 1

Find the complement of each angle.

A. 17°   B. 24°   C. 87°   D. 60°

Solution

A. $90° - 17° = 73°$
B. $90° - 24° = 66°$
C. $90° - 87° = 3°$
D. $90° - 60° = 30°$

Example 2

Find the supplement of each angle.

A. 156°   B. 95°   C. 103°   D. 135°

Solution

A. $180° - 156° = 24°$
B. $180° - 95° = 85°$
C. $180° - 103° = 77°$
D. $180° - 135° = 45°$

- **Vertical angles** are two nonadjacent angles formed when two lines intersect.
- **Two lines are perpendicular** when they intersect to form right angles. This can be written as line $a \perp$ line b.
- **Two lines** in same plane **are parallel** if they do not intersect. This can be written as line $a \parallel$ line b.

When two lines intersect, the angles in each pair of vertical angles formed have equal measures. When two parallel lines are intersected by a third line, several special types of angles are formed. In Figure 8.3, lines a and b are parallel; line t is called a transversal.

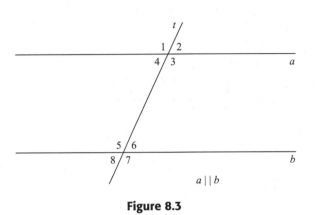

Figure 8.3

In Figure 8.3, $\angle 1$ and $\angle 5$ are a pair of **corresponding angles.** The other pairs of corresponding angles are $\angle 2$ and $\angle 6$, $\angle 3$ and $\angle 7$, and $\angle 4$ and $\angle 8$. Because $a \parallel b$, $\angle 1 = \angle 5$, $\angle 2 = \angle 6$, $\angle 3 = \angle 7$, and $\angle 4 = \angle 8$. Another pair of special angles is $\angle 3$ and $\angle 5$, which are **alternate interior angles**, and so are $\angle 4$ and $\angle 6$. Lines $a \parallel b$, $\angle 3 = \angle 5$, and $\angle 4 = \angle 6$. The **alternate exterior angles** are $\angle 1$ and $\angle 7$, and $\angle 2$ and $\angle 8$, which are equal since the lines are parallel. Angles 4 and 5 and angles 3 and 6 are interior angles on the same side of the transversal. Since $a \parallel b$, $\angle 4$ is supplementary to $\angle 5$ and $\angle 3$ is supplementary to $\angle 6$. Thus, $\angle 3 + \angle 6 = 180°$ and $\angle 4 + \angle 5 = 180°$.

If the measure of $\angle 1$ is $140°$, you can find the measure of all the other angles in Figure 8.3.

$\angle 1$ and $\angle 3$ are a pair of vertical angles so $\angle 1 = \angle 3$, then $\angle 3 = 140°$.

$\angle 1$ and $\angle 5$ are corresponding angles, $\angle 1 = \angle 5$, then $\angle 5 = 140°$.

$\angle 5$ and $\angle 7$ are vertical angles, $\angle 5 = \angle 7$, then $\angle 7 = 140°$.

$\angle 3$ and $\angle 6$ are interior angles on the same side of the transversal t, so $\angle 3$ supplements $\angle 6$, $\angle 3 + \angle 6 = 180°$, $140° + \angle 6 = 180°$, $\angle 6 = 180° - 140° = 40°$.

$\angle 6$ and $\angle 2$ are corresponding angles, so $\angle 6 = \angle 2$ and $\angle 2 = 40°$.

$\angle 6$ and $\angle 4$ are alternate interior angles, so $\angle 6 = \angle 4$ and $\angle 4 = 40°$.

$\angle 4$ and $\angle 8$ are corresponding angles, so $\angle 4 = \angle 8$ and $\angle 8 = 40°$.

When $a \parallel b$ and $\angle 1 = 140°$, $\angle 3 = \angle 5 = \angle 7 = 140°$ and $\angle 2 = \angle 4 = \angle 6 = \angle 8 = 40°$.

Angles 1 and 2 are adjacent angles, and the noncommon sides form a straight line; thus, $\angle 1$ and $\angle 2$ are a linear pair and are supplementary.

PRACTICE PROBLEMS

1. Find the supplements of these angles.
   A. $127°$ B. $90°$ C. $28°$ D. $30°$ E. $57°$

2. Find the complement of these angles.
   A. $71°$ B. $12°$ C. $76°$ D. $30°$ E. $45°$

3. Find the angles requested.
   A. An angle is 4 times its complement. Find the angle.
   B. An angle is 8 times its supplement. Find the angle.
   C. An angle is $10°$ less than its complement. Find the angle.
   D. An angle is $30°$ more than its supplement. Find the angle.
   E. An angle is $10°$ more than 3 times its complement. Find the angle.
   F. If twice an angle is added to $45°$, you get the supplement of the angle. Find the angle.

4. Using Figure 8.3 with $a \parallel b$, find all the angles 2 through 8.
   A. $\angle 1 = 72°$ B. $\angle 1 = 90°$ C. $\angle 1 = 125°$

5. In Figure 8.3 with $a \parallel b$, $\angle 1 = 4x° + 20°$, and $\angle 4 = 4x°$, find the measures of angles 1 through 8.

6. In Figure 8.3 with $a \parallel b$, $\angle 3 = 5x°$ and $\angle 4 = 3x° - 20°$, find the measures of angles 1 through 8.

7. In Figure 8.3 with $a \parallel b$, $\angle 7 = 3x° + 10°$ and $\angle 2 = x° - 30°$, find the measures of angles 1 through 8.

SOLUTIONS

1. A. $180° - 127° = 53°$
   B. $180° - 90° = 90°$
   C. $180° - 28° = 152°$
   D. $180° - 30° = 150°$
   E. $180° - 57° = 123°$

2. A. $90° - 71° = 19°$
   B. $90° - 12° = 78°$
   C. $90° - 76° = 14°$
   D. $90° - 30° = 60°$
   E. $90° - 45° = 45°$

3. A. $n =$ the complement, $4n =$ the angle
   $n + 4n = 90°$
   $5n = 90°$
   $n = 18°$
   $4n = 72°$
   The angle is $72°$.
   B. $n =$ complement, $8n =$ angle
   $n + 8n = 180°$
   $9n = 180°$
   $n = 20°$
   $8n = 160°$
   The angle is $160°$.
   C. $n =$ complement, $n - 10° =$ angle
   $n + n - 10° = 90°$
   $2n - 10° = 90°$
   $2n = 100°$
   $n = 50°$
   $n - 10° = 40°$
   The angle is $40°$.

D. $n =$ angle, $n - 30° =$ supplement
   $n + n - 30° = 180°$
   $2n - 30° = 180°$
   $2n = 210°$
   $n = 105°$
   The angle is $105°$.
E. $n =$ complement, $3n + 10° =$ angle
   $n + 3n + 10° = 90°$
   $4n + 10° = 90°$
   $4n = 80°$
   $n = 20°$
   $3n + 10° = 70°$
   The angle is $70°$.
F. $n =$ angle, $2n + 45° =$ supplement
   $n + 2n + 45° = 180°$
   $3n = 135°$
   $n = 45°$
   The angle is $45°$.

4. A. $\angle 1 = 72°$, $\angle 2$ supp $\angle 1$ so $\angle 2 + \angle 1 = 180°$,
   $\angle 2 = 180° - 72° = 108°$
   Vertical angles $\angle 1 = \angle 3$, $\angle 3 = 72°$; $\angle 4 = \angle 2$, $\angle 4 = 108°$
   Corresponding angles $\angle 1 = \angle 5$, $\angle 4 = \angle 8$, $\angle 2 = \angle 6$, $\angle 3 = \angle 7$,
   $\angle 5 = 72°$, $\angle 8 = 108°$, $\angle 6 = 108°$, $\angle 7 = 72°$
   $\angle 2 = 108°$, $\angle 3 = 72°$, $\angle 4 = 108°$

B. $\angle 1 = 90°$, $\angle 2$ supp $\angle 1$, so $\angle 2 + \angle 1 = 180°$, $\angle 2 = 180° - 90° = 90°$
Vertical angles $\angle 1 = \angle 3$, $\angle 3 = 90°$; $\angle 4 = \angle 2$, $\angle 4 = 90°$
Corresponding angles $\angle 1 = \angle 5$, $\angle 4 = \angle 8$, $\angle 2 = \angle 6$, $\angle 3 = \angle 7$
$\angle 5 = 90°$, $\angle 8 = 90°$, $\angle 6 = 90°$, $\angle 7 = 90°$
$\angle 2 = 90°$, $\angle 3 = 90°$, $\angle 4 = 90°$

C. $\angle 1 = 125°$, $\angle 2$ supp $\angle 1$ so $\angle 2 + \angle 1 = 180°$, $\angle 2 = 180° - 125° = 55°$
Vertical angles $\angle 1 = \angle 3$, $\angle 3 = 125°$; $\angle 4 = \angle 2$, $\angle 4 = 55°$
Corresponding angles $\angle 1 = \angle 5$, $\angle 2 = \angle 6$, $\angle 3 = \angle 7$, $\angle 4 = \angle 8$
$\angle 5 = 125°$, $\angle 6 = 55°$, $\angle 7 = 125°$, $\angle 8 = 55°$
$\angle 2 = 55°$, $\angle 3 = 125°$, $\angle 4 = 55°$

5. $\angle 1$ and $\angle 4$ are supplementary.
$\angle 1 + \angle 4 = 180°$
$4x° + 4x° + 20° = 180°$
$8x° + 20° = 180°$
$8x° = 160°$
$x° = 20°$
$\angle 1 = 4x° + 20° = 100°$, $\angle 4 = 80°$
$\angle 1 = \angle 3 = \angle 5 = \angle 7 = 100°$
$\angle 2 = \angle 4 = \angle 6 = \angle 8 = 80°$

6. $\angle 3$ and $\angle 4$ are supplementary.
$\angle 3 + \angle 4 = 180°$
$5x° + 3x° - 20° = 180°$
$8x° - 20° = 180°$
$8x° = 200°$
$x° = 25°$
$\angle 3 = 5x° = 125°$, $\angle 4 = 3x° - 20° = 55°$
$\angle 1 = \angle 3 = \angle 5 = \angle 7 = 125°$,
$\angle 2 = \angle 4 = \angle 6 = \angle 8 = 55°$

7. $\angle 2$ and $\angle 7$ are supplementary.
$\angle 7$ supp $\angle 2$
$\angle 7 + \angle 2 = 180°$
$x° - 30° + 3x° + 10° = 180°$
$4x° - 20° = 180°$
$4x° = 200°$
$x° = 50°$
$\angle 7 = 3x° + 10° = 160°$, $\angle 2 = x° - 30° = 20°$
$\angle 1 = \angle 3 = \angle 5 = \angle 7 = 160°$,
$\angle 2 = \angle 4 = \angle 6 = \angle 8 = 20°$

POLYGONS

A **polygon** is a closed figure whose sides are line segments.

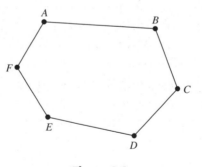

Figure 8.4

Two consecutive sides of a polygon share a common endpoint. The common endpoints are called the **vertices** of the polygon. A polygon is named by naming the vertices as you go around the polygon. In Figure 8.4, the polygon has six sides and can be named *ABCDEF*.

- A **diagonal of a polygon** is a line segment that joins two nonconsecutive vertices.
- An **equiangular polygon** is a polygon with all angles having the same measure.
- An **equilateral polygon** is a polygon with all sides having the same length.
- A **regular polygon** is a polygon that is both equiangular and equilateral.

Types of Polygons

Number of Sides	Name
3	Triangle
4	Quadrilateral
5	Pentagon
6	Hexagon
8	Octagon

The sum of the interior angles of a polygon with n sides is $S = (n-2)(180°)$.

Example 3

Find the sum of the interior angles of a polygon with the given number of sides.

A. 3   B. 4   C. 5   D. 10   E. 15

Solution

A. $n = 3, S = (n - 2)(180°) = (3 - 2)(180°) = 1 \times 180° = 180°$
B. $n = 4, S = (n - 2)(180°) = (4 - 2)(180°) = 2 \times 180° = 360°$
C. $n = 5, S = (n - 2)(180°) = (5 - 2)(180°) = 3 \times 180° = 540°$
D. $n = 10, S = (n - 2)(180°) = (10 - 2)(180°) = 8 \times 180° = 1,440°$
E. $n = 15, S = (n - 2)(180°) = (15 - 2)(180°) = 13 \times 180° = 2,340°$

- Two polygons are **congruent** if the angles of the first polygon are equal to the corresponding angles of the second polygon and the sides of the first polygon are equal to the corresponding sides of the second polygon.
- Two polygons are **similar** if the angles of the first polygon are equal to the corresponding angles of the second polygon and the sides of the first polygon are proportional to the corresponding sides of the second polygon.
- The **altitude**, or **height**, of a polygon is a line segment from one vertex of a polygon that is perpendicular to the opposite side, or to the opposite side extended.

To show that sides are of the same length, mark them with the same number of tick marks. To show that angles have the same measure, mark them with the same number of arcs.

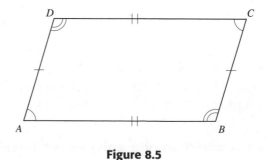

Figure 8.5

In Figure 8.5, the quadrilateral *ABCD* has sides that are marked to show $AD = BC$ and $AB = CD$. The angles are marked to show $\angle A = \angle C$ and $\angle B = \angle D$.

PRACTICE PROBLEMS

1. Find the sum of the interior angles of each polygon.
   A. Quadrilateral   B. Hexagon   C. Octagon

2. Find the measure of one angle for each polygon.

A. Equiangular triangle
B. Equiangular quadrilateral
C. Regular pentagon
D. Regular octagon

SOLUTIONS

1. A. A quadrilateral has 4 sides, so $n = 4$.
   $S = (n - 2)(180°) = (4 - 2)(180°) = 2 \times (180°) = 360°$
   B. A hexagon has 6 sides, so $n = 6$.
   $S = (n - 2)(180°) = (6 - 2)(180°) = 4 \times 180° = 720°$
   C. An octagon has 8 sides, so $n = 8$.
   $S = (n - 2)(180°) = (8 - 2)(180°) = 6 \times 180° = 1080°$

2. A. An equiangular triangle is a polygon with 3 sides, and the angles are equal.
   $S = (3 - 2)180° = 180°$, each angle is equal, so each is one-third of the sum. $180° \div 3 = 60°$. Each angle is 60°.

B. An equiangular quadrilateral is a polygon with 4 sides and all four angles are equal.
   $S = (4 - 2)(180°) = 360°$, $360° \div 4 = 90°$
   Each angle is 90°.
C. A regular pentagon is a polygon with 5 sides that are equal and 5 angles that are equal.
   $S = (5 - 2)(180°) = 540°$, $540° \div 5 = 108°$
   Each angle is 108°.
D. A regular octagon is a polygon with 8 equal sides and 8 equal angles.
   $S = (8 - 2)(180°) = 1080°$, $1080° \div 8 = 135°$
   Each angle is 135°.

TRIANGLES

A **triangle** is a polygon with three sides. Figure 8.6 shows triangle ABC (written as $\triangle ABC$).

Figure 8.6

Triangles can be classified by the number of equal sides they have. If no two sides have the same length, the triangle is a **scalene triangle**. If at least two sides have the same length, it is an **isosceles triangle**. When all three sides have the same length, the triangle is an **equilateral triangle**.

In Figure 8.6, if $AC = BC$, then $\triangle ABC$ is isosceles. The equal sides are called the legs of the isosceles triangle. Side AB, the unequal side, is called its base. The angles A and B are the base angles, and $\angle C$ is the vertex angle. In an isosceles triangle, the base angles are equal, $\angle A = \angle B$.

Triangles can also be classified by the size of their largest angle. If a triangle has an obtuse angle, the triangle is called an **obtuse triangle**. If a triangle has a right angle, the triangle is a **right triangle**. When all three angles of the triangle are acute, the triangle is an **acute triangle**.

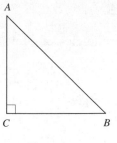

Figure 8.7

In Figure 8.7, $\triangle ABC$ is a right triangle since angle C is marked with the block ⌐. This is the symbol used to indicate right angles. The sides AC and BC are the legs of the right triangle. Side AB is the hypotenuse. In a right triangle, the sides that form the right angle are the legs, and the side opposite the right angle is the hypotenuse.

Properties of Triangles

In a triangle, the sum of the angles is $180°$. In $\triangle ABC$, if $AB > BC > AC$, then $\angle C > \angle A > \angle B$. That is, if the sides of a triangle are unequal, then the angles opposite the angles are unequal in the same order. Also, in $\triangle ABC$, if $\angle A > \angle B > \angle C$, then $BC > AC > AB$. In any $\triangle ABC$, $AB + BC > AC$, $AC + CB > AB$, and $CA + AB > BC$; that is, in any triangle the sum of the lengths of any two sides is greater than the third side.

Example 4

Can the three given lengths be the sides of a triangle?

A. 3, 8, 12   B. 3, 8, 11   C. 3, 8, 10

Solution

A. The first check is to add the two smaller numbers to see if they exceed the length of the third side. Here $3 + 8 = 11$ and $11 < 12$. A triangle cannot have sides of lengths 3, 8, and 12.
B. $3 + 8 = 11$ and $11 = 11$. A triangle cannot have sides of lengths 3, 8, and 11.
C. $3+8 = 11$ and $11 > 10$. $3+10 = 13$ and $13 > 10$. $8+10 = 18$ and $18 > 10$. A triangle can have sides of lengths 3, 8, and 10.

Example 5

Can these be the angles of a triangle?

A. 20°, 50°, 130°   B. 30°, 60°, 90°   C. 40°, 40°, 100°
D. 35°, 50°, 95°   E. 40°, 90°, 110°   F. 61°, 60°, 50°

Solution

A. $20° + 50° + 130° = 200°$ $200° \neq 180°$ These are not the angles of a triangle.

B. $30° + 60° + 90° = 180°$ $180° = 180°$ These are the angles of a triangle.

C. $40° + 40° + 100° = 180°$ $180° = 180°$ These are the angles of a triangle.

D. $35° + 50° + 95° = 180°$ $180° = 180°$ These are the angles of a triangle.

E. $40° + 90° + 110° = 240°$ $240° \neq 180°$ These are not the angles of a triangle.

F. $61° + 60° + 50° = 171°$ $171° \neq 180°$ These are not the angles of a triangle.

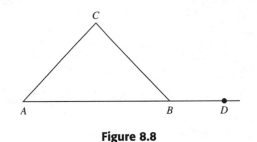

Figure 8.8

- An **exterior angle** of a triangle is created when a side of the triangle is extended through a vertex. In Figure 8.8, $\angle CBD$ is an exterior angle for $\triangle ABC$.

The interior and the exterior angles at the same vertex are supplementary. In Figure 8.8, $\angle ABC$ supp $\angle CBD$. The exterior angle at one vertex of a triangle has the same measure as the sum of the measures of the interior angles at the other two vertices. In Figure 8.8, $\angle CBD = \angle A + \angle C$.

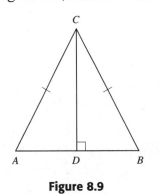

Figure 8.9

In Figure 8.9, $\triangle ABC$ is isosceles with altitude CD. The base is AB. Line CD bisects the base AB and the vertex $\angle C$. Also $\angle ACD = \angle BCD$ and $AD = BD$. Since AC and BC are marked as the equal sides, $\angle A = \angle B$.

An equilateral triangle is also an equiangular triangle. The measure of each angle of an equilateral triangle is $60°$. An equilateral triangle is also an isosceles triangle.

The right triangle in Figure 8.10 has legs a and b and hypotenuse c. In a right triangle ABC with right angle at C, $\angle A$ and $\angle B$ are complementary.

- **Pythagorean theorem:** In a right triangle, the square of the hypotenuse is equal to the sum of the squares of the legs. For Figure 8.10, $c^2 = a^2 + b^2$.

In a $30°$–$60°$–$90°$ right triangle, the hypotenuse is twice the length of the side opposite the $30°$ angle, and the side opposite the $60°$ angle is $\sqrt{3}$ multiplied by the side opposite the $30°$ angle. If $\angle A = 30°$ in Figure 8.10, then $\angle B = 60°$ and $c = 2a$ and $b = a\sqrt{3}$.

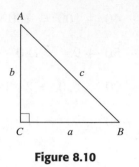

Figure 8.10

In a 45°–45°–90° right triangle, the two legs have the same length, and the hypotenuse is $\sqrt{2}$ times the length of the legs. If $\angle A$ is 45° in Figure 8.10, then $\angle B$ is 45° and $b = a$ and $c = a\sqrt{2}$.

Example 6

In a 30°–60°–90° right triangle, side a is opposite the 30° angle. Find the lengths of the other sides.

A. $a = 5$ B. $a = 8$ C. $a = \sqrt{3}$

Solution

A. $a = 5, b = a\sqrt{3} = 5\sqrt{3}, c = 2a = 10$
B. $a = 8, b = a\sqrt{3} = 8\sqrt{3}, c = 2a = 16$
C. $a = \sqrt{3}, b = a\sqrt{3} = 3, c = 2a = 2\sqrt{3}$

Example 7

In a 45°–45°–90° right triangle, the leg has length a. Find the lengths of the other sides.

A. $a = 8$ B. $a = 10$ C. $a = \sqrt{2}$

Solution

A. $a = 8, b = a = 8, c = a\sqrt{2} = 8\sqrt{2}$
B. $a = 10, b = a = 10, c = a\sqrt{2} = 10\sqrt{2}$
C. $a = \sqrt{2}, b = a = \sqrt{2}, c = a\sqrt{2} = \sqrt{2} \times \sqrt{2} = 2$

Example 8

Could a right triangle have sides of the lengths given?

A. 3, 4, 5   B. 5, 10, 12   C. 5, 12, 13

Solution

A. The hypotenuse is the longest side, so $c = 5, a = 3, b = 4$.
   $a^2 + b^2 = 3^2 + 4^2 = 9 + 16 = 25$ and $c^2 = 5^2 = 25$
   Since $a^2 + b^2 = c^2$, these can be the sides of a right triangle.
B. $c = 12, a = 5, b = 10$
   $a^2 + b^2 = 5^2 + 10^2 = 25 + 100 = 125$ and $c^2 = 12^2 = 144$
   Since $a^2 + b^2 \neq c^2$, these are not the sides of a right triangle.

C. $c = 13, a = 5, b = 12$
$a^2 + b^2 = 5^2 + 12^2 = 25 + 144 = 169$ and $c^2 = 13^2 = 169$
Since $a^2 + b^2 = c^2$, these can be the sides of a right triangle.

Two triangles are **similar** when two angles of one triangle are equal to the corresponding two angles of the other triangle.

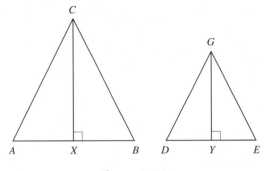

Figure 8.11

In Figure 8.11, the two triangles are similar. $\triangle ABC \sim \triangle DEF$. Line CX is the altitude to AB, and FY is the altitude to DE. Since $\triangle ABC \sim \triangle DEF$, the corresponding sides are proportional, so

$$\frac{AB}{DE} = \frac{BC}{EF} = \frac{CA}{FD} \quad \text{and} \quad \frac{AB}{DE} = \frac{CX}{FY}$$

PRACTICE PROBLEMS

1. Which sets of lengths can be the sides of a triangle?
   A. 5, 8, 17   B. 6, 8, 12   C. 5, 12, 17
   D. 12, 18, 20

2. Which sets of angles can be the angles of a triangle?
   A. 70°, 80°, 30°   B. 75°, 45°, 60°
   C. 18°, 72°, 90°   D. 70°, 30°, 40°

3. If triangle ABC is isosceles and $\angle A$ is a base angle, find the measure of the other base angle and the vertex angle. Use Figure 8.8.
   A. $\angle A = 40°$ B. $\angle A = 32°$ C. $\angle A = 75°$

4. If triangle ABC is isosceles and $\angle C$ is the vertex angle, find the measure of the base angles. Use Figure 8.8.
   A. $\angle C = 160°$ B. $\angle C = 90°$ C. $\angle C = 70°$

5. In a 30°–60°–90° triangle, the hypotenuse has length c. Find the lengths of the legs of the triangle.
   A. $c = 18$ B. $c = 24$ C. $c = 4\sqrt{3}$

6. In a 30°–60°–90° triangle, the hypotenuse has length c. Find the lengths of the legs of the triangles.
   A. $c = 20$ B. $c = 36$ C. $c = 6\sqrt{3}$

7. In a 45°–45°–90° triangle, the length of a leg is a. What are the lengths of the other two sides?
   A. $a = 8\sqrt{2}$ B. $a = 10$ C. $a = 16$

8. Could a right triangle have sides of the lengths given?
   A. 7, 24, 25   B. 10, 24, 26   C. 10, 15, 20

9. Find the missing side of the right triangle when the other two sides are as given.
   A. Leg = 11, leg = 60   B. Leg = 36, hypotenuse = 39

10.

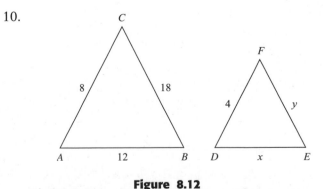

Figure 8.12

In Figure 8.12, triangle $ABC \sim$ triangle DEF with sides as indicated. Find x and y.

11.

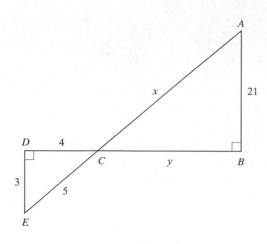

Figure 8.13

In Figure 8.13, triangle $DEC \sim$ triangle BAC with sides as indicated. Find x and y.

12.

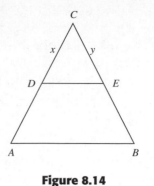

Figure 8.14

In Figure 8.14, triangle $ABC \sim$ triangle DEC, $AB = 10$, $BC = 14$, $AC = 18$, $DE = 5$, $CD = x$, and $CE = y$. Find x and y.

▮ SOLUTIONS

1. A. 17 is the longest side. $17 > 5 + 8$, so 5, 8, and 17 are not the sides of a triangle.
    B. 12 is the longest side. $12 < 6 + 8$, so 6, 8, and 12 are the sides of a triangle.
    C. 17 is the longest side. $17 = 5 + 12$, so 5, 12, and 17 are not the sides of a triangle.
    D. 20 is the longest side. $20 < 12 + 18$, so 12, 18, and 20 are the sides of a triangle.

2. A. $70° + 80° + 30° = 180°$. These are the angles of a triangle.
    B. $75° + 45° + 60° = 180°$. These are the angles of a triangle.
    C. $18° + 72° + 90° = 180°$. These are the angles of a triangle.
    D. $70° + 30° + 40° = 140°$. $140° < 180°$. These are not the angles of a triangle.

3. A. $\angle A = 40°, \angle B = 40°$, and $\angle C = 180° - 40° - 40° = 100°$
    B. $\angle A = 32°, \angle B = 32°$, and $\angle C = 180° - 32° - 32° = 116°$
    C. $\angle A = 75°, \angle B = 75°$, and $\angle C = 180° - 75° - 75° = 30°$

4. A. $\angle C = 160°, \angle A + \angle B = 180° - 160° = 20°$, $\angle A = \angle B = 10°$
    B. $\angle C = 90°, \angle A + \angle B = 180° - 90° = 90°$, $\angle A = \angle B = 45°$
    C. $\angle C = 70°, \angle A + \angle B = 180° - 70° = 110°$, $\angle A = \angle B = 55°$

5. A. $c = 18, c = 2a, a = 9, b = a\sqrt{3} = 9\sqrt{3}$
    B. $c = 24, c = 2a, a = 12, b = a\sqrt{3} = 12\sqrt{3}$
    C. $c = 4\sqrt{3}, c = 2a, a = 2\sqrt{3}, b = a\sqrt{3} = 2\sqrt{3} \times \sqrt{3} = 2 \times 3 = 6$

6. A. $c = 20, c = 2a, a = 10, b = a\sqrt{3} = 10\sqrt{3}$
    B. $c = 36, c = 2a, a = 18, b = a\sqrt{3} = 18\sqrt{3}$
    C. $c = 6\sqrt{3}, c = 2a, a = 3\sqrt{3}, b = a\sqrt{3} = 3\sqrt{3} \times \sqrt{3} = 3 \times 3 = 9$

7. $a = b, c = a\sqrt{2}$
    A. $a = 8\sqrt{2}, b = 8\sqrt{2}, c = 8\sqrt{2} \times \sqrt{2} = 8 \times 2 = 16$
    B. $a = 10, b = 10, c = 10\sqrt{2}$
    C. $a = 16, b = 16, c = 16\sqrt{2}$

8. A. $7^2 + 24^2 = 49 + 576 = 625, \ 25^2 = 625$
        $7^2 + 24^2 = 25^2$, so 7, 24, and 25 are the sides of a right triangle.
    B. $10^2 + 24^2 = 100 + 576 = 676, \ 26^2 = 676$
        $10^2 + 24^2 = 26^2$, so 10, 24, and 26 are the sides of a right triangle.
    C. $10^2 + 15^2 = 100 + 225 = 325, \ 20^2 = 400$
        $10^2 + 15^2 \neq 20^2$, so 10, 15, and 20 are not the sides of a right triangle.

9. A. $a^2 + b^2 = c^2, a = 11, b = 60$
        $11^2 + 60^2 = c^2$
        $121 + 3,600 = 3,721 = c^2$
        $\sqrt{3,721} = 61 = c$ (hypotenuse)
    B. $a^2 + b^2 = c^2$
        $36^2 + b^2 = 39^2$
        $1,296 + b^2 = 1521$
        $b^2 = 1,521 - 1,296 = 225$
        $b = \sqrt{225} = 15$ (second leg)

10. Triangle $ABC \sim$ triangle DEF, $AC = 8$, $AB = 12$, $BC = 18$, $DE = x$, $EF = y$, $DF = 4$

$$\frac{AB}{DE} = \frac{BC}{EF} = \frac{AC}{DF}$$

$$\frac{12}{x} = \frac{8}{4} \qquad \frac{18}{y} = \frac{8}{4}$$

$$8x = 48 \qquad 8y = 72$$
$$x = 6 \qquad y = 9$$

11. Triangle $DEC \sim$ triangle BAC, $DE = 3$, $EC = 5$, $DC = 4$, $BA = 21$, $AC = x$, $BC = y$

$$\frac{DE}{BA} = \frac{EC}{AC} = \frac{DC}{BC}$$

$$\frac{3}{21} = \frac{4}{y}, \qquad \frac{3}{21} = \frac{5}{x}$$

$$3y = 84 \qquad 3x = 105$$
$$y = 28 \qquad x = 35$$

12. Triangle $ABC \sim$ triangle DEC, $AB = 10$, $BC = 14$, $AC = 18$, $DE = 5$, $CD = x$, $CE = y$

$$\frac{AB}{DE} = \frac{BC}{EC} = \frac{AC}{DC}$$

$$\frac{10}{5} = \frac{14}{y} \qquad \frac{10}{5} = \frac{18}{x}$$

$$10y = 70 \qquad 10x = 90$$
$$y = 7 \qquad x = 9$$

QUADRILATERALS

A **quadrilateral** is a polygon with four sides. The sum of the angles of a quadrilateral is 360°.

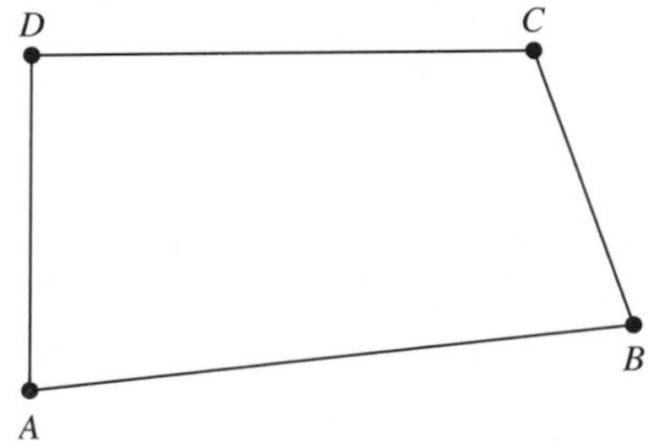

Figure 8.15

In quadrilateral $ABCD$ in Figure 8.15, $\angle A + \angle B + \angle C + \angle D = 360°$.

- A **trapezoid** is a quadrilateral with exactly one pair of parallel sides.

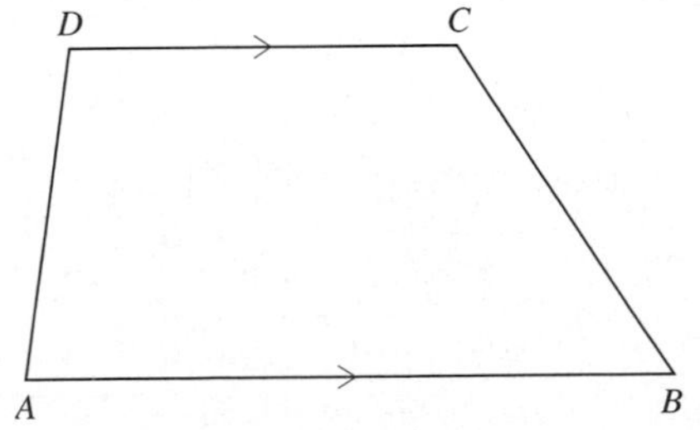

Figure 8.16

Quadrilateral $ABCD$ is a trapezoid since exactly one pair of sides, AB and CD, is parallel. The use of the > indicates which sides are parallel. See Figure 8.16. The parallel sides, AB and CD, are called the bases of the trapezoid. The nonparallel sides, AD and BC, are called the legs.

- A **parallelogram** is a quadrilateral with both pairs of opposite sides parallel.

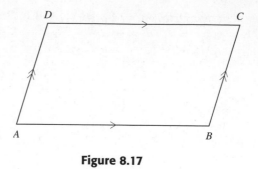

Figure 8.17

The quadrilateral in Figure 8.17 is a parallelogram because the figure is marked with $AB \parallel CD$ and $AD \parallel BC$.

Properties of a Parallelogram (See Figure 8.18)

1. The opposite sides are equal.
2. The opposite angles are equal.
3. The opposite sides are parallel.
4. The diagonals bisect each other.
5. The consecutive angles are supplementary.

$AB = CD$ and $AD = BC$
$\angle A = \angle C$ and $\angle B = \angle D$
$AB \parallel CD$ and $AD \parallel BC$
$AE = EC$ and $DE = EB$
$\angle DAB$ supp $\angle ABC$, $\angle ABC$ supp $\angle BCD$, $\angle BCD$ supp $\angle CDA$, $\angle CDA$ supp $\angle DAB$

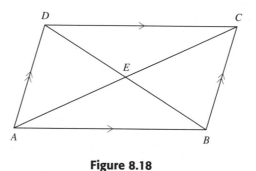

Figure 8.18

- A **rectangle** is a parallelogram that has right angles. See Figure 8.19.

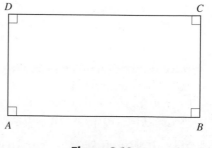

Figure 8.19

Properties of a Rectangle (See Figure 8.20)

1. Opposite sides are parallel.
2. Opposite sides are equal.
3. All angles are equal.
4. The diagonals are equal.
5. The diagonals bisect each other.
6. All angles are right angles.

$AB \parallel CD$ and $AD \parallel BC$
$AB = CD$ and $AD = BC$
$\angle A = \angle B = \angle C = \angle D = 90°$
$AC = BD$
$AE = EC = BE = DE$
$\angle A, \angle B, \angle C,$ and $\angle D$ are right angles.

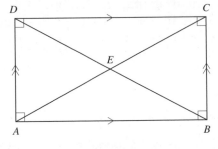

Figure 8.20

- A **rhombus** is a parallelogram with all sides equal. See Figure 8.21.

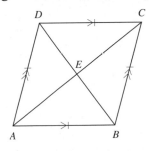

Figure 8.21

Properties of a Rhombus

1. Opposite sides are parallel.
2. Opposite angles are congruent.
3. All sides are equal.
4. The diagonals bisect the angles.

5. The diagonals bisect each other.
6. The diagonals are perpendicular.

$AB \parallel CD$ and $AD \parallel BC$
$\angle DAB = \angle BCD$ and $\angle ABC = \angle CDA$
$AB = BC = CD = DA$
$\angle DAC = \angle BAC, \angle DCA = \angle BCA$
$\angle CBD = \angle ABD$ and $\angle CDB = \angle ADB$
$AE = EC$ and $BE = ED$
$AC \perp BD$

- A **square** is a rectangle with all sides equal. See Figure 8.22.

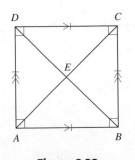

Figure 8.22

Properties of a Square

1. Opposite sides are parallel. $AB \parallel CD$ and $AD \parallel BC$
2. All angles are equal. $\angle DAB = \angle ABC = \angle BCD =$
                                          $\angle CDA = 90°$
3. All sides are equal. $AB = BC = CD = DA$
4. The diagonals bisect the angles. $\angle DAC = \angle BAC, \angle BCA = \angle DCA$
                                          $\angle CDB = \angle ADB$ and $\angle ABD = \angle CBD$
5. The diagonals are perpendicular. $AC \perp BD$
6. The diagonals are equal. $AC = BD$
7. The diagonals bisect each other. $AE = EC = BE = ED$
8. A square is a regular polygon.   All sides and angles are equal.

PRACTICE PROBLEMS

1. Which quadrilaterals have the sum of the angles equal to 360°?

2. Which quadrilaterals have only one pair of parallel sides?

3. Which quadrilaterals have two diagonals?

4. Which quadrilaterals have equal diagonals?

5. Which quadrilaterals have perpendicular diagonals?

6. Which quadrilaterals have two pairs of parallel sides?

7. Which quadrilaterals have diagonals that bisect each other?

8. Which quadrilaterals have diagonals that bisect the angles?

9. Which quadrilaterals have the opposite angles equal?

10. Which quadrilaterals are equiangular?

11. Which quadrilaterals are equilateral?

12. Which quadrilaterals have the consecutive angles supplementary?

13. Which quadrilaterals have opposite sides equal?

14. Which quadrilaterals are regular polygons?

SOLUTIONS

1. All quadrilaterals, trapezoid, parallelogram, rectangle, rhombus, square

2. Trapezoid

3. All quadrilaterals, trapezoid, parallelogram, rectangle, rhombus, square

4. Rectangle, square

5. Rhombus, square

6. Parallelogram, rectangle, rhombus, square

7. Parallelogram, rectangle, rhombus, square

8. Rhombus, square

9. Parallelogram, rectangle, rhombus, square

10. Rectangle, square

11. Rhombus, square

12. Parallelogram, rectangle, rhombus, square

13. Parallelogram, rectangle, rhombus, square

14. Square

PERIMETER AND AREA

Perimeter and area are measurements that are commonly the subject of GMAT math problems.

- The **perimeter** of a polygon is the distance around the polygon. Hence, the perimeter is the sum of the lengths of the sides of the polygon.

If a polygon has n sides, the perimeter P of the polygon is $P = s_1 + s_2 + s_3 + \cdots + s_n$, where each s is the length of a side. The perimeter P of a rectangle with length l and width w is $P = 2l + 2w$. The perimeter P of a square with sides of length s is $P = 4s$.

- The **area** of a polygon is the amount of the surface enclosed by the polygon. The area is expressed as the number of square units of surface inside the polygon.

Areas of Polygons

Polygon	Symbols Used in Formula	Area
Triangle	$b =$ base, $h =$ altitude to base	$A = 0.5bh$
Trapezoid	$h =$ distance between parallel sides a and b	$A = 0.5h(a + b)$
Parallelogram	$b =$ base side of parallelogram, altitude to base	$A = bh$
Rectangle	$l =$ length, $w =$ width	$A = lw$
Square	$s =$ side of square	$A = s^2$
Right triangle	a and $b =$ legs of right side of triangle	$A = 0.5ab$

The area of a general polygon can be found by dividing it into smaller regions, each of which is a polygon whose area can be found.

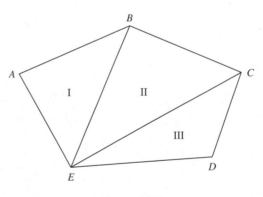

Figure 8.23

In Figure 8.23, polygon *ABCDE* was divided into three nonoverlapping regions by drawing all the diagonals from one vertex *E*. The area of polygon *ABCDE* equals the area of triangle I plus the area of triangle II plus the area of triangle III.

PRACTICE PROBLEMS

1. Find the perimeter of a square with side s.

   A. $s = 25$ cm   B. $s = 76$ mm   C. $s = 7.5$ ft
   D. $s = 2$ ft 9 in

2. Find the perimeter of a rectangle with length l and width w.

   A. $l = 16$ cm, $w = 9$ cm   B. $l = 63$ ft, $w = 49$ ft
   C. $l = 3.5$ m, $w = 9.75$ m

3. Find the perimeter of the triangle with these sides.

   A. 16 m, 8 m, 14 m   B. 20 in, 16 in, 28 in

   C. 6.22 m, 4.7 m, 5.84 m

4. Find the perimeter of the equilateral triangle with side s.

   A. $s = 40$ cm   B. $s = 14$ ft   C. $s = 4.75$ m

   D. $s = 8.4$ in

5. Find the perimeter of the pentagon whose sides are 24 in, 58 in, 32 in, 66 in, and 43 in.

6. Find the area of the parallelogram with the base b and altitude h.

   A. $b = 26$ in, $h = 14$ in   B. $b = 98$ cm, $h = 75$ cm

   C. $b = 25$ in, $h = 32$ in

7. Find the area of the triangle with the base b and altitude h.

   A. $b = 12$ cm, $h = 18$ cm   B. $b = 13$ m, $h = 10$ m

   C. $b = 5$ ft, $h = 7$ ft

8. Find the area of the square with side s.

   A. $s = 18$ ft   B. $s = 10$ ft   C. $s = 15$ cm

   D. $s = 6$ ft   E. $s = 8$ m

9. Find the area of the trapezoid with altitude h and bases a and b.

   A. $h = 8$ cm, $a = 4$ cm, $b = 10$ cm
   B. $h = 5$ mm, $a = 9$ mm, $b = 13$ mm
   C. $h = 18$ in, $a = 29$ in, $b = 36$ in
   D. $h = 7$ ft, $a = 8$ ft, $b = 14$ ft

10. Find the area of the right triangle with the given sides.
    A. 11 in, 60 in, 61 in   B. 7 cm, 24 cm, 25 cm

11.

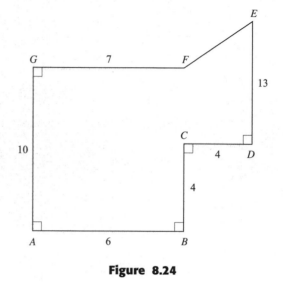

Figure 8.24

Find the area of figure $ABCDEFG$ using Figure 8.24.

SOLUTIONS

1. A. $P = 4s = 4(25 \text{ cm}) = 100$ cm
   B. $P = 4s = 4(76 \text{ mm}) = 304$ mm
   C. $P = 4s = 4(7.5 \text{ ft}) = 30$ ft
   D. $P = 4s = 4(2 \text{ ft } 9 \text{ in}) = 8 \text{ ft } 36 \text{ in} = 8 \text{ ft} + 3 \text{ ft} = 11$ ft

2. A. $P = 2l + 2w = 2(16 \text{ cm}) + 2(9 \text{ cm}) = 32$ cm $+ 18$ cm $= 50$ cm
   B. $P = 2l + 2w = 2(63 \text{ ft}) + 2(49 \text{ ft}) = 126 \text{ ft} + 98 \text{ ft} = 224$ ft
   C. $P = 2l + 2w = 2(3.5 \text{ m}) + 2(9.75 \text{ m}) = 7.0$ m $+ 19.5$ m $= 26.5$ m

3. A. $P = s_1 + s_2 + s_3 = 16 \text{ m} + 8 \text{ m} + 14 \text{ m} = 38$ m
   B. $P = 20 \text{ in} + 16 \text{ in} + 28 \text{ in} = 64$ in
   C. $P = 6.22 \text{ m} + 4.7 \text{ m} + 5.84 \text{ m} = 16.76$ m

4. A. $P = 3s = 3(40 \text{ cm}) = 120$ cm
   B. $P = 3s = 3(14 \text{ ft}) = 42$ ft
   C. $P = 3s = 3(4.75 \text{ m}) = 14.25$ m
   D. $P = 3s = 3(8.4 \text{ in}) = 25.2$ in

5. A. $P = 24 \text{ in} + 58 \text{ in} + 32 \text{ in} + 66 \text{ in} + 43 \text{ in} = 223$ in

6. A. $A = bh = (26 \text{ in})(14 \text{ in}) = 364 \text{ in}^2$
   B. $A = bh = (98 \text{ cm})(75 \text{ cm}) = 7{,}350 \text{ cm}^2$
   C. $A = bh = (25 \text{ in})(32 \text{ in}) = 800 \text{ in}^2$

7. A. $A = 0.5bh = 0.5(12 \text{ cm})(18 \text{ cm}) = 108 \text{ cm}^2$
   B. $A = 0.5bh = 0.5(13 \text{ m})(10 \text{ m}) = 65 \text{ m}^2$
   C. $A = 0.5bh = 0.5(5 \text{ ft})(7 \text{ ft}) = 17.5 \text{ ft}^2$

8. A. $A = s^2 = (18 \text{ ft})^2 = 324 \text{ ft}^2$
   B. $A = s^2 = (10 \text{ ft})^2 = 100 \text{ ft}^2$
   C. $A = s^2 = (15 \text{ cm})^2 = 225 \text{ cm}^2$
   D. $A = s^2 = (6 \text{ ft})^2 = 36 \text{ ft}^2$
   E. $A = s^2 = (8 \text{ m})^2 = 64 \text{ m}^2$

9. A. $A = 0.5h(a + b) = 0.5(8 \text{ cm})(4 \text{ cm} + 10 \text{ cm}) = 0.5(8 \text{ cm})(14 \text{ cm}) = 56 \text{ cm}^2$
   B. $A = 0.5h(a + b) = 0.5(5 \text{ mm})(9 \text{ mm} + 13 \text{ mm}) = 0.5(5 \text{ mm})(22 \text{ mm}) = 55 \text{ mm}^2$

C. $A = 0.5h(a + b) = 0.5(18 \text{ in})(29 \text{ in} + 36 \text{ in}) = 0.5(18 \text{ in})(65 \text{ in}) = 585 \text{ in}^2$

D. $A = 0.5h(a + b) = 0.5(7 \text{ ft})(8 \text{ ft} + 14 \text{ ft}) = 0.5(7 \text{ ft})(22 \text{ ft}) = 77 \text{ ft}^2$

10. A. $A = 0.5ab$ $A = 0.5(11 \text{ in})(60 \text{ in}) = 330 \text{ in}^2$

    B. $A = 0.5ab$ $A = 0.5(7 \text{ cm})(24 \text{ cm}) = 84 \text{ cm}^2$

11. Draw $FX \perp ED$, draw $CY \perp GF$, $AB + CD = GX = 6 + 4 = 10$
$GY = AB = 6$, $YX = CD = 4$, $FX = 10 - 7 = 3$,
$CY = GA - BC = 10 - 4 = 6$
Area of $ABCDEFG$ = area of $ABYG$ + area $CDXY$ + area FXE
Area $ABYG = lw = (10)(6) = 60$
Area $CDXY = lw = (6)(4) = 24$
Area $FXE = 0.5ab = 0.5(3)(7) = 10.5$ $ED - YD = 13 - 6 = 7$
Area $ABCDEFG = 60 + 24 + 10.5 = 94.5$ square units

CIRCLES

A **circle** is the set of all points in a plane that are at a fixed distance, or **radius**, from a given point, the **center**.

- Two circles are **concentric** if they have the same center.
- An **arc** is a part of a circle.
- A **semicircle** is an arc that is one-half of a circle.
- A **minor arc** is an arc that is less than a semicircle.
- A **major arc** is an arc that is greater than a semicircle.

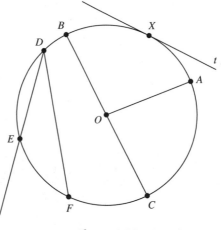

Figure 8.25

In circle O (Figure 8.25), AO is a radius, BC is a diameter, DF is a chord, $\angle AOB$ is a central angle, $\angle FDE$ is an inscribed angle, line t is a tangent to circle O at x, and line ED is a secant. Arc BAC is a semicircle, arc AC is a minor arc, and FDA is a major arc. In circle O, the region enclosed by arc AC, radius CO, and AD is called a sector of the circle.

- The **circumference** of a circle is the distance around the circle. $C = \pi d$. Pi (π) is the ratio of the circumference of a circle to its diameter. π is approximately 3.14 or $3\frac{1}{7}$.
- A **chord** of a circle is a line segment joining two points on the circle.
- A **diameter** is a chord that goes through the center of the circle.
- A **radius** is a line segment from the center of a circle to a point on the circle. A diameter is the same length as two radii.

- A **secant** is a line that intersects a circle in two points.
- A **tangent** is a line that intersects a circle in exactly one point.
- An **inscribed angle** is an angle whose sides are chords of a circle, and with its vertex on the circle.
- A **central angle** is an angle with its vertex at the center of the circle, and with sides that are radii.

The measure of a central angle is the same as the degree measure of its arc. However, the degree measure of an inscribed angle is one-half the measure of its arc. $\angle AOC$ = arc AC and $\angle FDE = 0.5$ arc EF. If an angle is inscribed in a semicircle, it is a right angle.

A diameter separates a circle into two semicircles. A semicircle is one-half of a circle, so it is one-half of 360°, or 180°. A minor arc is a part of a circle that is less than a semicircle, so it has a measure that is less then 180°.

The circumference of circle C equals π multiplied by the diameter. $C = \pi d$, or $C = 2\pi r$.

The area A of a circle is equal to π multiplied by the square of the radius. $A = \pi r^2$.

The area A of a sector of a circle is to the area of the circle as the central angle of the sector is to 360°. That is, find the ratio of the central angle of the sector to 360° and multiply that ratio by the area of the circle.

When two chords intersect inside a circle, the product of the segments of one chord is equal to the product of the segments of the other chord.

For Figure 8.26, $AE \times EB = CE \times ED$. Also, $\angle AED = 0.5$(arc AD + arc BC).

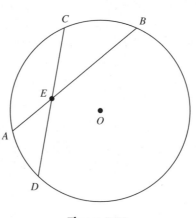

Figure 8.26

Example 9

If the diameter of a circle is 30 cm, what is the circumference of the circle?

Solution

$C = \pi d$
$C = 30\pi$ cm

Example 10

If the diameter of a circle is 40 feet, what is the area of the circle?

Solution

$d = 40$ ft, so $r = 20$ ft and use $\pi = 3.14$
$A = \pi r^2$
$A = (\pi)(20 \text{ ft})^2$
$A = 400\pi \text{ ft}^2$

Example 11

In Figure 8.26, if arc $AD = 42°$, arc $AC = 72°$, and arc $BC = 46°$, what is the measure of arc BD?

Solution

$$\text{arc } AD + \text{ arc } AC + \text{ arc } CD + \text{ arc } BD = 360°$$
$$42° + 72° + 46° + \text{ arc } BD = 360°$$
$$160° + \text{ arc } BD = 360°$$
$$\text{arc } BD = 200°$$

PRACTICE PROBLEMS

1. In Figure 8.27, if $AC = 12$ and $BC = 35$, what is the radius of the circle?

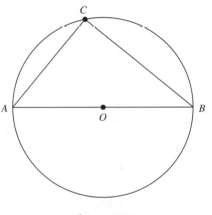

Figure 8.27

2. In Figure 8.27, if $AC = BC = 10$ cm, what is the length of the diameter of the circle?

3. In Figure 8.27, if $AC = AO = 5$, what is the area of triangle $\triangle ABC$?

4. In Figure 8.26, if $AE = 12$, $BE = 7$, and $CE = 6$, what is the length of CD?

5. In Figure 8.26, if $CE = ED$, $AE = 2$, and $EB = 6$, what is the length of CD?

6. In Figure 8.26, if arc $CB = 35°$ and arc $AD = 95°$, what is the measure of $\angle AED$?

7. In Figure 8.26, if arc $BC = 125°$ and arc $AD = 105°$, what is the measure of $\angle BEC$?

8. What is the circumference of a circle whose radius is 10 cm?

9. What is the area of a circle whose diameter is 10 inches?

10. What is the circumference of a circle whose area is 49π cm^2?

11. What is the area of a sector of a circle whose central angle is $60°$ and the radius is 12 ft?

12. What is the area of a circle whose radius is 12.2 cm?

13. Find the circumference of a circle when the radius is 18 cm.

SOLUTIONS

1. Triangle ACB is a right triangle. Line segment AB is the hypotenuse of the right triangle and the diameter of the circle. $12^2 + 35^2 = 144 + 1{,}225 = 1{,}369 = 37^2$ so $AB = 37$. The radius is one-half of the diameter. So $r = 0.5(37) = 18.5$.

2. $AC = BC = 10$ cm in right triangle ABC. $AC^2 + BC^2 = AB^2$, $10^2 + 10^2 = AB^2$, $100 + 100 = AB^2$, $200 = AB^2$, $\sqrt{200} = AB$, $AB = \sqrt{100}\sqrt{2} = 10\sqrt{2}$

Note: Right triangle ABC is an isosceles right triangle, so it is a $45°$–$45°$–$90°$ right triangle and $AB = AC\sqrt{2}$.

3. $AC = AO$, so $2AC = AB$, so it is a $30°$–$60°$–$90°$ right triangle and $BC = AC\sqrt{3} = 5\sqrt{3}$.
   $A = 0.5ab = 0.5(5)(5\sqrt{3}) = 12.5\sqrt{3}$

4. $AE * EB = CE * ED$
   $AE = 12, EB = 7, CE = 6$
   $ED = x$
   $12 \times 7 = 6x$
   $84 = 6x$
   $14 = x$
   $CD = CE + ED = 6 + 14 = 20$

5. $AE \times EB = CE \times ED$ $\quad$ $CE = ED, AE = 2,$
   $EB = 6$
   $2 \times 6 = y \times y$ $\qquad$ Let $CE = ED = y$
   $12 = y^2$ $\qquad\qquad$ $CE = 2\sqrt{3}, ED = 2\sqrt{3}$
   $\sqrt{12} = y$ $\qquad\qquad$ $CE + ED = 2\sqrt{3} + 2\sqrt{3}$
   $\sqrt{4}\sqrt{3} = y$ $\qquad\qquad$ $CD = 4\sqrt{3}$
   $2\sqrt{3} = y$

6. $\angle AED = 0.5(35° + 95°) = 0.5(130°) = 65°$

7. $\angle BEC = 0.5(125° + 105°) = 0.5(230°) = 115°$

8. $C = 2\pi r = 2\pi(10 \text{ cm}) = 20\pi$ cm

9. $A = \pi r^2 = \pi(5 \text{ in})^2 = \pi(25 \text{ in}^2) = 25\pi$ in^2

10. $A = \pi r^2 = 49\pi$ cm^2 so $r^2 = 49$ cm^2 $\quad r = 7$ cm
    $C = 2\pi r = 2\pi(7 \text{ cm}) = 14\pi$ cm

11. $360° \div 60° = 6$ $\qquad A = 2\pi r^2 = \pi(12 \text{ ft})^2 = \pi(144 \text{ ft}^2) = 144\pi$ ft^2
    Area of sector = area of circle $\div 6 = 144$ ft$^2 \div 6 = 24\pi$ ft^2

12. $A = \pi r^2 = \pi (12.2 \text{ cm})^2 = \pi (148.84 \text{ cm}^2) = 148.84\pi$ cm^2

13. $C = 2\pi r = 2\pi(18 \text{ cm}) = 36\pi$ cm

SOLID GEOMETRY

Solid geometry has to do with three-dimensional objects.

- A **solid** is a figure that encloses a portion of space.

The **volume** of a solid is the amount of space it encloses. The **surface area** of a solid is the area needed to cover the outside of the solid.

- A **polyhedron** is a solid made up of parts of planes.

The sides of a polyhedron are called **faces**. Two faces intersect in an **edge**. Two edges intersect in a **vertex**.

A **rectangular solid** is a polyhedron with all faces being rectangles. See Figure 8.28. Most rooms and boxes are rectangular solids. The dimensions of a rectangular solid are its length l, width w, and height h. The volume $V = lwh$. The surface area $S = 2lw + 2lh + 2wh$.

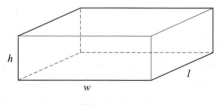

Figure 8.28

A **cube** is a rectangular solid with all faces being identical squares. See Figure 8.29. The edge e of any one of the squares is the length, width, and height for the cube.

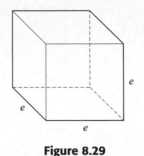

Figure 8.29

The volume $V = e^3$ and the surface area $S = 6e^2$.

A **right circular cylinder** has bases that are circles, and the curved surface is perpendicular to the bases. See Figure 8.30. The volume $V = \pi r^2 h$ and the surface area $S = 2\pi r h + 2\pi r^2$, where h is the height of the cylinder and r is the radius of the base.

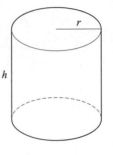

Figure 8.30

A **pyramid** is a solid with one base. See Figure 8.31. The vertices of the base are joined to the apex or vertex of the pyramid. The volume $V = \frac{1}{3}bh$, where b is the area of the base of the pyramid and h is the height from the base to the apex.

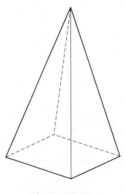

Figure 8.31

A **right circular cone** is a solid that has one circular base. See Figure 8.32. The vertex of the cone is a point on a line perpendicular to the circle at its center. The volume V of the cone $= \frac{1}{3}\pi r^2 h$, where r is the radius of the base and h is the height of the cone. The **start height** of a right circular cone is a line segment from the vertex to a point on the circumference of the base.

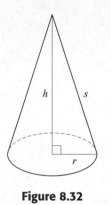

Figure 8.32

The surface area $S = \pi r^2 + \pi rs$, where s is the slant height and $s^2 = r^2 + h^2$.

A **sphere** is a ball-shaped solid. See Figure 8.33. The volume $V = \dfrac{4}{3}\pi r^3$, and the surface area $S = 4\pi r$, where r is the radius of the sphere.

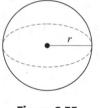

Figure 8.33

Volume and Surface Areas of Solids

Solid	Volume	Surface Area
Rectangular solid	$V = lwh$	$S = 2lw + 2lh + 2wh$
Cube	$V = e^3$	$S = 6e^2$
Right circular cylinder	$V = \pi r^2 h$	$S = 2\pi rh + 2\pi r^2$
Sphere	$V = \dfrac{4}{3}\pi r^3$	$S = 4\pi r^2$
Right circular cone	$V = \dfrac{1}{3}\pi r^2 h$	$S = \pi r^2 + \pi rs$
Pyramid	$V = \dfrac{1}{3}Bh$	—

Example 12

If the surface area of a cube is 1,176 in^2, what is the length of an edge of the cube?

Solution

$S = 6e^2$

$1{,}176 \text{ in}^2 = 6e^2$

$196 \text{ in}^2 = e^2$

$\sqrt{196 \text{ in}^2} = e$ Since e is the length of an edge of a cube, only the positive square root is used.

$14 \text{ in} = e$

Example 13

If the radius and height of a right circular cylinder are 8 cm and 10 cm, respectively, what is the surface area of the cylinder?

Solution

$$S = 2\pi rh + 2\pi r^2$$
$$S = 2(\pi)(8 \text{ cm})(10 \text{ cm}) + 2(\pi)(8 \text{ cm})^2$$
$$S = 160\pi \text{ cm}^2 + 128\pi \text{ cm}^2$$
$$S = 288\pi \text{ cm}^2$$

PRACTICE PROBLEMS

1. A rectangular solid has length l, width w, and height h. Find the volume of the solid.
   A. $l = 10$ ft, $w = 8$ ft, $h = 7$ ft
   B. $l = 30$ cm, $w = 24$ cm, $h = 12$ cm

2. A rectangular solid has length l, width w, and height h. Find the surface area of the solid.
   A. $l = 10$ in, $w = 6$ in, $h = 12$ in
   B. $l = 8$ m, $w = 7$ m, $h = 10$ m

3. A cube has edge e. Find the volume of the cube.
   A. $e = 0.4$ m   B. $e = 10$ in
   C. $e = 12$ cm   D. $e = 5$ m

4. A cube has edge e. Find the surface area of the cube.
   A. $e = 2$ in   B. $e = 7$ ft
   C. $e = 1.2$ cm   D. $e = 0.4$ m

5. A right circular cylinder has a radius r and height h. Find the volume of the cylinder.
   A. $r = 4$ in, $h = 8$ in   B. $r = 7$ cm, $h = 3.5$ cm

6. A right circular cylinder has radius r and height h. Find the surface area of the cylinder.
   A. $r = 8.4$ m, $h = 10.2$ m   B. $r = 8$ ft, $h = 7$ ft

7. A sphere has radius r. Find the volume of the sphere.
   A. $r = 6$ in   B. $r = 8$ cm   C. $r = 10$ m

8. A sphere has a radius r. Find the surface area of the sphere.
   A. $r = 5$ cm   B. $r = 1.4$ m   C. $r = 9$ in

9. A right circular cone has a radius r and height h. Find the volume of the cone.
   A. $r = 6$ in, $h = 10$ in
   B. $r = 4$ cm, $h = 12$ cm

10. A right circular cone has a radius r and slant height s. Find the surface area of the cone.
    A. $r = 6$ cm, $s = 12$ cm   B. $r = 10$ ft, $s = 8$ ft

11. Find the volume of a pyramid that has a rectangular base with length l and width w and the height of the pyramid is h.
    A. $l = 8$ in, $w = 6$ in, $h = 12$ in
    B. $l = 7$ cm, $w = 4$ cm, $h = 6$ cm

12. Find the volume of a pyramid that has a square base with side e. The height of the pyramid is h.
    A. $e = 6$ cm, $h = 10$ cm   B. $e = 9$ in, $h = 14$ in

13. The dimensions of a classroom are 24 feet by 17 feet by 12 feet. Find the number of cubic feet of air space that it contains.

14. Find the volume of a cube where the surface area is 54 square inches.

15. A cylindrical can is 6 inches tall, and the radius of the base is 3 inches. What is the surface area of the can?

16. A cylindrical tank holds 1,540 cubic feet of water. The base is a circle with a 7-foot diameter. To the nearest foot, what is the height of the cylinder?

17. Find the volume of a pyramid when the area of the base is 25 square inches and the height is 6 inches.

18. If the volume of a sphere is 288π cm^3, what is the radius?

19. What is the surface area of a rectangular solid whose dimensions are 17 cm, 19 cm, and 20 cm?

20. What is the surface area of a cube whose edge is 14 mm?

SOLUTIONS

1. A. $V = lwh = (10 \text{ ft})(8 \text{ ft})(7 \text{ ft}) = 560 \text{ ft}^3$
   B. $V = lwh = (30 \text{ cm})(24 \text{ cm})(12 \text{ cm}) = 8,640 \text{ cm}^3$

2. A. $S = 2lw + 2lh + 2wh = 2(10 \text{ in})(6 \text{ in}) + 2(10 \text{ in})(12 \text{ in}) + 2(6 \text{ in})(12 \text{ in})$
   $S = 120 \text{ in}^2 + 240 \text{ in}^2 + 144 \text{ in}^2 = 504 \text{ in}^2$
   B. $S = 2lw + 2lh + 2wh = 2(8 \text{ m})(7 \text{ m}) + 2(8 \text{ m})(10 \text{ m}) + 2(7 \text{ m})(10 \text{ m})$
   $S = 112 \text{ m}^2 + 160 \text{ m}^2 + 140 \text{ m}^2 = 412 \text{ m}^2$

3. A. $V = e^3 = (0.4 \text{ m})^3 = 0.064 \text{ m}^3$
   B. $V = e^3 = (10 \text{ in})^3 = 1,000 \text{ in}^3$
   C. $V = e^3 = (12 \text{ cm})^3 = 1,728 \text{ cm}^3$
   D. $V = e^3 = (5 \text{ m})^3 = 125 \text{ m}^3$

4. A. $S = 6e^2 = 6(2 \text{ in})^2 = 6(4 \text{ in}^2) = 24 \text{ in}^2$
   B. $S = 6e^2 = 6(7 \text{ ft})^2 = 6(49 \text{ ft}^2) = 294 \text{ ft}^2$
   C. $S = 6e^2 = 6(1.2 \text{ cm}) = 6(1.44 \text{ cm}^2) = 8.64 \text{ cm}^2$
   D. $S = 6e^2 = 6(0.4 \text{ m}) = 6(0.16 \text{ m}^2) = 0.96 \text{ m}^2$

5. A. $V = \pi r^2 h = \pi(4 \text{ in})^2(8 \text{ in}) = \pi(16 \text{ in}^2)(8 \text{ in}) = 128\pi \text{ in}^3$
   B. $V = \pi r^2 h = \pi(7 \text{ cm})^2(3.5 \text{ cm}) = \pi(49 \text{ cm}^2)(3.5 \text{ cm}) = 171.5\pi \text{ cm}^3$

6. A. $S = 2\pi r^2 + 2\pi rh = 2(\pi)(8.4 \text{ m})^2 + 2(\pi)(8.4 \text{ m})(10.2 \text{ m}) = 141.12\pi \text{ m}^2 + S = 312.48\text{m}^2 \ 171.36\pi \text{ m}^2 = 312.48\pi \text{ m}^2$
   B. $S = 2\pi r^2 + 2\pi rh = 2\pi(8 \text{ ft})^2 + 2\pi(8 \text{ ft})(7 \text{ ft}) = 2(64\pi \text{ ft}^2) + 2\pi(56 \text{ ft}^2) = 128\pi \text{ ft}^2 + 112\pi \text{ ft}^2 = 240\pi \text{ ft}^2$

7. A. $V = \frac{4}{3}\pi r^3 = \frac{4}{3}\pi(6 \text{ in})^3 = \frac{4}{3}\pi \ (216 \text{ in}^3) = 288\pi \text{ in}^3$
   B. $V = \frac{4}{3}\pi r^3 = \frac{4}{3}\pi(8 \text{ cm})^3 = \frac{4}{3}\pi(512 \text{ cm}^3) = 682.7\pi \text{ cm}^3$
   C. $V = \frac{4}{3}\pi r^3 = \frac{4}{3}\pi(10 \text{ m})^3 = \frac{4}{3}\pi(1,000 \text{ m}^3) = 1,333.3\pi \text{ m}^3$

8. A. $S = 4\pi r^2 = 4\pi(5 \text{ cm})^2 = 100 \text{ cm}^2$
   B. $S = 4\pi r^2 = 4\pi(1.4 \text{ m})^2 = 7.84\pi \text{ m}^2$
   C. $S = 4\pi r^2 = 4\pi(9 \text{ in})^2 = 324 \text{ in}^2$

9. A. $V = \frac{1}{3}\pi r^2 h = \frac{1}{3}\pi(6 \text{ in})^2(10 \text{ in}) = 120\pi \text{ in}^3$
   B. $V = \frac{1}{3}\pi r^2 h = \frac{1}{3}\pi(4 \text{ cm})^2(12 \text{ cm}) = 64\pi \text{ cm}^3$

10. A. $S = \pi r^2 + \pi rs = \pi(6 \text{ cm})^2 + \pi(6 \text{ cm})(12 \text{ cm}) = 36\pi \text{ cm}^2 + 72\pi \text{ cm}^2 = 108\pi \text{ cm}^2$
    B. $S = \pi r^2 + \pi rs = \pi(10 \text{ ft})^2 + \pi(10 \text{ ft})(8 \text{ ft}) = 100 \ \pi\text{ft}^2 + 80 \ \pi\text{ft}^2 = 180 \ \pi\text{ft}^2$

11. A. $V = \frac{1}{3}bh = \frac{1}{3}(lw)h = \frac{1}{3}(8 \text{ in})(6 \text{ in})(12 \text{ in}) = 192 \text{ in}^3$
    B. $V = \frac{1}{3}bh = \frac{1}{3}(lw)h = \frac{1}{3}(7 \text{ cm})(4 \text{ cm})(6 \text{ cm}) = 56 \text{ cm}^3$

12. A. $V = \frac{1}{3}bh = \frac{1}{3}(e^2)h = \frac{1}{3}(6 \text{ cm})^2(10 \text{ cm}) = 120 \text{ cm}^3$
    B. $V = \frac{1}{3}bh = \frac{1}{3}(e^2)h = \frac{1}{3}(9 \text{ in})^2(14 \text{ in}) = 378 \text{ in}^2$

13. A room is a rectangular solid. Find the volume.

$$V = lwh = (24 \text{ ft})(17 \text{ ft})(12 \text{ ft}) = 4,896 \text{ ft}^3$$

There is 4,896 cubic feet of air space in the room.

14. Surface area of the cube is 54 in^2.

$S = 6e^2$	$V = e^3$
$54 \text{ in}^2 = 6e^2$	$V = (3 \text{ in})^3$
$9\text{in}^2 = e^2$	$V = 27 \text{ in}^3$
$3\text{in} = e$	

The volume of the cube is 27 cubic inches.

15. $S = 2\pi r^2 + 2\pi rh = 2\pi(3 \text{ in})^2 + 2\pi(3 \text{ in})(6 \text{ in}) = 18\pi \text{ in}^2 + 36\pi \text{ in}^2 = 54\pi \text{ in}^2$
    The surface area of the can is 54π in^2.

16. Cylinder with circular base, volume is 1,540 ft^3.
    Diameter = 7 feet, so radius is 3.5 feet.
    $V = \pi r^2 h$
    $1,540 \text{ ft}^3 = 3.14(3.5 \text{ ft})^2 h$
    $1,540 \text{ ft}^3 = 38.465 \text{ ft}^2 h$
    $40.0036 \text{ ft} = h$
    The height of the cylinder is 40 feet.

17. $V = \frac{1}{3}bh = (25 \text{ in}^2)(6 \text{ in}) \div 3 = 150 \text{ in}^3 \div 3 = 50 \text{ in}^3$
    The volume of the pyramid is 50 in^3.

18. $V = \dfrac{4}{3}\pi r^3 = 288\pi \text{ cm}^3$

   $4\pi r^3 = 864\pi \text{ cm}^3$
   $r^3 = 216 \text{ cm}^3$
   $r = 6 \text{ cm}$
   The radius of the sphere is 6 centimeters.

19. $S = 2lw + 2lh + 2wh = 2(17 \text{ cm})(19 \text{ cm}) + 2(17 \text{ cm})(20 \text{ cm}) + 2(19 \text{ cm})(20 \text{ cm}) = 646 \text{ cm}^2 + 680 \text{ cm}^2 + 760 \text{ cm}^2 = 2{,}086 \text{ cm}^2$
   The surface area of the rectangular solid is 2,086 square centimeters.

20. $S = 6e^2 = 6(14 \text{ mm})^2 = 6(196 \text{ mm}^2) = 1{,}176 \text{ mm}^2$
   The surface area of the cube is 1,176 square millimeters.

COORDINATE GEOMETRY

Coordinate geometry is the branch of geometry that deals with planes on a coordinate system. Each point in the plane has a unique **coordinate** (x, y). The horizontal number line is the **x axis**, and the vertical number line is the **y axis**. The zeros on each number line match up, and the point is called the **origin** for the coordinate system. The plane is divided into four parts, which are called **quadrants** and are numbered I, II, III, and IV in counterclockwise order from the upper right. See Figure 8.34.

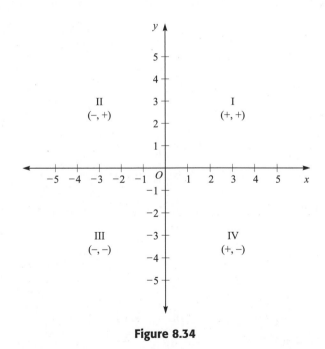

Figure 8.34

Points in quadrant I have both coordinates positive, (positive, positive). In quadrant II, the x coordinate is negative, but the y coordinate is positive (negative, positive). Points in quadrant III have both coordinates negative (negative, negative). Points in quadrant IV have a positive x coordinate and a negative y coordinate (positive, negative).

   To locate a point, such as $(5, -3)$, in the plane, start at the origin and move 5 units in the positive x direction (right). Then move from that location 3 units in the negative y direction (down). The point $(-3, 5)$ is 3 units left from the origin on the x axis and then 5 units up on the y axis. See Figure 8.35.

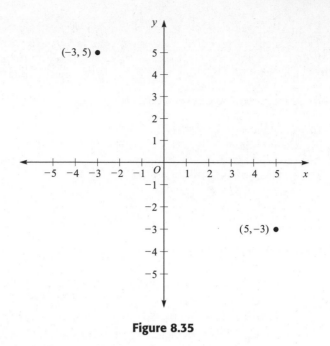

Figure 8.35

Let $P = (x_1, y_1)$ and $Q = (x_2, y_2)$. The **distance** from P to Q, denoted by d, can be found by the distance formula:

$$d = \sqrt{(x_2 - x_1)^2 + (y_2 - y_1)^2}$$

The **midpoint** M of the line segment PQ is:

$$M = \left(\frac{x_1 + x_2}{2}, \frac{y_1 + y_2}{2} \right)$$

The **slope** of the line through the points P and Q is

$$M = \frac{y_2 - y_1}{x_2 - x_1}, \quad \text{when } x_1 \neq x_2$$

Let l_1 with slope m_1 and l_2 with slope m_2 be any two nonvertical lines.
If $m_1 = m_2$, then $l_1 \parallel l_2$.
If $m_1 \times m_2 = -1$, then $l_1 \perp l_2$.
A vertical line does not have slope and has the form $x = k$, where k is a real number.
A horizontal line has a slope of zero and has the form $y = h$, where h is a real number.
Any two horizontal lines are parallel to each other.
Any two vertical lines are parallel to each other.
Any vertical line is perpendicular to any horizontal line.
If a line crosses the x axis, the point at which it crosses is called the **x intercept**. If a line crosses the y axis, the point at which it crosses is called the **y intercept**. The x intercept is the value of x when $y = 0$ for the line. The y intercept is the value of y when $x = 0$.

Let the slope of a line be m and the y intercept of the line be b. The **slope–intercept equation of a line** is

$$y = mx + b$$

Example 14

What is the slope of the line through the points $(6, -4)$ and $(-8, -6)$?

Solution

$$m = \frac{y_2 - y_1}{x_2 - x_1}$$

$$m = \frac{-6 - (-4)}{-8 - 6}$$

$$m = \frac{-6 + 4}{-14}$$

$$m = \frac{-2}{-14}$$

$$m = \frac{1}{7}$$

Example 15

What is the midpoint of the line segment with endpoints $(6, -4)$ and $(-8, -6)$?

Solution

$$M = \left(\frac{x_1 + x_2}{2}, \frac{y_1 + y_2}{2} \right)$$

$$M = \left(\frac{6 - 8}{2}, \frac{-4 - 6}{2} \right)$$

$$M = \left(\frac{-2}{2}, \frac{-10}{2} \right)$$

$$M = (-1, -5)$$

Example 16

What is the distance between the points $(6, -4)$ and $(-8, -6)$?

Solution

$$d = \sqrt{(x_2 - x_1)^2 + (y_2 - y_1)^2}$$

$$d = \sqrt{(-8 - 6)^2 + [-6 - (-4)]^2}$$

$$d = \sqrt{(-14)^2 + (-6 + 4)^2}$$

$$d = \sqrt{196 + (-2)^2}$$

$$d = \sqrt{196 + 4}$$

$$d = \sqrt{200}$$

$$d = \sqrt{100} \cdot \sqrt{2}$$

$$d = 10\sqrt{2}$$

Example 17

If a line has a slope of -3 and a y intercept of $(0, 4)$, what is the equation of the line?

Solution

$$y = mx + b$$
$$m = -3 \quad \text{and} \quad b = 4$$
$$y = -3x + 4$$

PRACTICE PROBLEMS

1. Name the quadrant or axis where each point is located.

   A. $(6, 1)$ B. $(-2, -4)$ C. $(-10, -2)$
   D. $(-8, 4)$ E. $(3, -6)$ F. $(-7, 5)$
   G. $(0, -8)$ H. $(3, 0)$

2. Locate each point on a coordinate grid.

   A. $A = (3, 2)$ B. $B = (-2, -3)$ C. $C = (5, 0)$
   D. $D = (4, -2)$ E. $E = (0, -2)$ F. $F = (-3, 3)$
   G. $G = (-3, 0)$ H. $H = (-1, 4)$

3. Find the slope of the line through the given points.

   A. $(-2, -3)$ and $(-1, 5)$ B. $(8, 1)$ and $(2, 6)$
   C. $(2, 4)$ and $(-4, 4)$ D. $(-3, 4)$ and $(-4, 3)$
   E. $(3, -13)$ and $(-6, -5)$ F. $(5, 4)$ and $(1, -2)$

4. Write the equation of the line with the given slope m and given y intercept b.

   A. $m = 1.5, b = -4$ B. $m = -4, b = 1.8$
   C. $m = 3, b = 0$ D. $m = -1.6, b = 4$

5. Write the equation of the line with the given slope m and intersection through the given point.

   A. $m = 0.5; (-3, 2)$ B. $m = -2; (0, 1)$
   C. $m = 1.25; (-2, -1)$ D. $m = -1.5; (2, 4)$

6. Determine if L_1 and L_2 are parallel, perpendicular, or neither.

   A. L_1 goes through $(4, 6)$ and $(-8, 7)$; L_2 goes through $(7, 4)$ and $(-5, 5)$.
   B. L_1 goes through $(9, 15)$ and $(-7, 12)$; L_2 goes through $(-4, 8)$ and $(-20, 5)$.
   C. L_1 goes through $(2, 0)$ and $(5, 4)$; L_2 goes through $(6, 1)$ and $(2, 4)$.
   D. L_1 goes through $(0, -7)$ and $(2, 3)$; L_2 goes through $(0, -3)$ and $(1, -2)$.

7. Find the distance between the given points.
   A. $(3, 4)$ and $(-2, 1)$ B. $(-2, 1)$ and $(3, 2)$
   C. $(-2, 4)$ and $(3, -2)$

8. Find the midpoint of the line segment between the points.
   A. $(7, -3)$ and $(-4, 2)$ B. $(0, -5)$ and $(4, -12)$
   C. $(5, -1)$ and $(-3, -7)$

SOLUTIONS

1. A. I   B. III   C. III
   D. II   E. IV   F. II
   G. Negative y axis   H. Positive x axis

2. See Figure 8.36. Note:
   $A = (3, 2)$ $B = (-2, -3)$ $C = (5, 0)$
   $D = (4, -2)$ $E = (0, -2)$ $F = (-3, 3)$
   $G = (-3, 0)$ $H = (-1, 4)$

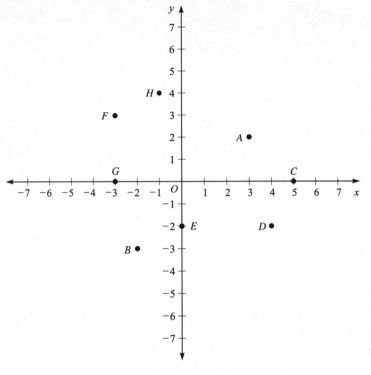

Figure 8.36

3. A. $m = \dfrac{y_2 - y_1}{x_2 - x_1} = \dfrac{5+3}{-1+2} = \dfrac{8}{1} = 8$

   B. $m = \dfrac{y_2 - y_1}{x_2 - x_1} = \dfrac{6-1}{2-8} = \dfrac{5}{-6} = \dfrac{-5}{6}$

   C. $m = \dfrac{y_2 - y_1}{x_2 - x_1} = \dfrac{4-4}{-4-2} = \dfrac{0}{-6} = 0$

   D. $m = \dfrac{y_2 - y_1}{x_2 - x_1} = \dfrac{3-4}{-4+3} = \dfrac{-1}{-1} = 1$

   E. $m = \dfrac{y_2 - y_1}{x_2 - x_1} = \dfrac{-5+13}{-6-3} = \dfrac{8}{-9} = \dfrac{-8}{9}$

   F. $m = \dfrac{y_2 - y_1}{x_2 - x_1} = \dfrac{-2-4}{1-5} = \dfrac{-6}{-4} = \dfrac{3}{2}$

4. $y = mx + b$

   A. $y = 1.5x - 4$
   B. $y = -4x + 1.8$
   C. $y = 3x - y = 3x$
   D. $y = -1.6x + 4$

5. A. $y = mx + b, (x, y) = (-3, 2), m = 0.5$
   $2 = 0.5(-3) + b$
   $2 = -1.5 + b$
   $3.5 = b$
   $y = 0.5x + 3.5$

B. $y = mx + b, (x, y) = (0, 1), m = -2$
   $1 = -2(0) + b$
   $1 = b$
   $y = -2x + 1$

C. $y = mx + b, (x, y) = (-2, -1), m = 1.25$
   $-1 = 1.25(-2) + b$
   $-1 = -2.5 + b$
   $1.5 = b$
   $y = 1.25x + 1.5$

D. $y = mx + b, (x, y) = (2, 4), m = -1.5$
   $4 = -1.5(2) + b$
   $4 = -3 + b$
   $7 = b$
   $y = -1.5x + 7$

6. A. L_1 has slope $m = \dfrac{y_2 - y_1}{x_2 - x_1} = \dfrac{7-6}{-8-4} =$
   $\dfrac{1}{-12} = \dfrac{-1}{12} = m_1$

   L_2 has slope $m = \dfrac{y_2 - y_1}{x_2 - x_1} = \dfrac{5-4}{-5-7} =$
   $\dfrac{1}{-12} = \dfrac{-1}{12} = m_2$

   Since $m_1 = m_2$, $L_1 \parallel L_2$.

B. $L_1 : m_1 = \dfrac{12 - 15}{-7 - 9} = \dfrac{-3}{-16}$

$L_2 : m_2 = \dfrac{5 - 8}{-20 + 4} = \dfrac{-3}{-16}$

Since $m_1 = m_2$, $L_1 \parallel L_2$.

C. $L_1 : m_1 = \dfrac{4 - 0}{5 - 2} = \dfrac{4}{3}$,

$L_2 : m_2 = \dfrac{4 - 1}{2 - 6} = \dfrac{3}{-4} = \dfrac{-3}{4}$

$m_1 \times m_2 = \dfrac{4}{3} \times \dfrac{-3}{4} = -1$

Since $m_1 \times m_2 = -1$, $L_1 \perp L_2$.

D. $L_1 : m_1 = \dfrac{3 + 7}{2 - 0} = \dfrac{10}{2} = 5$

$L_2 : m_2 = \dfrac{-2 + 3}{1 - 0} = \dfrac{1}{1} = 1$

$m_1 \neq m_2$, and $m_1 \times m_2 = 5 \times 1 = 5 \neq -1$
Since $m_1 \neq m_2$, and $m_1 \times m_2 \neq -1$, L_1 and
L_2 are neither parallel nor perpendicular.

7. A. $d = \sqrt{(x_2 - x_1)^2 + (y_2 - y_1)^2}$

$= \sqrt{(-2 - 3)^2 + (1 - 4)^2}$

$= \sqrt{(-5)^2 + (-3)^2}$

$= \sqrt{25 + 9} = \sqrt{34}$

$d = \sqrt{34}$

B. $d = \sqrt{(x_2 - x_1)^2 + (y_2 - y_1)^2}$

$= \sqrt{(3 + 2)^2 + (2 - 1)^2}$

$= \sqrt{(5)^2 + (1)^2} = \sqrt{25 + 1} = \sqrt{26}$

$d = \sqrt{26}$

C. $d = \sqrt{(x_2 - x_1)^2 + (y_2 - y_1)^2}$

$= \sqrt{(3 + 2)^2 + (-2 - 4)^2}$

$= \sqrt{(5)^2 + (-6)^2} = \sqrt{25 + 36} = \sqrt{61}$

$d = \sqrt{61}$

8. A. $M = \left(\dfrac{x_1 + x_2}{2}, \dfrac{y_1 + y_2}{2} \right)$

$= \left(\dfrac{7 - 4}{2}, \dfrac{-3 + 2}{2} \right) = \left(\dfrac{3}{2}, \dfrac{-1}{2} \right)$

B. $M = \left(\dfrac{x_1 + x_2}{2}, \dfrac{y_1 + y_2}{2} \right)$

$= \left(\dfrac{0 + 4}{2}, \dfrac{-5 - 12}{2} \right)$

$= \left(\dfrac{4}{2}, \dfrac{-17}{2} \right) = 2, \left(\dfrac{-17}{2} \right)$

C. $M = \left(\dfrac{x_1 + x_2}{2}, \dfrac{y_1 + y_2}{2} \right)$

$= \left(\dfrac{5 - 3}{2}, \dfrac{-1 - 7}{2} \right) = \left(\dfrac{2}{2}, \dfrac{-8}{2} \right)$

$= (1, -4)$

▁▁ GEOMETRY TEST

Use the following test to assess how well you have mastered the material in
this chapter. For each question, mark your answer by blackening the corresponding answer oval. An answer key and solutions are provided at the end
of the test.

1. Which is an angle with a measure between 90° and 180°?

   (A) Acute
   (B) Obtuse
   (C) Reflex
   (D) Right
   (E) Straight

2. Which is an angle with a measure of 180°?

   (A) Acute
   (B) Obtuse
   (C) Reflex
   (D) Right
   (E) Straight

3. Which is the supplement of a 72° angle?

    (A) 18°
    (B) 36°
    (C) 72°
    (D) 108°
    (E) 288°

4. What is the name for the opposite angles formed when two lines intersect?

    (A) Complementary
    (B) Supplementary
    (C) Vertical
    (D) Interior
    (E) Exterior

5. Which are complementary angles?

    (A) 32°, 58°
    (B) 20°, 51°, 19°
    (C) 74°, 26°, 80°
    (D) 130°, 50°
    (E) 37°, 63°

6. If two lines are cut by a transversal, which angles will always be equal?

    (A) Adjacent angles
    (B) Alternate exterior angles
    (C) Alternate interior angles
    (D) Corresponding angles
    (E) Vertical angles

7. If an angle is 5 times its complement, what is the measure of the angle?

    (A) 15°
    (B) 18°
    (C) 36°
    (D) 75°
    (E) 144°

8. Which angle is 10° less than its supplement?

    (A) 85°
    (B) 95°
    (C) 105°
    (D) 50°
    (E) 40°

9. When two parallel lines are cut by a transversal, which pair of angles will always be supplementary?

    (A) Alternate interior angles
    (B) Consecutive interior angles
    (C) Corresponding angles
    (D) Alternate exterior angles
    (E) Vertical angles

10. Which quadrilateral is equilateral but not always equiangular?

(A) Trapezoid
(B) Parallelogram
(C) Rectangle
(D) Square
(E) Rhombus

11. Which polygon always has diagonals of the same length?

(A) Pentagon
(B) Rectangle
(C) Parallelogram
(D) Rhombus
(E) Hexagon

12. Which polygon has exactly eight sides?

(A) Hexagon
(B) Quadrilateral
(C) Octagon
(D) Pentagon
(E) Triangle

13. If a polygon has seven sides, what is the sum of its interior angles?

(A) 450°
(B) 900°
(C) 1080°
(D) 1200°
(E) 1800°

14. What is the measure of one interior angle of a regular octagon?

(A) 45°
(B) 120°
(C) 135°
(D) 157.5°
(E) 1080°

15. Which is the fewest number of sides a polygon can have?

(A) 0
(B) 1
(C) 2
(D) 3
(E) 4

16. In which figure do the diagonals NOT bisect each other?

(A) Trapezoid
(B) Parallelogram
(C) Square
(D) Rhombus
(E) Rectangle

17. Which is NOT a property of parallelograms?

ⓐ The opposite sides are parallel.
ⓑ The opposite sides are equal.
ⓒ The consecutive angles are supplementary.
ⓓ The opposite angles are equal.
ⓔ The diagonals bisect the angles.

18. Which is a part of a line with one endpoint?

ⓐ Line
ⓑ Ray
ⓒ Line segment
ⓓ Angle
ⓔ Point

19. Which is NOT a requirement for adjacent angles?

ⓐ Two angles
ⓑ Common vertex
ⓒ Sum of angles is 180°
ⓓ No interior points in common
ⓔ Common side

20. Which is NOT a type of triangle?

ⓐ Scalene
ⓑ Equiangular
ⓒ Isosceles
ⓓ Reflex
ⓔ Regular

21. Which are the angles of a right triangle?

ⓐ 11°, 79°, 90°
ⓑ 33°, 67°, 90°
ⓒ 90°, 90°, 90°
ⓓ 10°, 20°, 60°, 90°
ⓔ 90°, 20°, 70°, 90°

22. In a triangle, two angles are 23° and 31°. What is the third angle in the triangle?

ⓐ 36°
ⓑ 54°
ⓒ 126°
ⓓ 216°
ⓔ 306°

23. Which lengths could be the sides of a triangle?

ⓐ 4, 9, 16
ⓑ 3, 4, 7
ⓒ 4, 6, 11
ⓓ 5, 7, 9
ⓔ 5, 5, 10

24. In $\triangle ABC$, $\angle A > \angle B > \angle C$, $AB = 31$ cm, and $AC = 50$ cm. Which could be the length of BC?

   (A) 25 cm
   (B) 30 cm
   (C) 40 cm
   (D) 45 cm
   (E) 80 cm

25. What is the smallest number of acute angles a triangle can have?

   (A) 0
   (B) 1
   (C) 2
   (D) 3
   (E) 4

26. In right $\triangle ABC$, angle C is the right angle. If $a = 57$ and $c = 185$, what is the length of b?

   (A) $\sqrt{37,474}$
   (B) 176
   (C) 128
   (D) 242
   (E) $\sqrt{242}$

27. Which set of lengths could be the sides of a right triangle?

   (A) 8, 15, 17
   (B) 4, 5, 6
   (C) 9, 12, 14
   (D) 1, 1, 2
   (E) 2, $2\sqrt{2}$, 4

28. If a base angle of an isosceles triangle is 32°, what is the measure of the vertex angle?

   (A) 26°
   (B) 58°
   (C) 64°
   (D) 116°
   (E) 148°

29. In a 30°–60°–90° triangle, if the hypotenuse is 10, what is the length of the side opposite the 60° angle?

   (A) $10\sqrt{3}$
   (B) $5\sqrt{3}$
   (C) $20\sqrt{3}$
   (D) 5
   (E) 20

30. In a 45°–45°–90° triangle, if the hypotenuse is $4\sqrt{6}$, what is the length of a leg?

   (A) $2\sqrt{6}$
   (B) $4\sqrt{3}$
   (C) $4\sqrt{2}$
   (D) $8\sqrt{6}$
   (E) $8\sqrt{3}$

31. $\triangle ABC \sim \triangle DEF$ and $DE = 6$, $AB = 3$, $BC = 7$, and $CA = 9$. What is the length of EF?

   (A) 1.5
   (B) 3.5
   (C) 4.5
   (D) 14
   (E) 18

32. What term is used to indicate the perimeter of a circle?

   (A) Diameter
   (B) Radius
   (C) Secant
   (D) Chord
   (E) Circumference

33. If the sides of a polygon are 2.5 cm, 3.8 cm, 11 cm, 4.9 cm, and 5.28 cm, what is the perimeter of the polygon?

   (A) 1.758 cm
   (B) 27.48 cm
   (C) 65.1 cm
   (D) 274.8 cm
   (E) 651 cm

34. If the length and width of a rectangle are 7 and 12, respectively, what is the perimeter of the rectangle?

   (A) 19
   (B) 38
   (C) 42
   (D) 84
   (E) 168

35. If the perimeter of a square is 36 cm, what is its area?

   (A) 81 cm^2
   (B) 324 cm^2
   (C) 36 cm^2
   (D) 12 cm^2
   (E) 24 cm^2

36. If the sides of a right triangle are 60 ft, 91 ft, and 109 ft, what is the area of the triangle?

   (A) 260 ft²
   (B) 3,270 ft²
   (C) 2,730 ft²
   (D) 5,460 ft²
   (E) 6,540 ft²

37. In a trapezoid, the bases are 17 cm and 25 cm. The legs are 14 cm and 18 cm. The altitude is 20 cm. What is the area of the trapezoid?

   (A) 840 cm²
   (B) 640 cm²
   (C) 94 cm²
   (D) 320 cm²
   (E) 420 cm²

38. Which line has exactly one point in common with a circle?

   (A) Radius
   (B) Chord
   (C) Diameter
   (D) Tangent
   (E) Secant

39. In a given circle, the diameter is 40 cm. What is the circumference?

   (A) 20π cm
   (B) 40π cm
   (C) 80π cm
   (D) 400π cm
   (E) $1,600\pi$ cm

40. If the circumference of a circle is 64π cm, what is its area?

   (A) 8π cm²
   (B) 16π cm²
   (C) 32π cm²
   (D) $1,024\pi$ cm²
   (E) $4,096\pi$ cm²

41. Two chords intersect inside a circle. The lengths of the two parts of one chord are 9 and 16. The lengths of the two parts of the second chord are 6 and x. What is the value of x? (See Figure 8.26.)

   (A) 24
   (B) 19
   (C) 13
   (D) 8
   (E) 2

42. A room is 20 ft by 30 ft by 8 ft. What is the surface area of the room?

    (A) 4,800 ft^2
    (B) 800 ft^2
    (C) 1,000 ft^2
    (D) 1,520 ft^2
    (E) 2,000 ft^2

43. If the edge of a cube is 6 cm, what is the volume of the cube?

    (A) 24 cm^3
    (B) 36 cm^3
    (C) 144 cm^3
    (D) 180 cm^3
    (E) 216 cm^3

44. If the altitude of a cylinder is 12 cm and the radius of the base is 9 cm, what is the volume of the cylinder?

    (A) 54π cm^3
    (B) 81π cm^3
    (C) 216π cm^3
    (D) 972π cm^3
    (E) $3,052\pi$ cm^3

45. If the area of the base of a pyramid is 24 cm^2 and the altitude of the pyramid is 18 cm, what is the volume of the pyramid?

    (A) 144 cm^3
    (B) 432 cm^3
    (C) 1,296 cm^3
    (D) 1,764 cm^3
    (E) 20,736 cm^3

46. If the radius of the base of a cone is 15 m and the slant height of the cone is 6 m, what is the surface area of the cone?

    (A) 225π m^2
    (B) 90π m^2
    (C) 630π m^2
    (D) 126π m^2
    (E) 315π m^2

47. What is the surface area of a sphere whose radius is 14 in?

    (A) 56π in^2
    (B) 196π in^2
    (C) 784π in^2
    (D) $2,744\pi$ in^2
    (E) $10,976\pi$ in^2

48. A cylinder has a height of 12 ft, and the radius of the base is 9 ft. What is the surface area of the cylinder?

   (A) 378π ft^2
   (B) 504π ft^2
   (C) 252π ft^2
   (D) 189π ft^2
   (E) 540π ft^2

49. What is the volume of a sphere whose radius is 15 cm?

   (A) $4{,}500\pi$ cm^3
   (B) $3{,}375\pi$ cm^3
   (C) $13{,}500\pi$ cm^3
   (D) $1{,}125\pi$ cm^3
   (E) 300π cm^3

50. What is the surface area of a cube when the length of an edge is 2.1 m?

   (A) 9.261 m^2
   (B) 4.41 m^2
   (C) 26.46 m^2
   (D) 17.64 m^2
   (E) 8.82 m^2

████████ # ANSWER KEY

```
    1.  B      11.  B      21.  A      31.  D      41.  A
    2.  E      12.  C      22.  C      32.  E      42.  E
    3.  D      13.  B      23.  D      33.  B      43.  E
    4.  C      14.  C      24.  E      34.  B      44.  D
    5.  A      15.  D      25.  C      35.  A      45.  A
    6.  E      16.  A      26.  B      36.  C      46.  E
    7.  D      17.  E      27.  A      37.  E      47.  C
    8.  A      18.  B      28.  D      38.  D      48.  A
    9.  B      19.  C      29.  B      39.  B      49.  A
   10.  E      20.  D      30.  B      40.  D      50.  C
```

████ **SOLUTIONS**

1. **B** Obtuse
   $90° <$ obtuse $< 180°$

2. **E** Straight
   Straight $= 180°$

3. **D** $108°$
   $180° - 72° = 108°$

4. **C** Vertical
   Vertical angles are the opposite angles.

5. **A** $32°$ and $58°$
   Complementary angles sum to $90°$. $32° + 58° = 90°$

6. **E** Vertical angles
   You are not told that the lines are parallel, so only vertical angles must be equal.

7. **D** $75°$
   $n + 5n = 90, 6n = 90, n = 15, 5n = 75, 75°$ is the angle.

8. **A** $85°$
   $n - 10° + n = 180°, 2n = 190°, n = 95°, n - 10° = 85°$ angle

9. **B** Consecutive interior angles
   The adjacent interior angles are always supplementary. The interior angles on the same side are transversal supplementary when the lines are parallel. So when the lines are parallel, consecutive interior angles are supplementary.

10. **E** Rhombus
    A square is both equilateral and equiangular. A rectangle is always equiangular, but only squares are equilateral. A rhombus is always equilateral, but only squares are equiangular.

11. **B** Rectangle
The diagonals of a rectangle are always equal.

12. **C** Octagon
An octagon is an eight-sided polygon.

13. **B** 900°
$n = 7, 5 = (n - 2)180° = (7 - 2)180° = (5)180° = 900°$

14. **C** 135°
$n = 8, 5 = (n - 2)180° = 6(180°) = 1080°, 1080° \div 8 = 135°$

15. **D** 3
A triangle has the fewest sides of any polygon, 3.

16. **A** Trapezoid
The diagonals of a parallelogram always bisect each other. The trapezoid is the only nonparallelogram listed.

17. **E** The diagonals bisect each other.
The diagonals of a rhombus bisect the angles but not for all parallelograms.

18. **B** Ray
A ray is a part of a line with one endpoint.

19. **C** Sum of angles is 180°.
Adjacent angles are two angles in the same plane that have a common vertex and a common side, and the common side separates the angles.

20. **D** Reflex
A reflex angle is an angle greater than 180° and less than 360°. No triangle can have a reflex angle in it.

21. **A** 11°, 79°, 90°
Every right triangle has a right angle, 90°, so the other two angles must have a sum of 90°, or $11° + 79° = 90°$.

22. **C** 126°
$23° + 31° = 54°, 180° - 54° = 126°$, the third angle is 126°.

23. **D** 5, 7, 9
In a triangle, any two sides must exceed the third side. Since $5 + 7 = 12 > 9$, and 9 is the longest side, these can be the sides of a triangle.

24. **E** 80 cm
Since $\angle A > \angle B > \angle C$, $BC > AC > AB$. So BC must be greater than $AC = 50$. $BC < AB + AC$, so $BC < 31 + 50 = 81$. Thus, $81 > BC > 50$ and only 80 is a choice.

25. **C** 2
An acute triangle has 3 acute angles. A right triangle has 1 right angle and 2 acute angles. An obtuse triangle has 1 obtuse angle and 2 acute angles. So every triangle has at least 2 acute angles.

26. **B** 176

$a^2 + b^2 = c^2$ and $a = 57$ and $c = 185$
$b^2 = c^2 - a^2 = 185^2 - 57^2 = 34{,}225 - 3{,}249 = 30{,}976$
$b^2 = 30{,}976$
$b = \sqrt{30{,}976} = 176$

27. **A** 8, 15, 17

In a right triangle, $a^2 + b^2 = c^2$ and c is the longest side.
$8^2 + 15^2 = 64 + 225 = 289 = 17^2$. So 8, 15, and 17 are the sides of a right triangle.

28. **D** 116°

The base angles of an isosceles triangle are equal. The three angles of a triangle have a sum of 180°. $180° - 32° - 32° = 116°$.

29. **B** $5\sqrt{3}$

In a 30°–60°–90° triangle, the sides are a, $a\sqrt{3}$, and $2a$. Side a is opposite the 30° angle, and $2a$ is the hypotenuse. $2a = 10$, $a = 5$, $a\sqrt{3} = 5\sqrt{3}$.

30. **B** $4\sqrt{3}$

In a 45°–45°–90° triangle, the sides are a, a, and $a\sqrt{2}$. The sides of length a are opposite the 45° angles, and $a\sqrt{2}$ is the hypotenuse. $a\sqrt{2} = 4\sqrt{6} = 4\sqrt{2}\sqrt{3} = 4\sqrt{3} \times \sqrt{2}$. So $a = 4\sqrt{3}$.

31. **D** 14

$\triangle ABC \sim \triangle DEF$, $AB : DE = BC : EF = AC : DF$. Both AB and DE are given. $DE = 6$, and $AB = 3$, so $AB : DE = 1 : 2$.
$BC = 7$ and you need EF. $BC : EF = 7 : EF = 1 : 2 = 7 : 14$, so $EF = 14$.

32. **E** Circumference

The perimeter of a circle is the circumference.

33. **B** 27.48 cm

$P = 2.5 \text{ cm} + 3.8 \text{ cm} + 11 \text{ cm} + 4.9 \text{ cm} + 5.28 \text{ cm} = 27.48 \text{ cm}$

34. **B** 38

For a rectangle, $P = 2l + 2w = 2(7) + 2(12) = 14 + 24 = 38$.

35. **A** 81 cm²

For a square, $P = 4s$ and $A = s^2$. New $P = 36$ cm, so $4s = 36$ cm and $s = 9$ cm.
$A = s^2 = (9 \text{ cm})^2 = 81 \text{ cm}^2$

36. **C** 2,730 ft²

In a right triangle, $A = 0.5ab$, where a and b are the legs. Side c is the longest side, so a and b are bases. $A = 0.5(60 \text{ ft})(91 \text{ ft}) = 2{,}730 \text{ ft}^2$.

37. **E** 420 cm²

For a trapezoid, $A = 0.5h(a + b)$, where a and b are bases.
$A = 0.5(20 \text{ cm})(17 \text{ cm} + 25 \text{ cm}) = 10 \text{ cm}(42 \text{ cm}) = 420 \text{ cm}^2$

38. **D** Tangent

A tangent is a line that intersects the circle in exactly one point.

39. **B** 40π cm
In a circle, $C = \pi d = \pi(40 \text{ cm}) = 40\pi$ cm.

40. **D** $1,024\pi$ cm²
$C = \pi d$ and $C = 64\pi$ cm, so $d = 64$ cm. And $d = 2r$, so $r = 32$ cm.
$A = \pi r^2 = \pi(32 \text{ cm})^2 = \pi(1,024 \text{ cm}^2) = 1,024\pi$ cm²

41. **A** 24
In a circle when two chords intersect inside a circle, the product of the segments, parts, of each chord is the same.
So, $9(16) = 6x \qquad 6x = 144 \qquad$ and $\qquad x = 24$

42. **E** 2,000 ft²
A room is a rectangular solid, so $S = 2lw + 2lh + 2wh$.
$S = 2(20 \text{ ft})(30 \text{ ft}) + 2(20 \text{ ft})(8 \text{ ft}) + 2(30 \text{ ft})(8 \text{ ft})$
$\quad = 1,200 \text{ ft}^2 + 320 \text{ ft}^2 + 480 \text{ ft}^2$
$S = 2,000$ ft²

43. **E** 216 cm³
$V = e^3, e = 6 \text{ cm} \qquad V = (6 \text{ cm})^3 = 216 \text{ cm}^3$

44. **D** $D = 972\pi$ cm³
$V = \pi r^2 h$
$V = (\pi)(9 \text{ cm})^2(12 \text{ cm}) = (\pi)(81 \text{ cm}^2)(12 \text{ cm}) = 972\pi$ cm³

45. **A** 144 cm³
$V = \dfrac{1}{3}bh = \dfrac{1}{3}(24 \text{ cm}^2)(18 \text{ cm}) = 8 \text{ cm}^2(18 \text{ cm}) = 144 \text{ cm}^3$

46. **E** 315π m²
$S = \pi r^2 + \pi rs = \pi(15 \text{ m})^2 + \pi(15 \text{ m})(6 \text{ m}) = 225\pi \text{ m}^2 + 90\pi \text{ m}^2$
$S = 315\pi$ m²

47. **C** 784π in²
$S = 4\pi r^2 = 4\pi(14 \text{ in})^2 = 4\pi(196 \text{ in}^2) = 784\pi$ in²

48. **A** 378π ft²
$S = 2\pi r^2 + 2\pi rh = 2\pi(r^2 + rh) = 2\pi[(9 \text{ ft})^2 + (9 \text{ ft})(12 \text{ ft})] =$
$2\pi(81 \text{ ft}^2 + 108 \text{ ft}^2) = 2\pi(189 \text{ ft}^2) = 378\pi$ ft²

49. **A** $4,500\pi$ cm³
$V = \dfrac{4}{3}\pi r^3 = \dfrac{4}{3}\pi(15 \text{ cm})^3 = \dfrac{4}{3}\pi(3,315 \text{ cm}^3) = 4,500\pi$ cm³

50. **C** 26.46 m²
$S = 6e^2 = 6(2.1 \text{ m}) = 6(4.41 \text{ m}^2) = 26.46$ m²

GMAT SOLVED PROBLEMS

For each question, select the best answer.

1. **Which of these are measures of angles that are supplementary?**

   A. 33°, 67°
   B. 35°, 55°
   C. 97°, 83°
   D. 108°, 92°
   E. 28°, 57°, 95°

2. **Which is the number of sides for an octagon?**

   A. 10
   B. 8
   C. 6
   D. 5
   E. 4

3. **Which is NOT the description of a possible triangle?**

   A. Scalene and right
   B. Equilateral and acute
   C. Isosceles and obtuse
   D. Scalene and acute
   E. Equilateral and obtuse

4. **Which is NOT a type of parallelogram?**

   A. Rectangle
   B. Square
   C. Trapezoid
   D. Rhombus
   E. Regular quadrilateral

5. **What is the circumference of a circle whose diameter is 20 centimeters? Use $\pi = 3.14$.**

   A. 62.8 cm
   B. 125.6 cm
   C. 314 cm
   D. 628 cm
   E. 1,256 cm

6. **Which solid has two bases that can be circles?**

   A. Cone
   B. Cylinder
   C. Prism
   D. Pyramid
   E. Cube

7. *N* is the number of sides of a polygon. What is *N*?

    1. **The sum of the interior angles is 1800°.**
    2. **The sum of the exterior angles is 360°.**

    A. Statement 1 ALONE is sufficient, but statement 2 is not sufficient.
    B. Statement 2 ALONE is sufficient, but statement 1 is not sufficient.
    C. BOTH statements TOGETHER are sufficient, but NEITHER statement ALONE is sufficient.
    D. EACH statement ALONE is sufficient.
    E. Statements 1 and 2 TOGETHER are not sufficient.

8. **If *K* is the area of a rectangle, then what is *K*?**

    1. **The length is 3 times the width.**
    2. **The perimeter is 80.**

    A. Statement 1 ALONE is sufficient, but statement 2 is not sufficient.
    B. Statement 2 ALONE is sufficient, but statement 1 is not sufficient.
    C. BOTH statements TOGETHER are sufficient, but NEITHER statement ALONE is sufficient.
    D. EACH statement ALONE is sufficient.
    E. Statements 1 and 2 TOGETHER are not sufficient.

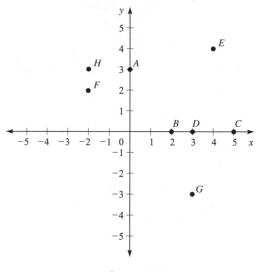

Figure 8.37

9. **Which pair of points listed in Figure 8.37 are 5 units apart?**

    A. *A* and *F*
    B. *B* and *G*
    C. *B* and *H*
    D. *F* and *G*
    E. *A* and *B*

10. **Which pair of points in Figure 8.37 lies on a line with a slope of −¹/₂?**

    A. *C* and *D*
    B. *E* and *F*
    C. *C* and *E*
    D. *B* and *F*
    E. *G* and *H*

▓▓ SOLUTIONS

1. **C** Supplementary angles are two angles that have a sum of 180°. This is only true for 97° and 83°, so the answer is C.

2. **B** Since the prefix *oct* means 8, an octagon is a polygon with eight sides.

3. **E** An equilateral triangle has all sides and angles equal. Since an obtuse angle has a measure greater than 90°, having three angles this large would mean that the sum of the angles was greater than 180°, which is the sum of all three angles in a triangle.

4. **C** A trapezoid is a quadrilateral with exactly one pair of parallel sides, so it is not a parallelogram. A regular quadrilateral is one with all sides equal and all angles equal, so it is a square, which is a parallelogram. The correct answer is C.

5. **A** The formula for the circumference of a circle is $C = \pi d$, so $C = 3.14(20 \text{ cm}) = 62.8$ cm. The answer is A.

6. **B** The bases of prisms, pyramids, and cubes must be polygons. A cone has only one base. A cylinder can have two bases that can be circles. The answer is B.

7. **A** The sum of the interior angles of a polygon is found by using the formula $S = (n-2)(180°)$, so if $S = 1800°$, then $n - 2 = 10$ and n is 12. So statement 1 alone is sufficient.

   The sum of the exterior angles of every polygon is 360°, so statement 2 is not sufficient. Thus, the answer is A.

8. **C** Since in statement 1 the length is 3 times the width, the area of the rectangle is $(3w)(w) = 3w^2$, but you can't find a specific value. Statement 1 alone is not sufficient.

   In statement 2, the perimeter is 80, so $l + w = 40$ and $l = 40 - w$. The area is $(40 - w)(w) = 40w - w^2$, but you still can't find a specific value. Statement 2 alone is not sufficient.

   If you take both statements together, you have $l = 3w$ and $2l + 2w = 80$. Combine to get $2w + 2(3w) = 80$. $2w + 6w = 80$. $8w = 80$. $w = 10$. $l = 30$.
   Thus, the area is 300. The answer is C.

9. **C** Point B is $(2,0)$, and point H is $(-2, 3)$, so $BH = \sqrt{(-2-2)^2 + (3-0)^2} = \sqrt{(-4)^2 + 3^2} = \sqrt{16+9} = \sqrt{25} = 5$.

10. **D** Point B is $(2,0)$ and point F is $(-2,2)$, so the slope of $BF = \dfrac{2-0}{-2-2} = \dfrac{2}{-4} = \dfrac{-1}{2}$.

GMAT PRACTICE PROBLEMS

For each question, select the best answer.

1. If an angle is 5 times its complement, what is the measure of the angle?

   A. 15°
   B. 18°
   C. 72°
   D. 75°
   E. 150°

2. What is the name of a triangle with exactly two sides equal?

   A. Isosceles
   B. Equilateral
   C. Acute
   D. Obtuse
   E. Scalene

3. If one leg of a right triangle is 3 and the hypotenuse is 4, how long is the other leg?

   A. 1
   B. $\sqrt{7}$
   C. 3.5
   D. 5
   E. 7

4. Which set of lengths could be the sides of a triangle?

   A. 2, 2, 7
   B. 4, 7, 8
   C. −6, −6, −6
   D. 6, 7, 0
   E. −2, −8, −9

5. If one angle of a right triangle is 57°, what is the measure of the other angle?

   A. 33°
   B. 43°
   C. 57°
   D. 123°
   E. 147°

6. Which solid has an apex and a polygon for a base?

   A. Cone
   B. Cylinder
   C. Cube
   D. Prism
   E. Pyramid

7. **If N is a polygon, what is the shape of the polygon?**

   1. *N* has 15 diagonals.
   2. When N is regular, each exterior angle is 60°.

   A. Statement 1 ALONE is sufficient, but statement 2 is not sufficient.
   B. Statement 2 ALONE is sufficient, but statement 1 is not sufficient.
   C. BOTH statements TOGETHER are sufficient, but NEITHER statement ALONE is sufficient.
   D. EACH statement ALONE is sufficient.
   E. Statements 1 and 2 TOGETHER are not sufficient.

8. **If X is the length of the radius of a circle, what is X?**

   1. The radius is one-half the length of the diameter.
   2. The ratio of the circumference to the diameter is π.

   A. Statement 1 ALONE is sufficient, but statement 2 is not sufficient.
   B. Statement 2 ALONE is sufficient, but statement 1 is not sufficient.
   C. BOTH statements TOGETHER are sufficient, but NEITHER statement ALONE is sufficient.
   D. EACH statement ALONE is sufficient.
   E. Statements 1 and 2 TOGETHER are not sufficient.

9. **In a square with an area of 64, what is the length of the diagonal?**

   A. 4
   B. $4\sqrt{2}$
   C. 8
   D. $8\sqrt{2}$
   E. 16

10. **In a 30°–60°–90° right triangle, the hypotenuse is 12. What is the length of the side opposite the 30° angle?**

    A. 6
    B. $4\sqrt{3}$
    C. $6\sqrt{2}$
    D. $6\sqrt{3}$
    E. 24

![grey bar] **ANSWER KEY**

1.	D
2.	A
3.	B
4.	B
5.	A
6.	E
7.	D
8.	E
9.	D
10.	A

SECTION IV

GMAT MATH PRACTICE TESTS

The questions on the following practice tests are designed to be just like questions that have appeared on the mathematics section of the GMAT. These questions were written specifically for these practice tests and are not endorsed by GMAT. Each practice test has a balance of questions over the content areas of arithmetic, algebra, and geometry.

GMAT MATH PRACTICE TESTS

Like the actual GMAT Quantitative section, each GMAT math practice test has 37 questions and a 75-minute time limit. The questions are divided into the following categories:

15 data sufficiency questions
22 general problem-solving questions

Each practice test will be an accurate reflection of how well you'll do on test day if you treat it as the actual examination. Here is how to take each test under conditions similar to the actual exam:

- Find a place where you can work comfortably and without interruption.
- Complete the test in one sitting.
- Tear out the answer sheet and mark your answers by blackening the corresponding answer oval. (Note that on the real tests, you will mark your answer by clicking on an answer choice oval on the computer screen.)
- Time yourself and observe the given time limits. Note how many questions remain, if any, when time runs out.
- Become familiar with the directions to the test and the reference information provided to test takers. You will save time on the actual test day if you are already familiar with this information.

Once you have completed a practice test, check your answers against the answer key provided. Then review the solutions to each problem, paying particular attention to the problems you missed. For those problems, you may want to go back and reread the corresponding topic review section in this book.

GMAT MATH PRACTICE TEST 1

➤ The numbers on this test are real numbers.

➤ You may assume that positions of points, lines, and angles are in the order shown.

➤ A figure accompanying a problem-solving question is intended to provide information useful in solving the problem. Figures are drawn as accurately as possible EXCEPT when it is stated in a specific problem that its figure is not drawn to scale. Straight lines may sometimes appear jagged. All figures lie in a plane unless otherwise indicated.

DIRECTIONS: Data sufficiency problems consist of a question and two statements, labeled (1) and (2), in which certain data are given. You have to decide whether the data given in the statements is sufficient for answering the question. Using the data given in the statements plus your knowledge of mathematics and everyday facts (such as the number of days in July or the meaning of counterclockwise), you must indicate whether

A. Statement (1) ALONE is sufficient, but statement (2) alone is not sufficient.
B. Statement (2) ALONE is sufficient, but statement (1) alone is not sufficient.
C. BOTH statements TOGETHER are sufficient, but NEITHER statement ALONE is sufficient.
D. EACH statement ALONE is sufficient.
E. Statements (1) and (2) TOGETHER are NOT sufficient.

➤ A figure accompanying a data sufficiency problem will conform to the information given in the question, but will not necessarily conform to the additional information given in statements (1) and (2).

➤ In data sufficiency problems that ask for the value of a quantity, the data given in the statements is sufficient only when it is possible to determine exactly one numerical value for the quantity.

Example 1

What is the value of $x + y$?

A B C D E
☐ ☐ ☐ ● ☐

(1) $0.5(x + y) = -1$
(2) $\frac{1}{5}x + \frac{1}{5}y = 2$

From (1): $x + y = -2$, so (1) is sufficient.
From (2): $x + y = 10$, so (2) is sufficient.

Example 2

N is a number in the set {35, 38, 41, 44, 47, 50}. What is N?

A B C D E
☐ ☐ ● ☐ ☐

(1) N is a multiple of 5.
(2) N is even.

From (1): $N = 35$ or 50, so (1) is not sufficient.
From (2): $N = 38$, 44, or 50, so (2) is not sufficient.
Taking (1) and (2) together, $N = 50$, so taken together (1) and (2) are sufficient.

1. A club wants to mix 20 pounds of candy worth $8.00 per pound with candy worth $5.00 per pound to reduce the cost of the mixture to $6.00 per pound. How many pounds of the $5.00 per pound candy should be used?

   A. 20
   B. 30
   C. 40
   D. 50
   E. 60

2. What is the solution of $n + 2 > 8$?

   (1) n is a positive integer less than 10.
   (2) n is a one-digit prime number.

3. If $p, q,$ and r are nonzero numbers and $p = q - r,$ which of the following is equal to 1?

A. $\dfrac{r - p}{q}$

B. $\dfrac{r + p}{q}$

C. $\dfrac{r + q}{p}$

D. $\dfrac{r - q}{p}$

E. $\dfrac{p + q}{r}$

4. If x to y equals 5 to 3, what is the value of $x + y$?

(1) $3x + y = 24$
(2) $y > 4$

5. Which is the value of $\dfrac{(1/3) + (1/4)}{1/2}$?

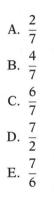

A. $\dfrac{2}{7}$

B. $\dfrac{4}{7}$

C. $\dfrac{6}{7}$

D. $\dfrac{7}{2}$

E. $\dfrac{7}{6}$

6. If N is a positive integer, is N divisible by 12?

(1) N is divisible by 6.
(2) N is divisible by 2.

7. Based on the figure, what is the measure of $\angle PRS$?

A. $50°$
B. $60°$
C. $70°$
D. $120°$
E. $180°$

8. In the equation $x^2 + bx + 10 = 0,$ x is a variable and b is a constant. What is the value of b?

(1) $x - 2$ is a factor of $x^2 + bx + 10 = 0.$
(2) 5 is a root of $x^2 + bx + 10 = 0.$

9. What is the product of the greatest prime factor of 160 and the greatest prime factor of 168?

A. 4
B. 15
C. 35
D. 80
E. 336

10. Is x^3 greater than x?

(1) $0 \le x \le 1$
(2) $x > 1$

11. Is the integer N divisible by 36?

(1) N is divisible by 9.
(2) N is divisible by 8.

12. Is the whole number N divisible by 3 or more positive integers?

(1) N is a prime number.
(2) $0 < N < 4$

13. A soccer team had no ties in the 25 games they played. If they won 60% of their games, how many more games did they win than they lost?

A. 5
B. 10
C. 15
D. 25
E. 40

14. Is x between 0 and 1?

(1) $x > x^2$
(2) $x > x^3$

15. Is $xy < 10$?

(1) $x < 5$ and $y < 2$
(2) $x < -3$ and $y < -1$

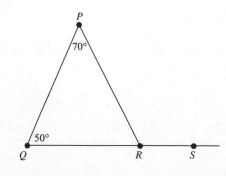

16. Carlos worked 40 hours last week, including 4 hours on Sunday. He earns $10.50 an hour regularly and $1\frac{1}{2}$ times that on Sunday. How much did he earn last week?

    A. $357
    B. $399
    C. $420
    D. $441
    E. $483

17. If $5w = x + y$, then what is the average (arithmetic mean) of w, x, and y in terms of w?

    A. $2w$
    B. $3w$
    C. $w + 2$
    D. $\frac{1}{3}w$
    E. $\frac{1}{2}w$

18. What is the ratio of P to Q?

    (1) P is 4 less twice Q.
    (2) $4P$ equals $7Q$.

19. If $\frac{2}{x} = 5$ and $\frac{y}{3} = 6$, what is the value of $\frac{2+y}{x+3}$?

    A. 11
    B. $\frac{100}{17}$
    C. $\frac{40}{11}$
    D. $\frac{20}{17}$
    E. $\frac{8}{11}$

20. Which has the least value?

    A. $\frac{8}{(2^3)(5^2)}$
    B. $\frac{10}{(2^2)(5^3)}$
    C. $\frac{28}{(2^3)(5^3)}$
    D. $\frac{16}{(2^2)(5^2)}$
    E. $\frac{140}{(2^4)(5^3)}$

21. What is N when N is an integer and $x < N < y$?

    (1) $y - x = 7$
    (2) x and y are integers.

22. A woman is 4 times as old as her daughter. In 3 years she will be 3 times as old as her daughter. How old is the woman now?

    A. 3 years
    B. 6 years
    C. 12 years
    D. 24 years
    E. 36 years

23. If a triangle has one side of 3 cm and another side of 4 cm, how long is the third side?

    (1) The triangle is a right triangle.
    (2) The third side is the longest side.

24. In $\triangle PQR$, PQ is an integer and $PQ > 6$. What is PQ?

    (1) $PR + QR = 8$
    (2) $\triangle PQR$ is equiangular and $PR = 10$.

25. What is the measure of the supplement of an angle with a measure of $42°$?

    A. $318°$
    B. $228°$
    C. $138°$
    D. $48°$
    E. $21°$

Questions 26 and 27 are based on the following graph.

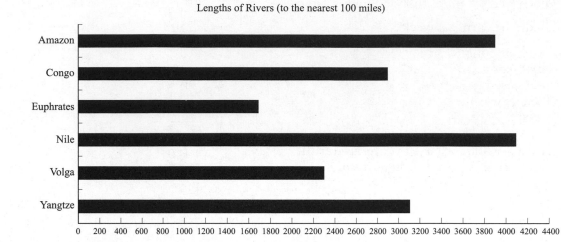

Lengths of Rivers (to the nearest 100 miles)

26. Based on the graph, the Nile is longer than the sum of what two rivers?

    A. Congo and Euphrates
    B. Euphrates and Amazon
    C. Congo and Yangtze
    D. Volga and Congo
    E. Volga and Euphrates

27. Based on the graph, the Nile is how much longer than the Congo?

    A. 100 miles
    B. 200 miles
    C. 600 miles
    D. 800 miles
    E. 1,200 miles

28. A hat contains 12 cards marked with a star and 18 unmarked cards. What is the probability that one card selected at random will be marked with a star?

    A. $\dfrac{2}{5}$

    B. $\dfrac{3}{5}$

    C. $\dfrac{2}{3}$

    D. $\dfrac{3}{2}$

    E. $\dfrac{5}{2}$

29. What is the average (arithmetic mean) of the values 39, 40, 39, 45, 42, 35, 47?

    A. 39
    B. 41
    C. 42
    D. 45
    E. 47

30. A rectangular room that is 8 meters by 5 meters is to be carpeted using carpet costing $12.50 per square meter. How much will the carpet cost?

    A. $40
    B. $100
    C. $162.50
    D. $480
    E. $500

31. A rectangular box that is 7 inches long by 4 inches wide by 3 inches deep is carefully packed to hold the maximum number of blocks that are 1 inch by 1 inch by 2 inches. How many blocks can be packed into the box?

    A. 84 blocks
    B. 42 blocks
    C. 28 blocks
    D. 14 blocks
    E. 2 blocks

32. Is $n < 0$?

    (1) $\dfrac{1}{n} < 0$

    (2) $n^2 > 0$

33. The original funding to build a housing development was $1.75 billion. The funding was increased to $2.5 billion. By what percentage was the original funding increased?

    A. 38%
    B. 43%
    C. 52%
    D. 65%
    E. 71%

Questions 34 and 35 are based on the following graph.

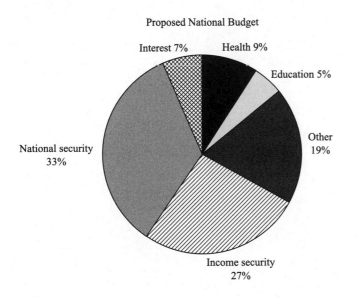

Proposed National Budget

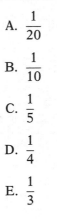

Interest 7%   Health 9%

Education 5%

National security 33%

Other 19%

Income security 27%

34. Based on the graph, what is the ratio of the proposed spending on national security compared to health?

    A. 11 to 3
    B. 3 to 1
    C. 33 to 5
    D. 1 to 3
    E. 3 to 11

35. Based on the graph, approximately what part of the proposed budget is for health, education, and interest combined?

    A. $\dfrac{1}{20}$

    B. $\dfrac{1}{10}$

    C. $\dfrac{1}{5}$

    D. $\dfrac{1}{4}$

    E. $\dfrac{1}{3}$

36. What is the value of $x^3 - y^3$?

    (1) $x - y = x + 3$
    (2) $x - y = 4 - y$

37. If the sale price of a television is $216 after a 10% reduction was made, what was the regular price of the television?

    A. $21.60
    B. $24.00
    C. $194.40
    D. $237.60
    E. $240.00

STOP

DO *NOT* GO BACK AND CHECK YOUR WORK.

ANSWER KEY

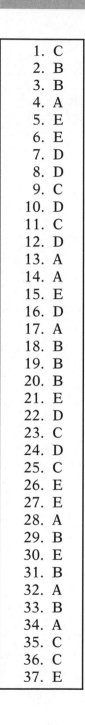

1. C
2. B
3. B
4. A
5. E
6. E
7. D
8. D
9. C
10. D
11. C
12. D
13. A
14. A
15. E
16. D
17. A
18. B
19. B
20. B
21. E
22. D
23. C
24. D
25. C
26. E
27. E
28. A
29. B
30. E
31. B
32. A
33. B
34. A
35. C
36. C
37. E

SOLUTIONS

1. **C** 40

   x = pounds of \$5.00 candy used
   $\$8.00(20) + \$5.00(x) = \$6.00(20 + x)$
   $\$160 + \$5x = \$120 + \$6x$
   $\$40 = \$1x$
   $40 = x$

2. **B** Only statement (2) is sufficient.

   $n + 2 > 8$ yields $n > 6$.

   (1) This statement says that n is a positive integer less than 10. So $n = 7, 8,$ or 9. Not sufficient.
   (2) This statement says that n is a one-digit prime number. The one-digit prime numbers are 2, 3, 5, and 7, and only $n = 7$ is greater than 6. Sufficient.

   So only statement (2) is sufficient.

3. **B** $\dfrac{r + p}{q}$

   $\dfrac{r + p}{q} = \dfrac{r + q - r}{q} = \dfrac{q}{q} = 1$

4. **A** Only statement (1) is sufficient.

   (1) $3x + y = 24$ means $y = -3x + 24$; x to $y = 5$ to 3 means $3x = 5y$, so $-3x = -5y$. $y = -5y + 24$, so $6y = 24$ and $y = 4$.
   $3x = 5(4) = 20$ and $x = 6\dfrac{2}{3}$
   $x + y = 4 + 6\dfrac{2}{3} = 10\dfrac{2}{3}$
   Sufficient.
   (2) $y > 4$ yields many values for y, and $x + y$ would also have many values. Not sufficient.

5. **E** $\dfrac{7}{6}$

   $\dfrac{1/3 + 1/4}{1/2} = \dfrac{12(1/3 + 1/4)}{12(1/2)} = \dfrac{4 + 3}{6} = \dfrac{7}{6}$

6. **E** Together the statements are not sufficient.

   (1) 18 is divisible by 6 but not by 12. Not sufficient.
   (2) 4 is divisible by 2 but not by 12. Not sufficient.

   Together the statements show only that N is divisible by 6, so not sufficient.

7. **D** 120°

   $\angle PRS$ is an exterior angle of $\triangle PQR$, so it is equal to the sum of $\angle P$ and $\angle Q$.
   $\angle P + \angle Q = 70° + 50° = 120° = \angle PRS$

8. **D** Each statement is sufficient alone.

   (1) If $x - 2$ is a factor of $x^2 + bx + 10 = 0$, then $x - 5$ is the other factor and $b = -7$. Sufficient.
   (2) If 5 is a root, then $x - 5$ is a factor of $x^2 + bx + 10 = 0$ and the other factor is $x - 2$ and $b = -7$. Sufficient.

   So each statement is sufficient alone.

9. **C** 35

   Prime factors of $160 = 2^5 \times 5$.
   Prime factors of $168 = 2^3 \times 3 \times 7$.
   $5 \times 7 = 35$

10. **D** Each statement is sufficient alone.

    (1) If $x = 0$, then $x^3 = 0$. If $x = \dfrac{1}{2}$, then $x^3 = \dfrac{1}{8}$. Thus, $x^3 \le x$. Sufficient.
    (2) If $x = 2$, then $x^3 = 8$. Sufficient.

11. **C** Together the statements are sufficient, but neither statement is sufficient alone.

    (1) 18 is divisible by 9, but 18 is not divisible by 36. Not sufficient.
    (2) 16 is divisible by 8, but 16 is not divisible by 36. Not sufficient.

    If a number is divisible by 9 and by 8, it will be divisible by 36. Together sufficient.

12. **D** Each statement is sufficient alone.

   (1) If N is prime, then N is divisible by 1 and N only. Sufficient.
   (2) If $0 < N < 4$, then $N = 1, 2,$ or 3, so N is not divisible by 3 or more positive integers. Sufficient.

13. **A** 5

   The team played 25 games and won 60% of them, or 15 games. The team lost $25 - 15 = 10$ games. So the team won $15 - 10 = 5$ more games than it lost.

14. **A** Only statement (1) is sufficient.

   (1) $x > x^2$, $x - x^2 > 0$, $x(1 - x) > 0$, so $0 < x < 1$. Sufficient.
   (2) $x > x^3$, $x - x^3 > 0$, $x(1 - x^2) > 0$, $x(1 + x)(1 - x) > 0$, so $0 < x < 1$ or $-1 < x < 0$. Not sufficient.

15. **E** Together the statements are not sufficient.

   (1) If $x < 5$ and $y < 2$, let $x = -8$ and $y = -6$. Then $xy = (-8)(-6) = 48 > 10$. But if you let $x = 1$ and $y = -6$, then $xy = 1(-6) = -6 < 10$. Not sufficient.
   (2) If $x < -3$ and $y < -1$, let $x = -10$ and $y = -8$. Then $xy = (-10)(-8) = 80 > 10$. But if you let $x = -4$ and $y = -2$, then $xy = (-4)(-2) = 8 < 10$. Not sufficient.

16. **D** 441

   $40 - 4 = 36$ regular hours
   $1.5(\$10.50) = \$15.75$ pay for Sunday hours
   Total pay $= 36(\$10.50) + 4(\$15.75) = \$441$

17. **A** $2w$

   $$\text{AVE} = \frac{x + y + w}{3} = \frac{w + 5w}{3} = \frac{6w}{3} = 2w$$

18. **B** Only statement (2) is sufficient.

   (1) $P = 4 - 2Q$ does not allow you to get a ratio of P to Q because of the constant. Not sufficient.
   (2) $4P = 7Q$, so $\frac{P}{Q} = \frac{7}{4}$. Sufficient.

   So only statement (2) is sufficient.

19. **B** $\dfrac{100}{17}$

   $\dfrac{2}{x} = 5$, so $2 = 5x$ and $0.4 = x$; $\dfrac{y}{3} = 6$, so $y = 18$.

   $$\frac{2 + y}{x + 3} = \frac{2 + 18}{0.4 + 3} = \frac{20}{3.4} = \frac{200}{34} = \frac{100}{17}$$

20. **B** $\dfrac{10}{(2^2)(5^3)}$

   $A = \dfrac{8}{200} = 0.04 \qquad B = \dfrac{10}{500} = 0.02$

   $C = \dfrac{28}{1,000} = 0.028 \qquad D = \dfrac{16}{100} = 0.16$

   $E = \dfrac{140}{2,000} = 0.07$

21. **E** Together the statements are not sufficient.

   (1) $y - x = 7$ means $y = x + 7$. So $x < N < x + 7$. If $x = 0.5$, then $0.5 < N < 7.5$, so N could be 1, 2, 3, 4, 5, 6, or 7. Not sufficient.
   (2) x and y are integers and $x < N < y$. Only when $y = x + 2$ is there just one value for N. Not sufficient.

   Together the statements are not sufficient.

22. **D** 24 years

   $x = $ age of daughter now
   $4x = $ age of woman now
   $4x + 3 = 3(x + 3)$
   $4x + 3 = 3x + 9$
   $x = 6$
   $4x = 24$ years

23. **C** Together they are sufficient but neither is sufficient alone.

   (1) Knowing the triangle is a right triangle does not tell you if 4 is the hypotenuse or not. The third side is limited to $1 < x < 7$. Not sufficient.
   (2) Knowing the third side is the longest side only tells you that the longest side, x, is $4 < x < 7$. Not sufficient.

   Together you have a right triangle with the third side, x, being the hypotenuse, so $x^2 = 3^2 + 4^2 = 25$ and $x = 5$. Together the two statements are sufficient.

24. **D** Each statement is sufficient alone.

    (1) PQ is an integer and $PQ > 6$. The third side of $\triangle PQR$ is less than the sum of the other two sides, so $6 < PQ < 8 = PQ + QR$. Thus, $PQ = 7$. Sufficient.
    (2) If $\triangle PQR$ is equiangular, then it is equilateral and each side is 10. Sufficient.

    So each statement is sufficient alone.

25. **C** $138°$

    Supplementary angles have a sum of $180°$. $180° - 42° = 138°$

26. **E** Volga and Euphrates

    Nile = 4,100
    Euphrates + Volga = $1,700 + 2,300 = 4,000$

27. **E** 1,200 miles

    Nile = 4,100 and Congo = 2,900
    $4,100 - 2,900 = 1,200$ miles

28. **A** $\dfrac{2}{5}$

    There are 12 marked and 18 unmarked cards, so 30 cards total.

    $$\frac{\text{Marked}}{\text{Total}} = \frac{12}{30} = \frac{6}{15} = \frac{2}{5}$$

29. **B** 41

    SUM $= (39 + 40 + 39 + 45 + 42 + 35 + 47) = 287$ $N = 7$
    AVE $=$ SUM $\div N = 287 \div 7 = 41$

30. **E** $500

    Floor area: 8 m $\times$ 5 m $= 40$ m^2
    $40 \times \$12.50 = \$500.00$

31. **B** 42 blocks

    Volume of box = 84 cu in; each block = $1 \times 1 \times 2$ cu in; $84 \div 2 = 42$ blocks maximum. On the bottom of the box you can lay 7 blocks across in 2 rows, so 14 blocks exactly cover the bottom. The box is 3 inches deep and a block is 1 inch high, so you can have 3 layers, $3 \times 14 = 42$ blocks. Thus, you can actually put 42 whole blocks in the box.

32. **A** Only statement (1) is sufficient.

    (1) If $\dfrac{1}{n}$ is negative, then n is negative. Sufficient.
    (2) If $n^2 > 0$, then $n < 0$ or $n > 0$. Not sufficient.

33. **B** 43%

    New funding ($2.5 billion) $-$ Original funding ($1.75 billion) = Gain ($0.75 billion)
    $\$0.75 \div \$1.75 = 0.4285$ or 43%

34. **A** 11 to 3

    National security = 33% and health = 9%
    33% to 9% = 11 to 3

35. **C** $\dfrac{1}{5}$

    Health = 9%, education = 5%, interest = 7%
    $9\% + 5\% + 7\% = 21\%$

    $$21\% \approx \frac{1}{5}$$

36. **C** Together the statements are sufficient, but neither is sufficient alone.

    (1) $x - y = x + 3$ yields $y = -3$ but does not allow you to evaluate $x^3 - y^3$. Not sufficient.
    (2) $x - y = 4 - y$ yields $x = 4$ but does allow you to evaluate $x^3 - y^3$. Not sufficient.

    Taken together you have $x = 4$ and $y = -3$, so $x^3 - y^3 = 4^3 - (-3)^3 = 64 - (-27) = 91$. Sufficient.

37. **E** $240.00

    10% discount, sale price $216
    $216 is 90% of regular price
    Regular price = $216 \div 0.90 = \$240.00$

GMAT MATH PRACTICE TEST 2

➤ The numbers on this test are real numbers.

➤ You may assume that positions of points, lines, and angles are in the order shown.

➤ A figure accompanying a problem-solving question is intended to provide information useful in solving the problem. Figures are drawn as accurately as possible EXCEPT when it is stated in a specific problem that its figure is not drawn to scale. Straight lines may sometimes appear jagged. All figures lie in a plane unless otherwise indicated.

DIRECTIONS: Data sufficiency problems consist of a question and two statements, labeled (1) and (2), in which certain data are given. You have to decide whether the data given in the statements is sufficient for answering the question. Using the data given in the statements plus your knowledge of mathematics and everyday facts (such as the number of days in July or the meaning of counterclockwise), you must indicate whether

A. Statement (1) ALONE is sufficient, but statement (2) alone is not sufficient.
B. Statement (2) ALONE is sufficient, but statement (1) alone is not sufficient.
C. BOTH statements TOGETHER are sufficient, but NEITHER statement ALONE is sufficient.
D. EACH statement ALONE is sufficient.
E. Statements (1) and (2) TOGETHER are NOT sufficient.

➤ A figure accompanying a data sufficiency problem will conform to the information given in the question, but will not necessarily conform to the additional information given in statements (1) and (2).

➤ In data sufficiency problems that ask for the value of a quantity, the data given in the statements is sufficient only when it is possible to determine exactly one numerical value for the quantity.

Example 1

What is the value of $x + y$?   A B C D E
□ □ □ ● □

(1) $0.5(x + y) = -1$
(2) $\frac{1}{5}x + \frac{1}{5}y = 2$

From (1): $x + y = -2$, so (1) is sufficient.
From (2): $x + y = 10$, so (2) is sufficient.

Example 2

N is a number in the set $\{35, 38, 41, 44, 47, 50\}$. What is N?   A B C D E
□ □ ● □ □

(1) N is a multiple of 5.
(2) N is even.

From (1): $N = 35$ or 50, so (1) is not sufficient.
From (2): $N = 38$, 44, or 50, so (2) is not sufficient.
Taking (1) and (2) together, $N = 50$, so taken together (1) and (2) are sufficient.

1. In a graduating class of 240 students, 80% apply to college. Of the students who apply to college, 75% actually attend college. How many students from the graduating class attend college?

   A. 48
   B. 144
   C. 180
   D. 192
   E. 372

2. If $x + 3y - 3 = 2y - 3x$, what is the value of x?

   (1) $y^2 = 25$
   (2) $y = 5$

3. The tens digit of a two-digit number is twice as large as the units digit. If the digits are reversed, the new number is 36 less than the original number. What is the original number?

   A. 4
   B. 8
   C. 42
   D. 48
   E. 84

4. If n is a member of the set {10, 15, 20, 25, 30, 35, 40}, what is the value of n?

   (1) n is a multiple of 3.
   (2) n is a multiple of 2.

5. If $8^{2x+4} = 4^{4x-3}$, what is the value of x?

   A. 1
   B. 3
   C. 6
   D. 9
   E. 10

6. If n is a positive integer, is $n + 1$ a prime?

   (1) n is a prime number.
   (2) n is even.

7. If $x^2 \neq 1$, which is equal to
   $$\frac{x}{x+1} - \frac{x}{x-1} + \frac{2}{x^2-1}?$$

   A. $\dfrac{-x+3}{x+1}$

   B. $\dfrac{2}{x+1}$

   C. $\dfrac{-2}{x+1}$

   D. $\dfrac{2}{x-1}$

   E. $\dfrac{-2}{x-1}$

8. If x and y are positive integers, what is the value of x?

   (1) Twice x equals 4 times y.
   (2) xy is the square of a positive integer.

9. If P and Q are positive integers, which CANNOT be the greatest common divisor of P and Q?

   A. $P + Q$
   B. PQ
   C. P
   D. Q
   E. 1

10. In a square, the length of a side is s and the diagonal is d. What is the perimeter of the square?

    (1) The area is 25 cm².
    (2) The diagonal is $10\sqrt{2}$ in.

11. Is $x > 0$?

    (1) $x^3 > 0$
    (2) $-3x < x$

12. A clothes dryer has a sale price of $203.15 after a 15% reduction. What is the regular price of the dryer?

    A. $274.85
    B. $239
    C. $233.62
    D. $172.68
    E. $35.85

13. x is a multiple of 12 that is less than 100. What is x?

    (1) x is a multiple of 4.
    (2) x is a multiple of 15.

14. Which fraction is equal to the decimal 0.0125?

    A. $\dfrac{1}{4}$

    B. $\dfrac{1}{8}$

    C. $\dfrac{1}{16}$

    D. $\dfrac{1}{32}$

    E. $\dfrac{1}{80}$

15. If x, y, and z are positive integers with the ratio $2 : 4 : 6$, what is the value of x?

 (1) $x + y + z = 60$
 (2) $y + z = 50$

16. What value is equal to $\dfrac{3/8}{3/4 + 2/3}$?

 A. $\dfrac{3}{4}$

 B. $\dfrac{15}{28}$

 C. $\dfrac{9}{34}$

 D. $\dfrac{3}{16}$

 E. $\dfrac{21}{20}$

17. If $x \neq 1$, which expression is equal to $\dfrac{x(x - 1) - 2(x + 1) + 3(x + 5)}{x - 1}$?

 A. $\dfrac{x^2 + 13}{x - 1}$

 B. $\dfrac{x^2 + 17}{x - 1}$

 C. $\dfrac{x^2 + x + 12}{x - 1}$

 D. $\dfrac{x^2 + x + 5}{x - 1}$

 E. $\dfrac{13}{x - 1}$

18. If $t \neq 0$, is r greater than zero?

 (1) $r - t = 8$
 (2) $-rt = 8$

19. What is the sum of the prime factors of 570?

 A. 29
 B. 30
 C. 65
 D. 66
 E. 67

20. Which number is divisible by 2, 3, 4, and 6 but is not divisible by 5?

 A. 138
 B. 644
 C. 1,020
 D. 1,428
 E. 4,620

21. If l is the length of a rectangle and w is the width of the rectangle, what is the perimeter of the rectangle?

 (1) $l + 2w = 80$
 (2) $l + w = 40$

22. If x is an integer and $y = 7x + 5$, which of the following CANNOT be a divisor of y?

 A. 10
 B. 11
 C. 12
 D. 13
 E. 14

23. At a discount wholesale store, a microwave is priced at a $x\%$ discount off the original warehouse price. Later, during a sale, the storeowner offers to sell the microwave at $y\%$ off the regular discount price. What was the original warehouse price?

 (1) $x = 15$
 (2) $x + y = 20$

24. One pump drains one-half of a pond in 3 hours, and then a second pump starts draining the pond. The two pumps working together finish emptying the pond in one-half hour. How long would it take the second pump to drain the pond if it had to do the job alone?

 A. 1 hour
 B. 1.2 hours
 C. 3 hours
 D. 5 hours
 E. 6 hours

25. Is p^2 an even integer?

 (1) p is an even integer.
 (2) $\sqrt{p}$ is an even number.

26. What is the value of $\dfrac{(-1.6)(1.5) - (1.2)(3.5)}{30}$?

 A. 0.24
 B. 0.22
 C. 0.06
 D. -0.06
 E. -0.22

27. In a rectangle, the length is l, the width is w, and the diagonal is d. What is the area?

 (1) $d = 13$ and $w = 5$
 (2) $d = 2l$

28. Which is equal to $(3 - \sqrt{2})(3 + \sqrt{2})$?

    A. $11 - 6\sqrt{2}$
    B. $7 - 6\sqrt{2}$
    C. 5
    D. 7
    E. 11

29. If $w = 3x - 4y^2$, what is w?

    (1) $x = \sqrt{324}$
    (2) $y^2 > 4$

30. The perimeter of a rectangular garden is 80 feet, and the area of the garden is 391 square feet. What is the length of the shorter side of the garden?

    A. 17 feet
    B. 23 feet
    C. 34 feet
    D. 40 feet
    E. 46 feet

31. The average of x, y, and z is 40. What is x?

    (1) $y = 2z$
    (2) $y + z = 75$

Questions 32 and 33 are based on the following graph.

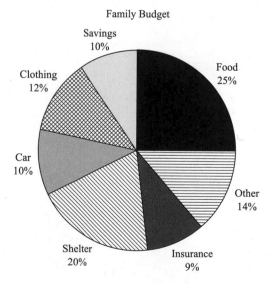

Family Budget

32. Based on the graph, what would be spent on clothing out of a budget of $2,500?

    A. $250
    B. $300
    C. $375
    D. $500
    E. $625

33. Based on the graph, how much more is being spent on food than on clothing?

    A. 5%
    B. 8%
    C. 10%
    D. 13%
    E. 15%

34. Which is equal to $\sqrt{25 + 25}$?

    A. $2\sqrt{5}$
    B. $5\sqrt{2}$
    C. 10
    D. 25
    E. 50

Questions 35 and 36 are based on the following graph.

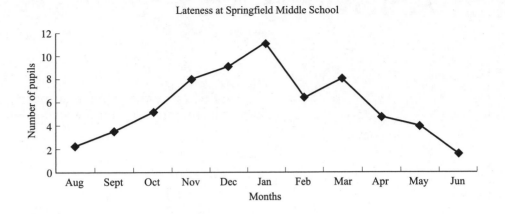

Lateness at Springfield Middle School

35. Based on the graph, how many students were late during August, September, and October combined?

   A. 14
   B. 12
   C. 10
   D. 8
   E. 6

36. Based on the graph, between which two consecutive months was the greatest change in lateness?

   A. March to April
   B. October to November
   C. May to June
   D. December to January
   E. January to February

37. What is the product of the roots of $x^2 - 15x + 36$?

   A. 36
   B. 15
   C. 9
   D. -15
   E. -36

STOP

DO *NOT* GO BACK AND CHECK YOUR WORK.

ANSWER KEY

1. B
2. B
3. E
4. C
5. D
6. C
7. C
8. E
9. A
10. D
11. D
12. B
13. B
14. E
15. D
16. C
17. A
18. C
19. A
20. D
21. B
22. E
23. E
24. B
25. D
26. E
27. A
28. D
29. E
30. A
31. B
32. B
33. D
34. B
35. C
36. E
37. A

SOLUTIONS

1. **B** 144

   80% of 240 apply to college. $0.8 \times 240 = 192$ apply to college. 75% of $192 = 144$ actually attend college.

2. **B** Only statement (2) is sufficient.

   $4x = -y + 3$

   (1) $y^2 = 25$ yields two values for y, $+5$ and -5. Not sufficient.
   (2) $y = 5$, then $4x = -5 + 3 = -2$ and $x = -0.5$. Sufficient.

3. **E** 84

   $U =$ units digit and $2U =$ tens digit, so $10(2U) + U =$ original number.

   $$10(2U) + U = 10U + 2U + 36$$
   $$20U + U = 12U + 36$$
   $$9U = 36$$
   $$U = 4$$
   $$2U = 8$$
   $$10(2U) + U = 10(8) + 4 = 80 + 4 = 84$$

4. **C** Together the statements are sufficient, but neither is sufficient alone.

   (1) n is a multiple of 3 yields 15, 30. Not sufficient.
   (2) n is a multiple of 2 yields 10, 20, 30, 40. Not sufficient.

   Taken together you want multiples of both 2 and 3. This yields 30. Together they are sufficient.

5. **D** 9

   $$8^{2x+4} = 4^{4x-3}$$
   $$(2^3)^{2x+4} = (2^2)^{4x-3}$$
   $$2^{6x+12} = 2^{8x-6}$$
   So $6x + 12 = 8x - 6$
   $-2x = -18 \qquad x = 9$

6. **C** Together the statements are sufficient, but neither is sufficient alone.

   (1) n is prime, so if $n = 2$, then $n + 1 = 3$ is prime. But if $n = 5$, then $n + 1 = 6$ is not prime. Not sufficient.
   (2) n is even, so if $n = 2$, then $n + 1 = 3$ is prime. But if $n = 8$, then $n + 1 = 9$ is not prime. Not sufficient.

   Together, n is even and n is prime, which means $n = 2$. If $n = 2$, then $n + 1 = 3$ which is prime. Together the statements are sufficient.

7. **C** $\dfrac{-2}{x+1}$

   $$\frac{x}{x+1} - \frac{x}{x-1} + \frac{2}{x^2-1} =$$
   $$\frac{x(x-1) - x(x+1) + 2}{(x-1)(x+1)} =$$
   $$\frac{x^2 - x - x^2 - x + 2}{(x+1)(x-1)} =$$
   $$\frac{-2x+2}{(x+1)(x-1)} = \frac{-2(x-1)}{(x+1)(x-1)} = \frac{-2}{x+1}$$

8. **E** Together the statements are not sufficient.

   (1) $2x = 4y$ so $x = 2y$, but there are no fixed values so you cannot determine the value of x. Not sufficient.
   (2) $xy = k^2$ has multiple possible values. Not sufficient.

   Taking the two statements together, you still do not have a way to fix a value for x or y.

9. **A** $P + Q$

   GCD $(8, 9) = 1$
   GCD $(4, 8) = 4 = P$
   GCD $(100, 10) = 10 = Q$
   GCD$(1, 1) = 1 = P \times Q$
   Not $P + Q$ since $P + Q$ is greater than P and greater than Q.

10. **D** Each statement is sufficient alone.

    (1) $A = s^2 = 25$ cm^2, $s = 5$ cm, and
    $P = 4s = 4(5) = 20$ cm. Sufficient.
    (2) $d = s\sqrt{2}$ $10\sqrt{2} = s\sqrt{2}$, so $s = 10$
    inches and $P = 4s = 4(10) = 40$ inches.
    Sufficient.

11. **D** Each statement is sufficient alone.

    (1) $x^3 > 0$ so $x > 0$. Sufficient.
    (2) $-3x < x$ so $-4x < 0$ and $x > 0$.
    Sufficient.

12. **B** $239

    The sale price is $203.15 after a 15%
    discount.
    So 0.85 times regular price = $203.15.
    Regular price = $230.15 ÷ 0.85 = $239

13. **B** Only statement (2) is sufficient.

    x is a positive multiple of 12 that is less than
    100, so x could be 96, 84, 72, 60, 48, 36, 24,
    or 12.

    (1) x is a multiple of 4, so all the values of x
    are possible. Not sufficient.
    (2) x is a multiple of 15, so only 60 is
    selected out of the x values. Sufficient.

14. **E** $\dfrac{1}{80}$

    $\dfrac{1}{80} = 1 \div 80 = 0.0125$

15. **D** Each statement is sufficient alone.

    $x : y : z = 2 : 4 : 6$ and $x = 2n$, $y = 4n$, and
    $z = 6n$

    (1) $x + y + z = 60$ $2n + 4n + 6n = 60$
    $12n = 60$ $n = 5$ $x = 2n = 10$
    Sufficient.
    (2) $y + z = 50$ $4n + 6n = 50$ $10n = 50$
    $n = 5$ $x = 2n = 10$ Sufficient.

16. **C** $\dfrac{9}{34}$

    $\dfrac{3/8}{3/4 + 2/3} \times \dfrac{24}{24} = \dfrac{9}{18 + 16} = \dfrac{9}{34}$

17. **A** $\dfrac{x^2 + 13}{x - 1}$

    $\dfrac{x(x + 1) - 2(x + 1) + 3(x + 5)}{x - 1} =$
    $\dfrac{x^2 - x - 2x - 2 + 3x + 15}{x - 1} = \dfrac{x^2 + 13}{x - 1}$

18. **C** Together the statements are sufficient,
    but neither is sufficient alone.
    $t \neq 0$

    (1) $r - t = 8$, so $r = t + 8$. If $t = -9$, then
    $r = -1$; if $t = 1$, then $r = 9$. Not
    sufficient.
    (2) $-rt = 8$, so $rt = -8$. If $t = 8$, then
    $r = -1$; if $t = -8$, then $r = 1$. Not
    sufficient.

    Together, $rt = -8$ and $t = r - 8$ yield
    $r(r - 8) = -8$ and $r^2 - 8r = -8$. Solve for r
    and you get $r = 4 \pm \sqrt{8}$, and both values for
    r are greater than 0. Together the statements
    are sufficient.

19. **A** 29

    $570 = 10 \times 57 = 2 \times 5 \times 3 \times 19$
    $2 + 5 + 3 + 19 = 29$

20. **D** 1,428

    138 is not divisible by 4.
    644 is not divisible by 3.
    1,020 and 4,620 are divisible by 5.
    $1,428 = 2 \times 714 = 3 \times 476 = 4 \times 357 =$
    $6 \times 238 = 5 \times 285.6$
    So 1,428 is divisible by 2, 3, 4, and 6 but not
    by 5. It would have been enough to test for
    divisibility by 12.

21. **B** Only statement (2) is sufficient.

    (1) $l + 2w = 80$ does not allow you to get a
    value for l or w or $l + w$. Not sufficient.
    (2) $l + w = 40$, so $2l + 2w = 80$ and
    $P = 2l + 2w$. $P = 80$. Sufficient.

22. **E** 14

    Since $7x$ is divisible by 7, $7x + 5$ is not
    divisible by 7 for any choice of x. Also,
    $7x + 5$ is not divisible by any multiple of 7,
    which includes 14.

23. **E** Together the statements are not sufficient.

    $P - xP - y(P - xP) = P - xP - yP - xyP =$
    $P(1 - x - y - xy)$. This means knowing x and
    y will not yield a dollar amount for P, the
    original warehouse price. Thus, knowing x
    or y or x and y will not yield a value for P.
    Not sufficient.

24. **B** 1.2 hours

    $x = $ number of hours for second pump alone
    $\dfrac{3.5}{6} + \dfrac{0.5}{x} = 1$
    So $3.5x + 3 = 6x$
    $3 = 2.5x$ and $x = 1.2$

25. **D** Each statement is sufficient alone.

    (1) p is even, so even $\times$ even = even. Thus $p \times p = p^2$ is even. Sufficient.
    (2) $\sqrt{p}$ is even, so $\sqrt{p} \times \sqrt{p} = p$, so p is even and p^2 is even. Sufficient.

26. **E** -0.22

    $$\frac{-1.6(1.5) - (1.2)(3.5)}{30} = \frac{-2.4 - 4.2}{30} =$$
    $$\frac{-6.6}{30} = -0.22$$

27. **A** Only statement (1) is sufficient.

    (1) In a rectangle, $d^2 = l^2 + w^2$, so $13^2 = l^2 + 5^2$ and $144 = l^2$, $l = 12$. $A = lw = 12(5) = 60$. Sufficient.
    (2) $d = 2l$ does not give any numerical value. Not sufficient.

28. **D** 7

    $(3 - \sqrt{2})(3 + \sqrt{2}) = 3^2 - (\sqrt{2})^2 = 9 - 2 = 7$

29. **E** Together the statements are not sufficient.

    (1) $x = \sqrt{324} = 18$, so $w = 3(18) - 4y^2$ and w does not have numerical value. Not sufficient.
    (2) $y^2 > 4$ does not yield a value for w. Not sufficient.

30. **A** 17 feet

    $P = 80 = 2l + 2w$ So $l + w = 40$
    $l = 40 - w$
    $A = 391 = l \times w = w(40 - w) = 40w - w^2$
    $w^2 - 40w + 391 = 0$
    $(w - 17)(w - 23) = 0$
    $w = 17$ or $w = 23$
    $l = 40 - w = 23$ or $l = 40 - w = 17$

31. **B** Only statement (2) is sufficient.

    $(x + y + z) \div 3 = 40$ and $x + y + z = 120$

    (1) $y = 2z$ $x + 2z + z = 120$
        $x = 120 - 3z$ Not sufficient.
    (2) $y + z = 75$ $x + 75 = 120$ $x = 45$
        Sufficient.

32. **B** $300

    Clothing = 12%, budget = $2,500
    $0.12(\$2,500) = \$300$

33. **D** 13%

    Food = 25%, Clothing = 12%
    25% − 12% = 13%

34. **B** $5\sqrt{2}$

    $\sqrt{25 + 25} = \sqrt{50} = \sqrt{25} \times \sqrt{2} = 5\sqrt{2}$

35. **C** 10

    August: 2 pupils late
    September: 3 pupils late
    October: 5 pupils late
    $2 + 3 + 5 = 10$

36. **E** January to February

    From January to February there was a decline of 5 latenesses.

37. **A** 36

    $x^2 - 15x + 36 = 0$
    $(x - 3)(x - 12) = 0$
    $x = 3, x = 12$
    $(3)(12) = 36$